Berlin and its environs : handbook for travellers

Karl Baedeker, Karl Baedeker

BERLIN

AND

ENVIRONS

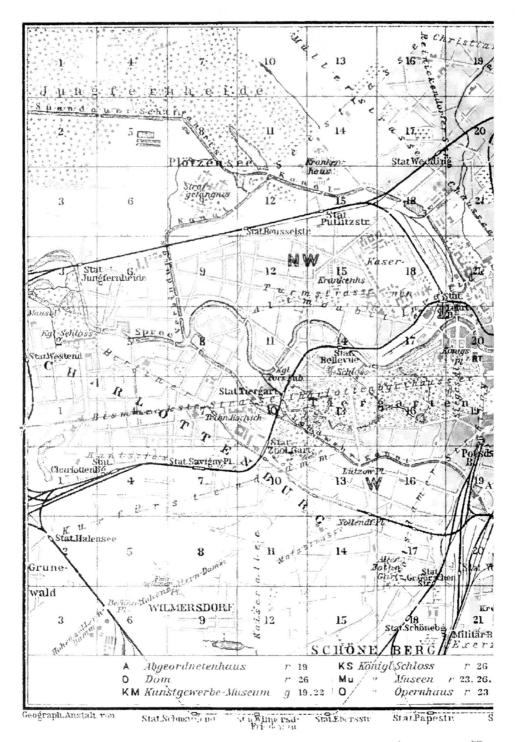

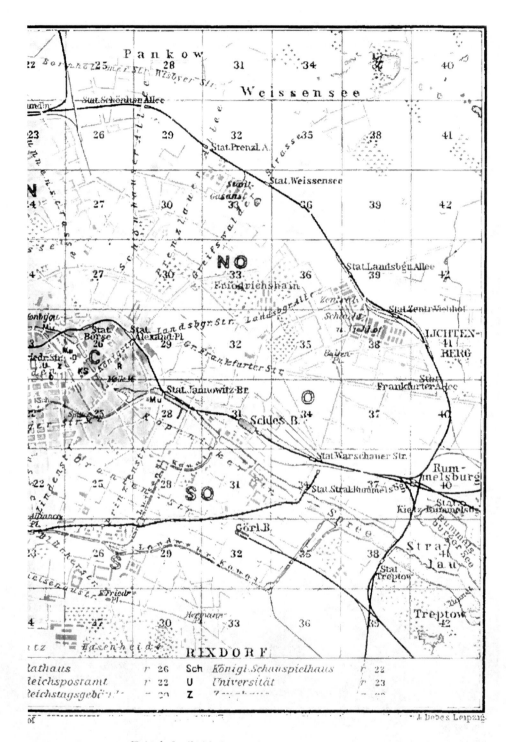

BERLIN

AND ITS

ENVIRONS

HANDBOOK FOR TRAVELLERS

BY

KARL BAEDEKER

WITH 6 MAPS AND 19 PLANS

THIRD EDITION.

LEIPSIC: KARL BAEDEKER, PUBLISHER

1908

Preface.

\-\-\-

The present Handbook for Berlin, which corresponds with the fifteenth German edition, incorporates, in a much expanded and carefully revised form, information heretofore included in the Handbook for Northern Germany. Its chief object, like that of the Editor's other guides, is to render the traveller as nearly as possible independent of the services of guides and others and to enable him to employ his time, his money, and his energy to the best advantage

Though Berlin does not compete in antiquity or historical interest with the other great European capitals, its position as the metropolis of the German empire and its wealth of art-treasures, both ancient and modern, invest it with high importance in addition to its special and characteristic interest as the greatest purely modern city in Europe. While devoting particular attention to the description of the imposing imperial and national edifices and of the great public collections, the Editor has not forgotten this last-mentioned phase, and has endeavoured to include as comprehensive a selection as possible of other objects of general interest for the cultivated traveller. No one is better aware than the Editor himself of the difficulty of securing absolute accuracy in a guidebook; and he will therefore gratefully welcome the continuance of those valuable corrections and suggestions with which travellers have long been in the habit of favouring him.

The utmost care has been bestowed upon the Maps and Plans. The subdivision of the large *Plan of Berlin* (at the end of the book) into three sections of different colours will be found materially to facilitate reference, as it obviates the necessity of unfolding a large sheet of paper at each consultation The area shown on this plan coincides with that given in reduced scale on the *Tramway Plan* at p. 14, so that reference from one plan to the other presents no difficulty. The numbers appearing on the Tramway Plan correspond with the official numbers of the tramway-lines. A plan of the inner town on a larger scale has been added to the present edition.

The list of Hotels and Restaurants given in the Handbook comprises the most important establishments and many of humbler pretensions. Those which the Editor has reason to believe especially worthy of commendation in proportion to their charges are denoted by asterisks The Editor has distributed these marks of commendation (the value of which is relative only as fully and impartially as his knowledge warrants, but there are doubtless many equally deserving establishments among those not starred or even mentioned. The charges are stated in accordance with information supplied by the proprietors themselves.

To hotel-keepers, tradesmen, and others the Editor begs to intimate that a character for fair dealing towards travellers is the only passport to his commendation, and that advertisements of every kind are strictly excluded from his Handbooks. Hotel-keepers are also warned against persons representing themselves as agents for Baedeker's Handbooks.

Abbreviations.

R = Room (including light and attendance).
B. = Breakfast
L = Light
Dej = Déjeuner.
D. = Dinner.
Pens. = Pension (i. e. board, lodging and attendance).
Rfmts. = Refreshments.
M. = English mile.
ft = English foot.
r = Right.
l = Left

N. = North, northern.
S. = South, southern
E. = East, eastern.
W. = West, western.
hr. = Hour.
min = Minute.
omn. = Omnibus
carr. = Carriage
M. = Mark.
pf. = Pfennig.
Str. = Strasse.
ca. = circa, about
p. = Page

The letters b or d, with a date, after a name indicate respectively the year of the person's birth or death.

Asterisks are used as marks of commendation.

CONTENTS.

- - —

I. Berlin.

Page

Maps and Plans.

I. BERLIN.

a. Railway Stations. Arrival and Departure.

Railway Stations. There are five TERMINUS RAILWAY STATIONS at Berlin, exclusive of the 'Stadtbahn' (see below). 1. *Anhalt Station* (Pl. G, 19), for Dresden, Leipzig, Halle (Austria, Bavaria, Thuringia, Frankfort on the Main). — 2. *Potsdam Station* (Pl. G, 19), for Potsdam, Magdeburg, Cassel, Cologne, and the Lower Rhine (junction with the 'Stadtbahn' at Potsdam). — 3. *Lehrte Station* (Pl. R, 18, 21), for all trains to Hamburg and slow trains to Lehrte, Hanover, Bremen, etc (junction with the 'Stadtbahn' at Spandau). — 4. *Stettin Station* (Pl. R, 24), for Rostock (and Copenhagen), Stettin, and Dantsic (viâ Stargard). — 5. *Görlitz Station* (Pl. G, 32), for the Spreewald, Gorlitz, and the Giant Mts. (junction with the 'Stadtbahn' at Nieder-Schoneweide). — The following five STATIONS OF THE 'STADTBAHN' (see p. 12) are also used for general traffic 1. *Charlottenburg Station* (Pl. G, 4). — 2. *Zoological Garden Station* (Pl. G, 10). — 3. *Friedrich-Strasse Station* (Pl. R, 23; with the heaviest traffic). — 4. *Alexander-Platz Station* (Pl. R, 26). — 5. *Silesian Station* (Pl. R, 31). — The express trains from Hanover, Bremen, Cologne and all the trains from Nordhausen-Frankfort on the Main, Königsberg, Posen, and Breslau arrive at these stations.

The *Custom House Examination* of registered luggage, arriving from abroad at the stations of the Stadtbahn or at the Stettin Station, is at the Friedrich-Strasse Station (daily 11-12 a.m.). — *Head Custom House*, Alt-Moabit 145.

Arrival. — Cabs are to be found on the S side at the stations of the Stadtbahn (except at Charlottenburg and Alexander-Platz), and on the arrival (right) side at the terminus stations (except at the Gorlitz Station where they are straight in front). A policeman, posted at the exit from each railway-station, hands the traveller a metal ticket with the number of a cab, on his stating whether he wishes a cab (*'Droschke'*) or a luggage cab (*'Gepäck-Droschke'*). Travellers with luggage should entrust the summoning of the vehicle to the porter (20 pf. for luggage up to 55 lbs., 10 pf. for every 55 lbs more). Cab fares see p. 23; in addition to the fare a charge of 25 pf. is made for the ticket securing the cab. 'Gepack-Droschken'

House numbers in Berlin generally begin at the end of the street nearest where the old town gate originally stood and then run consecutively along the right-hand side of the street. or turning on the left-hand side. so that the highest number is opposite to No. 1.

are necessary if luggage is heavy (over 240 lbs.); see p. 24. — Most of the TRAMWAYS stop near the stations: *Zoological Garden*, see p. 177; *Friedrich-Strasse*, see p. 145 (a few min. from the station); *Alexander-Platz*, see p. 153; *Silesian Station*, see p. 167; *Anhalt Station*, see p. 128; *Potsdam Station*, see p. 127; *Lehrte Station*, see p. 140; *Stettin Station*, see p. 166; *Görlitz Station*, see p. 169. — *Hotels near the Railway Stations*, see pp. 4, 5.

Travellers may avoid the necessity of taking a cab by having then luggage delivered by the *Parcel Delivery Co* (*Paketfuhrt-Gesellschaft*, see p. 26; offices at all the large stations). For registered luggage forms may be obtained from the guard of the train during the journey, and after filling these up the traveller gives up his luggage-ticket in exchange for a receipt. Luggage reaching Berlin between 7 a.m. and 7 p.m. should be delivered within 3 or 4 hrs., luggage arriving after 7 p.m. is delivered before 10 a.m. the next day. Tariff: small luggage (up to 20 lbs.) 30, two pieces 40, three 60 pf., etc.; trunks up to 20 lbs 30, 20-40 lbs 50, 40-60 lbs. 70, 80-100 lbs 90 pf., every 20 lbs. more 10 pf. — The Parcel Delivery Co. conveys luggage to the station on receiving 5 working hours' notice, together with an exact statement of the address of the sender, the number and approximate weight of the packages, and the station and the hour of departure. Luggage for trains starting between 10 p.m. and 10 a.m. is sent for between 6-8 the previous evening. Tariff see above, additional charge 20 pf.

Tourist Agencies, where railway tickets also may be obtained: *Amtliches Reisebureau at the Potsdam Station* (open 8-7, Sun. 9-1); *Office of the Hamburg-America Linie* (agency of the *American Express Co.*), Unter den Linden 8, *Weltreisebureau Union*, Unter den Linden 5-6 (agents for *Thomas Cook & Son, London*, and for the *North German Lloyd*); the *Internationale Reisebureau of the Sleeping Car Co.*, Unter den Linden 57, 58; the *Reisebureau des Westens* (booking-office for New York), Potsdamer-Str. 6; the *Office of the Austrian State Railways*, Unter den Linden 47 (also agency of the Austrian Lloyd). Railway tickets may be obtained also at several first-class hotels (see below).

Tickets for London viâ Flushing may be had from *Brasch & Rothenstein*, Unter den Linden 17, Mohren-Str. 33, Lunebuger-Str. 22, etc.; at the *Reisebureau of the Hollandische Eisenbahngesellschaft* (Hook of Holland Route), Unter den Linden 5-6, tickets are issued for London and other English towns.

b. Hotels. Boarding Houses. Furnished Apartments.

For alphabetical list see Index. — *List of Streets*, p. 227.

In the following list of **Hotels** mention is first made of the large establishments of the highest class, all of which are comfortably fitted up, with steam or hot-water heating, electric light, lifts, baths, and first-class restaurants, and with proportionate charges. The hotels in or near the Linden are the most conveniently situated for tourists.

Hôtel Adlon Pl. a: R, 19. Unter den Linden 1, in the Pariser-Platz, a magnificent new building (see p. 56), 325 R. from 6 *M* (140 with baths, from 12 *M*), B. 1½, déj. 3, D. 6 *M*, with gardens, palm-house and tourist office of the Hamburg-America Linie (tickets sold and luggage forwarded). — *Kaiserhof* (Pl. k; R, 22), Wilhelm-Platz, facing the Zieten-Platz, 250 R. from 6 (100 with baths), B. $1^1/_2$, déj. 3, D. 6 $\mathcal{M}$, with railway-ticket and luggage offices. — *Hôtel Bristol* (Pl. b, R, 19, 20), Unter den Linden 5-6, 350 R. from $4^1/_2$, B. $1^1/_2$, déj. $2^1/_2$, D. 6, S. (9-11.30 p.m.) 5 $\mathcal{M}$, with garden, railway-ticket and luggage-offices. — *Continental Hotel* (Pl. g, R, 23), Neustädtische Kirch-Str. 6-7, near the Friedrich-Strasse Station, 200 R. from 4, B. $1^1/_2$, déj. 3, D. 6, board 9 $\mathcal{M}$. — *Savoy Hotel* (Pl. s; R, 23), Friedrich-Str. 103, with garden, 200 R. from 4, B. $1^1/_4$, déj. $2^1/_2$, D. 5 $\mathcal{M}$. — *Monopol Hotel* (Pl. m; R, 23), Friedrich-Str. 100, opposite the Friedrich-Strasse Station, 200 R. from 4, B. $1^1/_4$, déj. $2^1/_2$, D. 5, pens. from $12^1/_4$ $\mathcal{M}$. — *Palast Hotel* (Pl. p; R, 19), Leipziger-Platz 18-19, near the Potsdam Station, 120 R. from 4, B. $1^1/_2$, déj. 3, D. 5, pens. from $12^1/_2$ $\mathcal{M}$. — *Hôtel Esplanade* (Pl. e; R, 19), Bellevue-Str. 17-18, near the Potsdam Station, 300 R. from 5 $\mathcal{M}$ (many of them with baths); to be opened in 1908. — *Grand Hôtel de Rome & du Nord* (Pl. r; R, 23), Unter den Linden 39, corner of the Charlotten-Str., 120 R. from 4, B. $1^1/_2$, déj. $2^1/_2$, D. 5, S. 3, pens. from 12 $\mathcal{M}$, with winter garden. — *Fürstenhof* (Pl. f; R, 19), Potsdamer-Platz, 300 R. from 4 $\mathcal{M}$ (100 with baths), B. $1^1/_4$, déj. $2^1/_2$, D. $4^1/_2$, S. $3^1/_2$, pens. from 12 $\mathcal{M}$. — *Hôtel Excelsior* (Pl. x; G, 19), Königgratzer-Str 112, opposite the Anhalt Station, 200 R at 3-8, B $1^1/_4$, déj. $2^1/_2$, D. 4, S. 3 $\mathcal{M}$. — *Central Hotel* (Pl. h; R, 23), Friedrich-Str. 143-149, near the Friedrich-Strasse Station, 500 R. from 3, B. $1^1/_4$, déj. $2^1/_2$, D. 5, S. 4, pens. from 10 $\mathcal{M}$, with railway-ticket office. — *Elite Hotel* (Pl. t; R, 23), Neustädtische-Kirch-Str. 9, near the Friedrich-Strasse Station, 130 R. from $4^1/_2$ $\mathcal{M}$ (many of them with baths), B. $1^1/_2$, déj. $2^1/_2$, D $4^1/_2$ $\mathcal{M}$.

Of the other hotels the following are probably the best adapted for the users of Baedeker's Handbooks (comp. p. 2). The prices given will be some guide as to their standing and importance.

UNTER DEN LINDEN. S. side: Nos. 17-18, *Hôtel Westminster* (Pl. w; R, 22, 23); No. 3, *Hôtel Royal*, corner of the Wilhelm-Str., 60 R. at 4-10, B. $1^1/_4$, déj. $2^1/_2$, D. 4 $\mathcal{M}$; No. 20, *Hôtel Métropole*, 50 R. from 3, B. $1^1/_4$ $\mathcal{M}$; No. 32, corner of the Charlotten-Str., *Carlton Hotel* (Pl. o; R, 23), with the Astoria Restaurant (p. 8), 100 R. from $3^1/_2$, B $1^1/_2$, déj. $2^1/_2$, D. 5, pens. $10^1/_2$-20 $\mathcal{M}$. — N. side: No. 46, *Hôtel Victoria* (Pl v; R, 23), corner of the Friedrich-Str., 32 R. at $2^1/_2$-6, B 1 $\mathcal{M}$; No. 68a, *Hôtel Minerva*, 50 R. at $3^1/_2$-6, B. $1^1/_4$, déj $2^1/_2$, D. $3^1/_2$, board $6^1/_4$ $\mathcal{M}$.

To the S. of the Linden. Wilhelm-Str. 44 near the Leipziger-Str., *Wilhelmshof*, 32 R. at 2^1 4 B 1 D. $2^1/_2$ $\mathcal{M}$. a good old-fashioned house, without lift or electric light. Behren-Str.:

No 64-65, *Hôtel Windsor*, patronized by the gentry; No. 45, corner of the Charlotten-Str., ¯*Hôt. Phönix*, 60 R at 3-10, B 1, D. 2½ *M* (Swedish cuisine). — Jäger-Str. 17, corner of the Friedrich-Str., *Schlösser s Hotel*, 42 R. at 3-7, B. 1¼ *M* — Friedrich-Str. No 178, corner of Jäger-Str., *⁺Kaiser-Hotel* (Pl. d; R, 22), 180 R. from 3½, B. 1¼, D. 2½-4 *M* (in connection with the Kaiser-Keller, see p. 8); No. 180, corner of the Tauben-Str., *Nürnberger Hof* (Pl. n; R, 22), 100 R. from 3, B. 1¼, D. 2-3 *M*; No.50-51, near the Schützen-Str., *Hôtel Britannia*, 60 R at 3-7½, B 1 *M*. — Krausen-Str 6, *Werner's Hotel*. — Prinz Albrecht-Str. 9, near the Wilhelm-Str., *Hôtel Prinz Albrecht*, 70 R. at 2¾-6, B. 1¼, déj. 2½, D. 4 *M*. — Markgrafen-Str. 55-56, corner of the Gendarmen-Markt *Hôtel de France*, 70 R. at 2-5½, B. 1 *M*; No. 49, in the Gendarmen-Markt, *Fursten-Hotel*, 50 R. at 2½-6, B. 1¼ *M*. — Charlotten-Str. 71, *Hôtel Brandenburg*, 45 R. at 2-6, B 1 *M*. — Niederwall-Str. 11, *Krebs' Hotel*, 26 R. at 1½-10, B. ¾ *M*.

Near the Friedrich-Strasse Station: *Hotels Continental, Savoy, Monopol. Central, Elite*, see p 3; *⁺Grand Hôtel de Russie*, Georgen-Str. 21-22, 200 R. from 3, B 1¼, déj. 2½, D. 3½ *M*; *Hôtel Silesia*, Friedrich-Str. 96, 52 R. at 2½-4½, B. 1 *M* (no lift); *Friedrichshof*, Friedrich-Str. 93, 40 R. at 2½-6, B. 1¼ *M*; *Rheinischer Hof*, Friedrich-Str. 150, 36 R. at 2½-5, B 1 *M*, *Berliner Hof*, Neustädtische-Kirch-Str 10, 46 R at 3-10, B 1 *M* *Westfälischer Hof*, Neustädtische-Kirch-Str. 13, 50 R. at 2½-8, B. 1 *M*, well spoken of (no central heating) *Schmidt's Hotel*, Neustädtische-Kirch-Str. 14, 55 R. at 2½-8, B. 1-1¼ *M*; *Stadt Magdeburg*, Georgen-Str. 24, *Terminus Hotel*, Friedrich-Str. 101, to the N of the station, 45 R at 2½-6, B. 1¼ *M* (no central heating).

To the N. of the Linden. Dorotheen-Str.: No. 16, *Prinz Wilhelm*, 70 R. at 2½-6½, B. 1¼ *M*, recommended No. 22, *Dorotheenhof*, 100 R. at 3-7, B. 1 *M*; No. 81, *Prinz Friedrich Karl*, 21 R. at 2½-6, B. 1 *M*; No. 90, *Prinzenhof*, 25 R. at 2-4, B. 1 *M*; No.91, *Stadt Kiel*, 25 R at 2-4 *M*, B. 90 pf.; Nos. 92-93, *Splendid Hotel*. — Mittel-Str. No. 5, *Frankfurter Hof and Helvetia*, 75 R. at 2-4 *M*, B.80 pf.; No. 12, *Stadt Riga*, 40 R. at 2-4½, B. 1 *M*; No.16, *Alexandra Hotel*, 100 R. at 2½-6, B. 1¼, D 3½ *M*; No. 54, *Hôtel Janson*, 45 R. at 2-4½, B. 1 *M*; Nos. 57-58, near the Friedrich-Str., *Hôtel Stadt London*, 75 R. at 2½-5, B. 1 *M*; No. 61, *Hôtel du Pavillon*, 36 R. at 2-6, B 1 *M*, well spoken of — Neue Wilhelm-Str. 10, 11, *Hôtel Königshof*, 60 R. at 3-6, B. 1 *M*, frequented by officers. — Luisen-Str. 30, corner of the Schiffbauerdamm, *Hôtel Kronprinz*, 40 R. at 2½-10, B. 1, D. 2½ *M* (no lift nor central heating). — Am Zirkus 11, corner of the Schiffbauerdamm, *Hôtel Moskau*. 30 R. at 2½-6, B. 1 *M* patronised by Russians.

In the Old Town, frequented by business-men: *Grand Hôtel Alexander-Plat.* Pl. l R, 29, Alexander-Str. 46-48, a huge hôtel garni (200 R. at $2^1/_2$-5, B. 1 $\mathcal{M}$), with restaurant and café — Heiligegeist-Str. 17-18, *Hôtel de Hambourg*, 60 R. at 2-4, B 1 $\mathcal{M}$.

Near the Potsdam Station. *Palast-Hotel* and *Furstenhof*, see p. 3. ×*Grand Hôtel Bellevue & Tiergarten-Hotel* (Pl. i: R, 19), Potsdamer-Platz 1, 120 R. at $3^1/_4$-$7^1/_2$, B $1^1/_4$, déj. $2^1/_2$, D. $3^1/_2$-5, pens. $9^1/_2$-14 $\mathcal{M}$; *Hôtel Sanssouci*, Link-Str. 27, 80 R. from 2, B. 1 $\mathcal{M}$.

Near the Anhalt Station. *Hot. Excelsior*, see p. 3· *Habsburger Hof*, Askanischer-Platz 1, 120 R. at 3-8, B. $1^1/_4$. pens. from 10 $\mathcal{M}$, with restaurant. — Königgratzer-Str : No. 21, *Askanischer Hof*, 50 R. at $3^1/_2$-8 (incl. B.), D. $1^1/_2$-3 $\mathcal{M}$; No. 23, *Westend Hotel*, 60 R. at $2^1/_2$-$7^1/_2$, B. 1, D. 2, pens. from $7^1/_2$ $\mathcal{M}$· No. 25, *Deutscher Kaiser*, 40 R at 2-5, B. 1 $\mathcal{M}$; No 32, *Hôtel Union*, 60 R. at $2^1/_2$-5, B. 1, D. 2 $\mathcal{M}$; No. 38, corner of Mockern-Str , *Hôtel Hollstein*, 50 R. at $2^1/_2$-5. B 1, D. $1^3/_4$ $\mathcal{M}$; No. 107, *Wettiner Hof*, 30 R at 2-3 $\mathcal{M}$, B. 75 pf.; No. 117a, *Preussischer Hof*, 50 R. at $2^1/_2$-5, B. 1 $\mathcal{M}$. — Hedemann-Str. 8, *Thüringer Hof*, 40 R. at 2-$3^1/_2$, B $^3/_4$ $\mathcal{M}$.

In the West: Kurfürsten-Str. 105, *Kurfürsten-Hotel*, 40 R. at 2-5, B 1 $\mathcal{M}$ (no lift nor central heating). — Hotels at Charlottenburg, see p. 179.

Near the Lehrte Station· Invaliden-Str. 84-85, *Schwarz's Hotel*, 21 R. at $1^1/_2$-3, B. $^3/_4$ $\mathcal{M}$.

Near the Stettin Station Invaliden-Str. 126, *Nordischer Hof*, 120 R at 2-5, B. 1 $\mathcal{M}$.

Hospices, so-called, of a religious character, generally well spoken of; recommended also to ladies travelling alone. Wine not compulsory An addition of 10-15 per cent of the total amount is made to the bill in lieu of tips — *Hospiz des Westens*, Marburger-Str. 4, 70 R. at $2^1/_2$-$6^1/_2$, B. 1, D. $1^1/_4$-2, pens. from 5 $\mathcal{M}$. — *Hospiz der Berliner Stadtmission*, Mohren-Str. 27-28, corner of the Gendarmen-Markt, 85 R. at 2-5, B. 1, D. 2-$2^1/_2$ $\mathcal{M}$. — *Hospiz am Brandenburger Tor*, Königgratzer-Str. 5, 40 R. at $2^1/_2$-10 $\mathcal{M}$. — *Hospiz im Centrum Berlins*, Holzgarten-Str. 10, near the Kur-Str., 76 R. at $1^3/_4$-4, B. $^3/_4$ $\mathcal{M}$, D $1^1/_2$. pens. 5-8 $\mathcal{M}$. — *Hospiz St. Michael*, Wilhelm-Str. 34, 55 R. at $2^1/_2$-$6^1/_2$, B. $^3/_4$, D. 2, pens. 6-10 $\mathcal{M}$. — *Hospiz des Nordens*, Borsig-Str. 5, near the Stettin Station, R $1^1/_2$-3 $\mathcal{M}$ — *Ranke Hospiz*, Ranke-Str. 4, close to Zoolog Garden Station, R. & B. from $3^1/_2$ $\mathcal{M}$. — *Allianz-Hospiz*, Schluter-Str. 55-56, at Charlottenburg, 38 R. from 2, B. $^3/_4$-1, D. $1^1/_4$-$1^1/_2$, pens. from $4^1/_2$ $\mathcal{M}$.

Hôtels Garnis (B supplied in all; some also with hot and cold cuisine). Kleine Kirchgasse 2-3, *Linden Hotel*, 50 R. from $2^1/_2$ $\mathcal{M}$, B 80 pf. — Unter den Linden 26. *Hotel Bauer*, 30 R. at $2^3/_4$-6, B. 1 , Mauer-Str 1, *Schweizer Hof*. Schadow-Str. 1a, *Berg's Hotel*, 30 R. at $2^1/_2$, 5 B. 1 . — Schiffbauer-

damm 13. *Hôtel Kosmos*, 30 R. at 2¹/₂-6, B. 1 ℳ. — Behren-Str. 28,
Pettke's Private Hotel, 20 R at 2-3¹/₂ ℳ, B. 75 pf. — Charlotten-
Str. 59, corner of the Gendarmen-Markt, *Eichberg*, 18 R. at 2-5,
B. 1 ℳ. — Friedrich-Str.. No. 66, corner of Mohren-Str., *Mohren-
hof* (Pl. g; R, 33), 70 R. at 3-6, B. 1¹/₄ ℳ, very fair; No. 134, *Dutch
Private Hotel*, 20 R. at 1¹/₂-3, B ¹/₂ ℳ; No. 29, corner of Koch-
Str., *Pariser Hof*, 50 R. at 3-7, B. 1¹/₄ ℳ. — Krausen-Str.:
Nos. 56-58, *Zum Grünen Baum*, 106 R. at 2-3, B. ³/₄ ℳ; Nos. 67-68,
Kleiner Kaiserhof, 75 R. at 2¹/₂-7, B. ³/₄ ℳ. — Koch-Str. 74,
Wieland, 10 R. at 1³/₄-4 ℳ, B. 60 pf., with baths. — Breite-Str. 27,
Krüger, 30 R. at 1¹/₂-3, B. ³/₄, D. 1¹/₂ ℳ. — Near the Anhalt
Station: Askanischer-Platz 1, *Eichberg* (family hotel). 8 R. at
2¹/₂-4, B. ³/₄ ℳ; Anhalt-Str. 12, *Stuttgarter Hof*, 50 R at 3-12 ℳ;
Wilhelm-Str. 35, *Wittelsbacher Hof*, 35 R at 2¹/₂-6, B 1 ℳ.

Boarding Houses ('*Pensionate*'; usually managed by ladies)
are to be found in great numbers; the following are among the best
known.

Unter den Linden: No. 29 (3rd floor), *Stern*, 7 R., pens. 5-8 ℳ;
No. 33, *Residenz-Pension* (Stark), 17 R., pens 5-12 ℳ. No. 43,
Radtke, 17 R., pens. 4-7 ℳ: Nos. 62-63 (3rd floor), *Fritz*, 25 R.,
pens. 5-9¹/₂ ℳ; No. 70, *Pens. Daheim* (Frau Ida Schmidt), 28 R.,
pens. 5-12 ℳ.

To the S. of the Linden. Charlotten-Str.: No. 48 (3rd floor),
corner of the Behren-Str., *Talkenberg*, 24 R., pens. 5-7¹/₂ ℳ,
Nos. 50-51 (3rd floor; lift), corner of the Gendarmen-Markt, *Porsch*,
25 R., pens. 4-8 ℳ. — Französische-Str. 21 (3rd and 4th floors),
Schultz & Vielhauck, 15 R., pens 4-8 ℳ. — Markgrafen-Str. 39-40,
Ludwig, 17 R., pens. 5-7 ℳ. — Jäger-Str. 27 (2nd floor), *Schmidt-
Heinritz*, 16 R., pens. 5-8 ℳ.

To the N. of the Linden. Neue Wilhelm-Str. 2 (2nd floor),
Gretsel- von Behr, 16 R., pens. 5-9 ℳ; same house (3rd floor), *Von
Ehrenthal*, 16 R., pens. 4¹/₂-9 ℳ. — Schadow-Str. 4-5 (3rd floor),
Rinkel, 12 R., pens. 4-8 ℳ. — Dorotheen-Str. 36, *Von Engelbrecht*,
18 R., pens. 4-6 ℳ. — Schiffbauerdamm 5 (3rd floor), *Wallraff*,
15 R., pens. 5-7 ℳ. — Karl-Str 31, *Jendritza*, 7 R., pens. 5-7 ℳ.

Near the Potsdam and Anhalt Stations (Pl. G, 19, 22; R, 19).
Köthener-Str. 32 (1st floor), *Bauer*, 12 R., pens. 4-7 ℳ. — Potsdamer-
Str.: No. 13 (2nd-4th floors; lift), *Kirstein*, 33 R., pens. 5-8¹/₂ ℳ;
No. 14, *Hoenke*, 14 R., pens. 4-8 ℳ, No. 103a (1st floor), *Leh-
mann-Herzberg*, 17 R., pens. 4-8 ℳ; No. 105 a, *Buschhammer*,
40 R., pens. 4¹/₂-8 ℳ; No 123 a (2nd and 3rd floors), *Von Finck*,
44 R., pens. from 5¹/₂ ℳ. — Bernburger-Str. 15-16 (3rd floor),
Von Hauen, 12 R., pens 4¹/₂-5¹/₂ ℳ. — Anhalt-Str. 15 (3rd floor),
Mätzky. 12 R.. pens per month from 100 ℳ. — Wilhelm-Str.:
No. 30-31. *Ruscheweyh-Seyfried*, 23 R., pens. 4¹/₂-10 ℳ; No. 49
(2nd-4th floors, *Gerling* English, 20 R., pens. 5-8, per month

120-230 *M*; No. 114 (1st and 2nd floors), *Herpich*, pens. 5-7 *M*
— Koniggratzer-Str.: No. 109, *Mahlendorf*, 11 R., pens. 4-7 *M*;
No. 62. *Lessel*, 10 R , pens. 3-8 *M*. — Hallesche-Str.: No 17 (1st
floor), *Spranger*, 10 R., pens. 2¹/₂-4¹/₂ *M*; No. 20, *Wilda*, 19 R,
pens 4¹/₂-9 *M*.

In the West (Pl. G, 16. 13, 10), between the Tiergarten and
the Electric Elevated and Underground Railway. Potsdamer-Str :
No. 39a (2nd floor), *Volckmann*, 16 R., pens 4¹/₂-8 *M*: No. 40, *Otto*,
10 R., pens. 4-6 *M*; No. 41, *Welle*, 13 R , pens. 4-8 *M*. — Eichhorn-
Str 9, *Senstius*, pens. 4-6 *M*. — Lutzow-Str.: No. 20 (1st floor),
Von Göckel, 12 R , pens from 4 *M*; No 93 (3rd floor), *Boelicke*.
12 R — Lutzow-Platz 12 (2nd and 3rd floors), *Gubitz*, 20 R., pens.
4-8 *M*. — Lutzow-Ufer 33 (1st floor), *Giereke*, 10 R., pens 5¹/₂-
10 *M*. — Keith-Str. 16, *Van Heuckelum*, 80 R , pens. 7¹/₂-15 *M*
— Dornberg-Str. 1, *Grau*, 12 R., pens. 4¹/₂-7 *M* — Magdeburger-
Str 14 (2nd and 3rd floors), *Meinshausen*, 15 R., pens. 4-6 *M* —
Steglitzer-Str.: No. 21, *Naether*, 9 R., pens. 4-6 *M*; No. 69,
Jacoby, 17 R., pens. 4¹/₂-6¹/₂ *M* — Kurfursten-Str . No. 81b
(2nd floor), *Linde*, 9 R , pens. 4¹/₂-7 *M*; No 106 (2nd and 3rd
floors), *Von Spitz*, 14 R , pens 5¹/₂-10 *M*; No 111 (1st floor),
Volhard, 11 R., pens. 5-10 *M*; No 112, *Tscheuschner*, 50 R.,
pens 5-8 *M*. — Nettelbeck-Str. 21. *Von Schelepin*, 12 R., pens
4-5 *M*. — Bulow-Str. 100 (2nd floor), *Frommhold*, 6 R., pens.
5-7 *M*. — Kleist-Str.. No. 3 (3rd floor), *Radloff & Ramland*,
19 R , pens. 4¹/₂-10¹/₂ *M*; No. 28. *Kährn*, 25 R , pens. 5-9 *M*:
No. 27, *Starkmann*, 28 R., pens from 8 *M*; No. 23, *Klamroth*,
11 R., pens. 5-8 *M*, No. 26 (3rd floor), *Peters*, pens 5-7 *M*; No. 32
(3rd floor), *Witte*, 9 R , pens. 5-8 *M*. — Tauenzien-Str.: No. 1
(2nd floor), *Reichel*. 20 R , pens 4-7 *M*: No 18, *Gansel*, 17 R ,
pens. 4¹/₂-8 *M*. — Genthiner-Str 32, *De Bourdeaux*, 14 R., pens.
4-8 *M*. — Von-der-Heydt-Str. 1, *Medenwaldt & Stubenranch*,
16 R., pens. 5-10 *M*. — Friedrich-Wilhelm-Str. 4, *Krause*, 40 R.,
pens. from 8 *M* — Luther-Str. 12, corner of Kleist-Str., *Frau
Marie Dollen*, 10 R.. pens. 4-8 *M*.—Nurnberger-Str.: No 3, *Kahle*.
8 R., pens. monthly 120-180 *M*. No. 6, *Kietz*, 12 R., pens. 4-6 *M*.

To the S. of the Elevated and Underground Railway. Eisenacher-
Str. 10 (3rd floor), *Ferber*, 9 R , pens. 4-5 *M*. — Motz-Str. 72,
Von Laurenz, 16 R , pens 4-5¹/₂ *M* — Viktoria-Luise-Platz:
No. 7, *Stolzenberg*, 8 R., pens 4¹/₂-10 *M*; No. 10, *Belmont* (Eng-
lish), pens. 6-10 *M*. — Luitpold-Str. 37: *Miss Edman*, pens. 4-6 *M*.
— Heilbronner-Str. 25: *Pens Clare* (Mrs Bennett). pens. 5-8 *M*.
— Bayreuther-Str. 39 (2nd floor), *Polckow*, 7 R., pens. 5-10 *M*. —
Nurnberger-Str. 37 (1st floor), *Scheringer*, 6 R., pens 5-8 *M*. —
Ranke-Str.: Nos. 31-32 (1st and 2nd floors), *Heym*, 22 R., pens from
5 *M*; No. 8 *Pension des Westens*. 14 R , pens 5-10 *M*. Angs-
burger-Str No. 63, *Stossinger*. 16 R.. pens. 5-8 *M* Nos 59-60.

Frau Anna Duncan, pens. 32 ℳ weekly; Nos. 68-69, *Scheele,* 7 R., pens. monthly 120-175 ℳ; No. 81, *Pens Mayfair;* No. 100 (1st floor), *Von Langen,* 6 R., pens. 5-7 ℳ.

To the N. of the Stadtbahn, in Charlottenburg: Uhland-Str. 197, Stein-Platz, *Moraht,* 50 R., pens. 7-16 ℳ.

At Grunewald, Hubertus-Allée 16: *Sprague-Koch-Kaschke,* 20 R., pens. 6-12 ℳ.

Furnished Apartments (30-45 ℳ per month) are plentiful between the Karl-Str. to the N. of the Linden and the Koch-Str. to the S. of the Leipziger-Str., as well as in the neighbourhood of the Potsdamer-Str. (see p. 173). If rooms are occupied for more than one month, notice must be given on the 15th if it is desired to leave on the 1st of the following month.

c. Restaurants. Wine Houses. Beer.

For alphabetical list see Index. — *List of Streets,* p. 227.

Wine Restaurants. — *Hôtel Adlon,* Unter den Linden 1, S. side (see p. 2); *Hôtel Kaiserhof,* Wilhelm-Platz (p. 3); *Hôtel Bristol,* Unter den Linden 5-6, S. side (p. 3); *Savoy Hotel,* Friedrich-Str. 103 (p 3); *Monopol Hotel,* Friedrich-Str. 100 (p. 3); *Continental Hotel,* Neustädtische-Kirch-Str. 6-7 (p. 3); *Hôtel de Rome,* Unter den Linden 39, N. side (p. 3); *Hiller,* Unter den Linden 62-63, N. side; *Dressel,* Unter den Linden 50, N. side; *Astoria,* Unter den Linden 32, S. side, in the Carlton Hotel (p 3); *Central Hôtel,* Friedrich-Str. 143-149 (p. 3); *Hôtel Fürstenhof,* Potsdamer-Platz (p. 3); *Palast-Hotel,* Leipziger-Platz 18-19 (p 3); *Borchardt,* Französische-Str. 48; *Ewest,* Behren-Str. 26a; *Restaurant Royal,* Unter den Linden 33. S side. — *Restaurant at the Zoological Garden* (p 177) — All these establishments are of the first class and may be visited by ladies; evening dress customary. At most of them visitors may dine either *à la carte* or *à prix fixe;* déj (11-2) 2½-3 ℳ, D. (3-8) 5-6 ℳ, S. 3½-5 ℳ. Prices of wines generally high.

The following are somewhat less expensive. *Haus Trarbach,* Behren-Str 47 (p. 120), D. (1-5) 2½, S (7-11) 3 ℳ; *Kempinski & Co.,* Leipziger-Str. 25. much frequented; *Rheingold* (p. 127), Bellevue-Str. 19-20, near the Potsdam Station (with beer restaurant, Potsdamer-Str. 3); *Traube,* Leipziger-Str 117-118; *Zum Treppchen,* Unter den Linden 56, N. side, D. (1-7) 2½-3½ ℳ; *Zum Rudesheimer,* Friedrich-Str. 80, D. (1-5) 3 ℳ, *Kaiser-Keller* (p. 121), Friedrich-Str. 178, D. (1-7) 2½ ℳ, both to the S. of the Linden; *Restaurant F. Schanke* (Hôtel Royal, p. 3), D. 3½ and 5, S. 3 ℳ.

Next follow: Unter den Linden 29-30 (S. side), *Habel,* an old-fashioned house, much frequented for luncheon. — To the N. of the Linden: Friedrich-Str. No. 96, *Rheinische Winzerstuben,* D. (1-4) 1½ ℳ, good; No. 95, *Eggebrecht.* — Dorotheen-Str.: No. 16. *Prinz*

Wilhelm; No. 81, *⁺Töpfer* (Hôtel Prinz Friedrich-Karl); No. 84, *⁻Stadt Berlin* (beer also at these three). — To the S. of the Linden Franzosische-Str. 18, *⁺L. Mitscher*, Moselle wines, D. (1-8) 1¹/₂-2 *M.* — Charlotten-Str.: Nos. 29-30, *Helmut Schmidt;* No. 49, near the Gendarmen-Markt, *⁺Lutter*, an old-established firm (p. 122); No. 59, *Nadolny*, D. (1-5) 1¹/₂ *M.* — Markgrafen-Str. 48, near the Gendarmen-Markt, *×Trarbach Nachfolger*, Rhine and Moselle wines, D (1-4) 1¹/₂ *M.* — Jager-Str. 5, *⁺Haussmann*, D. 1¹/₂ *M*, Rhenish cuisine, Moselle wines. — Kronen-Str. 21, *Höhn's Oyster Saloon*, D. (1-5) 2 *M.* — Leipziger-Str.: Nos. 31-32, *Rheinische Winzerstuben* (p. 8); No. 33, *Steinert & Hansen*, D. 1¹/₂ *M.* — Krausen-Str. 41, corner of the Dönhoff-Platz, *⁺J. H. D. Becker's Söhne* (good claret), D. 1¹/₂ *M.* — Zimmer-Str. 29, *Trierischer Winzerverein.* — Potsdamer-Str. No. 139, *Huth & Sohn;* No. 12, *'Frederich* (good claret); Nos. 136-137, *Fr. Muller;* Nos. 127-128, *Roland von Berlin* (comp p. 173) — Bülow-Str. 20, *Steinert & Hansen*, D. 1¹/₂ *M.* — Kurfurstendamm: No. 22, *Eugen Steinert;* No. 237, *Georg Meyer* (oysters). — Werderscher Markt 4, *'Kühn*, D. (1-5) 1¹/₂ *M.* — Burg-Str. 14, *Valentin.* — König-Str. 40, *⁺Mitscher & Caspary*, Rhine and Moselle wines. — Alexander-Platz, Dirksen-Str. 21, *⁻J. Knoop Söhne*, D. (1-4) 1 *M* 60.

ITALIAN WINES: *Unione Cooperativa di Milano*, Tauben-Str. 16-18; *Zum Vesuv* (Dalbelli), Potsdamer-Str. 13. — SPANISH & PORTUGUESE WINES *The Continental Bodega Company*, Friedrich-Str. 94, Alexander-Str 71, Jerusalemer-Str. 17, and Ranke-Str. 1 (at these cold viands only).

DUTCH LIQUEURS: *Erven Lucas Bols*, Friedrich-Str. 169; *C. S. Gerold Sohn* (Cognac rooms), Unter den Linden 19, Friedrich-Str. 153a, and Leipziger-Str. 103.

Beer Restaurants. The following are restaurants where genuine ('echt') Bavarian beer (litre generally 50, ¹/₂ litre 30 pf.), Pilsen (Bohemian), or locally brewed beer, with meals *à la carte* or *à prix fixe* (1-2 *M*) may be obtained. Some of these establishments are very handsomely fitted up, and most of them may be visited by ladies, though smoking is generally permitted.

UNTER DEN LINDEN: No. 13 (S. side), *Stadt Pilsen* (Pilsen beer), D. (12-5) 1¹/₂ *M*, Austrian cuisine, with garden: No. 44 (N. side), *Linden-Restaurant*, D. 1 and 1¹/₂ *M.*

S. OF THE LINDEN. Behren-Str. 23-24, *＊Siechen* (Nuremberg beer). — Friedrich-Str.: No. 84, *Augustiner-Bräu;* No. 165, corner of the Behren-Str., *＊Pschorrbräu:* No. 172, *⁺Sedlmayr 'Zum Spaten';* Nos. 176-178, corner of the Jager-Str., *'Weihenstephan.* D. (12-4) 1¹/₄ *M·* No. 180, *＊Tucher-Bräu* (Nuremberg beer). — Französische-Str. No. 21 *Ermitage* Russian cuisine Nos. 25-26, corner of the Charlotten-Str., *Löwenbräu.* Kronen-Str. 55,

Mönchshof (Kulmbach beer), D. 1 *M* 10 pf. — Niederwall-Str. 25, corner of the Spittelmarkt, *Münchner Bürgerbräu.* — Leipziger-Str.: No. 85, near the Donhoff-Platz, *Münchner Hofbräu;* No. 109, *Dortmunder Unionbräu,* D. (12-4) 1 *M.* — Krausen-Str. 64, **Zum Klausner* (Pilsen beer). — Wilhelm-Str. 92-93, *Architektenhaus* (p. 123). — Belle-Alliance-Platz 15, *Erlanger Reifbräu,* D. (12-4) 1 *M* 10 pf. — Belle-Alliance-Str. 89, ** Wahlstatt* (Nuremberg beer), D. (12-5) 1 *M.*

Outside the Potsdam Gate. — In the Potsdamer-Platz: **Zum Schultheiss,* with terrace. — Königgrätzer-Str. 123a, *Potsdamer Garten* — Potsdamer-Str. Nos. 10-11, **Alt-Bayern (Weihen-stephan;* handsome Romanesque 'Minstrels' Hall', comp. p. 173); No. 124, by the bridge, *Großer Kurfürst,* D. (12-5) 1¼ *M.* — Schöneberger Ufer 23, by the Potsdamer Brücke, *Weihenstephan,* with garden. — Bülow-Str. 1, near the Nollendorf-Platz, *Voges.* — Motz-Str. 81, *Restaurant Neues Schauspielhaus* (p. 28; with wine rooms). — Kurfürsten-Str. 91, close to the Zoological Garden, *Burggrafenhof.*

N. of the Linden. Mittel-Str.: Nos 16-17, *Saalburg;* Nos 57-58, corner of the Friedrich-Str., 1st floor, *Krzinanerk,* Austrian cuisine, D. (12-5) 1¼-2½ *M.* — Dorotheen-Str 92-93, *Splendid Hotel* (p. 4). — Georgen-Str. 13, in an arch of the Stadtbahn, *Zum Franziskaner,* D. (12-4) 1½ *M,* with garden. — Friedrich-Str.: No. 101, *Terminus;* Nos. 143-149, *'Zum Heidelberger,* in the Central Hotel (p 3); No. 150, *Oesterreichischer Hof* (in the Hôtel Rheinischer Hof, p 4). — Kaiser Wilhelm-Str. 49, *Schloss-Restaurant,* D. (12-4) 1 *M* 10-1 *M* 50 pf. — Luisen-Str. 46, *Schünemann* (Nuremberg beer). — Invaliden-Str. 40, *Zur Hochschule* (Spatenbräu). — Alt-Moabit 138, near the Exhibition Park, **Printz* (Pschorrbräu).

In the Old Town. — In the Rathaus: **Ratskeller* (p. 152), also wine-room, D. 1½-3 *M.* — Burg-Str. 20, *Schloss-Restaurant,* D. 1 *M* 10-1 *M* 50 pf. — Neuer Markt 8-12, corner of Kaiser Wilhelm-Str., *Altstädter Hof.* — Alexander-Platz: *Zum Prälaten,* in an arch of the Stadtbahn.

In the East: **Alhambra,* Andreas-Str. 6, in an arch of the Stadtbahn.

In the Tiergarten: The *Zelte* (Pl. R, 17; comp. p. 176); *'Charlottenhof* (Pl. R, 10, 13; p. 176), near the Charlottenburger Chaussée, *Tiergartenhof,* near the Tiergarten Station (Pl. R, 10), all with gardens.

Light luncheons may be obtained quickly and simply at *Aschinger's Bierquellen,* Friedrich-Str. 97, 88, and 151, a little to the S. of the Linden, and at the *Automatic Restaurants,* of which there are several in the Friedrich-Str. and other important centres of traffic. — Jäger-Str. 11, *Niquet & Co.* (good sausages; limited space) Friedrich-Str. 95, *Restaurant Skandinavia.*

BERLIN BEER (15 pf. per glass; D. generally *à la carte*): *Zum Schultheiss*, Behren-Str. 49, corner of the Friedrich-Str.; also at Alt-Moabit 15. — Tauben-Str. 36, corner of Friedrich-Str., *Ausschank Friedrichshöhe* (see below). — Oranien-Str. 150, at the Moritz-Platz, *Neumann*. — Friedrich-Str. 100, *Botzow's Brauerei-Ausschank* (in the Monopol Hotel, p. 3).

WEISS-BIER: *Clausing*, Zimmer-Str. 80; *Haase*, Ross-Str. 6.

VEGETARIAN RESTAURANTS: *Behnke*, Friedrich-Str. 151; *Kronberg*, Prinz Louis-Ferdinand-Str. 2, near the Friedrich-Strasse-Station; *Kammerer*, Kronen-Str. 47, 1st floor; *Jaschke*, Scharren-Str. 8; *Freya*, Charlottenburg, Bismarck-Str. 8.

Breweries with Gardens, situated on the outskirts of the town, in many of which military bands play in summer. IN THE S.: *Zum Schultheiss am Kreuzberg* (Pl. G, 21), to the E. of the monument; *Berliner Bock-Brauerei* (Pl. G, 24), Fidicin-Str. 2-3; *Habel* (Pl. G, 24), Bergmann-Str. 5-7. — IN THE S.E.: Hasenheide (Pl. G, 30), Nos. 32-38, *Happoldt*; Nos. 22-31, *Union*; Nos. 108-114, *Bergschloss* (Neue Welt). — IN THE N.E.: *Aktien-Brauerei Friedrichshain* (Pl. R, 33), Friedrichshain 16-23 (see p. 30); *Aktien-Brauerei Friedrichshöhe* (Pl. R, 35), Landsberger Allée 24-27; *Böhmisches Brauhaus* (Pl. R, 32), Landsberger Allée 11-13. — IN THE N.: *Pfefferberg* (Pl. R, 27), Schönhauser Allée 176; *Schultheiss* (Pl. B, 30), Schönhauser Allée 36-39; *Berliner Bock-Brauerei* (Pl. B, 21), Chaussee-Str. 64. — IN THE N.W.: *Aktien-Brauerei Friedrichshöhe* (Pl. R, 15), Strom-Str. 11-16. — IN THE W.: *Schöneberger Schloss-Brauerei* (Pl. G, 15), see p. 174.

d. Cafés. Confectioners.

Cafés. *Bauer* (Pl. R, 23), Unter den Linden 26, corner of the Friedrich-Str.; *Josty* (Pl. R, 23), Bellevue-Str. 21-22, corner of the Potsdamer-Platz, with terrace, both in the centre of traffic; *Monopol* (p. 3), these three well provided with German and foreign newspapers; *Café Westminster*, Unter den Linden 17-18; *Victoria-Café*, Unter den Linden 46; *Café Klose*, Leipziger-Str. 19, corner of the Mauer-Str., 1st floor; *Kaiser-Café*, with the Kaiser-Buffet (American bar), Friedrich-Str. 176-178; *Café Fürstenhof*, Potsdamer-Platz, in the Hôtel Fürstenhof (p. 3); *Reichshallen-Café*, Leipziger-Str. 77, near the Donhoff-Platz; *Café Kerkau*, Friedrich-Str. 59-60 (billiards); *Café Friedrichshof*, Friedrich-Str. 41-42, corner of the Koch-Str.; *Café Central-Hôtel* (p. 3); *Mohren-Café*, Mohren-Str. 47; *Café Schiller*, Markgrafen-Str. 55-56, near the Gendarmen-Markt; in the *Grand Hôtel Alexander-Platz* (p. 4); *Börsen-Café*, Burg-Str. 27, *Café Austria*, Potsdamer-Str. 28, *Romanisches Café*, Kurfürstendamm 238, *Josty*, Joachimsthaler-Str. 44, *Mandl*, Kant-Str. 165-166, these three near the Kaiser Wilhelm-Gedächtnis-

Kirche Luncheons and beer (generally Pilsen) may be procured at all these cafés. Cup of coffee 25-30, 'mélange' (glass of milk, coffee, and whipped cream) 35 pf., baskets with cakes, etc., stand on the tables. The waiter expects 5-10 pf. per person.

Confectioners (cup of coffee 25-30, chocolate 40-50, ices 50-60 pf.). Payment is usually made at the cashier's desk; smoking allowed in special smoking rooms only. *Kranzler*, Unter den Linden 25, S. side, corner of the Friedrich-Str.; *Schilling*, Friedrich-Str. 209, corner of the Koch-Str., with branch at Kurfürstendamm 231; *Hillbrich*, Leipziger-Str. 24; *Telschow*, Potsdamer-Platz 3; *Mericke*, Tauenzien-Str. 13; *Gumpert*, König-Str. 22-24. *Aschinger*, Friedrich-Str. 79a, Alexander-Platz, etc.; *Lagergren*, Schloss-Platz 3 (frequented by Scandinavians). — *Bullock's American Candy Shop* (ice-cream, etc.), Potsdamer-Str. 126. — *Indian Tea Rooms*, Leipziger-Str. 94. — Frequented by ladies only. *Salis*, Friedrich-Str. 162, and the tea-rooms in the stores mentioned on p. 31.

c. Stadtbahn and Ringbahn. Electric Elevated and Underground Railway.

Comp. Plans opposite the title-page and at p 13, and the Map at p. 185.

The **Stadtbahn**, or *City Railway*, built in 1874-82, is 10 M in length and stretches through the N. half of the inner city from Westend-Charlottenburg on the W. to Stralau-Rummelsburg on the E. It is connected with the **Ringbahn**, built in 1867-77, which runs through the N. suburbs and makes a wide sweep round the S. portion of the city. Trains run on the Stadtbahn from about 5 a.m. till after midnight at intervals of 2-5 minutes, and on the Ringbahn every 10-20 minutes. There are only second and third class carriages. Fares for any 5 stations 15 and 10 pf. (monthly tickets $4\frac{1}{2}$ and 3 *M*), beyond that distance 30 and 20 pf. (monthly tickets 7 and $4\frac{1}{2}$ *M*). No time should be lost in taking seats, as the stoppages are extremely brief. Notice-boards indicate the point at which second-class carriages come to a stand, the name of the station, and the direction in which the trains run Passengers accidentally carried past their destination may return thither without extra charge on applying at once to the station-master.

The STADTBAHN has four tracks, of which the two northernmost are used for the intramural traffic and by the Ringbahn trains (see below), while the two southernmost are traversed by mainline trains (see p. 1; special entrances) All four tracks are used by the suburban trains. The stations are (from W. to E.) *Charlottenburg* (Pl. G, 4), *Savigny-Platz* (Pl. G, 7), *Zoologischer Garten* (Pl. G, 10), *Tiergarten* (Pl. R, 10), *Bellevue* (Pl. R, 14), *Lehrter Bahnhof* Pl. R, 18, 21, *Friedrich-Strasse* (Pl. R, 23), *Börse* (Pl. R, 26), *Alexander-Platz* Pl. R 26, *Jannowitz-Brücke* (Pl. R, 28),

Schlesischer Bahnhof (Pl R, 31), *Warschauer-Strasse* (Pl. G, 34), and *Stralau-Rummelsburg* (Pl. G, 37, 40).

Suburban Trains of the Stadtbahn. On the S. tracks trains run (from the chief stations) eastwards to *Strausberg* (p. 208), with junction for *Rüdersdorf* (p. 202); westwards to *Spandau* (p. 200) — On the N. tracks they run (from all stations) eastwards to *Nieder-Schöneweide*, with connection to *Grünau* (p. 203) or *Königs-Wusterhausen* (p 202), viâ *Lichtenberg* (p. 168) to *Kaulsdorf*, and to *Erkner* (p. 202; junction for *Fürstenwalde*); westwards to *Grunewald* (p. 184). — Suburban trains also run from the *Potsdam Station* viâ Potsdam to Wildpark or Werder (comp. p 199); from the *Wannsee Station* (Pl G, 19) viâ Schlachtensee and Wannsee to Potsdam (comp. p 186); from the *Ring-Bahnhof* (Pl. G, 19; to the left behind the Potsdam Station) to Gross-Lichterfelde (p 185) and Zossen; from the *Stettin Station* to Tegel, Oranienburg, and Bernau; and from the *Lehrte Station* to Nauen.

Tickets by suburban trains are cheaper than tickets to the same place by main-line trains On Sun afternoons in summer the suburban trains are usually overcrowded, and in the evening it is almost impossible to find a place at stations near Berlin in trains returning to the capital.

The RINGBAHN consists of the 'Nord-Ring' and the 'Süd-Ring', both mostly used in connection with the Stadtbahn (stations, see above), from which they diverge at *Stralau-Rummelsburg* (Pl. G, 37, 40; comp. above) and *Charlottenburg* (Pl. G, 4). — The NORD-RING (11 M.) passes the following stations: *Frankfurter Allee* (Pl. R, 40; p. 168), *Zentral-Viehhof* (cattle-market; Pl. R, 38; p. 168), *Landsberger Allée* (Pl. R, 39), *Weissensee* (Pl. B, 33, 36; p. 168), *Prenzlauer Allée* (Pl. B, 32), *Schönhauser Allée* (Pl. 29; p 167), *Gesundbrunnen* (Pl. B, 23; p. 167). *Wedding* (Pl. B, 17. 20, p. 168), *Putlitz-Strasse* (Pl. B, 15), *Beussel-Strasse* (Pl. B, 12; p. 165), *Jungfernheide* (Pl. R, 3), and *Westend* (Pl. R, 2; p. 183). — The SÜD-RING (13$\frac{1}{2}$ M) stops at the stations of *Halensee* (Pl. G, 2: p. 184), *Schmargendorf*, *Wilmersdorf-Friedenau* (pp 181, 185), *Ebers-Strasse*, *Schöneberg* (Pl. G, 18; p. 174), *Pape-Str.*, *Tempelhof* (p. 173), *Hermann-Strasse*, *Rixdorf* (p. 172), and *Treptow* (Pl. G, 38; p. 170). Carriages are changed at Schoneberg; the trains proceed or come from the *Potsdamer Ring-Bahnhof* (Pl. G, 19; p. 127).

The **Electric Elevated and Underground Railway,** built in 1896-1902 by Siemens & Halske (p. 182) and subsequently extended, traverses the S. quarters of Berlin from E. to W. The underground portion begins at the Nollendorf-Platz and runs thence to the W. to Charlottenburg. From the central junction (see p. 128) a branch line, descending a steep incline, leads to the underground platform at the Leipziger-Platz. The stations are: *Warschauer-Brücke* (Pl G, 34, close to the Stadtbahn Station, see above), *Stralauer Tor* (Pl. G, 34; Oberbaum-Brücke, p. 170), *Schlesisches Tor* (Pl. G, 34; p. 169), *Oranien-Strasse* (Pl. G, 31, 31; Görlitz Station, p 169), *Kottbuser Tor* (Pl. G, 28, 29), *Prinzen-Strasse* (Pl. G, 26), *Hallesches Tor* Pl. G, 23: p 170, *Mockern-Brücke* Pl. G, 20). — *Leipziger-Platz*. Pl. G, 19: underground, access at the E. end of the

Platz or to the left in front of the Potsdam Station; comp. pp. 124, 127).   *Bülow-Strasse* (Pl. G, 17; p. 174), *Nollendorf-Platz* (Pl. G, 13; p. 174), then (underground) *Wittenberg-Platz* (Pl. G, 13), *Zoologischer Garten* (Pl. G, 10; close to the Stadtbahn Station, p. 12), *Charlottenburg-Knie* (Pl R, 7; p. 182), *Bismarck-Strasse* (Pl. R, 4), *Wilhelm-Platz* (Pl R, 5)   From Bismarck-Strasse Station an underground branch leads to the W. viâ the stations of *Sophie-Charlotte-Platz* (Pl R, 1) and *Kaiserdamm* (Pl R, 1) to the *Reichs-Kanzler-Platz* (West End, beyond Pl. R, 1)   — Before the end of 1908 the underground line from the Leipziger-Platz to the Spittel-Markt will be opened; entrances to the stations: Wilhelm-Platz and Trinity Church, Mohren-Str. (cor. of Friedrich-Str.) and Gendarmen-Markt, Tauben-Str. and Hausvogtei-Platz, Spittel-Markt and Spindlershof (comp. Pl. R, 22, 25). The trains run viâ Leipziger-Platz Station (not reckoned for travellers not alighting there) or direct to their terminal stations. — The regulations are similar to those of the Stadtbahn. There is no 1st class; tickets on the main line 2nd class 15-35, 3rd class 10-25 pf.; trains every 3-7 minutes.

f. Electric Tramways.

The various lines of the Berlin Tramway Co. (*Grosse Berliner Strassenbahn - Aktien - Gesellschaft*) are divided into groups and numbered or designed by large initials   The numbers and letters shewn in the list below and on the opposite plan correspond with these official numbers A few lines which have no numbers are marked at p. 22 with small letters. On certain busy routes extra cars are run, marked with an E beneath the route-number, these are not marked in our list. Cars run every $7\frac{1}{2}$ min. or oftener except when otherwise indicated. Fare 10 pf., 10-20 pf. on certain lines. Monthly ticket for one line $7\frac{1}{2}$, for two lines 10, all lines (except a-h) 30 ℳ

The lines radiating from the chief points of intersection will be found specially mentioned in our description of the city

1. STADTRING: from the Rosenthaler Tor viâ Schönhauser Tor, Prenzlauer Tor, Königs-Tor, Landsberger Tor, Andreas-Str. (Silesian Station), Moritz-Platz, Hallesches Tor, Anhalt Station, Potsdam Station, Brandenburger Tor, Kronprinzen-Brücke, Oranienburger Tor back to the Rosenthaler Tor.

2. AUSSENRING: from the Rosenthaler Tor to the Moritz-Platz as in No. 1, then Gneisenau-Str., Katzbach-Str. (Kreuzberg), Schöneberg Station, Nollendorf-Platz, Lützow-Platz, Grosser Stern, Hansa-Platz, Lehrte Station, Neues Tor, Stettin Station, Rosenthaler Tor; every $\frac{1}{4}$ hr.

3. GROSSER RING: from the Rosenthaler Tor viâ Alexander-Platz, Andreas-Str. (Silesian Station), Kottbuser Tor, Gneisenau-Str., Yorck-Strasse Station, Winterfeldt-Platz, Nollendorf-Platz, Lützow-Platz, Grosser Stern, Hansa-Platz, Moabit, Wedding, Garten-Platz, and Rosenthaler Tor.

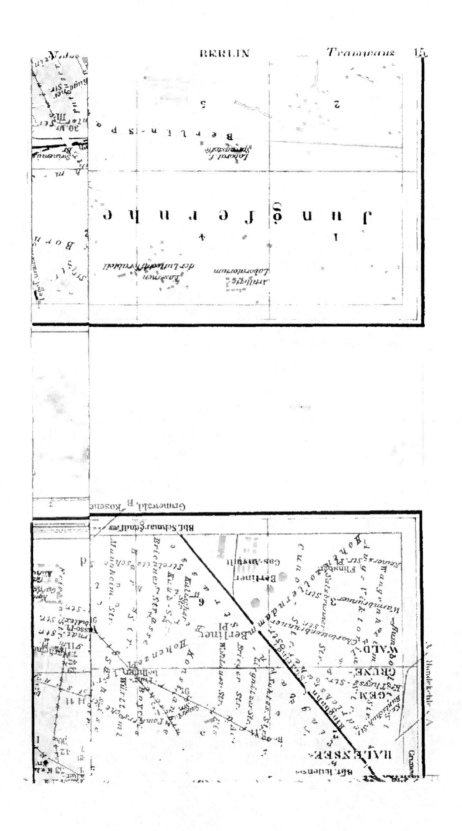

4. East-and-West Ring from the Rosenthaler Tor to the Hallesches Tor as in No. 1, then Yorck-Strasse Station, Hohenstaufen-Str., Zoological Garden, Grosser Stern, Hansa-Platz, Turm-Str., Lehrte Station, Kronprinzen-Brücke, Oranienburger Tor, Rosenthaler Tor; every $1/4$ hr.

5. Gerichts-Ring (not complete). Pankow, Schonhauser Allée Station, Alexander-Platz, Jannowitz-Brücke Station, Kottbuser Tor, Hasenheide, Yorck-Strasse Station, Winterfeldt-Platz, Wilmersdorf, Charlottenburg Station, Turm-Str., Wedding Station, Pank-Str. (corner of Bad-Str.); every $1/4$ hr.

6. *Küstriner-Platz* (Pl. R, 31, 34)-*Moabit* (Gotzkowski-Str.; Pl. R, 12): viâ Gruner Weg, Andreas-Str. (Silesian Station), Jannowitz-Brücke Station, Jakob-Str., Spittel-Markt, Leipziger-Str., Potsdam Station, Brandenburger Tor, Lehrte Station; every $1/4$ hr.

7. *Rixdorf* (Hertha-Str., near Pl. G, 3)-*Moabit* (Bremer-Str.; Pl. R, 12): viâ Rixdorf Station, Hasenheide, Hallesches Tor, Anhalt Station, Potsdam Station, Brandenburger Tor, Lehrte Station; every $1/4$ hr.

8. *Gesundbrunnen* (Pank-Str.; Pl. B, 19)-*Charlottenburg* (Amtsgericht; Pl. G, 1): viâ Wedding Station, Moabit, and Charlottenburg Palace; every $1/4$ hr.

9. *Silesian Station* (Pl. R, 31)-*Moabit* (Gotzkowski-Str.; Pl. R, 12): as in No 6, every $1/4$ hr.

10. *Schonhauser Allée* (Pappel-Allee; Pl B, 29, 30)-*Moabit* (Beussel-Strasse; Pl. R, 12): viâ Zions-Kirche, Stettin Station, Neues Tor, Lehrte Station; every $1/4$ hr.

11. *Görlitz Station* (Pl. G, 31)-*Moabit* (Wiebe-Str.; Pl. R, 12): viâ Oranien-Platz, Jannowitz-Brücke Station, Alexander-Platz, Rosenthaler Tor, Stettin Station, and as in No 10: every $7^1/_2$-15 minutes.

12. *Görlitz Station* (Pl. G, 31)-*Plötzensee* (Pl. B, 9, 12). viâ Donhoff-Platz, Opern-Platz, Georgen-Str., Lehrte Station, Moabit, and Beussel-Str. Station; every $1/4$ hr.

13. *Schlesische Brücke* (Pl. G, 35)-*Moabit* (Bremer-Str.; Pl R. 12): viâ Skalitzer-Str. (Görlitz Station), Ritter-Str., Donhoff-Platz, Opern-Platz, Dorotheen-Str. (Friedrich-Strasse Station), Königs-Platz, and Lehrte Station; every $1/4$ hr.

14. *Marheineke-Platz* (Pl. G, 24)-*Moabit* (Beussel-Str.; Pl. R, 12): viâ Hallesches Tor, Anhalt Station, Potsdam Station, Brandenburger Tor, Karls-Platz, Lehrte Station.

15. *Rixdorf Station* (near Pl. G, 33)-*Moabit* (Bremer-Strasse); viâ Hasenheide, Hallesches Tor, and thence as in No. 14, every $1/4$ hr.

16. *Küstriner Platz* Pl. R, 31, 34 - *Moabit* Bremer-Str., Pl. R, 12): viâ Gruner Weg, Silesian Station, Alexander-Platz Station, Rat-

haus, Exchange Station, Chaussee-Str. (Stettin Station), Neues
Tor, and Lehrte Station; every $1/4$ hr.

17. *Moabit* (Beussel-Str.; Pl R, 12)-*Greifswalder-Strasse* (Pl
B, 33): viâ Hansa-Platz, Grosser Stern, Lutzow-Platz, Anhalt
Station, Donhoff-Platz, Schloss-Platz, Rathaus, and Alexander-
Platz Station, every $1/4$ hr

18. *Görlitz Station* (Pl. G, 31)-*Charlottenburg* (Jungfern-Heide
Station; Pl. R, 3): viâ Donhoff-Platz, Opern-Platz, Georgen-Str.
(Friedrich-Strasse Station), Lehrte Station, Turm-Str , every
$1/4$ hr.

19. *Moabit* (Putlitz-Strasse Station; Pl B, 15)-*Silesian Gate* (Pl.
G, 34); viâ Jannowitz-Brucke, Alexander-Platz and as in No. 16;
every $1/4$ hr.

22. *Rixdorf* (Canner-Str.; near Pl G, 33)-*Müller-Strasse* (Gericht-
Str ; Pl. B, 17; some cars run on to See-Str.) viâ Gorlitz Station,
Bethanien, Andreas-Str. (Silesian Station), Alexander-Platz,
Rosenthaler Tor, and Garten-Platz; every $1/4$ hr.

23. *Schöneberg* (Goten-Str.; Pl. G, 18)-*Gesundbrunnen* (Pank-
Str.; Pl. B, 19). viâ Potsdamer-Str. and Station, Brandenburger
Tor, Lehrte Station, Moabit, and Wedding Station; every $1/4$ hr.

24. From the *Potsdamer-Str.* (Grossgörschen-Str.; Pl. G, 17) to
the *Nettelbeck-Platz* (Pl. B, 17, 20), as in No. 23; every $1/4$ hr.

25. *Charlotten-Str.* (Unter den Linden; Pl. R, 23)-*Tegel:* viâ
Georgen-Str. (Friedrich-Str. Station), Chaussee-Str. (Stettin
Station), and Wedding Station; every $1/4$ hr.

26. *Oranienburg Gate* (Pl. R, 24)-*Tegel,* as in No. 25; every $1/4$ hr.

28. *Rixdorf* (Mariendorfer Weg; near Pl. G, 30)-*Wittenau* (Dalldorf Lunatic Asylum, near Pl B, 10) viâ Kottbuser Tor, Oranien-
Platz, Jannowitz-Brucke Station, Rathaus, Exchange Station,
Chaussée-Str. (Stettin Station), Wedding-Station, and Reinickendorf-West; every $1/4$-$1/2$ hr.

29. From *Britz* to *See-Strasse* (Virchow-Krankenhaus; Pl. B, 13);
every $1/4$ hr.

30. *Swinemunder-Strasse* (Ramler-Strasse; Pl. B, 23)-*Rixdorf*
(Hermann-Platz; Pl. G, 30): viâ Rosenthaler Tor, Exchange Station, Rathaus, Jannowitz-Brucke Station, Oranien-Platz; every
$1/4$ hr.

31. *Silesian Station* (Pl. R, 31)-*Reinickendorf-West* (Pl. B, 10):
viâ Alexander-Platz, Rosenthaler Tor, Garten-Platz, Wedding
Station (some cars running on to Tegel); every $1/4$ hr.

32. *Charlotten-Strasse* (Unter den Linden; Pl. R, 23)-*Reinickendorf* beyond (Pl B, 16): viâ Georgen-Str. (Friedrich-Str. Station)
Chaussée-Str (Stettin Station), and Wedding Station; every
$7 1/2$-15 minutes.

33. *Charlottenburg* (Leibnitz-Str.; Pl. G, 7)-*Pappel-Allée* (Schön-hauser Allée; Pl. G, 29, 30): viâ Zoological Garden, Lützow-Platz, Potsdam Station, Gendarmen-Markt, Opern-Platz, Exchange Station, and Rosenthaler Tor.

34. *Kreuzberg* (Viktoria Park; Pl. G, 21)-*Gesundbrunnen* (Pank-Str.; Pl. B, 19): viâ Hallesches Tor, Koch-Str., Gendarmen-Markt, Opern-Platz, Georgen-Str. (Friedrich-Strasse Station), Chaussée-Str. (Stettin Station), and Wedding Station; every ¼ hr.

35, 36, 37. *Kreuzberg* (Viktoria Park; Pl. G, 21)-*Reinickendorf* (near Pl B, 16): viâ Gneisenau-Str., Moritz-Platz, Jannowitz-Brücke Station, Alexander-Platz, Rosenthaler Tor, Brunnen-Str (Demminer-Str), and Gesundbrunnen Station; every ¼ hr. — 36. To *Schönholz Station* (near Pl. B, 19): viâ Gesundbrunnen, as in No. 35, every ¼ hr. — 37. *Kreuzberg* (Bergmann-Str; Pl. G, 24)-*Brunnen-Strasse* (Demminer-Str.; Pl. B, 24; some cars to Schönholz Station); every ¼ hr.

38. *Kreuzberg* (Viktoria Park, Pl. G, 21)-*Gesundbrunnen* (Ex-erzier-Str.; Pl. B, 19): viâ Hallesches Tor, Dönhoff-Platz, Spittel-markt, Rathaus, Exchange Station, Rosenthaler Tor, and Ge-sundbrunnen Station; every ¼ hr.

39. *Marheineke-Platz* (Pl. G, 24)-*Gesundbrunnen* (Exerzier-Str.; Pl. B, 19): viâ Hallesches Tor, Dönhoff-Platz, Hausvogtei-Platz, Opern-Platz, Exchange Station, and as in No. 38; every ¼ hr.

40. *Schöneberg* (Eisenacher-Strasse; Pl. G, 15)-*Swinemünder-Strasse* (Ramler-Str.; Pl. B, 23): viâ Grossgörschen-Str. Station, Dennewitz-Platz, Potsdam Station, Gendarmen-Markt, Opern-Platz, Exchange Station, and Rosenthaler Tor; every ¼ hr.

41. *Schöneberg* (Pape-Strasse Station; near Pl. G, 21)-*Gesund-brunnen* (Exerzier-Str.; Pl. B, 19; some cars running as far as Reinickendorf): viâ Katzbach-Str. (Kreuzberg), Gneisenau-Str., and as in No. 35; every ¼ hr.

42. *Marheineke-Platz* (Pl G, 24)-*See-Strasse* (Virchow-Kranken-haus; Pl. B, 14), as in No 39; every ¼ hr.

43. *Schöneberg* (Eisenacher-Strasse; Pl. G, 15)-*Gesundbrunnen* (Pank-Str.; Pl. B, 19), as in No 34; every ¼ hr.

46. *Rixdorf* (Cauner-Strasse; near Pl. G, 33)-*Schönhauser Allée* (Kaiser-Friedrich-Str.; Pl. B, 28): viâ Görlitz Station, Andreas-Str. (Silesian Station), Alexander-Platz: every ¼ hr.

47, 48. *Britz* (Rudower-Strasse; near Pl. G, 33)-*Nieder-Schön-hausen* (near Pl B, 28): viâ Rixdorf Station, Kottbuser Tor, Moritz-Platz, Spittelmarkt, Rathaus, Exchange Station, Schön-hauser Tor Schönhauser Allée Station, and Pankow: every ½ hr. —48. *Rixdorf* Julius--... Schönhausen Str. Kaiser-Fried-rich-Str.; Pl. B, 28 ... . , P

BAEDEKER's Berlin. 3rd Edit.   2

49. *Rixdorf* (Hermann-Platz; Pl. G, 30)-*Nieder-Schönhausen* (near Pl. B, 28): viâ Fichte-Str., Kottbuser Tor, Bethanien, Jannowitz-Brucke Station, Alexander-Platz, Schonhauser Tor, Schonhauser Allée Station, and Pankow; every ¹/₄ hr.

51. *Schöneberg* (Viktoria-Luise-Platz; Pl. G, 11, 14)-*Pankow* (Breite-Str.; near Pl. B, 28): viâ Nollendorf-Platz, Bülow-Str., Potsdam Station, Brandenburger Tor, Neues Tor, Stettin Station, Zionskirch-Platz, and Schonhauser Allée Station; every ¹/₄ hr.

52. *Wilmersdorf* (Wilhelms-Aue, Pl. G, 9)-*Danziger-Strasse* (Weissenburger-Str.; Pl. B, 30): viâ Winterfeldt-Platz, Nollendorf-Platz, Geuthiner-Str., Potsdam Station, Brandenburger Tor, Karl-Str., Oranienburger-Str., Hackesche Markt (Exchange Station), and Schonhauser Tor; every ¹/₄ hr.

53. *Rixdorf* (Hermann-Platz; Pl. G, 30)-*Danziger-Strasse* (Weissenburger-Str.; Pl. B, 30): viâ Hasenheide, Hallesches Tor, Gendarmen-Markt, Opern-Platz, Exchange Station, and Schonhauser Tor; every ¹/₄ hr.

54. *Charlottenburg* (Jungfernheide Station; Pl. B, 3)-*Schönhauser Allée* (Glein-Str.; Pl. R, 29): viâ Charlottenburg Palace, Savigny-Platz Station, Lutzow-Platz, Potsdam Station, Charlotten-Str., Gendarmen-Markt, Opern-Platz, and Exchange Station.

55. *Britz* (near Pl. G, 30)-*Danziger-Strasse* (Weissenburger-Str.; Pl. B, 30): viâ Hasenheide, etc., as in No. 53; every ¹/₄ hr.

56. *Schöneberg* (Mühlen-Strasse; Pl. G, 15)-*Danziger-Strasse* (Weissenburger-Str., Pl. B, 30), viâ Winterfeldt-Platz, an das in No 52; every ¹/₄ hr.

57. *Nieder-Schönhausen* (Church; near Pl. B, 28)-*Schöneberg* (Viktoria-Luise-Platz; Pl. G, 11, 14), as in No. 51; every ¹/₄ hr.

58. *Rixdorf* (Hermann-Strasse Station; near Pl. G, 30)-*Central Cattle Market* (Pl. R, 38): viâ Kottbuser Tor, Moritz-Platz, Spittelmarkt, Alexander-Platz Station, Friedrichshain, Petersburger-Str.; every ¹/₄ hr.

59. *Weissensee* (Rennbahn-Strasse; Pl. B, 37)-*Steglitz* (near Pl. G, 15): viâ Weissensee Station, Friedrichshain, Alexander-Platz Station, Rathaus, Spittelmarkt, Donhoff-Platz, Prinz-Albrecht-Str., Anhalt Station, Lützow-Str., and Potsdamer-Str.; every ¹/₄ hr.

60, 61. *Schöneberg-Friedenau* (near Pl. G, 15)-*Weissensee* (Schloss; Pl. B, 37): viâ Wartburg-Platz, Viktoria-Luise-Platz, Nollendorf-Platz, Bulow-Strasse, Potsdam Station, Kanonier-Str, Gendarmen-Markt, Schloss-Platz, Rathaus, Alexander-Platz Station, and Prenzlauer Allée Station; every ¹/₄ hr. —
61. From *Schöneberg* (Wartburg-Platz; Pl. G, 15), every ¹/₄ hr.

62. *Wilmersdorf* (Prager-Platz; Pl G, 11) - *Weissensee* (Renn-bahn-Str.; Pl. B, 37): viâ Hohenstaufen-Str. and as in No. 59; every 1/4 hr

63. *Hansa-Platz* (Tiergarten; Pl. R, 14) - *Greifswalder-Strasse* (Danziger-Str., Pl B. 33), as in No. 17: every 1/4 hr.

64. *Charlottenburg* (Palace; Pl. R, 5) - *Landsberger Allée Station* (Pl. R, 39) viâ Zoological Garden Station, Nollendorf-Platz, Yorck-Str. Station, Hallesches Tor, Donhoff-Platz, Spittelmarkt, Rathaus, Alexander-Platz Station, and Friedrichshain.

65. *Moritz-Platz* (Pl. G, 25) - *Zentral-Viehhof* (Pl. R, 38) · as in No. 58; every 1/4 hr.

66, 67. *Wilmersdorf* (Kaiser-Platz, near Pl. G, 12) - *Lichtenberg* (Dorf-Str.; Pl. R, 41): viâ Augsburger-Str., Lützow-Platz, Potsdam Station, Leipziger-Str., Spittelmarkt, Rathaus, Alexander-Platz Station, Zentral-Viehhof, every 1/4 hr -- **67.** *Wilmers-dorf* (Wilhelms-Aue; Pl. G, 9) - *Zentral-Viehhof* (Samariter-Str.; Pl. R, 38); every 1/4 hr.

68. *See-Strasse* (Virchow-Krankenhaus; Pl. B, 14) - *Frankfurter Chaussée* (near Pl. R, 40) · viâ Wedding Station, Stettin Station, Rosenthaler Tor, Alexander-Platz, Lichtenberg: every 1/4 hr.

69, 70, 71. *Schöneberg* (Wartburg-Platz; Pl G, 15) - *Friedrichs-felde* (near Pl. R, 41): viâ Winterfeldt-Platz, Potsdam Station, Leipziger-Str, Dönhoff-Platz, Spittelmarkt, Rathaus, Alexan-der-Platz Station, and Frankfurter Allée Station; every 1/4 hr. -- **70.** From the *Kanonier-Str.* (Behren-Str.; Pl. R, 22): viâ Gendarmen-Markt, Schloss-Platz, Rathaus, and as in No. 69; every 1/4 hr. -- **71.** *Wartburg-Platz - Herzberge* (Lunatic Asy-lum; near Pl. R, 42), as in No. 69, finally viâ Lichtenberg (Dorf-Str.); every 1/4 hr.

72. *Prenzlauer Allée* (Danziger-Strasse; Pl. B, 33) - *Potsdamer-Strasse* (Gr.-Görschen-Str.; Pl G, 17): viâ Alexander-Platz Sta-tion, Rathaus, Schloss-Platz, Gendarmen-Markt, and Hallesches Tor: every 1/4 hr.

73. *Prenzlauer Allée* (Danziger-Strasse, Pl. B, 33) - *Marheineke-Platz* (Pl B, 33): viâ Alexander-Platz, König-Str., Schloss-Platz, Gendarmen-Markt, and Hallesches Tor; every 1/4 hr

74. *Schöneberg* (Ebers-Str. Station; near Pl G, 15) - *Kniprorler-Str* (Pl. R, 36): to Alexander-Platz Station as in No. 69, then Friedrichshain.

75. *Zoological Garden* (Kurfurstendamm, Pl G, 13) - *Zentral-Viehhof* (Pl. R, 38): viâ Nollendorf-Platz, Yorck-Str. Station, Hallesches Tor, Gendarmen-Markt, Royal Palace, Rathaus, Alexander-Platz Station, Friedrichshain: every 1/4 hr.

76. *Halensee Station* (Pl G, 2 Rummelsburg (Near Prinz Alb-recht-St ... and Pl. R, 4... via Zoologi... Garden, Wurten-berg-Pl... Lützow Plat, Potsdam Station, Leipziger Str.,

Donhoff-Platz, Spittelmarkt, Grüner Weg (Silesian Station), Boxhagen; every ¹/₄ hr.

78. *Wilmersdorf* (Olivaer-Platz; Pl. G, 4, 7)-*Frankfurter Allée
Station* (Pl. R, 40): viâ Ludwigs-Kirch-Platz, Zoological Garden, Lützow-Platz, and as in No. 76.

79. *Halensee Station* (Pl. G, 2)-*Rummelsburg* (Rathaus; Pl. G, 40):
viâ Zoological Garden, Wittenberg-Platz, Lützow-Platz, Potsdam Station, Leipziger-Str., Dönhoff-Platz, Spittelmarkt, Gruner
Weg (Silesian Station), Boxhagen; every ¹/₄ hr.

80, 81. *Charlottenburg* (Westend Station; Pl. R, 2)-*Silesian
Station* (Pl. R, 31): viâ Amtsgericht, Savigny-Platz Station,
Zoological Garden, Lützow-Platz, Potsdam Station, Kanonier-
Str., Gendarmen-Markt, Schloss-Platz, Mühlendamm, and Jannowitz-Brücke Station; every ¹/₄ hr. — **81.** To the *Zentral-Viehhof* (Pl R, 28): as far as the Schloss-Platz as in No. 80; thence
viâ Rathaus, Alexander-Platz Station, and Friedrichshain; every
¹/₄ hr.

82. *Zoological Garden Station* (Pl. G, 10)-*Silesian Gate* (Pl.
R, 31): viâ Prager-Platz, Winterfeldt-Platz, Yorck-Strasse Station, Hallesches Tor, Skalitzer-Str. (Gorlitz Station); every
¹/₄ hr.

83, 84. *Friedrich-Strasse* (Behren-Strasse; Pl. R, 22)-*Treptow* (Spree-Tunnel, Pl. G, 42)· viâ Dönhoff-Platz, Spittelmarkt,
Jakob-Str., Schlesische Brücke, and Treptow Station; every
¹/₂ hr. — **84.** To the *Schlesische Brücke* (Pl. G, 35).

87, 88. *Schöneberg* (Eisenacher-Strasse; Pl. G, 15)-*Treptow Station* (Pl. G, 38), viâ Potsdam Station, Donhoff-Platz, and as
in No. 83; every ¹/₄ hr. — **88.** *Schöneberg-Friedenau* (near
Pl. G, 15)-*Schlesische Brücke* (Pl. G, 35); every ¹/₄ hr.

89, 90. *Treptow* (Spree-Tunnel; Pl. G, 42)-*Wilmersdorf* (Pariser-
Str.; Pl. G, 8): as in No. 83, every ¹/₂ hr. — **90.** To the *Silesian Gate* (Pl. G, 34); every ¹/₂ hr.

91, 92. *Halensee Station* (Pl. G, 2)-*Gorlitz Station* (Pl. G, 32):
viâ Wilmersdorf, Viktoria-Luise-Platz, Nollendorf-Platz, Genthiner-Str., Potsdam Station, Leipziger-Str., Donhoff-Platz,
Spittelmarkt, Dresdener-Str., and Bethanien; every ¹/₄ hr. —
92. *Wilmersdorf* (Wilhelms-Aue; Pl. G, 9)-*Görlitz Station*
(Pl. G, 32): as in No. 91; every ¹/₄ hr.

93. *Charlottenburg* (Witzleben-Strasse; Pl. G, 1)-*Gorlitz Station*
(Pl. G, 32): viâ Savigny-Platz Station, Zoological Garden,
Lützow-Platz, Potsdam Station, Anhalt Station, Koch-Str., and
Moritz-Platz; every ¹/₄ hr.

94. *Dönhoff-Platz* (Pl. R, 22, 25)-*Rixdorf* (Knesebeck-Strasse):
viâ Kottbuser Tor, Thielen-Brücke, and Hermann-Strasse Station;
every ¹/₄ hr.

95. *Friedrich-Strasse* (Behren-Strasse; Pl. R, 22)-*Hasenheide*
(Fichte-Str., Pl. G, 30), viâ Koch-Str., Moritz-Platz, and Kottbuser Tor.

96, 97. *Friedrich-Strasse* (Behren-Str.; Pl. R, 22)-*Mariendorf*
(Lichtenrader Chaussée: near Pl G, 24)· viâ Gendarmen-Markt,
Koch-Str., Hallesches Tor, Belle-Alliance-Str. (Kreuzberg), and
Tempelhof Station; every ¹/₄ hr. — **97.** To *Mariendorf* (near
Pl. G, 24), every ¹/₄ hr.

98. *Charlottenburg* (Amtsgericht; Pl. G, 1)-*Görlitz Station* (Pl
G, 32): as in No. 93; every ¹/₄ hr.

  I. Süd-Ring (13 M. long): From the *Hallesches Tor* (Blucher-
Platz; Pl. G, 23) viâ Hasenheide, Kaiser Friedrich-Str., Rixdorf
Station, Britz, Tempelhof, Ebers-Str. Station, Schöneberg (Rat-
haus), Schöneberg Station, Military Station, and Katzbach-Str.
(Kreuzberg) back to the *Hallesches Tor*; every 24 minutes

  II. *Schöneberg* (Eisenacher-Str.· Pl. G, 15)-*Rixdorf Station*:
viâ Hallesches Tor, as in No. I., every 8-16 minutes.

  III. *Swinemünder-Strasse* (Ramler-Str.; Pl. B, 23)-*Schöneberg*
(Pape-Strasse Station· Pl. G, 18, 21), as in No. 40, finally viâ
Kolonnen-Str. (Schöneberg Station); every ¹/₄ hr.

  IV. *Tempelhof Station* (Pl. G, 21)-*Gross-Lichterfelde-East*:
viâ Sudende and Lankwitz; every 24 minutes.

  V. *Rixdorf Station* (near Pl. G, 23)-*Steglitz* (near Pl. G, 15): viâ
Britz, Tempelhof, Schöneberg, and Friedenau, every ¹/₄ hr

  A. *Potsdamer-Platz* (Link-Str.; Pl. R, 19)-*Hundekehle* (Grune-
wald suburb; near Pl. G, 2, 3): viâ Flottwell-Str., Kurfursten-
Str., Nollendorf-Platz, Zoological Garden, Kurfurstendamm,
Halensee Station; hence through the suburb of Grunewald (viâ
Hundekehle or St. Hubertus), returning viâ Halensee Station:
every ¹/₄ hr., to Halensee every 7¹/₂ minutes

  B. *Potsdamer-Platz* (Link-Str.; Pl. R, 19)-*Grunewald* (Roseneck; near Pl. G, 9)· viâ Grossgorschen-Str. Station, Wilmersdorf (Aue), Schmargendorf, and Roseneck; every ¹/₄ hr.

  D. *Zoological Garden Station* (Pl. G, 10)-*Steglitz* (near Pl. G,
15), viâ Nollendorf-Platz, Winterfeldt-Platz, Schöneberg, and
Friedenau; every 10 minutes.

  E. *Potsdamer-Platz* (Link-Str.; Pl. R, 19)-*Steglitz* (near Pl G,
15): viâ Dennewitz-Platz, Grossgörschen-Str. Station, Schöneberg, and Friedenau, every 10 minutes.

  F. *Zoological Garden Station* (Pl. G, 10)-*Steglitz* (near Pl. G, 15):
viâ Kaiser-Allée and Wilmersdorf-Friedenau Station, every
10 minutes

  G. *Zoological Garden Station* Pl. G, 10 *Wilmersdorf* Wil-
helms Au Pl. G, 9 viâ Uhland-Strasse

H. *West Ring:* Grunewald-Str., Winterfeldt-Platz, Nollendorf-Platz, Zoological Garden Station, Wilmersdorf, Grunewald-Str.; every $\frac{1}{4}$ hr.

N. *Kupfergraben* (Pl. R, 23)-*Charlottenburg* (Westend Station; Pl. R, 2): viâ Brandenburger Tor, Grosser Stern, Tiergarten Station, Knie, Wilhelm-Platz, and Charlottenburg Palace.

O. *Kupfergraben* (Pl. R, 23)-*Wilmersdorf* (Wilhelms-Aue; Pl. G, 9): viâ Brandenburger Tor, Grosser Stern, Zoological Garden, and Uhland-Strasse; every $\frac{1}{4}$ hr.

P. *Dönhoff-Platz* (Pl R, 22, 25)-*Westend* (Kirsch-Allée, near Pl. R, 2): viâ Zimmer-Str., Potsdam Station, Lützow-Platz, Zoological Garden, Berliner-Str., and Charl. Palace; every $\frac{1}{4}$ hr.

Q. *Kniproder-Strasse* (Pl. R, 36)-*Halensee Station* (Pl. G, 2): viâ Friedrichshain, Rosenthaler Tor, Stettin Station, Neues Tor, Lehrte Station, Alt-Moabit, March-Str, Wilhelm-Platz, Charlottenburg Station, and Amtsgericht; every $\frac{1}{4}$ hr.

R. *Dönhoff-Platz* (Pl. R, 22, 25)-*Spandauer Bock* (near Pl. R, 2), as in Route P, and farther along the Spandauer Chaussée; every $\frac{1}{4}$ hr.

S. *Kupfergraben* (Pl. R, 23)-*Wilmersdorf-Friedenau Station* (near Pl G, 12), as in Route O; every $\frac{1}{4}$ hr.

T. *Kupfergraben* (Pl. R, 23) — *Halensee Station* (Pl. G, 2): to the Knie as in Route N, then Leibnitz-Str., Kant-Str., Amtsgericht; every 10 minutes.

V. *Schönhauser Allee Station* (Pl. B, 29)-*Wilmersdorf-Friedenau Station* (near Pl. G, 12): viâ Stettin Station, Lehrte Station, Gotzkowski-Brücke, and Wilmersdorf: every $\frac{1}{4}$ hr.

Lines without numbers or letters.

a. *Mittel-Strasse* (Friedrich-Str.; Pl. R, 23)-*Pankow* (Mendel-Str., near Pl. B, 28) or *Nieder-Schönhausen:* viâ Georgen-Str. (Friedrich-Str. Station), Eberts-Brücke, Garten-Str. (Stettin Station), Humboldthain, and Gesundbrunnen.

b. *Wassmann-Strasse* (Pl. R, 29, 32)-*Hohen-Schönhausen* (near Pl. B, 42) viâ Friedrichshain, Landsberger Allée Station, and Wilhelmsberg; every $\frac{1}{4}$ hr

c. *Warschauer-Strasse Station* (Pl. G, 34)-*Zentral-Viehhof* (Pl. R, 38), in connexion with the Elevated Railway.

d. *Silesian Station* (Pl. R, 31)-*Treptow* (Pl. G, 42) viâ Warschauer Brücke, Stralau, and Spree-Tunnel; every $\frac{1}{4}$ hr., to Stralau every $7\frac{1}{2}$ minutes.

e. *Behren-Strasse* (Mauer-Str.; Pl. R, 19)-*Treptow* (Pl. G, 42)· viâ Schutzen-Str, Wassertor-Str., Gorlitz Station, Wiener Brücke, and Kopenicker Landstrasse.

f. *Bad-Strasse* Prinzen-Allée; Pl. B, 19 - *Französisch-Buchholz,* viâ Pankow, every 35 minutes.

g, h. (under construction). *Balten-Platz* (Pl. R, 35)-*Elsasser-Strasse* (Borsig-Str.; Pl. R, 24): viâ Friedrichshain, Danziger-Str., Strelitzer-Str., Stettin Station. — h. From the Strelitzer-Str. on to the *Virchow-Krankenhaus* (Pl. B, 14, 15).

g. Omnibuses.

Omnibuses (fare 10 pf., two tickets 15, five tickets 30 pf.) traverse the city in every direction, but the following are perhaps the only lines likely to be of service to the visitor. 1. From the *Stettin Station* (Pl. R, 24) to the *Bülow-Strasse* (Pl. G, 17), viâ Friedrich-Str., Leipziger-Str., and Potsdam Station. — 2. From the *Stettin Station* to the *Kreuzberg* (Grossbeeren-Str.; Pl. G, 21), viâ the Friedrich-Str. Station, and a second line viâ the Anhalt Station. — 3. From the *Stettin Station* to the *Görlitz Station* (Pl. G, 32), viâ the Exchange Station and the Schloss-Platz. — There are also a few motor lines (fares 10-15 pf.).

NIGHT OMNIBUSES run from the *Chaussée-Strasse* (corner of Liesen-Str.) to the *Hallesches Tor*, viâ Friedrich-Str. Station, every 7 min. from 10.35 p.m. to 6.50 a.m.; from the *Stettin Station* to the *Bülow-Strasse* (corner of Potsdamer-Str.), viâ Friedrich-Str. and Potsdam Station, every 17 min. from 10.45 p.m. to 4.30 a.m.; etc. (fares 10-20 pf.).

MOTOR-OMNIBUSES in summer on Sun. (several also on week-days) ply to *Grunewald* (p. 184). *Wannsee*, *Potsdam* (Sanssouci); *Plötzensee* (Kaislhof), *Tegel*, *Wandlitz* (Bernau, Lanke, Liepnitz-See). Comp. the advertisements.

h. Cabs.

The cab-district under the control of the Berlin police comprises also those parts of Charlottenburg, Schoneberg, and Rixdorf which lie within the Ringbahn. — Complaints should be directed to the 'Verkehrs-Commissariat' of the Polizei-Präsidium, see p. 26. — Lost Property Office, see p. 27. — Night fares from 12 to 6 in summer and to 7 in winter.

Taximeter Cabs	by day		at night
Within the limits of the police-district	1 or 2 pers.	3—5 pers.	1—5 pers.
HORSE CABS.			
For the minimum fare of 70 pf. hirers are entitled to drive	800 mètres	600 m.	400 m.
For each additional 10 pf.	400 „	300 „	200 „
MOTOR CABS.			
For 70 pf.	600 „	400 „	400 „
For each additional 10 pf	300 „	200 „	200 „

Outside the police-district: horse-cabs, 1-2 pers. by day 600 (3-5 pers., at night 1-5 pers. 400) mètres for 70 pf., every additional 300 (200) mètres 10 pf. motor-cabs, day or night 1-5 pers. 400 mètres for 70 pf., every additional 200 mètres 10 pf.

Ordinary Cabs, without taximeter: 1-2 persons for $^1/_4$ hr. 60 pf. (3-5 pers. 1 $\mathcal{M}$), $^1/_2$ hr. 1 (1$^1/_2$) $\mathcal{M}$, every additional $^1/_4$ hr. 50 pf.; at night double fares; for each addit. $^1/_4$ hr., or fraction thereof, 50 pf.

Waiting: 8 min. 50 pf., each additional 4 min 10 pf., per hr. 1$^1/_2$ $\mathcal{M}$, motor-cabs 2 (3) $\mathcal{M}$. Luggage: 22 lbs. inside the cab free; 23-55 lbs., 25 pf.; 56-110 lbs, 50 pf.; 111-165 lbs., 75 pf., 166-220 lbs., 1 $\mathcal{M}$. Luggage over 240 lbs. may be taken only in a luggage-cab (Gepack-Droschke, see p. 1; two seats only); fares as for taximeter cabs (see p. 23).

For drives from a railway-station, a charge of 25 pf. in addition to the fare is made in every case for the metal ticket securing the cab (see p 1).

Circular Drives through the town: *H. Kase*, starting at 10 a.m and 3 p.m. from the Hôtel Viktoria, Unter den Linden 46 (duration, 3 hrs.; fare 3$^1/_2$ $\mathcal{M}$); *Union* (see p. 2; motor-cars), starting at 10 and 3 from Unter den Linden 5-6 (3 hrs.; fare 5 $\mathcal{M}$).

Private Carriages 15-20 $\mathcal{M}$ per day, 8-12 $\mathcal{M}$ per $^1/_2$ day, fee 1-2 $\mathcal{M}$. *Schultze*, Georgen-Str 4; *Kornfeld*, Zimmer-Str 83 — **Motor Cars** may be hired from *E. Dommenz*, Holsteiner Ufer 15-16; *P Burmeister*, Linden-Str. 92; *Bedag*, Chaussee-Str 28; *K. Melchior*, Waldemar-Str. 55: per hour 6-15, whole day 40-150 $\mathcal{M}$; for longer excursions, 50-60 pf per kilomètre.

Excursion Trips. To Potsdam: *H Kase*, starting at 9 30 a m. from the Hôtel Viktoria. Unter den Linden 46; fare 12 $\mathcal{M}$, including fees for visiting the royal palaces, dinner, etc. — *Union* (see p. 2; motor-cars), starting at 10 a.m. from Unter den Linden 5-6, 15 $\mathcal{M}$.

i. Steamboats on the Upper Spree and Dahme.

Comp the *Time Tables* (often posted on the advertising-pillars).

From the *Jannowitz-Brücke* (N. side, p. 155; Pl. R, 28; pier also at the Silesian Gate, see p 169) at 10.30 a.m., and every $^1/_2$ hr. from 1.30 p.m. to *Stralau, Treptow, Eierhäuschen, Tabbert's Waldschlösschen, Loreley, Blumengarten, Neptunshain, Sadowa, Köpenick,* and *Grünau* (fares 20-55 pf.). — From *Grünau* (p. 203) from 10 23 a.m. hourly to *Waldrestaurant, Marienlust* (Muggel-turm), *Karolinenhof, Krampenburg,* and *Schmöckwitz* (fares 10-30 pf.). — From *Köpenick* (p. 201) at 12.10, 2.05, 3, etc. to *Hirschgarten, Friedrichshagen, Rahnsdorfer Mühle,* and *Restaurant Rübezahl* (fare 10-30 pf.) — From *Friedrichshagen* (p 202) from 10 a.m. every hour across the *Muggel-See* (15 pf.) to the *Rübezahl Restaurant* (visit to the *Muggel-Berge*).

From the *Jannowitz-Brücke* (p. 155; S. end; Pl. R, 28) separate trips on week-days (except Sat.) in summer: at 9 a.m. to *Woltersdorfer Schleuse* return-ticket 75 pf.; at 2 or 2.15 p m. (return-ticket 50 pf.) also to *Woltersdorfer Schleuse,* and on certain days to *Rauchfangswerder*, *Neue Mühle* (near Konigs-Wusterhausen), and *Hessenwinkel*.

k. Post, Telegraph, and Telephone Offices.

The addresses of the nearest post-offices, etc., are given on the letter-boxes and advertising-pillars Inquiry Office for all postal matters, Konig-Str 61 Official postal guide ('Postbuch') for Berlin and neighbourhood, 50 pf.

Post Offices. The CENTRAL POST OFFICE is at Spandauer-Str. 19-24 (Pl. R, 26, p. 151). The town is divided into nine postal districts, designed by letters, *C, N, NO, O,* etc. (comp. the list of streets, p. 229). Letters for Berlin should contain the district initial in their address and, if possible, also the number of the post-office by which they are delivered. There are 113 post-offices and branch-offices, almost all of which have telegraph, pneumatic post, and tele-phone offices. No parcels are received by the branch-offices. The most important post-offices are the following: *C1*, Hof-Postamt, Spandauer-Str. 19-24; *C2*, Heiligegeist-Str. 24-33· letters to be call-ed for *('Postlagernd' or 'Poste Restante')* and *Money Orders*, when not addressed to any particular post-office, are distributed here Then, *N3*, Paket-Postamt *(Parcel Post Office)*, Oranienburger-Str 70-72; *NW7*, Dorotheen-Str. 23-24; *W8*, Tauben-Str. 8-9; *SW12*, Zim-mer-Str. 27; *SW19*, Beuth-Str. 18-21; *C25*, Am Konigsgraben 17; and the offices at the six chief railway stations (Anhalt, Potsdam, Lehrte, Stettin, Silesia, and Gorlitz). The post-offices are open from 7 (in winter from 8) a.m to 8 p.m (branch-offices from 8 a.m. to 7 p.m.); for parcels till 7 p.m.; on Sundays and holidays the dis-trict offices are open from 7 (in winter 8) to 9 a.m., and 12 to 1 p.m., the branch-offices remaining closed. The postage for letters within the city and its neighbourhood is 5 pf., for post-cards also 5 pf.· for other parts of Germany 10 and 5 pf.; for abroad 20 and 10 pf. Parcels from abroad are examined by custom-house officers at Ritter-Str. 7, Kloster-Str. 76, Köthener-Str. 28, or Schiffbauerdamm 22, according to the district of the city in which the addressee lives.

A system of **Pneumatic Tubes** *(Rohrpost)* also exists, for the rapid transmission of letters and post-cards from one part of Berlin to another (including Charlottenburg). Letters (30 pf.), which must not exceed a certain size and weight, or post-cards (25 pf., reply post-cards 50 pf.) intended for transmission by this service must be marked 'Rohrpost' in the upper left-hand corner of the address. Post-offices with pneumatic service (open from 7 or 8 a.m. till 10 p.m.) are distinguished by a red lamp (comp. above). Letters and post-cards sent by this service reach their destination in 1-2 hrs., but only when posted at a pneumatic post office.

Telegraph Offices. C d Ode Pl R 22 Oberwall-Str. 4a, a d e s b k n c t with the above-named post-offices. The Central Office, that at Goethe-Str. 3 (Charlottenburg), and the offices at the six chief railway stations (see above) are open day and night; the offices at the General Post Office, Exchange, and a few others from 7 or 8 a.m. till 10 p.m.; the remainder, from 7 or 8 a.m. to 9 p.m. Telegrams within Berlin cost 3 pf. per word (minimum 30 pf.), to other parts of Germany 5 pf. (minimum 50 pf.). Telegrams to Great Britain 15 pf. (minimum 80 pf.), to the United States and Canada from 1 ℳ 5 pf. to 1 ℳ 75 pf., to British India 2 ℳ 60 pf. per word, etc.

Telephone Offices (open 7 a.m. till 10 p.m.) at Französische-Str. 33 b and c (head-office) and the above-named post-offices, where lists of subscribers to the 'Telephonic Exchange' are provided. Fee for 3 min. conversation within the city, 10 pf.; environs, 20 pf.; for longer distances, 25 pf.- 4 ℳ.

l. Parcel Delivery Co. Commissionaires.

The BERLIN PARCEL DELIVERY COMPANY (*Starke & Co.;* office: Berlin S., Ritter-Str. 98-99) delivers parcels in the town and suburbs at a moderate charge. The numerous offices are recognizable by their red signs. For luggage to be conveyed to the station see p. 2.

COMMISSIONAIRES (*Dienstmänner*): for parcels up to 11 lbs. (5 kg.) and for letters and messages taking not more than 20 min., 30 pf., and 10 pf. for every additional 10 min.; for parcels of 11-55 lbs. (5-25 kg.), up to 20 min. 60 pf., and 15 pf. for every further 10 min. *Commissionaires with bicycles:* for 1 M. (1_6 km.), 30 pf., with a parcel, 40 pf. and 10 or 15 pf. for every further $^1/_2$ M. (800 m.). — The charge should be arranged beforehand when possible; and it is safer always to demand the porter's number

The *Berlin Messenger Boy Company* undertakes messages of every kind. Stations. Bayreuther-Str. 38 (head office), Unter den Linden 23 (Passage, shop No. 1), König-Str. 1 (Kurfürsten-Brücke), Leipziger-Str. 46-49 (Tietz), etc. Telephone Central Office Amt VI, 9783 Fee. up to 2 kilomètres 50 pf., one hour 60 pf.

m. Police.

The address of the nearest police-station is given on each advertising-pillar

HEAD POLICE OFFICE (*Polizei-Präsidium*), Alexander-Platz 5-6 (Pl. R, 29; p 153). The *Passport Office* is at Eingang IV. beside the Stadtbahn (office hours 8-3). On the third floor at the same address is the *Einwohner-Meldeamt*, where the address of any resident in Berlin may be obtained for a fee of 25 pf. The *Office for Public Conveyances* (*'Verkehrs-Commissariat'*) is at Eingang II in the Alexander-Str (complaints are received daily 8-4 in room 80). — All strangers arriving in Berlin must be reported at the police-office by their landlord within six days. — The 111 police-offices are open day and night.

Lost Property Offices· of the *Police*, especially for articles left in cabs, at the Polizei-Präsidium, Eingang II, Room 79 (9 1 on week-days; a list of articles that have been found is posted up); of the *Railways* at the Silesian Station, N Arch 10 (8-3 on week-days) and at the terminus stations (p. 1; after the eighth day at the Silesian Station only); of the *Elevated Railway* at Köthener-Str 12 (10-4 on week-days), of the *Tramways* at Leipziger-Platz 14 (10-4 on week-days).

n. Theatres. Concerts.

Theatres. Plans may be consulted in the Berlin 'Adressbuch', or Directory Performances at the royal theatres and the Deutsches Theater begin at 7 30 p m., at all the others generally at 8 p.m. Weekly repertoire in the daily papers. Seats may be procured in advance at the box offices or at the *Invalidendank*, Unter den Linden 24 (9-4.30, on Sun. 9-10 and 12-2); at *Wagner's*, Markgrafen-Str. 72, at *Wertheim's* (p. 31; 1st floor), and for several theatres also at the *Kaufhaus des Westens* (p. 31), the three last-mentioned not for the royal theatres). In winter Sunday afternoon performances at reduced prices are given at most of the private theatres.

1. *Royal Opera House (Königliches Opernhaus;* Pl. R, 23; p 58), for operas and ballets; 1574 seats. Best boxes 12 *M*, orchestra boxes 10 *M*, parquet, front boxes, and 1st balcony 8 *M*, 2nd balcony and boxes 6 *M*, 3rd balcony and boxes 4 *M*, gallery $2^{1}/_{2}$ *M* (standing room $1^{1}/_{2}$ *M*) Prices are raised for grand opera.

2 *Royal Theatre (Königliches Schauspielhaus;* Pl. R, 22; p. 121), chiefly for classical dramas; 1000 seats. Best boxes 10 *M*, 1st balcony boxes and orchestra fanteuils 8 *M*, 1st balcony, parquet, and parquet-boxes $6^{1}/_{2}$ *M*, balcony 4 *M*, 2nd balcony $2^{1}/_{2}$ *M*, gallery 1 *M*.

3. *New Royal Opera Theatre (Neues Opern-Theater,* formerly Kroll's Theatre; Pl. R, 17; comp. p. 140), in the Königs-Platz; 1523 seats. Admission to the garden (concerts) 50 pf , sometimes 1 *M*.

Tickets for the royal theatres may be obtained in advance at the ticket-offices daily 10.15-1 (booking-fee 50 pf). In the evening the ticket-offices are open 1 hr. before the beginning. When very popular pieces are to be performed, a great number of the tickets are purchased by speculators, from whom they can be obtained only at exorbitant prices. In such cases the porter of the traveller's hotel will often be found useful in preventing excessive extortion. — The royal theatres are closed in July and August

4. *Deutsches Theater* (Pl. R, 20), Schumann-Str. 13 a, for dramas and comedies; 1028 seats Best boxes 8 *M* 20, 1st balcony and boxes, and parquet boxes 6 *M* 20, parquet 6 *M* 20 (1st-12th row) and 4 *M* 70 pf. (13th-21th row; standing room 3 *M*), 2nd balcony and boxes 3 *M* (gallery at back $2^{1}/_{2}$ *M*), lateral seats $1^{1}/_{2}$ *M*. Box-office 10-1.30· booking-fee 50 pf. *Kammerspiele* of the Deutsches Theater, Schumann Str. 14 320 seats at 15, 10 , and 5 *M*; box-office 10-2

5. *Lessing-Theater* (Pl. R, 20), Friedrich-Karl-Ufer 1, near the Kronprinzen-Brücke, for modern dramas and comedies; 1146 seats. Orchestra and best boxes 8 *M*, 1st balcony (front row) and side boxes 6½ *M*, parquet 6 and 5 *M*, parquet (standing room), 2nd balcony boxes 3 *M*, 2nd balcony (side seats) 3½ and 2½ *M*, gallery 2 *M*. Box-office 10-1.30; booking-fee 30-50 pf.

6. *Komische Oper* (Pl R, 23; p 145), Friedrich-Str. 104; 1250 seats. Stage and orchestra boxes, 1st balcony side-boxes 10 *M*, 1st balcony 1st row 8½ *M*, 1st balcony and parquet stalls 7½ *M*, parquet 6½ and 5½ *M*, 2nd balcony 1st row 4½, middle and side seats 3½ and 2¼ *M*, 3rd balcony 2¼-1¼ *M*. Box-office 10-2; booking-fee 30-50 pf.

7 *Neues Schauspielhaus* (Pl. G, 14; p. 121), Motz-Str 80-82, Nollendorf-Platz, for dramas and comedies. 1200 seats Orchestra boxes 8 *M* 20, orchestra stalls 7 *M* 70 (back rows 5 *M* 70), 1st balcony boxes 6 *M* 20, 1st balcony stalls 5 *M* 20, parquet stalls 4 *M* 70, 1st balcony 4 *M* 20-3 *M* 20, 2nd balcony 3 *M* 10-1 *M* 60 pf Box-office from 10 a.m.; booking-fee 30-50 pf.

8 *Hebbel-Theater* (Pl. G, 22; p 128), Königgratzer-Str 57-58, for dramas. 800 seats. Orchestra stalls 8 *M*, parquet stalls 6 *M*, 1st balcony 6-6½ *M*, 2nd balcony 2-3½ *M*. Box-office 11-2, booking-office 30-50 pf

9. *Theater des Westens* (Pl. G, 10; p. 181), Kant-Str. 12, for operas and operettas. 1650 seats. Best boxes 8 *M* 20, balcony boxes 6 *M* 70, orchestra stalls 6 *M* 20, parquet boxes and 1st balcony 5 *M* 20, parquet stalls and 1st balcony 4 *M* 20, 2nd balcony 2 *M* 80, 3rd balcony 1 *M* 30 pf. Box-office 10-1.30; booking-fee 30-50 pf.

10. *Berliner Theater* (Pl. G, 22), Charlotten-Str. 90-92, for dramas and comedies; 1600 seats. Orchestra and best boxes 8 *M* 35, parquet boxes and 1st balcony boxes 6 *M* 35, stalls, 1st balcony centre boxes and stalls 5 *M* 35-3 *M* 85, 1st balcony 3 *M* 35-2 *M* 85, 2nd balcony 2 *M* 35 and 1 *M* 85, parterre (pit) 1 *M* 85. Box-office 10-2; booking-fee 30-50 pf.

11. *Schiller-Theater Ost* (Pl. R, 28), Wallner-Theater-Str. 35, seats 90 pf.-2 *M* 70 pf. — 12. *Schiller-Theater Charlottenburg* (Pl. R, 7; p. 182), Bismarck-Str. 117-120; seats 50 pf.-2 *M* 10 pf.

13. *Neues Theater* (Pl. R, 23), Schiffbauerdamm 4a; seats 1½-8½ *M*. — 14. *Residenz-Theater* (Pl. R, 29), Blumen-Str. 9, French farces; seats 2-8 *M*. — 15. *Neues Operetten-Theater* (Pl. R, 20; p. 161), Schiffbauerdamm 25; 1100 seats at 2-8½ *M*. — 16. *Metropol-Theater* (Pl R, 23; p 120), Behren-Str. 55-57, spectacular pieces with ballet; seats 2-10 *M*. — 17. *Lustspielhaus*, Friedrich-Str. 236; seats 2 *M* 70-7 *M* 70 pf.

18. *Kleines Theater*, Unter den Linden 44, seats 2 *M* 20-10 *M* 20 pf 19. *Luisen-Theater* Pl. G 29). Reichenberger-

Str 34; seats 1-4 *M.* — 20. *Lortzing-Theater* (Pl G 23), Belle-Alliance-Str. 7-8, for popular operas; seats 1 *M* 40-4 *M* 85 pf. — 21. *Zentral-Theater* (Pl. G, 25), Alte Jakob-Str. 30, operettas; seats 1 *M* 10-6 *M* 20 pf

22. *Thalia-Theater* (Pl. R, 25), Dresdener-Str. 72-73; farces; seats 1 *M* 30-7 *M* 50 pf. — 23. *Bernhard-Rose-Theater* (Pl. R, 23), Grosse Frankfurter-Str. 132; seats 1-3 *M.* — 24. *Friedrich-Wilhelmstädtisches Schauspielhaus* (Pl. R, 21), Chaussée-Str. 30-31; seats 1 *M*-2 *M* 80 pf. — 25 *Trianon-Theater*, Georgen-Str. 9. — 26. *Theater an der Spree*, Köpenicker-Str. 68 (pieces in Berlin dialect). — 27 *Gebrüder Herrnfeld Theater*, Kommandanten-Str. 57 (pieces in Jewish dialect).

THEATRES OF VARIETIES. *Wintergarten*, Dorotheen-Str. 18, in the Central Hotel (p. 3); *Reichshallen-Theater* (Pl. R, 22), Leipziger-Str. 77, Donhoff-Platz; *Apollo-Theater* (Pl. G, 22), Friedrich-Str. 218; *Walhalla-Theater*, Weinbergs-Weg 19-20; *Passage-Theater*, see Panopticums (p. 38); *Folies Bergère*, Jäger-Str. 63 a.

CABARETS (frequently changing; performances generally from 11 or 12 p.m, adm. 1$^1/_2$-3 *M*)· *Chat noir*, Friedrich-Str. 165 (Castan's Panopticum); *Roland von Berlin*, Potsdamer-Str. 127; *Linden-Cabaret*, Unter den Linden 22, in the Kaiser-Galerie.

CIRCUSES (in winter only) *Circus Busch* (Pl R, 26), Burg-Str., near the Exchange Station; boxes 5 *M*, parquet 3 *M*, balcony 2 *M*, 1st tier 1$^1/_2$ *M*, 2nd tier 1 *M.* — *Circus Schumann* (Pl. R, 23), Karl-Str., boxes 5-6 *M*, reserved seats 3 *M*, balcony 2$^1/_2$ *M*, ordinary seats 1$^1/_2$ and 1 *M.*

Concerts. Tickets and concert-lists at *Bote & Bock's*, Leipziger-Str 37, and at *Wertheim's* (p. 31), 1st floor. Visitors admitted also to the rehearsals of several of the following concerts (moderate charges).

Symphony Soirées of the Royal Orchestra, a series of 10 concerts given during the winter (generally on Frid.) in the concert-room of the Opera House. As all the seats are taken by subscription, strangers are admitted to standing-room only (pit; 1 *M*). Rehearsals (Symphony-Matinees) usually at noon on concert-days.

Philharmonic Concerts, in the Philharmonie (p. 127), Bernburger-Str. 22, ten concerts in winter (director, Professor Arthur Nikisch). Rehearsals at noon on the previous day.

Philharmonic Choir, in the Philharmonie (p. 127); director, Prof. S. Ochs. Three concerts in winter. Foreign visitors admitted to the rehearsals on application to the director.

Sing-Akademie (p. 59), six or seven concerts in winter, rehearsals Tues. 5-7 p.m., to which visitors are admitted on application to the director after 1 p.m.

Mozart-Saal p 17   such   three   in and   adm. 2-5 *M*, to the rehearsals   2 .

Recitals are also given in the *Hochschule für Musik* (p. 181); *Beethoven-Saal* (p. 127), Köthener-Str. 32; *Bechstein-Saal*, Link-Str. 42, *Bluthner-Saal* (p. 174) and *Klindworth-Scharwenka-Saal*, Lutzow-Str. 76; *Choralion-Saal*, Bellevue-Str. 4; and at the *Philharmonie* (p. 127).

Cathedral Choir, instituted by Fred. William IV. in 1843 for the promotion of sacred music; director, Prof. Prüfer. Musical services in the Cathedral (p. 63) on Sun. at 10 a.m. and on the eves of great festivals.

Stern's Gesang-Verein, in the Philharmonie (p. 127); director, Prof. Oscar Fried. — *Berliner Lehrer-Gesang-Verein* (director Prof. Felix Schmidt) and *Berliner Liedertafel* (director, Herr Wagner), both also in the Philharmonie. Three concerts in winter

Philharmonic Orchestra: concerts in the Philharmonie (p. 127), on Sun., Tues., and Wed. during the winter; tickets 75 pf. (Sundays 1 *M*), 12 tickets 7 *M* 20 pf.

Organ recitals on Wed. evenings in the *Marien-Kirche* (p 154), on Thurs evenings in the *Kaiser-Wilhelm-Gedächtnis-Kirche* (p. 180); in the *Petri-Kirche, Zions-Kirche*, etc.

Bands play in summer in the *Zoological Garden* (p. 177; usually 5-11 p.m.); in the *Exhibition Park* (p. 141); in the garden of the *New Opera Theatre* (p. 140); in the *Zelten* (p. 176) and most of the brewery gardens outside the city gates (p. 11); in winter in the hall of the *Aktien-Brauerei Friedrichshain* (p. 11) and in the *Zoological Garden* (p. 177; daily, 4-7; best on Thurs.; adm. 1 *M* extra). See notices on the advertising-pillars.

o. Sport. Military Spectacles.

Horse Races. Flat-races at Hoppegarten (Ostbahn; p. 208). — Steeplechases in spring, summer and autumn, at Karlshorst (Niederschlesische Bahn; p. 202) and near Strausberg Station (Ostbahn; p. 208). — Trotting Matches at Weissensee (p. 168) and Westend (p. 183).

Cycling Races on the tracks at Steglitz (near Friedenau Station, p. 185), Zehlendorf (p. 186), and Treptow (p. 170).

Regattas. Rowing regattas in June on the Lange See at Grunau (p. 203); sailing regattas in May and Sept. on the Wannsee (p. 186) and on the Muggelsee near Friedrichshagen (p. 202).

Skating In the Tiergarten near the Rousseau-Insel (p. 177); on the Neue See; and at the West-Eisbahn near the Zoological Garden Station. Also on the Berlin-Spandau Canal from Plotzensee to Spandau and Tegel, and on the Karpfenteich at Treptow.

Berlin Golf Club. Sec., Dr Ed. D. Barrows. Königgratzer-Str. 140.

Military Reviews ('Paraden'). A magnificent military spectacle is afforded every year, at the end of May and beginning of
September, by the review of the various regiments of Guards held
by the Emperor on the Tempelhofer Feld (p. 173). Admission to
the tribunes (6000 seats; tickets at the Invalidendank, p. 27), 3-
10 *M*; programme 20 pf. For carriages a special permit from the
'Polizei-Präsidium' is necessary, for which visitors should apply in
good time; if no answer is received, the applicant must understand
that all space available has already been assigned. The troops,
with the Emperor at the head, march back through the Belle-
Alliance-Strasse.

GUARD MOUNTING at the Royal Guard House (p. 59) takes place
daily at 12.45 p.m. (during the manœuvres, at 2.45 p.m.), after
which, when the weather is good, the band plays in the Lustgarten,
near the statue of Frederick William III. (p. 63).

p. Baths.

BATH ESTABLISHMENTS. All the following establishments have
hot and shower baths; some have swimming-baths also. *Admirals-
garten-Bad* (Pl. R, 23), Friedrich-Str. 102, near the Friedrich-Str
Station, with swimming-bath, open from 8 a.m. (Sun. till 1 p.m.
only); 1st class hot bath 1 *M* 75 pf., 2nd class 75 pf.; subscribers
1 *M* 25 pf. & 50 pf.; *Augusta-Bad*, Kopenicker-Str. 60-61. Both
establishments have medicinal, vapour, and Turkish baths; the Ad-
miralsgarten-Bad and its branch establishments (Friedrich-Str. 8,
Alexander-Platz 3, Luisen-Ufer 22. Lützow-Str. 71, Paul-Str. 6,
Reinickendorfer-Str. 3) also brine-baths. — Medicinal baths: *Verein
der Wasserfreunde*, Königgratzer-Str. 19; *Belle-Alliance-Bad*,
Gneisenau-Str. 3: *City-Bad*, Dresdener-Str. 52-53. — Municipal
popular baths, with swimming-basins: Turner-Str. 85a, at the
Schillings-Brücke, Dennewitz-Str. 24a, Barwald-Str. 65, etc

RIVER BATHS. *Flussbad*, An der Stralauer-Brücke (Pl. R, 28;
also for ladies); *Sachse* (Pl. G, 35), at the Schlesische Brucke. —
In the inner town (water not very clear): *Runge*, An der Schleuse 6
(also for ladies).

q. Shops. Art Dealers and Show Rooms. Banks.

The best shops are in Unter den Linden, the Leipziger-Str., the
Friedrich-Str., and the vicinity.

STORES (large establishments for all kinds of dress, millinery,
household utensils, furniture, fancy articles, etc.): *A. Wertheim*,
Leipziger-Str. 132-137 and Rosenthaler-Str. 23-31 (pp. 125, 166);
F. Tietz Leipziger-Str. 46-50 and Alexander-Str. 61-70 (p. 126,
153); *Kaufhaus des Westens*, 177, Wittenberg-Platz

ANTIQUITIES: *Van Dam*, Wilhelm-Str. 46; *A. Fröschels*, Wilhelm-Str. 88; *M. Heilbronner*, Mohren-Str. 61; *Krumschmidt*, Prinz-Albrecht-Str. 3; *M. Wollmann*, Königgrätzer-Str. 28.

ARTISTS' MATERIALS: *G. Bormann Nachfolger*, Bruder-Str. 39; *Keltz & Meiners*, Leipziger-Str. 130.

BOOK-BINDINGS AND ALBUMS: *W. Collin*, Leipziger-Str. 19; *G. Hulbe*, Leipziger-Str. 121.

BRONZES (originals and copies)· *Aktiengesellschaft, late H. Gladenbeck & Sohn*, Leipziger-Str. 111; *R. Bellair & Co*, Mauer-Str. 13-14; *E. Kayser*, Leipziger-Str. 124; *Ad. Névir*, Unter den Linden 14; *Rakenius & Co.*, Unter den Linden 62 — ENAMELLED BRONZES: *A. Stübbe*, Wall-Str. 86.

CABINET MAKING (ARTISTIC). *Joh. Pingel*, Wilhelm-Str 130; *C. Pohl & Sohn*, Friedrich-Karl-Str. 32; *Siebert & Aschenbach*, Horn-Str. 11; *G. Wenkel Nachfolger*, Potsdamer-Str. 19.

CARPETS· see Upholstery.

CHINESE AND JAPANESE WARES AND TEA: *L. Glenk*, Unter den Linden 59 *J. L. Rex*, Leipziger-Str. 22; *R. Wagner*, Potsdamer-Str. 20a.

CIGARS· *Otto Boenicke*, Französische-Str. 21; *Continental Havanna Co.*, Friedrich-Str. 203; *C G. Gerold*, Unter den Linden 24; *Loeser & Wolff*, Alexander-Str 1; *J. Neumann*, Konig-Str. 56,57.

GERMAN COLONIAL PRODUCTS: *Deutsches Kolonialhaus* (Bruno Antelmann), Lützow-Str. 89, 90.

CUTLERY: *J. A. Henckels*, Leipziger-Str. 117.

DRUG STORES: *Anglo-American Drug Store*, Potsdamer-Str. 134, *Klaehre*, Am Prager Platz, *O. Sasse*, Kleist-Str. 22.

ENGRAVINGS: *Amsler & Ruthardt*, Behren-Str. 29a.

FANCY ARTICLES: *J. Demuth*, Unter den Linden 3a; *Van Santen*, Unter den Linden 24; *Gebr. Nathan*, Unter den Linden 5-6.

FANS. *C. Sauerwald*, Leipziger-Str. 22.

FURNITURE DEALERS AND UPHOLSTERERS: *Bauer Brothers*, Bellevue-Str 5; *Hess & Rom*, Leipziger-Str. 106; *Keller & Reiner*, Potsdamer-Str. 122; *Karl Müller & Co.*, Friedrich-Str. 77; *J. C. Pfaff*, Französische-Str. 38-39; *Thonet*, Leipziger-Str. 89. — See also Upholstery.

FURRIERS: *C. A. Herpich Söhne*, Leipziger-Str. 9-11; *C. Salbach*, Unter den Linden 67.

GOLDSMITHS. *Friedländer*, Unter den Linden 4a; *J. H. Werner*, at the Hôt. Adlon (p. 2); *L. Posen*, Unter den Linden 5, *Sy & Wagner*, Werder-Str. 7; *D. Vollgold & Sohn*, Unter den Linden 34; *Hugo Schaper*, Potsdamer-Str. 8; *Joh. Wagner & Sohn*, Unter den Linden 30. — ELECTRO-PLATE· *Henniger & Co.*, Leipziger-Str. 126; *Württembergische Metallwarenfabrik*, Leipziger-Str. 112.

HOSIERS. *Bruno Nordberg*, Französische-Str. 20; *Mosich*, Friedrich-Str. 63a, *Th. Lindner*, Post-Str. 2-3.

JEWELLERS· see Goldsmiths.

LACE. *J. Link*, Jager-Str. 25; *Wechselmann*, Behren-Str. 36.

LEATHER GOODS (cut and stamped leather)· *G. Halbe*, Leipziger-Str. 121; see also trunk-makers.

LINENDRAPERS: *F. V. Grunfeld*, Leipziger-Str. 20-21 and Mauer-Str 9-11; *N. Israel*, Spandauer-Str. 26-32; *Rudolf Hertzog*, Breite-Str. 12-18; *Gebruder Mosse*, Jager-Str. 47.

MARBLE WARES AND CHIMNEY-PIECES *G. Schleicher & Co.*, Lutzow-Str. 82; *Schumacher & Co.*, Leipziger-Str. 97-98.

MILLINERY AND COSTUMES: *J. Bister*, Unter den Linden 64; *Hermann Gerson*, Werderscher Markt 5-6; *Rud. Hertzog*, Breite-Str. 12-18; *Jean Landauer*, Behren-Str. 51; *V. Manheimer*, Oberwall-Str. 6-7. — CHILDREN's CLOTHES. *Arnold Müller*, Leipziger-Str. 95.

MOURNING WAREHOUSE: *Otto Weber*, Mohren-Str. 34-35.

OPTICIANS: *P. Dorffel*, Unter den Linden 44; *Paetz & Flohr*, Unter den Linden 59a; *Robert A. Thompson*, Wilhelm-Str. 59.

ORNAMENTAL IRONWORK: *A. L. Benecke*, Mittel-Str. 16; *P. Marcus*, Schoneberg, Monumenten-Str. 19; *B. Miksits*, Heide-Str. 14; *Ed. Puls*, Tempelhof, Germania-Str.; *Schulz & Holdefleiss*, Fenn-Str. 13.

PAINTINGS ON ENAMEL: *E. Bastanier*, Prinz-Albrecht-Str. 8.

PERFUMERS. *Gustav Lohse*, Unter den Linden 16; *J. F. Schwarzlose Söhne*, Markgrafen-Str. 29; *Treu & Nuglisch*, Werder-Str. 7.

PHOTOGRAPHS (see p. 34): *Amsler & Ruthardt*, Behren-Str. 29a; *Quaas*, Stechbahn 2; *H. Maes*, Kronen-Str. 15, corner of Friedrich-Str.

PHOTOGRAPHERS: *O. Anschütz*, Leipziger-Str. 131; *E. Bieber*, Leipziger-Str. 130. *W. Fechner*, Potsdamer-Str. 13; *H. Rückwardt*, Gross-Lichterfelde, Knesebeck-Str. 3-4 (buildings and interiors). — PHOTOGRAPHIC MATERIALS *O. Anschütz*, Leipziger-Str. 131; *Kodak*, Unter den Linden 26; *H. Klein*, Victoria-Luise-Platz 8.

PLASTER OF PARIS FIGURES: *Micheli*, Unter den Linden 76a.

PORCELAIN: *Royal Porcelain Manufactory*, Leipziger-Str. 2; *F. Hengstmann*, Leipziger-Str. 39 (Dresden china).

PRESERVED FRUIT AND CHOCOLATES: *Von Hövell*, Unter den Linden 12; *Sarotti*, Leipziger-Str. 129; *T. Hildebrand & Son*, Leipziger-Str. 100; *Sawade*, Unter den Linden 19.

SILK MERCERS· *H. Gerson*, Werderscher Markt 5-6; *Rud. Hertzog*, Breite-Str. 12-18; *Michels & Co.*, Leipziger-Str. 43-44.

STATIONERS· *A. W. Faber*, Friedrich-Str. 79; *M. Adler & Co.*, Friedrich-Str. 90; *Jul. Rosenthal*, Behren-Str. 30; *H. Schultze Nachfolger*, Behren-Str 28· *Aug. Zeiss & Co.*, Leipziger-Str. 126.

TAPESTRY *W. Zirsch & Co.*, Bethanien Ufer 3.

TRUNK MAKERS: *Ed. Lehrmann*, Unter den Linden 21: *J. De-*

muth, Unter den Linden 3a; *M. Mädler*, Leipziger-Str. 101-102; *Turner & Glanz*, Friedrich-Str. 193a, *Wellhausen & Co.*, Mohren-Str. 29-30; *B. Wisniewski*, Potsdamer-Str. 106.

UNDERCLOTHING: *Goschenhofer & Rösicke*, Leipziger-Str. 58; *Heinrich Jordan*, Markgrafen-Str. 104-107; *E. E. Mezner*, Markgrafen-Str. 39-40; *Mosse Brothers*, Jäger-Str. 47; *W. Wolffenstein*, Leipziger-Str. 124.

UPHOLSTERY AND CARPETS. *Hermann Gerson*, Werder-Str. 9-12; *Grunow, Gebhardt & Roessel Nachfolger*, Markgrafen-Str. 53-54; *R. Holstein*, Wilhelm-Str. 59, corner of Leipziger-Str.; *J. L. Rex*, Leipziger-Str. 22; and the stores of *Wertheim* and *Tietz* (p. 31.)

Art Dealers and Show Rooms: *Ed. Schulte*, Unter den Linden 75; *Keller & Reiner*, Potsdamer-Str. 122, also industrial art; *Paul Cassirer*, Viktoria-Str. 31; *Wertheim* (p. 31; entrance in the Voss-Str.); *Fritz Gurlitt*, Potsdamer-Str. 113; *Mathilde Rabl*, Potsdamer-Str. 134c; adm. at all these 1 *M.*, annual ticket 3 (at Cassirer's 5) *M.* — AUCTIONS OF WORKS OF ART at *Rud. Lepke's*, Koch-Str. 28-29. — Good collections of works of nearly all branches of industrial art are on sale also at the *Hohenzollern-Kunstgewerbehaus* (Hirschwald), Leipziger-Str. 13 (adm. 50 pf.-1 *M*, for 1 year 2-3 *M*), and *Keller & Reiner* (see above).

ARTISTIC REPRODUCTIONS, PHOTOGRAPHS, ETC. *Photographische Gesellschaft*, Stechbahn 1, near the Royal Palace, *Neue Photographische Gesellschaft*, Leipziger-Str. 131, 1st floor, *Vereinigung der Kunstfreunde*, Markgrafen-Str. 57 (copies in colours of paintings in the National and other Galleries); *Amsler & Ruthardt*, Behren-Str. 29a (original etchings and drawings). Adm. free.

Banks: *Reichsbank*, Jäger-Str. 34; *Deutsche Bank*, Behren-Str. 8-13; *Bank für Handel und Industrie*, Schinkel-Platz 1-2; *Berliner Bank*, Behren-Str. 46; *Berliner Handels-Gesellschaft*, Behren-Str. 32; *S. Bleichröder*, Behren-Str. 62-63; *Delbrück, Leo & Co.*, Mauer-Str. 61-62; *Diskonto-Gesellschaft*, Unter den Linden 35 and Behren-Str. 43-44; *Dresdner Bank*, Behren-Str. 37-39; *Mendelssohn & Co.*, Jäger-Str. 49; *Nationalbank für Deutschland*, Voss-Str. 31; *Schaaffhausen'scher Bankverein*, Französische-Str. 53-54; *Königliche Seehandlung*, Jäger-Str. 21.

r. Newspapers. Reading Rooms.

Newspapers. Upwards of 1100 newspapers and periodicals are published at Berlin. Among the leading daily papers may be mentioned: *Deutscher Reichs- und Staats-Anzeiger*, Wilhelm-Str. 32, *Berliner Tageblatt*, Jerusalemer-Str. 46-49; *Berliner Lokal-An-*

zeiger, Unter den Linden 3 (p. 56); *Vossische Zeitung*, Breite-Str. 8-9 (p. 157); *Berliner Zeitung*, Koch-Str. 23; *Post*, Zimmer-Str. 94; *Norddeutsche Allgemeine Zeitung*, Wilhelm-Str. 32; *Kreuz-Zeitung*, Kothener-Str. 2; *National-Zeitung*, Mauer-Str. 86-88; *Germania*, Stralauer-Str 25; *Tägliche Rundschau*, Zimmer-Str. 7-8; *Berliner Börsen-Zeitung*, Kronen-Str. 37; *Berliner Börsen-Courier*, Benth-Str. 8; *Der Tag*, Zimmer-Str. 37-41, etc.

The *Continental Times* and the *English and American Register* are English weekly papers published at Berlin.

Reading Rooms. — *Royal Library*, Opern-Platz and (for newspapers) Behren-Str 42. see pp. 39, 58. — *University Library*, Dorotheen-Str. 9 (p. 57; 9-7; free). — *Akademische Lesehalle*, see pp 36, 58. — *Öffentliche Bibliothek und Lesehalle*, Alexandrinen-Str. 26. — Reading-room at the office of the *Chicago Daily News*, in the Equitable Building (p 126), Friedrich-Str. 59-60 (week-days 9-6, adm. free). — *American Exchange* (Brasch & Rothenstein), Hausvogtei-Platz 2 (week-days 9-6; free).

American Association of Commerce and Trade, Leipziger-Str. 101 — *American Woman's Club*, Münchener-Str. 49-50.

s. Embassies and Consulates.

GREAT BRITAIN. Ambassador, *Sir Frank C. Lascelles*, Wilhelm-Str. 70 (office-hours 11-1). — Consul-General, *Dr. P. v. Schwabach*, Behren-Str. 63 (office-hours, 10-12 and 4-5).

UNITED STATES OF AMERICA. Ambassador, *Dr David J. Hill*, Hôtel Adlon (p 2); office, Unter den Linden 68 (10-1). — Consul-General, *Alexander M. Thackara*; vice-consul-general, *Frederick W. Cauldwell*, Friedrich-Str. 59-60 (office-hours, 10-3).

The following are the present addresses of the Ministers and Consuls of other countries, but changes of residence sometimes take place.

Austria-Hungary, Kronprinzen-Ufer 11; Consulate-General, Schoneberger Ufer 40 (10-1).

Belgium, Roon-Str. 12; Consulate-General, Oberwall-Str 20a (10-12).

China, Kurfürsten-Damm 218.

Denmark, Königgrätzer-Str. 140; Consulate-General, Jager-Str 49 (10-12).

France, Pariser-Platz 5 (also Consulate-General, 10 30-1, 3-4).

Greece, Ranke-Str 16; Consulate-General. Unter den Linden 71 (9 30-1, Sat. 9.30 2).

Holland, Voss-Str. 10, Consulate-General, Unter den Linden 8 (10-1).

Italy, Viktoria-Str 36, Consulate-General, Dorotheen-Str. 32 (9-1).

Japan, Blumeshof 12 (10.30 1.30).

Norway, Alsen-Str. 2; Consulate General, Spandauer-Str 59-60 (10 2).

Portugal, Potsdamer-Str.118a; Consulate-General,Muhlen-Str.6-7(11-1)

Roumania,Moltke-Str 2, Consulate-General, Unter den Linden 35 (11-1)

Russia, Unter den Linden 7; Consulate-General, Schiffbauerdamm 30 (10-2).

Sweden, Bellevue-Str. 7; Consulate-General Jager-Str. 49-50 (11-1).

Spain, Regenten-Str. 15, Consulate-General, Wilhelm-Str. 70b (9-11 and 4-5)

Swit... ... ... Wilhelm-Str. 70 1.

Turk... Ranke-Str ... Consulate-General, Behren-Str. ... -1).

t. English Churches.

St George's Church (Episcopal; Pl. R, 23), Monbijou Garden
(p. 146); services on Sun. at 9 and 11 a.m. and 6 p.m. — Chaplain,
Rev. J. H. Fry, M. A., Savigny-Platz 7, Charlottenburg.

American Church (Pl. G, 13, 14), Motz-Str. 6 (p. 175); service
on Sun. at 11.30 a.m. — Pastor, *Rev. J. F. Dickie, D. D.,* Luitpold-
Str. 30

First Church of Christ, Scientist, Choralion-Saal, Bellevue-
Str. 4; English service on Sun. at 11.30 a.m.

u. Collections and Places of Interest. Diary.

Several of the collections are closed on the chief holidays, *viz.* Jan. 1st,
Good Friday, Easter Sunday, Whitsunday, Ascension Day, Christmas
Day, and the national Day of Repentance (Busstag)

Abgeordneten-Haus (Prussian Chamber of Deputies; p. 135),
Prinz-Albrecht-Str. 5-6. Cards of admission to the meetings may
be obtained on the E. side and in the passage through the Herrenhaus, Leipziger-Str., from 5-7 p.m. on the previous evening, as well
as on the day of meeting. Plan showing the distribution of the 433
deputies, 1 *M.* The house is shown to visitors on week-days out of
session between 9 and 10 a.m. (fee).

Agricultural Museum (p. 162), Invaliden-Str. 42; open free,
daily except Wed. and Sun., 10-3; also on the 3rd Sun. of each
month, 11-3.

Akademische Lesehalle (Students' Reading Room), behind the
University (p. 58), open on week-days in summer 8-7.30, in winter
9-8, Sun 9-1; in vacation 9-3, Sun. 10-1, adm. for the day, 25 pf.

Aquarium (p. 56), Unter den Linden 68a, entrance Schadow-
Str. 14, open daily 9-7, on week-days in winter 9-6. Adm. 1 *M,*
Sun. 50 pf., on the last Sunday in each month (crowded) 25 pf.

Architectural Museum, see Technical Academy.

Arsenal (p. 59), open free, daily except Sat., 10-3 (Nov. to Feb.,
10-2), Sun. and second holidays 12-3; closed on the Emperor's birthday (Jan 27th).

Bellevue, royal château in the Tiergarten (p. 176), shown in summer 11-5, Sun. 12-4; adm. 25 pf.

Beuth-Schinkel Museum, see Technical Academy (p. 42).

Botanical Garden (p. 185) at Steglitz Adm., from April to 15th
Oct., on Sun., Tues., Wed., and Frid. 2-7, free; on other days 8-7 by
buying one of the catalogues (*e. g.* Alpine flora, 1 *M*), to each of
which 4-16 tickets of admission are attached. Hot-houses: 3-6 (in
winter 1-4), except Saturday. The mere walk between the S. and N.
gates, indicated by arrows requires 1 hr.; plan, 20 pf. — The Botanical Museum on the Dahlem-Chaussée will be opened in 1908.

Cathedral (p. 63), Lustgarten, on week-days 10-6 or till dusk; free.

Charlottenburg: The *Royal Mausoleum* (p. 183) and *Palace* (p. 182) are open on week-days 10-6, Sun. and holidays 11-6, in winter till 4 p.m. Cards of admission for both (25 pf. for each) are issued in the right wing of the palace.

Colonial Museum (p. 140), Alt-Moabit 1; adm. from 9 to 7 or till dusk, 1 *M.* Sun. 50 pf. (including lecture). Lectures with photographic illustrations in winter on Sun. at 5 p m. (25 pf.).

Column of Victory (Sieges-Saule; p. 136); ascent to the platform daily, in summer 7-7, in winter 9-5 or till dark. Admission 50 pf.

Emperor Frederick Museum (p. 96), open Tues. to Sat. from 10 (Sun 12, Mon. 1) to 6 (Oct. to March 10-5, Nov. and Feb. 10-4, Dec. and Jan. 10-3). Adm. on Sun., Thurs., Frid. and Sat. free, Mon 1 *M,* Tues and Wed. 50 pf. On Sun. generally crowded.

Emperor William Memorial Church (p. 180), in Charlottenburg, near the Zoological Garden; open on week-days 9-1 and usually also 3-6 (free). Entrance near the sacristy (S. E. side).

Ethnographical Museum (p.128), Koniggratzer-Str. 120; open free, as the Museum of Industrial Art (p 38).

Exchange (p. 154), Burg-Str. 25-26; on week-days 12-2. Cards of admission (30 pf.) and entrance to the gallery at Neue Friedrich-Str. 51, 1st floor.

Exhibition of Art (Grosse Berliner Kunstausstellung), in the Exhibition Park (p. 141; with restaurant), daily from the end of April till the end of Sept., 10-8 (after August 1st 10-7); adm. 50 pf., Mon. 1 *M,* season-ticket 6 *M.*

Exhibition of the Academy of Arts (p. 55), Pariser - Platz 4, several times in winter, 10-4 or 6: adm. 1-5 *M.*

Exhibition of the Berliner Sezession, Kurfursten-Damm 208, Charlottenburg (p. 181; tramway-station Uhland-Str.), several times yearly, in summer daily 9-7, in winter 10-6; adm. 1 *M,* Sun after 2 30 p.m. 50 pf.

Exhibition of the Society of Berlin Artists (Verein Berliner Künstler), in the Künstler-Haus (p. 141), Bellevue-Str. 3, open the whole year; week-days 10-6, Sun. 11-2, adm. 1 *M,* season-ticket 3 *M*

Exhibition Park (p. 141). Moabit. Several bands play in the summer during the exhibition; adm. 50 pf., Mon. 1 *M;* season-ticket for park and exhibition 6 *M.*

Giant Telescope in the Astronomical Museum at Treptow (p. 170); inspection of the collections and explanation of the telescope daily 2-8 (for strangers in the morning also), 50 pf.; use of the telescope. 2-12 p.m. (in winter 2-10 p.m.). 1 *M.* Lectures with photographic illustrations Sun. 5 and 7 M . . . 50 pf.

Hall of Fame . . .

Herrenhaus (Upper Chamber of the Prussian Diet; p. 125), Leipziger-Str 3-4. Cards of admission to the meetings may be obtained in the left angle of the fore-court ¹/₂ hr. before the beginning of the meeting and while it is going on The Herrenhaus is shown to visitors out of session on week-days at noon (cards of adm . 25 pf.) See also Abgeordneten-Haus (p. 36).

Hohenzollern Museum (p. 146), Monbijou-Platz 6-9; open Mon. to Frid. 10-3, Sun. 11.30-2. Admission 25 pf. Closed on Sat., the chief holidays, and the Emperor's birthday.

Märkisches Provinzial-Museum (p. 155), Märkischer Platz; open Sun. 11-1.30, Mon.-Thurs. 11-2 30; adm. on Tues. 50 pf., other days free.

Mining Museum (p. 164), Invaliden-Str. 44; open free on week-days (except Mon.) 12-2 p.m., Sun. 12-4 (in winter 12-3).

Old and New Museums (pp. 71, 74); adm. as to the Museum of Industrial Art (see below). — For the *Asiatic Antiquities* see p. 84. Adm. free.

Museum of German National Costumes and Domestic Industries (p. 155), Kloster-Str. 36; open daily, except Wed., 11-2. Admission 50 pf.

Museum of Industrial Art (p. 132), Prinz-Albrecht-Str.; open on Sun 12-6 (in winter 12-3), week-days (except Mon.) 10-4 (in winter 10-3). Exhibitions in the central court, lighted by electricity, Tues.-Sat. 7.30-9.30 p m. (except in June, July, and August) The library is open on week-days, 10-10; the costume library 10-1 and (on Tues. and Frid.) 6-8 p.m. Admission free.

Museum of Natural History (p. 162), Invaliden-Str. 43; open free on Sun. 12-4 (in winter 12-3), on week-days, except Tues. and Frid., 10-4 (in winter 10-3).

Museum of Traffic and Engineering (p. 164), Invaliden-Str. 50-51, Sun. 11-4, Tues., Thurs., and Frid. 10-4, Wed. and Sat. 2-8; closed on Mon. and the chief holidays.

National Gallery (p. 85); open on Mon , Tues., Wed., Frid., and Sat. from 10 (Sun. from 12, Thurs. from 1) till 6 (Oct. and March till 5, Nov and Feb. till 4, Dec. and Jan. till 3); adm. on Sun. (generally crowded), Mon., Tues., and Frid. free, Thurs. 1 ℳ, Frid. and Sat. 50 pf.

Oceanographical Museum (p. 144), Georgen-Str. 34-36, open on Sun. 12-3, week-days 11-4 (in winter 10-3), free. Lectures in winter at 8 p m (adm 25 pf.).

Palace of Emperor William I. (p. 57); open Sun. 10-1, week-days 10-2. Admission 50 pf.

Panopticums (waxworks; variety performances in the evening): *Castan's Panopticum* (p 120) corner of Behren-Str. and Friedrich-Str.. *Passage Panopticum*, in the Kaiser Galerie p. 56 , both open daily from 9 a m till 10 p.m.; adm. 50 pf.

Pergamon Museum (p. 82; entrance behind the National Gallery), open free, as the Museum of Industrial Art (p. 38).

Picture Exhibitions, see p. 37.

Postal Museum (p. 125), Leipziger Str. 16, open free daily, except Wed. and Sat., 10-2; on Sun. and holidays 12-2. Closed on the chief holidays.

Rathaus, Berlin (p. 151); open free daily, except Thurs. and Frid., 10-3. Ascent of the tower daily from Apr. 1st to Oct. 1st, 20 pf.

Rathaus, Charlottenburg (p 182), week-days 10-3, Sun. 11 and 1; adm. 20 pf. including tower (in summer daily 11 and 1).

Rauch Museum (p. 156), Kloster-Str. 75-76; open free on week-days 10-4 (in winter 10-3).

Ravené's Picture Gallery (p. 160), Wall-Str. 5-8 (Portal II); open free on Tues. and Frid. 10-2; closed on the chief holidays.

Reichstags-Gebäude (Hall of the Imperial Diet; p. 136); adm. to view the building (Portal V, on the N. side) on Sun. at 1 and 1.30 p.m., on week-days at 9 a.m., and after the close of the session also at 9.30, 12, and 2 30. Adm. 25 pf.; the inspection occupies $3/4$ hr. — Cards of adm. to the galleries (10 seats; free) are issued on the day of session at 10 a.m. (Portal V), but are generally at once exhausted (access easier by applying to a member).

Royal Library (p. 58), in the Opern-Platz, shown to visitors, Mon.-Frid., 1 to 2 p.m.

The *Large Reading Room* on the 2nd floor is open daily from 9 a.m. to 9 p.m., and visitors on application to the official in charge are allowed freely to consult the books and periodicals there. Books are lent to strangers under certain restrictions only (comp. the regulations hung at the entrance) — The *Newspaper Reading Room* (open 9-9) and the *Music and Map Rooms* (open 9 3) are at Behren-Str. 42.

Royal Collection of Musical Instruments (p. 181), in the Academy of Music, Charlottenburg, Fasanen-Str. 1 (Portal IV), open free during term, Tues. 11-1, Wed. & Sat 12-2.

Royal Palace (p. 65); open on week-days 10-1, Sun. and holidays 11.30-1.30. Adm 50 pf. Entrance from the Lustgarten at Portal IV, which is opened by a sentry. Visitors receive their tickets in the inner court, to the left, and are conducted through the state-rooms in parties every half-hour. The visit lasts $3/4$ hr.

Royal Porcelain Factory (p. 179), Wegely-Str., near the Tiergarten Station; open Tues. to Frid. 9-12. Visitors are shown the process of manufacture and (by special permission of the director) also the ceramic room (fee). — Shop, see p. 33.

Royal Stables (p. 70; entrance Breite-Str. 37); daily 11 30-1.30; adm. 50 pf. Parties conducted every $1/4$ hr.; duration $3/4$ hr.

New Synagogue (p. 116) Oranienburger Str. 30; admission 9-5 (in winter 9 4) on application to the sacristan; closed on Jan. 1st,

Comp. pp. 36-42.   **Diary.**

	Sundays and Holidays	Monday	Tuesday	Wednesday
Aquarium (p. 56)	9-7(6)	9-7(6)	9-7(6)	9-7(6)
Arsenal (p. 59)	12-3	10-3(2)	10-3(2)	10-3(2)
Exchange (p. 154)	—	12-2	12-2	12-2
Giant Telescope (p. 170)	2-12(10)	2-12(10)	2-12(10)	2-12(10)
Library, Royal (p. 58)	—	1-2	1-2	1-2
Mausoleum at Charlottenburg(p.183)	11-6(4)	10-6(4)	10-6(4)	10-6(4)
Monument of Victory (p. 136) . . .	7-7(5)	7-7(5)	7-7(5)	7-7(5)
Museum, Agricultural (p. 162) . . .	—	10-3	10-3	—
—, Architectural (p. 180)	—	10-3	12-3	10-12
—, Colonial (p. 140)	9-7(5)	9-7(5)	9-7(5)	9-7(5)
—, Emperor Frederick (p. 96) . .	12-6(3)	1-6(3)	10-6(3)	10-6(3)
—, Ethnographical (p. 128)	12-6(3)	—	10-4(3)	10-4(3)
— of German Costumes (p. 155) .	12-6(3)	—	10-4(3)	10-4(3)
—, Hohenzollern (p. 146)	11.30-2	10-3	10-3	10-3
— of Industrial Art (p. 132) . . .	12-6(3)	—	10-4(3)	10-4(3)
—, Märk. Provinzial (p. 155) . . .	11-1.30	11-2.30	11-2.30	11-2.30
—, Mining (p. 164)	12-4(3)	—	12-2	12-2
—, Natural History (p. 162) . . .	12-4(3)	10-4(3)	—	10-4(3)
—, Oceanographical (p. 144) . . .	12-3	11-4(3)	—	—
—, Old and New (pp. 71, 74) . . .	12-6(3)	—	10-4(3)	10-4(3)
—, Pergamon (p.82)	12-6(3)	—	10-4(3)	10-4(3)
—, Postal (p. 125)	12-2	10-2	10-2	—
—, Rauch (p. 156)	—	10-4(3)	10-4(3)	10-4(3)
— of Traffic (p. 164)	11-4	—	10-4	2-8
National Gallery (p. 85)	12-6(3)	10-4(3)	10-6(3)	10-6(3)
Palace, Royal (p. 65)	11.30-1.30	10-1	10-1	10-1
— of Emperor William I. (p. 57) .	10-1	10-2	10-2	10-2
Picture Exhibition, Annual (p. 37)	10-8	10-8	10-8	10-8
— — (Berlin Artists; p. 37)	11-2	10-6	10-6	10-6
— — (Secession; p. 37) . .	9-7(6)	9-7(6)	9-7(6)	9-7(6)
Rathaus, Berlin (p. 151)	10-3	10-3	10-3	10-3
Ravené's Picture Gallery (p. 160) .	—	—	10-2	—
Reichstags-Gebäude (p. 136)	1 & 1.30	9 & 9.30	9 & 9.30	9 & 9.30
Stables, Royal (p. 70)	11.30-1.30	11.30-1.30	11.30-1.30	11.30-1.30
Workmen's Welfare Exhibition (p. 182)	1-5	—	10-1	10-1
Zoological Garden (p. 180)	6-10	6-10	6-10	6-10

Diary.   Comp. pp. 36-40.

Thurs-day	Friday	Satur-day	Admission free except when otherwise stated.
9-7(6)	9-7(6)	9-7(6)	Adm. 1 *M.*; Sun. 50 pf.
10-3(2)	10-3(2)	—	Closed on the chief holidays and the Emperor's birthday (27th Jan.).
12-2	12-2	12-2	Adm. 30 pf.
2-12(10)	2-12(10)	2-12(10)	Adm. 1 *M.*
1-2	1-2	—	
10-6(4)	10-6(4)	10-6(4)	Adm. 25 pf.
7-7(5)	7-7(5)	7-7(5)	Closed in winter at dusk.
10-3	10-3	10-3	Closed on the chief holidays.
12-3	10-3	—	
9-7(5)	9-7(5)	9-7(5)	Adm. 1 *M.*, Sun. 50 pf.
10-6(3)	10-6(3)	10-6(3)	Adm. Mon. 1 *M.*, Tues. & Wed. 50 pf.; closed on the chief holidays.
10-4(3)	10-4(3)	10-4(3)	Closed on the chief holidays.
10-4(3)	10-4(3)	10-4(3)	Closed on the chief holidays.
10-3	10-3	—	Adm. 25 pf.; closed on the chief holidays and the Emperor's birthday (27th Jan.).
10-4(3)	10-4(3)	10-4(3)	Closed on the chief holidays.
11-2.30	—	—	Adm. Tues. 50 pf.; other days free.
12-2	12-2	12-2	
10-4(3)	—	10-4(3)	Closed on the chief holidays.
—	—	11-4(3)	
10-4(3)	10-4(3)	10-4(3)	} Closed on the chief holidays.
10-4(3)	10-4(3)	10-4(3)	
10-2	10-2	—	
10-4(3)	10-4(3)	10-4(3)	
10-4	10-4	2-8	
10-6(3)	10-6(3)	10-6(3)	Adm. Thurs. 1 *M.*, Frid. & Sat. 50 pf.; closed on the chief holidays.
10-1	10-1	10-1	Adm. 50 pf.; closed on the chief holidays.
10-2	10-2	10-2	Adm. 50 pf.
10-8	10-8	10-8	In summer only. Adm. 50 pf., Mon. 1 *M.*
10-6	10-6	10-6	Adm. 1 *M.*
9-7(6)	9-7(6)	9-7(6)	Adm. 1 *M.*, Sun. 50 pf.
—	—	10-3	Tower daily in summer 10-3 (20 pf.).
—	10-2	—	Closed on the chief holidays.
9 & 9.30	9 & 9.30	9 & 9.30	Adm. 50 pf.
10.30-1.30	11.30-1.30	11.30-1.30	Adm. 50 pf.
10-1	10-1	10-1	
6-10	6-10	6-10	In winter till dusk. Adm. 1 *M.*, Sun. and holidays 50 pf.

and the Day of Atonement, when cards, a tariff for which is shown by the sacristan, are necessary. Ordinary services after dusk on Fridays.

Technical Academy (p. 179), in Charlottenburg. *Architectural Museum* and *Beuth-Schinkel Museum* (on the second floor of the E. wing, entrance Room 314), open free on Mon. and Frid. 10-3, Tues. and Thurs. 12-3, Wed 10-12.

Urania, two branches. — *a.* Tauben-Str. 48, 49 (p. 121); admission to collections from 10 a m., 50 pf.; to the Scientific Theatre at 8 p.m., 1-3 *M*, including adm. to collections; tickets taken in advance (10-4) 25 pf. extra; to scientific lectures (including adm. to collections) at 8 p.m , adm. 3-8 *M*. — *b.* Invaliden-Str. 57-62 (p. 141); open daily 7.15-11 p.m.; observatory 50 pf., half-year's ticket 3 *M*.

Workmen's Welfare Exhibition (p. 182), in Charlottenburg, Fraunhofer-Str. 11, open free Tues. to Sat. 10-1, Sun. 1-5, also Tues. and Thurs. 6-9 p m.

Zoological Garden (p. 177); open daily in summer (April-Sept. 30th) 6 a.m -10.30 p.m., in winter 7 or 7.30 a.m till 7 p.m. Adm. 1 *M*, Sun. and holidays (generally full) and on week-days after 6 p.m. in summer (after 4 p.m. in winter), 50 pf.; on the first Sun. in each month 25 pf. (crowded). Concerts see p. 30.

v. A Week in Berlin.

For the days and hours of admission to the museums, palaces, and other places of interest comp pp. 36-42.

A fair knowledge of Berlin may be gained in a single week. The most important places and objects of interest in the city are to be found in the space enclosed between the Tiergarten to the W., the Alexander-Platz to the E., the Spree to the N. and the Leipziger-Strasse to the S. A fine day should be reserved for Potsdam (comp. p. 187).

1st DAY. Walk by the Unter den Linden from the Brandenburger-Tor (p. 55) to the Lustgarten, visiting the *Arsenal* (p. 59) and the *Royal Palace* (p. 65) on the way. Then drive past the Old and New Museums (pp. 71, 74) and the National Gallery (p. 85), cross the Friedrichs-Brucke, and proceed viâ the Burg-Str. (Exchange, p. 154) and Kaiser Wilhelm-Str. to the Alexander-Platz (p. 153). Thence follow the König-Str (inspection of the *Rathaus*, with the view from its tower, p. 152), the Kurfürsten-Brucke (p. 70), and the Schloss-Platz (p. 69) to the *National Monument to Emperor William I* (p. 69). Crossing the Werdersche-Markt (p. 159) and the Gendarmen-Markt (p. 121), take the Friedrich Str. and Mohren-Str. to the *Wilhelm-Platz* (p. 123) and thence the Wilhelm-Str. and

Leipziger-Str. to the Potsdamer-Platz (p. 127), and proceed by the Bellevue-Str. to the *Sieges-Allée* (p. 141). Finally, walk through the last to the Reichstag Building (p 136) and the *Bismarck Monument* (p. 139).

2ND DAY. *Emperor Frederick Museum* (p 96). In the afternoon (before 6 p.m.) visit the *Emperor William Memorial Church* (p. 180) and the *Mausoleum* at *Charlottenburg* (p. 183).

3RD DAY. *Cathedral* (p. 63), *National Gallery* (p. 85), and *Pergamon Museum* (p. 82). In the afternoon, the *Märkisches Museum* (p. 155), after which a drive may be taken through the S.E. quarters (viâ Jannowitz-Brucke, Oranien-Platz, Kaiser-Friedrich-Platz, comp. p. 169) to the *Kreuzberg* (p. 172).

4TH DAY. *Reichstag Building* (9 a.m., comp. p. 136), *Palace of Emperor William I* (p. 57), *Old* and *New Museums* (pp. 71, 74). In the afternoon the *Exhibition Park* (p. 141).

5TH DAY. *Museum of Industrial Art* (p. 132) and *Ethnographical Museum* (p. 128). Drive through the Tiergarten Quarter (p. 173) and walk through the S. part of the *Tiergarten* (p 175). *Zoological Garden* (p. 177).

6TH DAY. *Hohenzollern Museum* (p. 146) and *Natural History Museum* (p. 162). In the afternoon to the suburb of *Grunewald* (p. 184) and excursion to the *Kaiser-Wilhelm-Turm* (p. 184).

7TH DAY. *Potsdam* (p. 187). The first fine day should be devoted to this excursion, without which a correct impression of Berlin can scarcely be obtained.

w. Hints for Cyclists.

Cyclists resident in Berlin must be provided with a permit (to be obtained from the district police authorities), but for a short visit that is not necessary. The rule of the road in Germany is the reverse of that in England; riders keep to the right side of the street in meeting, and to the left in overtaking traffic.

In Berlin the following streets are closed to cyclists, but may be crossed: *Unter den Linden* (including the *Pariser-Platz* and the *Lustgarten*), *Friedrich-Strasse* (from the Leipziger-Str. to the station of the Stadtbahn), *Leipziger-Strasse* (including the *Spittel-Markt* and the *Potsdamer-Platz*), and *Potsdamer-Strasse* (from the Potsdamer-Platz to the Potsdamer-Brucke).

The business offices for Section 20 of the *Deutsche Radfahrer-bund* are at Berlin S.W., Wilhelm-Str. 15 (9-5).

Bicycles cannot be sent through the town by the Stadtbahn or Ringbahn, and the following regulations are in force as to the transporting of unpacked machines to and in the suburbs and on the Berlin-Tegel Kremmen line. The machines must be presented at the

luggage office not later than $^1/_4$ hr. before the departure of the
train; the bicycle ticket (30 or 20 pf.) may be taken either here or
at the ticket office. For the convenience of those who wish personally to see their machines into the van, there are special des-
patching offices at the Friedrich-Str. Station (entrance Georgen-
Str.) and at the Silesian Station (E. entrance). The journey may
not be interrupted.

Several bicycle excursions are indicated on pp. 189-208. For further
information see *E. Richter's* 'Wegweiser durch die Mark Brandenburg'.

Berlin (110-160 ft above the sea-level; 13° 23′ 54″ E long.,
52° 30′ 17″ N. lat.), the capital of Prussia, the residence of the
German Emperor, and the seat of the imperial government as well
as of the highest Prussian authorities, contains upwards of 3,000,000
inhab.†, and thus occupies the third place among the cities of
Europe. Lying in a sandy plain about halfway between the S.W. and
N E. extremities of the Empire (465 M. from Mulhausen in Alsace, and
405 M. from Memel), equidistant from the mid-German mountains
and the sea, and connected with N E. Germany and Poland by the
navigable *Spree*, it is at the same time an important centre of the
railway-system of Germany, one of the foremost seats of commerce
in the country, and perhaps the greatest manufacturing town in continental Europe. The staple commodities of its trade are grain,
spirits, and wool; the principal branches of its industry are iron-
founding, the construction of machinery, locomotives, and railway-
carriages, and the manufacture of arms, chemicals and textiles, furniture, china, carpets, linoleum, linen, household and fancy goods,
and articles of clothing, the cheaper qualities of which last find
their way to all parts of the world. The money-market of Berlin
is also of great importance, and the city has of late taken a leading
place in the utilization of electric power and the improvement of
lighting facilities.

The boundaries of the city now enclose an area of about 25 sq M.
The oldest quarters are *Alt-Berlin* (on the right bank of the Spree,
bounded by the Ringbahn), *Alt-Kölln* (on an island in the river),

---

† The census of Berlin proper for Dec. 1905 gave its population as
2,035,815, of whom about 83 per cent were Protestants, 11 per cent Roman
Catholics, and 5 per cent Jews, and this number had increased to upwards
of 2,100,000 in Dec., 1907. To this total must, however, be added about
1,000,000 inhabitants of suburbs which, though not yet incorporated, really
form an integral part of the city. There are 80,000 Poles in Berlin, of
whom 10,000 are not German subjects. Of other foreigners there are
ca. 21,000 from Austria-Hungary (4000 Hungarians), ca. 15,000 Italians,
8000 English and Americans, 3200 Russians, 3000 Scandinavians, 1300
Swiss, 600 Dutch, 550 Roumanians, 500 French, etc. — The *Garrison* of
23,000 men consists of the 2nd, 3rd, and 4th regiments of Foot Guards,
the 1st, 2nd, and 4th Grenadier Guards, the Fusilier and Cuirassier Guards,
the 1st and 2nd Dragoon Guards, the 2nd Lancer Guards (Uhlans), the 1st
and a part of the 3rd Field Artillery Guards, the battalions of Pioneer
and Train Guards, the 1st, 2nd, and 3rd Railway Regiments, the 1st Telegraph Battalion, etc. Berlin is the seat not only of the Commander-in-
Chief of the Mark of Brandenburg, but also of the 1st Army Inspector,
the Chief Commander of the Guards, and the Commander of the 3rd Army
Corps. — The 3rd Grenadier Guards is quartered at Charlottenburg, and
a battalion of Riflemen of the Guards in Gross-Lichterfelde.

Friedrichs-Werder (on the left bank of the Spree, between the Arsenal and the Spittel-Markt), and *Neu-Kölln* (the Wall-Strasse and its neighbourhood) These form the heart of the city and were originally enclosed by fortifications. Round them in the 17th and 18th cent. rose an inner zone of new quarters, bounded until 1868 by a customs-wall 9 M in length (almost corresponding with the present 'Stadtring' of the electric tramway, p. 14): the *Dorotheenstadt* (stretching from the Spree to the Behren-Strasse), *Friedrichstadt* (to the S. of the Behren-Strasse), *Luisenstadt* (to the E. of the Linden-Strasse), etc. To these a large number of suburbs now incorporated in the town were added during the 19th century.

The government of the city is shared by the Royal Police Department, the Civic Magistracy, and the Town Council, under a Chief Burgomaster and a Burgomaster. The magistracy consists of 34 members, of whom 18 are salaried. There are 144 town councillors. The municipal revenues for 1908 were estimated at 8 millions sterling. — Berlin is divided into six electoral districts for the Reichstag (Imperial Diet), and four for the Landtag (Prussian Chamber of Deputies), in the latter of which it is represented by nine deputies.

History. Berlin first appears in history in the early part of the 13th cent., when it was already a double town of some importance (Berlin and Kölln) In all probability the original Wendish settlements had been taken possession of by German colonists at the end of the preceding century. The name also is doubtless of Wendish origin, and its connection with the bear *(Bär)* which appears in the city arms is merely an etymological fancy of later date. The name of *Kölln* is mentioned for the first time in a document of 1237, that of *Berlin* in 1244, after which the town soon began to be regarded as one of the most considerable in the Mark, ranking with Brandenburg (p. 205), the residence of the Margraves. The two towns were united in 1307, and by their prudent policy during the troublous times of the 14th cent. raised themselves to a position of great importance. Berlin-Kölln even became head of a confederation of towns of the Mark, which it represented in dealings with the Hanseatic League Such a position, however, almost amounting to the independence of a free imperial town, could not be maintained against the might of the *Hohenzollern* family, who became masters of the Mark in 1415. In consequence of its unsuccessful opposition to *Frederick 'with the Iron Tooth'* (1440-70), the second Elector, the town was deprived of its privileges (1442, 1448), and a fortified castle was erected to keep it in check *Elector John Cicero* (1486-99) made Berlin-Kölln his permanent abode, and since that period the fortunes of the town have been interwoven with those of the Hohenzollern family and their other dominions. In 1539 the townspeople and *Joachim II.* (1535-71) embraced the Reformed faith. This splendour-loving prince and his successor *John George* (1571-98) began the alteration and extension of the palace in the Renaissance style.

To FREDERICK WILLIAM, the 'Great Elector' (1640-88), the founder of the modern Prussian state, Berlin is chiefly indebted for its modern importance. He incorporated the settlement of *Friedrichs-Werder* with Berlin-Kölln, fortified the city on the Dutch system (1658-83), and founded the new town, which he named *Dorotheenstadt* in honour of his second wife. The forest which extended on this side of the town nearly as far as the Spree was now removed, and on its site was planted a double avenue of lime-trees, on each side of which gradually sprang up the handsome modern street named *Unter den Linden* (p 55). Owing to the introduction of foreign settlers, particularly of French Protestant refugees (after the Revocation of the Edict of Nantes in 1685), the population of the town increased to 20,000. It now became the seat of an independent industrial activity, while the Court zealously promoted artistic enterprise and strove to embellish the town, chiefly with the aid of Dutch architects. The nucleus of the royal library and art-collections was also formed at this period.

Frederick III. (1688-1713), who became KING FREDERICK I. in 1701, erected the *Friedrichstadt*, constituted Berlin a royal residence, and united the administration of the five quarters of the city. In 1694 he founded the *Academy of Art*, and in 1700 the *Academy of Science* (p. 57), the first president of the latter being the celebrated *Leibnitz;* while in the province of architecture he was fortunate in obtaining the services of *Andreas Schlüter* (b. at Hamburg in 1664, d. at St. Petersburg in 1714), the greatest artist of his period. First employed as a sculptor on the *Lange Brücke*, in the *Royal Palace* (p 65), and on the *Arsenal* (p. 60), begun by *J. A. Nering* (d. 1695), Schlüter afterwards erected the *Palace of Charlottenburg* (p. 182), and in 1699 began the reconstruction of the *Royal Palace*, which was not completed until long after his death. He was also the sculptor of the *Equestrian Statue of the Great Elector* (p. 70) in 1703. In 1710 the population, which had been steadily augmented by French and Walloon immigrants, was 61,000.

Under the patriarchal government of FREDERICK WILLIAM I. (1713-40) the city made no less substantial, though less striking progress. This monarch completed the royal palace, enlarged the Friedrichstadt and the Dorotheenstadt, began to pull down the fortifications, and added the N. and E. suburbs to the town, enclosing them with the customs-wall mentioned on p. 16. All these operations, however, were conducted in so economical a spirit, that the buildings are ....ally ..st.....ed in appearan... In 1740 the population had increased to 90,000, including 2000 Bohemian Protestants.

FREDERICK THE GREAT (1740-86) was unwearied in his efforts to extend and embellish his capital, though he seldom made it his residence. In *G. W. von Knobelsdorff* (1699-1753) he found an architect who was eminently capable of executing his plans. Thus in 1743 he erected the *Opera House* (p. 58) in a noble, almost classical style, which presented a marked contrast to the capricious and degraded taste of the age. As the great monarch, however, had a strong predilection for designing his new buildings in person and for materially altering the designs submitted to him, he found the less independent successors of Knobelsdorff more subservient to his wishes. The *Palace of Prince Henry* (now the University; p. 58), the *Church of St. Hedwig* (p 59), the *Royal Colonnades* (p. 152), the *Library* (p. 58), and the *Domed Towers* in the Gendarmen-Markt (p. 121) are the principal edifices of this period. Frederick also presented his citizens and officials with several hundred building-sites, but characteristically insisted that, however modest the houses erected on them might be, they should present palatial façades towards the street. Commerce and industry (banking, maritime commerce, the manufacture of china, silk-culture, weaving) were fostered; the Academy of Sciences, under the auspices of French savants, awoke to new life; and the collections of art were materially increased. At the same time a new intellectual era began to dawn, and to this period belong the authors *Lessing* (1729-81), *Moses Mendelssohn* (1729-86), and *Nicolai* (1733-1811), and the painter and engraver *Chodowiecki* (1726-1801). Although Berlin suffered severely during the Seven Years' War, having been twice occupied by foreign troops (1757 and 1760), the population had increased by the end of Frederick's reign to 145,000.

Under FREDERICK WILLIAM II. (1786-97), Frederick's successor, the population increased much more rapidly, and in the year 1800 it amounted to no fewer than 172,000. Considerable progress was also made in the province of art. In 1793 *K. G. Langhans* (1733-1808), following the example of Knobelsdorff, erected the *Brandenburg Gate* (p 55) in the classical style, while *G. Schadow's* Quadriga, with which it was adorned, achieved a new triumph in the province of sculpture. The architects *Gentz* and *Gilly* also adopted the classical style, while *J. A. Carstens*, a native of Schleswig, who began his career in 1788 as professor at the Berlin Academy, inaugurated the revival of classical taste in painting. The theatre, formerly devoted to French plays, was now dedicated to the national German drama, which was zealously cultivated from the year 1796 onwards under the auspices of *Iffland* (d. 1814).

The Napoleonic disasters by which Berlin was overtaken during the reign of FREDERICK WILLIAM III. (1797-1840), presented only a temporary obstacle to the progress of the city. The crushing impression produced by the defeat of the Prussian army in 1806 and by the French occupation of the city, which lasted till the end of 1808, was largely counterbalanced by the foundation of the *University* in 1809. After the establishment of peace in 1815, art, science, and commerce began to flourish anew. The university took the highest rank among the learned institutions of Germany. *William* and *Alexander von Humboldt*, *Karl Ritter*, *Hegel*, *Savigny*, *Schleiermacher*, *Boeckh*, *Lachmann*, and many other famous men lived and worked at Berlin, and the dramatic art also attained a high standard. At this period the most distinguished architect was *Friedrich Schinkel* (1781-1841), who was equally capable as a painter, as his sketches for the frescoes of the hall of the old museum testify (see p. 72), and many admirable buildings, both in the classical and Gothic style, were erected by this great master in Berlin and the environs. It was his aim to build as the ancient Greeks would have built had they lived among us, and it was due to his teaching that the foundation-stone of a national artistic revival was laid. He was the architect of the *Royal Guard House* (1818; p 59), the *Royal Theatre* (1821; p. 124), the *Old Museum* (1828; p. 71), the *Academy of Architecture* (1834; p. 158), and the *Friedrichs-Werder Church* (p. 159, in the Gothic style) at Berlin, of the *Palaces of Babelsberg* (p. 198), *Glienicke* (p 198), and *Charlottenhof* (p. 196), and the *Church of St. Nicholas* at Potsdam (p. 192), while his numerous designs exercised no inconsiderable influence on the architecture of other countries. Berlin architects long counted it the highest fame to be reckoned among his pupils. As Schinkel reigned supreme at Berlin in the province of architecture, so did *Chr. D. Rauch* (1777-1857) in that of sculpture, eclipsing his senior, G. Schadow, and still more so his contemporary, *Fr. Tieck*. In him the hero-worship of the period of the wars of independence found an admirable illustrator, and portrait-sculpture now received a new impulse. Far inferior to these architects and sculptors were the painters of this period (*Wach, K. Begas, Hensel, Klöber, K. Blechen,* and *F. Krüger*), whose names are hardly known out of their native place. — The long years of peace in the latter part of this reign contributed materially to the external prosperity of Berlin Commerce and industry, the latter stimulated by the exertions of *Beuth*, were greatly benefited by the construction of highroads, the foundation of the Zollverein, and the abolition of the monopoly of the guilds; and the city now began to lose the official and garrison-like air with which it had hitherto been pervaded. In 1838 the railway to Potsdam was opened. From 201,000 in 1819 the population had in 1840 increased to 329,000

During the following reign, that of FREDERICK WILLIAM IV. (1840-61), the cultivation of art seemed likely to progress far more rapidly. The favourable conditions of that monarch's reign were enhanced by the enthusiasm and refined artistic taste of the king himself, who often acted as his own architect. The prospect, however, was not entirely realised. The building of a cathedral, the king's favourite project, and of the royal burial vault (Campo Santo) was never carried out; and although the architecture of the city was enriched by the completion of the New Museum, the dome of the palace, and numerous other edifices, most of them lack the imposing grandeur of Schinkel's creations. The leading architects of this period were *F. A. Stüler* (d 1865), to whom most of the government-buildings were entrusted, *Soller* (d. 1853; St. Michael's Church; p 169), *K. F. Langhans* (d. 1869; remodelling of the Opera House; p 58), *Strack* (d. 1880; St. Peter's; p. 158), *Knoblauch* (d. 1865), and *Hitzig* (d. 1881), the last two chiefly eminent in the field of domestic architecture. — In the department of painting also the revival which had been anticipated from the presence of *Cornelius* (from 1841; d. 1867; p. 92) and *Kaulbach* (d. 1874, p. 78) was never realised; while the originality of *Ad. Menzel* (p. 92) was not duly appreciated. To the labours of *Rauch*, on the other hand, whose masterpiece, the statue of Frederick the Great, is justly admired, and to those of his numerous pupils (*Drake, Bläser, A. Wolff, Kiss*, etc.), the art of sculpture was indebted for its high repute during this reign. — After the introduction of railways Berlin increased rapidly in importance as a commercial and industrial centre. In 1849 the population was 421,000, and in 1860 it had increased to 496,000.

During the reign of the Emperor William I. (Prince Regent from 1858, King 1861-88) the prosperity of Berlin made still more rapid strides. In 1871, indeed, began that marvellous activity in industry and commerce which has obtained for Berlin a place among the great capitals of the world with a rapidity hitherto unknown except in the case of American towns. The population (826,000 in 1871, 1,000,000 in 1877, 1,500,000 in 1888) was trebled, and by the end of the 19th cent., under the Emperors Frederick III. (1888) and William II. (ascended the throne June 5th, 1888), it had risen to a sum total (including the suburbs) of 3,000,000.

Art also has revived, especially in the department of architecture. The Rathaus or Town Hall (begun in 1859; p. 151), the Exchange (p 154), and the New Synagogue (p. 145) were the first of a long series of imposing edifices, in which a complete revolution in taste manifests itself. The prevailing tendency is to attach more importance to solidity of material and the artistic ornamentation of the interior, and to use colour more freely. Since 1870 the classic tradition of Schinkel has been supplanted by a strong leaning towards the Renaissance, though the Italian style proper has seldom been followed. The baroque-like forms of the later German Renaissance were found more congenial, and the pronounced baroque style associated with the name of Schluter became ultimately the dominating feature in domestic architecture. The Building of the Imperal Diet (p. 136), by *Wallot*, marks a distinct advance in the standard of architectural forms. The Italian baroque style applied in the Cathedral (p. 63) makes a somewhat foreign impression. On the other hand mediæval styles of architecture have been most in vogue for the numerous churches built since 1890, especially the Romanesque style, which is well illustrated in the Emperor William Memorial Church (p. 180). More important than these examples of varying fashion in architecture are the creations produced by the specific demands of modern times, such as the railway stations with their enormous departure-halls (nearly all entirely rebuilt since 1870), the hospitals built on the pavilion system, and especially the palatial business offices and warehouses. This last type of building, which has already changed the appearance of whole streets, was initiated by *Kayser & von Groszheim* in the Rosen-Strasse (p. 151), and carried to its height by *Messel* in Wertheim's Emporium (p. 125). Suburban villas show a leaning towards forms borrowed from England and the North of Europe. The Ministerial Offices (pp. 123-24), the Chamber of Deputies (p 135), the Royal Stables (p. 70), the Emperor Frederick Museum (p. 96), and other palatial edifices usually follow the beaten track. *Ludwig Hoffmann*, the designer of the High Court of Justice at Leipzig, who has held the post of city-architect since 1896, has adopted a happy compromise, typically exemplified in the schools, hospitals, municipal offices, and baths built under his supervision. *Lucae, Adler, Ende, Gropius, Raschdorff, Grisebach*, and *Ihne* may also be mentioned among the creators of the most successful buildings of recent date. -- In sculpture *Siemering* and *Schaper* adhered to the noble repose of the school of Rauch, while *Reinhold Begas* exhibits a pictorial style, with motives bordering on the baroque.. The wholesale production of monumental statuary has rather expanded the field of sculpture than added to its intrinsic merit. Among the many younger masters may be mentioned *Tuaillon, Lederer, Eberlein, Herter, Brütt, Manzel, Lessing*, and *Uphues*. — In painting the movement towards monumental art expected after the summoning of *A. von Werner* to Berlin in 1871 did not take place. *Geselschap's* paintings in the cupola of the Arsenal found no imitators. Of the members of the Society of Berlin Artists we may mention the painters *L. Knaus, Paul Meyerheim, F. Skarbina, H. Herrmann, Hertel, Kallmorgen, A. Kampf*, and the gifted portrait-painter *Hugo Vogel*. *Max Liebermann* started the 'Secession', an 'impressionist' movement emanating from the Munich society of that name, and has been followed by *Leistikow, Slevogt, L. Corinth*, the sculptors *Klimsch* and *Gaul*, and many others among the younger artists.

Contemporaneously with the rise of architecture the APPLIED ARTS, which since the misfortunes of Napoleon's time had made no progress, received a stimulating impetus towards the picturesque style of the Renaissance The increasing prosperity of the town after 1870 caused a demand for more luxurious and more artistic domestic interiors. The *Museum of Industrial Art* (p. 132), founded in 1868, made its influence strongly felt in this field The increased activity in this branch of art is shown not only by the extraordinary multiplication of artistic upholsterers and the like, but also by the long list of excellent artists who devote themselves in whole or part to decorative art. Among these may be mentioned, besides architects, the painters *Doepler, Koch, Lechter*, and the sculptors *O. Lessing, Wiedmann*, and *Vogel*. Chandeliers and artistic designs in brackets for gas and electric lighting are nowhere better made than in Berlin; while cabinet-making and carpet-weaving hold a high place among the industries of the city. The arts of the jeweller and the goldsmith, enamelling, and the manufacture of brass and bronze articles, are also carried on very successfully. The Royal Porcelain Factory is mentioned at p. 181.

As regards the **General Aspect,** Berlin suffers from the dead level of its site, and also, since three-quarters of its buildings are quite modern, from a certain lack of historical interest. The Church of St. Nicholas (p. 157), the Church of St. Mary (p. 153), the Kloster-Kirche (p. 156), and the Chapel of the Holy Ghost (p 154) are practically the only buildings remaining of the old town (p. 46), which consisted of some narrow, crooked streets of dwelling-houses (pp 147, 152), and a few larger cloisters and hospitals grouped round the two Town Halls. With improved means of locomotion the inner town has now gradually become the commercial nucleus of Berlin, like the City in London. Immense and palatial buildings have arisen, occupied from floor to ceiling by business offices and warerooms alone The approaches to the old town have been widened, new ones have been built, and the Spree has been cleared of obstructions. The neighbourhood of the *Royal Palace* (p. 65) has been remodelled in harmony with the baroque forms of the palace itself. The Lustgarten, the Opern-Platz, and the Linden together form a broad and magnificent thoroughfare of the first rank, such as may possibly be paralleled in Vienna, but certainly not in either London or Paris. The street known as *Unter den Linden* (p. 55), which had hardly lived up to its ancient reputation, has again become one of the chief arteries of traffic. The old houses are disappearing, magnificent hotels and business premises have sprung up, while the avenues of trees and the footpaths have been altered and modernized. The system on which the *Friedrichstadt*, to the S. of the Linden, is laid out, points to its origin in the mere will of

the sovereign (p. 18). The regular streets crossing each other at
right angles were not caused by the needs of traffic; the few squares,
such as the Gendarmen-Markt, have been arbitrarily inserted. Here
also, however, the old houses have been replaced by magnificent new
buildings, notably in the chief streets. The Behren-Strasse, the
chief residence of the diplomats down to 1870, the Mauer-Strasse
and the Kanonier-Strasse, all now contain numerous banking-houses
and insurance offices. The Spittel-Markt and the Hausvogtei-Platz
(p. 159) are commercial centres, while the invasion of the residential
quarters by business premises progresses steadily towards the W.
and already extends far up in the neighbourhood of the Leipziger-
Strasse.

Neither the expansion of the town in the 18th century, nor the
system of building adopted in 1860, was conducive to originality
or variety in the different quarters. For miles the whole ground
was systematically marked out, without any great consideration of
the characteristic difference between the wide main arteries and
such smaller side-streets as might be found necessary. The enormous
prices of the large building-lots, which were generally very narrow
in proportion to their depth, necessitated the building of high houses
with narrow courts. All over the town we find on the same plots
expensive residences in front and cheaper ones behind, thus causing
a great mixture of all classes of the inhabitants, and great mono-
tony of street effects. It is only within recent years that some of
the suburbs have been laid out on the villa-system.

Just as in London, Paris, and other capitals, so in Berlin, the
upper classes tend on the whole to live in the W. end of the town,
while the E. end is given over to factories and workshops. The
SOUTH-EASTERN QUARTER is the seat of the more skilled industries,
such as cabinet-making and the manufacture of articles in bronze
and other metals. The place of the old building-yards and factories
is gradually being taken by the so-called *Höfe*, huge, many-storied
buildings, often enclosing three or four interior courts, and airy
and well lighted from floor to ceiling, while the motive power for
the machinery is furnished by steam or electricity. Similar erec-
tions serve as warehouses for industrial samples sent from every
part of Germany. The permission to run their waste into the Spree
being denied them, all the tanneries, fulling-mills, and dye-works
situated on the river will soon be transplanted to the upper Spree
at Köpenick (p. 201). Single imposing buildings, such as hospitals
and churches, are to be seen more towards the centre of the town,
and large barracks are found in the S. quarters, near the large
parade-ground on the Tempelhofer Feld, which here marks the
limit of the town's development. The NORTH-EASTERN QUARTER is
the seat of much new woollen and cotton industry and contains
little worth seeing. The Friedrichshain (p. 151) forms a

pleasant oasis here. Farther out is the Central Slaughter House, with its attendant industries.

The NORTHERN QUARTER was from 1860 to 1880 the seat of great machine works and foundries. Since then the manufactories have been transferred to the N.W. as far as the neighbourhood of Tegel, and the buildings containing the Physical Science Schools and their collections now stand on the site of the old royal iron-foundry. In the extreme N. are the suburbs of *Pankow* and *Nieder-Schönhausen*. — The NORTH-WEST QUARTER is being given over more and more to barracks, courts-of-law, medical institutes, and hospitals. The district of *Moabit* is surrounded by them, while the *Hansa Quarter* (p. 176), which lies beyond the Spree and adjoins the park of *Schloss Bellevue*, can boast of several streets of high-class residences.

The WESTERN QUARTER is the favourite residence of the well-to-do inhabitants on account of its proximity to the Tiergarten. In place of the large park and small villas which once surrounded the woods, the aristocratic *Tiergarten Quarter* has arisen since 1850, with its handsome villas, gardens, and private roads, stretching on the S. to the Landwehr Canal and on the W. to the Zoological Garden. The gardens, however, are gradually disappearing before the encroachments of bricks and mortar, the ground to the S. of the canal being almost entirely built over. In the *Potsdamer-Strasse* the business life of the Leipziger-Strasse extends as far as Schöneberg. The *Kurfürsten-Damm*, a magnificent street beginning on the S. side of the Zoological Garden, runs to the S.W. to the Grunewald. The surroundings of the *Grunewald* (p. 184), which marches with *Halensee*, are given over to villas. To the N. the W. end of Berlin borders on *Charlottenburg*, to the S. on *Schöneberg* and *Wilmersdorf*, the space once intervening between the city and these suburbs being now entirely built over.

Almost every part of Berlin offers a pleasing picture. Its streets enjoy a model cleanliness, and a system of main drainage, radiating in twelve directions, carries off all its sewage to distant fields. There are few dark lanes or alleys even in the old part of the city. Nearly all the newer houses have balconies, gay in summer with flowers and foliage. The public squares are embellished with gardens, monuments, and fountains, and the newer churches also are generally surrounded by small pleasure-grounds. Numerous bridges are beautified by sculpture. The centres of traffic, such as the Jannowitz-Brucke, the Trebbiner-Strasse, the Lehrte Station, etc., with their network of railway-lines, and the navigation on the river, offer scenes of remarkable animation.

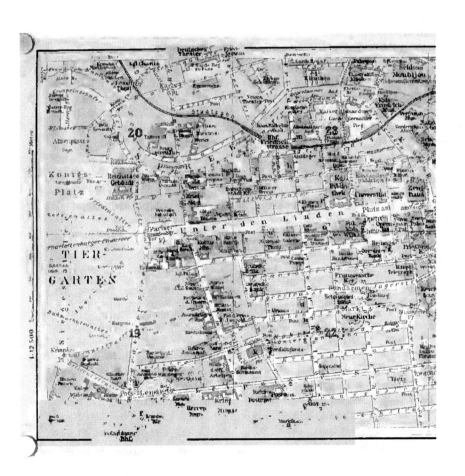

1. Unter den Linden. Platz am Opernhaus.

The handsomest and busiest part of Berlin, which likewise comprises the most interesting historical associations, is the line of streets extending from the Brandenburg Gate to the Royal Palace, consisting of '**Unter den Linden** (Pl. R, 20, 23), the *Platz am Opernhaus*, and the *Platz am Zeughaus*. The Linden, a street 198 ft. in width, deriving its name from the lime-trees (interspersed with chestnuts) with which it is planted, resembles the Boulevards of Paris, although inferior in length, and is flanked with handsome palaces, spacious hotels and restaurants, and attractive shops, which since the end of the 19th. cent. have gradually replaced the older buildings (see p. 52). The Linden is to Berlin what Bond Street and Piccadilly are to London, the corner of the Friedrich-Strasse presenting a most animated picture, especially in the afternoon and evening. The length of the street from the Brandenburg Gate to the Monument of Frederick the Great is about $^2/_3$ M., to the palace-gate about 1 M.

The **Brandenburg Gate* (Pl. R, 20, 19), at the W. end of the Linden, forms the entrance to the town from the Tiergarten (see p. 136). It was erected in 1789-93 by *K. G. Langhans* in imitation of the Propylæa at Athens, and has five different passages, separated by massive Doric columns. The material is sandstone. The structure (85 ft. in height, including the figure, and 205 ft. in width) is surmounted by a *Quadriga of Victory*, in copper, by *G. Schadow* (1794). This was taken to Paris by the French in 1807, but restored in 1814. The iron cross (under the eagle) was added after its return. The gate is flanked with open *Colonnades* for foot-passengers, built by Strack in 1868; the statue of Mars in that to the S. is by *Schadow*.

TRAMWAYS (pp. 14-22) run from the Brandenburg Gate and the Reichstag Building (No. 13 from the latter only) to the Anhalt Station (Nos. 1, 7, 14, 15), Charlottenburg N., Dönhoff-Platz (6, 9, 13), Friedrich-Strasse Station (13, N, O, S, T), Gesundbrunnen (23), Görlitz Station (13), Hackescher Markt (52, 56), Halle Gate (1, 7, 14, 15), Lehrte Station and Moabit (6, 7, 9, 13, 14, 15, 23, 24), Museum Island (N, O, S, T), Neues Tor (51, 57), Nollendorf-Platz (51, 52, 56, 57), Opern-Platz (13), Potsdam Gate (1, 6, 7, 9, 11, 15, 23, 24, 51, 52, 56, 57), Rixdorf (7, 15), Silesian Station (1, 6, 9), Schöneberg (23, 24, 51, 56, 57), Spittelmarkt (6, 9), Stettin Station (51, 57), Zoological Gardens (O).

Between the gate and the beginning of the Linden lies the PARISER-PLATZ, so named after the victories of 1814, and embellished with pleasure-grounds. No. 4, on the S. side, is the *Royal Academy of Art*, in the former palace of Count Arnim. The Academy of Art was established in 1691 under Frederick I. by Schlüter and Terwesten. Exhibitions, see p. 37. No. 5, on the N. side, is the *French Embassy*.

Unter den Linden, No. 1 (S. side), at the corner of the Pariser-Platz, is the *Hôtel Adlon* (p. 2), erected by Gause & Leibnitz in 1905-7 on the site of a palace built by Schinkel. On the right, beyond it, diverges the Wilhelm-Strasse (p. 122), continued on the N. by the Neue Wilhelm-Strasse (p. 161). No. 3, on the right, contains the offices of the *Berliner Lokal-Anzeiger*, where the latest telegrams and original illustrations of events of the day are exhibited No. 4, with a sculptured frieze by Eberlein, is the office of the *Minister of Religion and Education;* Nos. 5 & 6 form the *Hôtel Bristol* (p. 3), by Gause; No. 7 is the palace of the *Russian Embassy*, erected by Knoblauch in 1840-41. On the N. side No. 75 is *Schulte's Art Shop* (p. 34), built in 1904-5 by Messel; No. 73 is occupied by the *Minister of the Interior;* and Nos. 57-58 are the premises of the *International Railway Sleeping Car Co* (p. 2), by Berndt (1908).

At No. 68a, on the N. side, is the *Aquarium (Pl. R, 20, 23; entrance in the Schadow-Str.), founded by *Prof. Brehm*, and opened in 1869 Director, *Dr. Hermes* (adm., see p 36; catalogue 50 pf).

The collection is exhibited in a grotto-like corridor about 300 yds. in length, which occupies two floors. We first enter the *Reptile House*, which contains gigantic lizards and snakes of all kinds, some of the poisonous varieties attaining a length of 12 ft. The *Geological Grotto*, which comes next, contains birds (gulls, cockatoos). This is followed by the large *Bird House*, among the inmates of which the weaver-birds are specially worthy of notice. Here also are the cages of the anthropoid apes, and, to the left and right of the entrance, tanks containing salamanders, crocodiles, and tortoises. After these comes the *Aquarium proper*, with an excellent collection of fresh and salt water fish. We finally descend, with breeding-tanks for salmon and trout on either side, to the lower rooms, containing other curiosities of the deep and a refreshment-bar.

Farther along the Linden, on the S. side (Nos. 17 & 18), is the *Hôtel Westminster* (p. 3), adjoined to the S in the Behren-Str. (passage) by the *Metropol-Theater* (p. 28). Near the corner of the Friedrich-Str. is the entrance to the *Passage* or **Kaiser-Galerie** (Pl. R, 23, 22), built in 1869-73 by *Kyllmann & Heyden*, which leads to the corner of the Friedrich-Strasse and Behren-Strasse (p. 120). The arcade (400 ft. long, 24 ft. broad, and 40 ft. high) contains a café, shops, the *Kaiser-Panorama* (stereoscopic views; open 9 a m. to 10 p m., 20 pf.), and the *Passage Panopticum* (p. 38).

At the corner of the Friedrich-Strasse (comp. p. 120) are *Kranzler's* confectioner's shop, and (No. 25) the *Café Bauer* (No. 26: p. 11).

Tramways from the Gendarmen-Markt (S E.) see p 121; from the corner of the Charlotten-Str and Dorotheen-Str. (N E) see p. 145.

Beyond the Friedrich-Strasse, on the S. side (No. 35), is the building of the *Diskonto-Gesellschaft*, by Ende & Böckmann. — On the N. side No. 39 stands the *Grand Hôtel de Rome* (p. 3). Close by Charlotten-Str. 43 is the building of the *Society of German Engineers*, by Reimer & Körte.

At the E. end of Unter den Linden rises the 'Monument of Frederick the Great (Pl. R, 23), 44 ft. in height, an impressive and masterly work by *Rauch*, erected in 1851. On the top the great king is represented on horseback, with an ermine mantle and his crutch-handled stick The pedestal is richly decorated with reliefs. The uppermost section contains scenes from Frederick's life and figures of Moderation, Justice, Wisdom, and Strength at the corners. At the corners of the central section are four equestrian figures· Prince Henry of Prussia and Duke Ferdinand of Brunswick on the E., and Generals Zieten and Seydlitz on the W. Between these are placed spirited lifesize groups of other contemporaries and officers of the king, including Prince August Wilhelm and Keith (E side), Kleist, Winterfeldt, and Tauentzien (N. side), Leopold of Anhalt-Dessau and Schwerin (S. side), Lessing, Kant, and Graun (W. side). The lowest section contains the dedication and the names of other distinguished men, chiefly soldiers of the time of Frederick.

To the right (S) of the monument is the **Palace of Emperor William I.** (Pl. R, 23; adm., see p. 38), at present belonging to Prince Heinrich, erected by *K. F. Langhans* (p 50) in 1834-36; the decorations of the interior are by *Strack*. Entrance on the right of the palace, between it and the adjacent 'Niederländische Palais' (where the cards of admission are obtained). Description with views 50 pf.

The Ground Floor contains the simple rooms of the Emperor, crowded with furniture and souvenirs of all kinds The *Fahnenzimmer*, to the E. of the main entrance, contains a picture by *Camphausen* (William I. entering Berlin in 1871). Beyond the Ministers' Room is the Emperor's *Study*, from the corner-window of which he was wont to watch the passing guard. It is preserved unchanged and contains many reminiscences of the old Kaiser Behind the library is the bedroom (not shown) in which he died on March 9th, 1888. — The Staircase is adorned with three Victories by *Rauch* and other sculptures — On the Upper Floor are the *Apartments of the Empress Augusta*, including her *Study*, containing a picture by *Pesne* of Frederick the Great as a child, and the room (not shown) in which she died on Jan. 7th, 1890. — The W. part of this floor is occupied by the handsome *Reception Rooms*.

Opposite the palace to the N. is the 'Academy Quarter' (Pl. R, 23), where new buildings in the baroque style after Ihne's designs are being erected for the *Academy of Science* (founded after Leibnitz's plan in 1700, see p. 47), the Royal Library (p. 58), and the University Library (p. 58).

To the N. of the Academy Quarter, Dorotheen-Str 7-8, is the *Berlin Chamber of Commerce*, a baroque building by Cremer & Wolffenstein. Adjacent, Nos 9 10, is the *University Library* (196,000 vols.); on No. 10 are busts of A. S. Margraf (d. 1782). the discoverer of beet-sugar, and of F. K Achard (d. 1821), the founder of the beet-sugar industry

Beyond the Monument of Frederick the Great the street expands, forming the Cantz am Opernhaus of Opern Platz The monumental buildings surrounding this Forum Fridericianum are together

with the towers on the adjacent Gendarmen-Markt (p. 121), the most
important creations of this King in his capital.

The **University Buildings** (Pl. R, 23), formerly the palace
of Prince Henry, brother of Frederick II., built by the elder Boumann in 1748-66 and fitted up in 1809 for the then recently-founded
university *(Friedrich Wilhelms-Universität)*, were remodelled in
the interior in 1891. In winter 1907-8 the university was attended by
ca. 8220 students and 1440 'hearers', and had a teaching-staff of 503.
The front garden is adjoined by seated figures of *William* (d. 1835)
and *Alexander von Humboldt* (d. 1859), the former by Paul Otto,
the latter by R. Begas. In the garden itself is a marble statue of
the physicist *Helmholtz* (d. 1894), by Herter (1899), which is to be
accompanied by others of the historians *Treitschke* (d. 1896), by
Siemering, and *Mommsen* (d 1903), by Brütt. The Aula, formerly
the banqueting-hall of Prince Henry, contains busts of celebrated
professors. The *Academic Inquiry Office* (week-days 10-1.30) is
in the University Building opposite the porter's lodge.

Behind the University to the left of the Students' Reading Room
(p. 33) is the *University Garden*, and to the right is the *Kastanien-
Wäldchen* (chestnut grove), with a bronze statue, by Hartzel, of *Mitscher-
lich* (d. 1863), the chemist. Beyond the grove, in the Dorotheen-Str., is
a colossal bust of *Hegel*, the philosopher (d. 1831), by Blaser

The **Royal Library** (*Königliche Bibliothek;* Pl R, 23, 22),
behind the Palace of Emp. William I. and facing the Opern-Platz,
was erected in 1775-80 by Boumann the Younger from plans drawn
by Unger, and is one of the most effective rococo structures in
Berlin, though sometimes likened to a chest of drawers. The building is copied from a design by Fischer von Erlach for the Vienna
Hofburg. The motto below the cornice, 'nutrimentum spiritûs', was
selected by Frederick the Great. Director, *Prof. Harnack*. Adm.,
see p. 39.

The Library, which was founded in 1661, now contains about 1,230,000
vols. and 30,000 MSS. Among the chief treasures may be mentioned part
of the MS. of *Luther's* translation of the Bible; early impressions of
the ninety-five Theses of 1517 and other works of Luther; *Melanchthon's*
report of the Diet of Worms; *Joh. Agricola's* letter from Eisleben on
Luther's death, *Gutenberg's* 42-line Bible on parchment, of 1450, the
first large book printed with movable types, the *Codex Wittekindi*, a MS.
of the Gospels of the 8th cent., said to have been presented by Charlemagne
to the Saxon duke Wittekind, water-colour portraits by *Lucas Cranach;*
Chinese books; a small octagonal Koran, important musical works, etc.
Some of the older pieces of music are of great historical interest.

Opposite the Library is the **Opera House** (Pl. R, 23; performances, see p. 27), erected by *Knobelsdorff* in 1741-43, and restored
by *K. F. Langhans* after a fire in 1843. The building is disfigured
by a number of iron staircases erected in 1904 to facilitate escape
in case of fire. The tympanum contains an admirable group in
zinc, by *Rietschel* (1844; in the centre the muse of music; on the
right the tragic and the comic muse with a satyr, the dramatic

poet with the arts of painting and sculpture; on the left a dancing
group with the Three Graces.

In the grounds between the Library and the Opera House stands
a marble monument, by Schaper, to the *Empress Augusta*, unveiled
in 1895. The reliefs on the pedestal represent the nursing of the
wounded in war and the education of children. — In the background
is the Roman Catholic **Church of St. Hedwig** (*Hedwigs-Kirche;*
Pl. R, 22), a simplified imitation of the Pantheon at Rome, erected
by Frederick the Great in 1747-73. The dome was sheathed with
copper in 1886-87 and provided with the lantern and cross demanded
by the spirit of the original design. The representation of the
Adoration of the Magi in the pediment was executed in 1898 by
N. Geiger. — Close by, Behren-Str. 38-39, is the *Dresdner Bank,*
built in 1887 by Heim and enlarged in 1902.

Five ***Statues** by *Rauch* embellish the Platz am Opernhaus
farther E. Between the Opera House and the palace of the crown-
prince is *Blucher* (d. 1819), a bronze figure, 11 ft. high, with drawn
sword, resting one foot on a cannon, erected in 1826. To the left and
right are bronze statues of *Yorck* (d. 1830) and *Gneisenau* (d. 1831),
both erected in 1855. In front of the guard-house are marble figures of *Bulow* (d. 1816) and *Scharnhorst* (d. 1813), erected in 1822.
The pedestals are adorned with reliefs referring to the wars of
1813-15.

The **Royal Guard House** (*Königswache;* Pl. R, 23) was constructed by *Schinkel* in the Doric style in 1816-18 in the form of a
Roman fortified gate. Adjoining it are three large cannon; the central one ('La belle Joséphine') was brought from Fort Mont Valérien
at Paris in 1871 and has been rechristened 'Valeria'.

At the back of the guard-house is the *Ministry of Finance.* —
To the left of this, and farther back, is the **Singing Academy**
(Pl. R, 23), erected in 1825 and renowned for the excellent acoustic
properties of its concert-hall. The academy was founded by *Fasch*
in 1791, and afterwards came under the management of *Zelter*
(d. 1832) Concerts, see p. 29.

TRAMWAYS (see pp. 11-22) run from the Opern-Platz and from the
Dorotheen-Str. (lines N, O, S, and T) to the Brandenburg Gate (N, O, S,
T, 13), Charlottenburg (N, T, 33, 51), Donhoff-Platz (12, 13, 18, 39, 42),
Gesundbrunnen (34, 39, 12, 43), Gorlitz Station (12, 13, 18), Hackescher-
Markt (33, 39, 10, 42, 53, 54, 55 III), Halle Gate (34, 43, 39, 42, 53, 55),
Kreuzberg (31, 43), Lehrte Station and Moabit (12, 13, 18), Lutzow-Platz
(33, 51), Potsdam Station (33, 40, 51, III), Rixdorf (53, 55), Schoneberg
(10, 43, III), Stettin Station (34, 43), Zoological Garden (O, S, 83). — The
lines 60, 61, 70, 73, 75, 80, 81, running through the Franzosische Str. (S.),
may also prove serviceable.

⸺ ⸺ ⸺ ⸺

To the E. of the Royal Guard House, see above, and fronting
to the S., is the **Arsenal** *Zeughaus;* Pl. R, 23, 26, one of the

best buildings in Berlin, begun by *Nering* in 1694 and carried to completion by *Grünberg, Schlüter* (1698-99), and *De Bodt* (1706). It is a square structure, each side of which is 295 ft. in length, enclosing a quadrangle 125 ft. square. The exterior is richly adorned with sculptures by *Schlüter*. The bronze bust of Frederick I. above the main portal and the allegorical figures to the right and left are by *Halot*. In 1877-80 the interior underwent a thorough alteration under the superintendence of *Hitzig* (d. 1881), and it was re-opened as a *Military Museum* and *Hall of Fame of the Prussian Army*. The artistic decoration was completed in 1891. The director of the collections is *Dr. von Ubisch* (adm., see p. 36; official handbook 50 pf.).

The rooms of the GROUND FLOOR, unfortunately somewhat poorly lighted, are separated by handsome iron railings and adorned with mural paintings in grisaille (siege operations) by *Burger*. The rooms to the right (E.) of the vestibule contain the *Museum of Artillery*, those to the left (W.) are devoted to the *Museum of Military Engineering*.

The collection of artillery is nearly complete from the end of the 11th century onwards, though the number of fine artistic specimens is comparatively small. The following objects are specially worthy of attention: (to the left) between pillars 1 and 2 Chinese guns captured in 1900, among them No. 603. Chinese gun, cast in 1689 by *Verbiest*, a Jesuit (comp. p 195). (to the right) old flint-lock muskets and orgues; No. 66. The 'Wild Man', the longest gun (19 ft.) in the collection, No 130 (in the corner), so-called golden cannon of 1611, adjacent, 17th cent cannon made of leather; No 157 richly chased 48-pounder, made at Lübeck in 1669 for Holland and discovered at Paris in 1811; Nos. 168, 169, 185, and 186 (between the pillars), cannon of the time of the Great Elector, the last covered with ornamentation; farther on, opposite a balloon-gun of 1870-71, a cannon dedicated to the Elector Albert Achilles, one of eleven cast by Jacobi in 1708 by command of King Frederick I., No. 361 (near the end of the room), orgue used by Schill's volunteers, who made in 1809 a brave but unsuccessful attempt to free Prussia from the French yoke.

The Museum of Military Engineering (left side) contains models of objects connected with pioneering and artillery. Here also are models of old French fortresses (including Sedan and Paris), brought from Paris in 1814, model-plans of the battles of Düppel (1864), Königgratz (1866), and St Privat (1870); and uniforms (to the left Austrian, French, British, etc., to the right Russian). At the end a magnificent Turkish tent, captured in 1683 before Vienna.

Opposite the vestibule is the entrance to the glass-roofed COURT, the centre of which is occupied by a colossal marble figure of Borussia, by *R. Begas*. The *Heads of Dying Warriors on the key-stones of the windows (widely known as the *Masks of Schlüter*) are very striking. The Chinese standards above were captured in 1900.

FIRST FLOOR. From the back of the court two flights of steps, adorned with sculptures by R. Begas, ascend to the HALL OF FAME, which occupies the N wing of the UPPER STORY and consists of three sections - the 'Herrscherhalle' in the middle and the two 'Feldherrnhallen' at the sides

The 'Hall of the Rulers', which is 70 ft. square and nearly 70 ft. high, is lighted from the roof. The "Triumphal Procession on the dome, the large "Paintings in the spandrels (Resuscitation of the German Empire, War, Peace, and Valhalla), and the four Virtues of Rulers (Bravery, Justice, Wisdom, and Moderation) in the corners, are all by *Geselschap*. In the side-niches are the following paintings: Homage of the Silesian Estates in 1741, by *Camphausen;* Assembling of the Volunteers at Breslau in 1813, by *Bleibtreu:* Coronation of Frederick I. at Königsberg in 1701, by *A. von Werner;* and the Proclamation of the German Empire at Versailles in 1871, also by *Werner.* The sculptures include a marble Victory by *Schaper* (in the central recess, opposite the entrance), eight bronze statues of Prussian rulers from the Great Elector to the Emperor William I., by *Encke, Brunow, Hilgers. Hundrieser, Schuler,* and *Siemering,* and busts of Scharnhorst. Stein, Bismarck, and Roon.

The 'Halls of the Generals' are each adorned with six mural paintings of battles. Those in the hall to the left (W.) are the Battle of Turin (1706), by *Knackfuss;* the Passage of the Kurische Haff by the Great Elector (1679). by *Simmler;* the Battle of Fehrbellin (1675), by *Janssen;* Torgau (1760), by *Janssen;* Hohenfriedberg (1745), by *Janssen;* and Frederick the Great before the battle of Leuthen (1757), by *Roeber.* Those in the hall to the right (E.) are the Capitulation at Sedan (1870), by *Steffeck;* the Storming of St. Privat (1870), by *Bleibtreu;* the Meeting of King William and the Crown Prince at Königgratz (1866), by *Hünten;* the Allied Monarchs at Leipsic (1813), by *Schuch:* Waterloo (Belle Alliance; 1815), by *Bleibtreu;* and Düppel (1864), by *Roeber.* The plastic ornamentation includes colossal bronze busts of 32 eminent leaders of the Prussian army and four allegorical figures in marble. Two of the latter, by *R. Begas* ('Science of War' and 'Power'), are in the W. hall, and two by *Schaper* ('Enthusiasm' and 'Loyalty') in the E. hall. The busts were executed under the superintendence of R. Begas by various sculptors. Those in the hall to the left represent Sparr and Derfflinger, Schöning and Treffenfeld, Prince Leopold of Dessau and Schwerin, Keith and Winterfeldt, Prince Maurice of Dessau and Gessler, Duke Ferdinand of Brunswick and Seydlitz, Prince Henry and Fouqué, Zieten and Belling. In the hall to the right are Blücher and Prince Louis Ferdinand, Yorck and Courbière, Bülow and Kalckreuth, Tauenzien and Gneisenau, Kleist and Wrangel, Goeben and Werder, Moltke and Manteuffel, Crown Prince Frederick William and Prince Frederick Charles.

The W., N., and E. wings of the upper floor are separated from the Hall of Fame by iron railings, and contain the COLLECTION OF WEAPONS AND ARMOUR which is divided into three sections. The numbers given below are those of the article in the order of the labels attached to the objects.

E. WING. On entering from the E Hall of the Generals, we have the Oriental weapons to our right and the European to our left. Special attention should be paid to the beautiful 15th cent. armour and the fine gala suits of the 16th cent., mostly bequeathed by Prince Charles of Prussia (d. 1883), and many of them adorned with reliefs. The chief specimens are on or near the central pillars and by the windows No. 60 a. helmet with the Judgment of Paris and Abduction of Helen; 59 a & b. state armour of Elector Joachim II, of 1539; 76. part of a suit of armour with Roman battles; (window-side) 64. shield with the Judgment of Paris (after Raphael), 73 with cavalry contest, 74. with engagement under the walls of a fortress, 75. armour of Emperor Charles V, 82 shields with Curtius and Hercules; 84. field suit of Joachim II, 1560; shields with Horatius Cocles (87), and the Fall of the Giants (95), 105. armour of the Margrave Hans of Küstrin. — In the corner: ornamented cross-bows (125, 133) and portable fire-arms (130-132), calendar blades (131)

S. WING. Chiefly Prussian arms and uniforms up to the time of Frederick the Great. In the middle of the side next the court are uniforms and orders of the Emperors William I. and Frederick III, orders of Bismarck and Moltke, and keys of the French fortresses captured in 1814 and 1870-71. — On the side next the street, near the middle; swords (197) of the Brandenburg Electors, and (198) with portraits of Emperors Leopold, Rudolph II, and Ferdinand II. — Beyond the centre, 232. souvenirs of Derfflinger, 233 standards of Henning von Tretteufeld with symbolic devices These are followed by uniforms of the 18th century, on case 278, ensign of a Prussian recruiting officer of the 18th century, tigerskin and bearskin-cap of Zieten; 302-7 figures of the soldiers of Frederick the Great On the adjoining pillars are portraits of the tall grenadiers of Frederick William I.

The W. WING is specially devoted to arms and uniforms of the time of the Wars of Liberation (1813-1815) At the end of the side next the street· 117. figures of Prussian soldiers of the period; 412 orders, hat, and pistols of Napoleon I, captured at Waterloo, 411 uniforms of Frederick William III., 123. souvenirs of Blücher. — On both sides of the central passage are 68 *Lifesize Figures of Prussian Soldiers* Those to the left represent soldiers from the time of the Great Elector down to 1806 and also the royal household troops; to the right, those from 1806 to the present time, ending with the troops in the colonies and the China expedition (1900).

On the S. side of the Zeughaus-Platz is the **Palace of the Crown Prince** (Pl. R, 23), which is connected with the so-called *Palace of the Princesses* by an arch over the Oberwall-Strasse. Built in 1663 as a private mansion, it was rebuilt in 1732 for Frederick the Great when Crown Prince, and from 1793 to 1840 was occupied by Frederick William III. In 1797 Emperor William I. was born here. It owes its present form to the alterations made in 1857 by *Strack*, who added the second story, and from 1858 to 1888 it was the winter residence of the Crown Prince Frederick William (Emp. Frederick III.).

The last house on this side is the *Residence of the Commandant of Berlin.* — Behind is the *Schinkel-Platz*, see p 158.

2. Cathedral. Royal Palace. National Monument to Emperor William I.

In a straight line with the E. prolongation of the Linden, and spanning the *Spree*, is the 'Schloss-Brücke (Palace Bridge; Pl. R, 26), 106 ft. in width, constructed in 1822-24 from designs by *Schinkel*. It was adorned by Frederick William IV. with eight groups in marble, over lifesize, illustrative of the life of a warrior. On the S . 1 Victory teaches the boy the history of the heroes, by *E. Wolff*; 2. Athena instructs the youth in the use of weapons, by *Schievelbein*; 3. Athena presents the combatant with arms, by *Möller*; 4. Victory crowns the conqueror, by *Drake*. On the N.: 5. Victory raises the wounded warrior, by *Wichmann*; 6. Athena protecting and aiding a combatant, by *Blaser*; 7. Athena inciting him to a new contest, by *A. Wolff*; 8. Iris conducts the victorious fallen warrior to Olympus, by *Wredow*.

Beyond the bridge extends the LUSTGARTEN (Pl. R, 26), an open space planted with trees, 247 yds. in length and 220 yds in width, originally a garden belonging to the palace, and afterwards converted into a drill-ground by Frederick William I. In the centre, on a pedestal of granite 20 ft. in height, rises the equestrian Statue of Frederick William III., by *A. Wolff*, 19 ft. in height, unveiled in 1871. The pedestal is adorned with allegorical figures of Clio (in front), Borussia with the Rhine and Memel on the right, Science with Industry and Art on the left, between them Legislation, and at the back Religion with the olive-branch, a reference to the Union of the Evangelical Confessions (1817). Military music at noon (p. 31). — Beyond the statue, in front of the steps of the Old Museum, is a huge *Granite Basin*, 22 ft. in diameter and 75 tons in weight, hewn out of a solid erratic block of ten times the weight.

The *Cathedral (*Dom;* open on week-days 10-6) dominates not only the Lustgarten and its environs, but with its lofty dome forms the distinguishing feature of any general view of Berlin. It occupies the site of another cathedral built in 1747-50, the poverty of whose appearance even Schinkel (1816-17) was unable to remedy, and of the beginnings of a royal vault ('Campo Santo'), dating from the time of Frederick William IV. (1845-48). The new building was erected in 1894-1905 in the style of the developed Italian Renaissance by *Julius Raschdorff* and his son, *Otto Raschdorff*, at an expense of $10\frac{1}{2}$ million marks (525,000 *l.*). Its dimensions are: length 344 ft., breadth 216 ft., height to the main cornice 102 ft., to the foot of the lantern 246 ft., and to the top of the cross on the dome 374 ft. The material is Silesian sandstone, with granite for the lower courses of stone and white the upper lanterns, and roofing are copper

The VESTIBULE on the Lustgarten side is two stories high and
262 ft. long. The chief entrance in the centre is high and vaulted;
over the arch are two bronze angels holding a shield. The piers on
both sides of the entrance are adorned with bronze reliefs (to the
right, Luther translating the Bible, by *Goetz;* to the left, Luther at
Worms, by *Janensch*); above them are bronze statues of SS. Luke
and John (right) and SS. Matthew and Mark (left). On the impost
to the right and left are bronze figures of Mercy and Truth, modelled
by *Widemann.* On the attic are two head-pieces ending in crowns
and a centre-piece containing a figure of Christ by *Schaper* in copper, 17 ft. in height. The domed towers at the corners, each 262 ft.
high, contain the bells. On the entablature are ten Apostles by
Manzel, Bratt, Baumbach, Herter, Calandrelli, and *Pfann-*
schmidt. — The CENTRAL DOME is octagonal in shape and measures
125 ft. in external and 102 ft. in internal diameter. The richly ornamented drum is surmounted by eight figures of angelic musicians,
17 ft. in height, by *Schott.* — The side towards the Spree, with
two vestibules adjoining the apse, ends in two smaller towers with
cupolas, beneath which, in niches, are two carved angels taken from
the old cathedral. Above, next the apse, are figures of Moses, by
Janensch, and John the Baptist, by *Vogel.*

The INTERIOR (adm., see p. 36) of the cathedral is tripartite. The CHURCH
PROPER, to which the main entrance admits, is surmounted by the dome.
The vaulting is adorned with mosaic representations of the Eight Beati-
tudes, after *A. von Werner;* the four spandrels with decorative carvings
from the history of the Apostles, by *O. Lessing.* Eight colossal statues
surround the base of the drum: Luther and Melanchthon (by *Pfannschmidt*),
Zwingli (by *Janensch*), Calvin (by *Calandrelli*), Frederick the Wise (by
K. Begas), Joachim II. (by *Magnussen*), Philip the Magnanimous (by
Schott), and Albert of Prussia (by *Baumbach*). The body of the church
is in the form of an irregular octagon, and has seats for 1960 worshippers.
In the semicircular niches on the shorter sides are the pulpit and galleries.
On the longer sides are galleries for the court (W.), the ministers (S.),
and the organ and choir (N.). On the E. is the semicircular apse, with
dark-red marble columns, sumptuously fitted up with sculpture and gilding, and lighted by beautiful stained-glass windows. — To the S. lies the
WEDDING AND BAPTISMAL CHURCH (not accessible), 59 ft. long and 30 ft.
wide; it is roofed with barrel-vaulting and is adorned with sculptures
on the exterior by *O. Lessing.* — To the N. is the MEMORIAL CHURCH,
115 ft. in length and breadth. The pentagonal central space is surrounded
by small chapels to contain various monuments. Among these are a monument of *Bismarck* by R. Begas, the bronze monument of *Elector John*
Cicero (d. 1499), by Peter Vischer and his son, finished in 1530, with
two representations of the deceased (see p. 151); the zinc state coffins of
the *Great Elector* (d. 1688) and his consort *Dorothea* (d. 1689), of *King*
Frederick I. (d. 1713) and his consort *Sophia Charlotte* (d. 1705), the last
two from designs by Schlüter; and the marble sarcophagus of *Emp. Fre-*
derick III., by R. Begas (comp. p. 193). — A staircase on the E. side
(with a Descent from the Cross by M. Lock) leads from the Memorial
Church down to the HOHENZOLLERN BURIAL VAULT (not accessible), extending beneath the whole cathedral and containing) 87 coffins of members
of the reigning family.

Between the Cathedral and the 'Schloss-Apotheke', a side-build-
ing of the palace (see p. 65) the *Kaiser-Wilhelm-Bruecke* (1886-89)

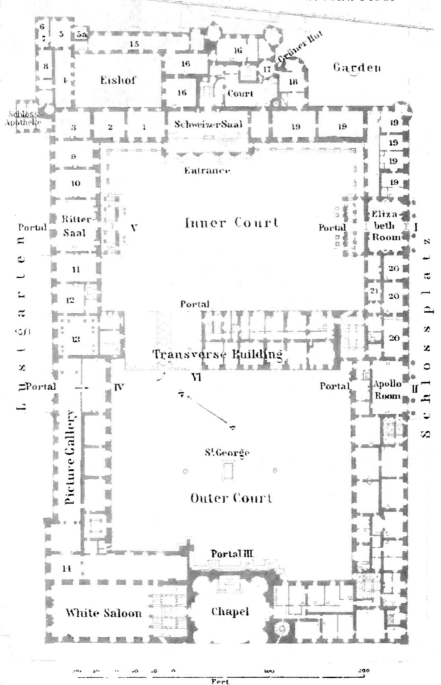

SPREE

ROYAL PALACE
Second Floor

6
7
3   5a
8
4   Eishof
15
16
16
16   Court
16
17 Grüner Hut
18
Garden

Schloss-Apotheke

3   2   1   Schweizer-Saal
19   19   19
19
19
19

9
Entrance

10

Portal
Ritter-Saal   V
Inner Court
Portal
Eliza-beth Room   I

20
21   20

11
Portal
Transverse Building   VI
Portal
20

12
Portal   Apollo Room   II

13

Portal   IV
Picture Gallery
St. George
Outer Court

14
Portal III

White Saloon   Chapel

Lustgarten

Schlossplatz

Feet

crosses the Spree to the Kaiser Wilhelm-Strasse, in which the lofty Marien-Kirche is visible (p. 153)

The *Royal Palace (*Königliches Schloss; Pl. R, 26) is in the form of a rectangle 630 ft. in length and 381 ft. in depth, enclosing two large courts, which are entered by five portals, each bearing a number. The façade rises in four stories to the height of 98 ft., while the dome above it is 232 ft. high. The original building was a castle erected by Elector Frederick II. on the Spree in 1443-51. Since 1538 Joachim II. converted it into a palace after the designs of *Kaspar Theyss*, with a tilting-yard on the S. side, the whole forming a handsome example of the German Renaissance, highly praised by contemporary critics. Elector John George finished the enclosure of the E. court in 1580-95; from his time date the water-front on the Spree with its corner-turrets (Pl. 16) and the 'Schloss-Apotheke' (chemist's shop), protruding towards the N and recently shortened. A second court was added (to the W) and the N.E. corner completed Under the Great Elector, who at first directed his energies to laying out the Lustgarten, *Nering* erected the round-arched gallery on the Spree (Pl. 15) in 1685. The Elector's successor, Frederick I., the first King of Prussia, determined to replace the irregular pile of buildings that had now arisen by a uniform structure of massive and imposing proportions, and confided the execution of this task to *Andreas Schlüter*, who began his work in 1698. The gigantic scheme of alteration thus projected has, however, never been fully carried out, the part of the building on the Spree and the transverse building still retaining their original form. In 1706 Schlüter retired from the direction of the work, as the rebuilding of the so-called 'Münzturm', which was to be some 300 ft high (at the N.W. corner, where the column with the eagle now stands), had failed. He was succeeded by *Johann Friedrich Eosander*, surnamed *von Goethe*, a native of Sweden, to whom is due the architecture of the largest court and of the W. façade. In 1716 the process of alteration was brought by *Böhme* to a conclusion for the nonce, and during the reigns of Frederick II. and Frederick William II. comparatively trifling additions only were made. In 1825-26 *Schinkel* restored the apartments of Frederick II. for the Crown Prince. The spacious chapel in the W. wing, with its dome, was constructed in the reign of Frederick William IV. by *Stüler* and *Schadow* (1845-52), and greatly enhances the effect of the exterior. A new period of building activity began under Emp. William II., who made the palace once more the actual residence of the reigning sovereign. Great gates of wrought iron were placed in the five outer portals; a terrace with a landing-stage was constructed on the river-side; and, finally, the W. wing, with the White Saloon (p. 68) and the neighbouring apartments has recently undergone a thorough reconstruction from the designs of *Ihne*.

The rooms occupied by the imperial family (no admittance), fitted up in 1888 89, are on the first floor, overlooking the Schloss-Platz. Those of the Emperor are between Portals 1 and 11, while the apartments of the Empress adjoin them to the W. Above Portal I is the 'Sternen-Saal' (Star Hall), with the 'Elisabeth-Saal' above it on the second floor; see plan of the Royal Palace), containing the colours and standards of the Berlin regiments. A purple banner, hoisted on the N. side, indicates the Emperor's presence.

The exterior of the palace exhibits in its two principal façades, both by Schluter, a pleasing diversity of style, that to the S. being distinguished by monumental severity, while that to the N., overlooking the Lustgarten (formerly the garden-front), is enlivened with light and elegant details. The statues on the balustrade of the latter are modern. They represent Emperor William I. as Jupiter, Empress Augusta as Juno, Emperor Frederick as Mars, and Empress Frederick as Minerva. The *Horse Tamers* at Portal IV, two large bronze groups by Baron Clodt, were presented by the Emperor Nicholas I. of Russia in 1841.   The W. Façade, by Eosander, with its great central portal, built in imitation of the arch of Septimius Severus, is colder in style, but highly effective. The two bronze reliefs by O. Lessing (1897) represent Elector Frederick II. as builder of the castle, and King Frederick I. as builder of the palace.

To the memory of the Netherlandish relations of the Great Elector, Emperor William II. has recently dedicated six bronze statues. In front of the 'Schloss-Apotheke' a statue of *Admiral Coligny*, by Count Gortz-Schlitz, was unveiled in 1905 (Coligny, murdered in the Night of St. Bartholomew in 1572, was the great-grandfather of Louise Henrietta, the first wife of the Great Elector). Five statues of members of the Orange family on the parapet of the palace-terrace followed in 1907: *William I the Silent* (1533-84), by Schott; *Maurice* (1567-1625), by Wolff; *Frederick Henry* (father of Louise Henrietta, 1584-1647), by Brütt, *William II.* (1626-50), by Haverkamp; and *William III.* (1650-1702; King of England from 1689), by Bancke.

By Portal IV of the N. façade, which is opened by a sentry, we enter the Outer Court, in the centre of which is a large bronze group of *St. George and the Dragon*, by Kiss (1865). A passage leads hence to the *Inner Court, which is considered one of Schluter's masterpieces; it is surrounded on three sides by arcades. To the left, in Portal V, is a *Statue of the Great Elector*, by Franz du Sart (1651).

Tickets of admission to the *Interior of the palace (comp. p. 39) are issued in the inner court, at the office on the groundfloor to the left. The entrance is in the E. wing. Sticks and umbrellas must be given up here and are returned at the exit (no fees). — The old 'Wendelstein' (winding staircase) leads to the —

Second Floor, where as a rule only the State Rooms overlooking the Lustgarten are shown to visitors. — In the E. Wing is the *Schweizer-Saal*, originally the old guard-room, and now used as a reception-room on festive occasions. - - Next come the two STATE ANTECHAMBERS. The first (1) contains portraits of the family of Frederick the Great and his queen, by *Pesne;* the second (2), with an old ceiling by Schluter, has portraits of the Great Elector and his family, Frederick William I. as Crown Prince, Peter the Great, and Catharine II. of Russia.

In the NORTHERN WING is the KÖNIGS-ZIMMER (3), renovated in the style of Schluter, and containing portraits of all the Prussian kings down to the Emperor Frederick (the first three by *Pesne*). — To the W of the Konigs-Zimmer follow the STATE ROOMS, built by *Schlüter* and gorgeously decorated, later somewhat modernized by *Stuler*. In the ʻROTE DRAP D'OR KAMMER (9) is *Camphausen's* picture of 'Emperor William I. at Gravelotte', while the fireplace is surmounted by a relief by *Schluter.* — This is followed by the ROTE ADLER, or BRANDENBURGER KAMMER (10), with silk wall-hangings; the chandeliers and tables are of wood covered with silver, the originals having been melted down by Frederick the Great; here is also *Camphausen's* picture of 'The Great Elector at Fehrbellin'. — In the ʻRITTER-SAAL (formerly the Throne Room) the gorgeous rococo decoration reaches its climax. The ʻGroups of the four quarters of the globe, above the side-doors, are among the best efforts of *Schluter*, while the carving of the large central door is also worthy of notice. The trumpeters' gallery was formerly (1739) of solid silver, but was melted down by Frederick the Great in 1745. The crystal chandelier was purchased from the city of Worms by Frederick William III. On the sideboard, designed by *Eosander* (1703), are the finest specimens of plate in the royal collection (including a tankard by Jamnitzer), mostly dating from the time of the first two Prussian kings, and forming the remains of a once considerable treasure, the rest of which was melted down in war-time. In this apartment court receptions and the distribution of orders take place. — The SCHWARZE ADLER KAMMER (11), decorated in the same style as the 'Rote Adler Kammer', contains *Camphausen's* picture of 'Frederick the Great at Leuthen'. The allegorical ceiling-painting represents 'The Founding of the Order of the Black Eagle', by *Leygebe*. — In the ROTE SAMT-KAMMER (12) are portraits of Frederick I. and his consort Sophia Charlotte, in handsome antique frames. The old velvet tapestry with silver borders (from which the room takes its name) and the gilded furniture are worthy of notice. — The former CHAPEL (13) was fitted up in 1879 as a hall for themeetings of the High Order of the Black Eagle, and contains a picture by *A. von Werner* representing the first investiture with the order by King Frederick I. on Jan. 18th 1701

The PICTURE GALLERY, 197 ft. in length, is used as a meeting-hall and court-chamber. It contains 100 windows (fine view of the Linden and the Lustgarten) are various pictures, including battle-scenes by *Röchling:* Hohenfriedberg (1745), Tres Forcas (1856), Zorndorf (1758), and Kolin (1757); also *Schöbel,* Generals of Frederick the Great before his dead body. Main wall: *Weidemann,* King Frederick I. and Queen Sophia Charlotte; *Menzel,* *Coronation of King William I at Königsberg in 1861; *Bülow,* Emp. William I; *Keinke,* Emp. Frederick; *Corcos,* Emp. William II. and Empress Augusta Victoria; *A. von Werner,* King William proclaimed Emperor at Versailles in 1871, and Emp. William II. opening the Imperial Diet for the first time. At the end of the gallery, to the right, is a sculptured ⸗Group of Queen Louise and her sister (1795), by *Schadow.*

We now reach the WEST WING and enter the GALLERY OF THE WHITE SALOON, the addition of which (see p. 65) remedied the former isolated position of the saloon. The gallery is adorned with Gobelins tapestry (scenes from 'Don Quixote; woven at Paris in 1774-76) and with portraits of members of allied reigning families. It communicates by several doors with the *WEISSE SAAL or WHITE SALOON, a large hall 105 ft. in length, 52 ft. in width, and 43 ft. high, begun in 1728, completed by *Stüler* in 1844, and completely remodelled by *Ihne* in 1894-95. The ceiling has been raised and has received a rich plastic decoration, the four central spaces being adorned with the arms of the Hohenzollerns as Burgraves, Electors, Kings, and Emperors. The reliefs on the vaulting between the walls and the ceiling are by *O. Lessing* and represent victorious war as the fosterer of art, science, trade, and industry. The walls are decorated in coloured marble and gilded bronze. Between the coupled pilasters on the long side are 9 marble statues of Prussian rulers as they appeared at the time of their accession to the throne: the Great Elector, by *Schaper,* Frederick I., by *Böse,* Frederick William I., by *Schott,* Frederick the Great, by *Magnussen,* Frederick William II., by *Calandrelli,* Frederick William III., by *Eberlein,* Frederick William IV., by *Unger,* William I., by *K. von Üchtritz,* and Frederick III., by *Baumbach.* The opening of the Reichstag and of the Landtag (Prussian Diet) as well as the chief court festivities take place in the White Saloon.

The adjoining staircase leads to the *PALACE CHAPEL (comp. p. 67), an octagonal edifice, 113 ft. in height, lined with marble of different colours, and adorned with frescoes on a gold ground. The altar with its four columns is of yellow Egyptian alabaster, and is backed by a richly gilded silver cross set with large precious stones.

The Palace contains altogether about 700 apartments, but permission is seldom accorded to view any others than those above mentioned Adjoining the Königs-Zimmer (Pl. 3, p. 67) on the SECOND FLOOR, and looking towards the river are the so-called Alte Parade Kammern' or 'Old Staa. Rooms occupied before the commencement of Schlüter's building by Elector Frederick III. and containing rich decorations of his

Gallery (4), with portraits of the Great Elector and his family This gallery leads into the *Kurfürsten-Zimmer* (5), with portraits of all the Hohenzollern Electors, this is adjoined by an antechamber containing those of the old Counts of Zollern and the Burgraves of Nuremberg. The following rooms include the *Chinesische Kabinett* or *Chinese Cabinet* (5a); the *Kron-Kabinett* or *Crown Cabinet* (6), in which the crown jewels used to be kept; the *Betkammer* or *Oratory of Frederick I* (7), and the *Bridal Chamber* (8), which still plays its historical part in weddings of the royal house — Farther on, on the river-front, is the *Neue Galerie* or *New Gallery* (15), with portraits of the female relatives of Frederick the Great, by Pesne, the *Braunschweigische Kammern* or *Brunswick Rooms* (16); the *Tower Room* in the 'Grüne Hut' (Green Hat; 17), hung with views of the Berlin Palace in the times of the Electors, by C. and P. Graeb; the adjoining *Kapellen-Zimmer* or *Chapel Room*; the *Kleist Rooms* (18), which have lately been restored in the German Renaissance style, and contain ten pictures by L. Cranach, the *Elizabeth Rooms* (19), formerly occupied by Queen Elizabeth Christina, consort of Frederick the Great, and later by Queen Elizabeth, consort of Frederick William IV., and the *Apartments of Princess Marie* (20). In an adjoining room (21) Frederick the Great was born on Jan. 14th, 1712. — Looking on to the Lustgarten on the FIRST FLOOR are the *Königs-Kammern* or *King's Rooms*, fitted up for Frederick William II by Gontard and Erdmannsdorf, and now used as guest-rooms for the most distinguished foreign princes In the S.E wing (extending from the old Palace Chapel, the chief remaining fragment of Joachim's building, as far as Portal II) are the *Apartments of Frederick the Great*, re-decorated in 1825 26 by Schinkel for Crown Prince Frederick William, and now partly used by the Emperor. — On the GROUND FLOOR OF THE NORTH WEST WING were the *Apartments of Frederick William I.*, the later 'Petits appartements' of Frederick William II, which are still fitted up in the style characteristic of their period

Opposite the W. side of the Schloss, on a raised platform, stands the —

*National Monument to Emperor William I. (Pl. R, 26, 25), an imposing work by *R. Begas*, unveiled in 1897 On a pedestal 66 ft. in height rises the colossal equestrian figure of the Emperor (30 ft. high), in bronze, attired in a field-cloak and holding a commander's bâton in his right hand, on a powerful horse led by a graceful figure of Peace. At the four corners of the base are Victories, and on the two principal sides are seated colossal figures of War (to the N.) and Peace (to the S.). Projecting from the corners of the base are four lions, amid trophies of weapons and banners. — A stone colonnade, with coupled Ionic columns, by *Halmhuber*, extends on three sides of the platform. The attic is adorned with sculptured groups representing the kingdoms of Prussia (by Brener), Bavaria (by Gaul), Saxony (by Kraus), and Wurtemberg (by Brener). The four groups at the back represent Commerce and Navigation (by I. Cauer), Art (by Hidding), Science (by K. Begas), and Agriculture and Industry (by L. Cauer). Each of the corner pavilions bears a bronze *Quadriga*, that to the N. with Borussia, by Götz, that to the S. with Bavaria, by Bernewitz -- The cost amounted to 200,000*l* The castings were made by Gladenbeck

In the Schinkel-Platz (Pl. R, 23, 26 , to the S , is the Palace

(tramways No. 17, 60, 61, 63, 70, 73, 78, 80, and 81; see pp. 16-20) is the **Schloss-Brunnen,** a monumental fountain by *R. Begas,* unveiled in 1891. In the centre is Neptune on a rocky throne, with Tritons and putti below. The basin, 59 ft in diameter, contains four marine animals, while round the brim are figures of the Rhine, Oder, Elbe, and Vistula.

On the S. side of the Schloss-Platz, between the Spree and the Breite-Str., are the **Royal Stables** (Pl. R, 25, 26), erected by *Ihne* in the Renaissance style in 1897-1900. The main front is 305 ft. long, while the river-front is 578 ft. in length. The building is adorned with sculptures by *Otto Lessing.* On the attic are horse-tamers and figures of ancient warriors, while at each end of the main front is a fountain inserted in the wall, that to the left with Prometheus and the Oceanidæ, that to the right with Perseus and Andromeda.

Adm. to the stables (entrance, Breite-Str 37), see p. 39. — The horses (350) are kept in two stories of the river-wing, with the carriages above. The small HISTORICAL MUSEUM arranged here contains the sledge on which the Great Elector pursued the Swedes across the Kurische Haff in 1679, the white charger which Frederick the Great bestrode at the battle of Mollwitz; Sadowa, a favourite horse of William I., and state carriages and sledges of the time of the first kings. — The main wing contains state carriages, saddle and harness rooms; in the middle the coronation coach, built at Strassburg in 1793

The *Kurfursten-Brücke* (Bridge of the Elector; Pl. R, 26) leads to the E. from the Schloss-Platz to the old town of Berlin. The bridge, built in 1692-95 after designs by Nering and rebuilt in the old style in 1895, affords a good view of the river-front of the Royal Palace (p. 65), the Cathedral (p. 63), etc.

The bridge is adorned with a bronze equestrian *Statue of the Great Elector (d. 1688),* designed by *Schlüter* and erected in 1703. This clever and artistic group is one of the few really good works of a period when art was generally in a very debased condition. In spite of the Roman costume, the figure is remarkable for its air of majestic repose, which is heightened by contrast with the movements of the four slaves round the pedestal intended to typify the hostile powers against whom the Elector had waged war. The reliefs on the sides represent (left) the Electorate and the Old Palace, and (right) the Kingdom and the New Palace (original pedestal in the Emp. Frederick Museum, see p. 97).

3. The Museum Island.

Tramways Nos 33, 39, 40, 12, 53, 54, 55, III, and from the neighbouring Kupfergraben N, O, S, T; see pp 17, 18, 21 and comp also p. 59.

To the N. of the Lustgarten (p. 63) rises the *Old Museum* (see p 71), with the *New Museum* (p. 78) behind it, the two buildings being connected by a passage carried across the street. To the right is the *National Gallery* (p. 85). The *Pergamon Museum* (p. 82) and a building for the *Antiquities from Western Asia* (p. 84) are situated between the New Museum and the Stadtbahn. Beyond the Stadtbahn, on the triangular piece of land between the two arms of the Spree and only thence accessible, is the *Emperor Frederick Museum* (p. 96).

The following pages contain a notice of the principal treasures of the Museums. Details will be found in the official catalogues sold inside the buildings. The catalogues offered for sale outside are untrustworthy.

The Director General of the Royal Museums (including the Ethnographical and Industrial Museums, pp. 128 and 132) is *Dr. Bode*, who is also director of the Picture Gallery and of the Collection of Christian Sculptures, *Dr. Kekule von Stradonitz* of the Collection of Antiquities, the Antiquarium, and the Pergamon Museum, *Dr. Friedländer* of the Cabinet of Engravings; *Prof. Menadier* and *Prof. Dressel* of the Collection of Coins; *Prof. Delitzsch* of the Asiatic Antiquities; *Prof. Erman* of the Egyptian and Assyrian Department, and *Dr H. von Tschudi* of the National Gallery.

a The Old Museum.

ADMISSION, see p 38. — The OFFICIAL GUIDE to the Old and New Museums (50 pf ; 12th edit, 1907) and also SPECIAL CATALOGUES and PHOTOGRAPHS may be bought in the North Room (p. 73).

The *Old Museum (Pl. R, 26), an admirable building in the Greek style, 285 ft. long, 175 ft. wide, and 62 ft. high, with an Ionic portico of eighteen columns, and approached by a broad flight of steps, was erected by *Schinkel* in 1824-28. The raised central part of the structure is adorned with colossal groups in bronze: in front, the Horse Tamers of the Piazza del Quirinale at Rome, copies by *Tieck;* at the back, Pegasus tamed and refreshed by the Horæ, by *Schievelbein* and *Hagen.* The steps also are flanked by two large groups in bronze: right, *Amazon on horseback, defending herself against a tiger, by *Kiss;* left, Youth on horseback, launching a spear at a lion, by *A. Wolff.*

The VESTIBULE contains marble statues of German artists and connoisseurs: to the right of the entrance are those of *Rauch* (d. 1857), by Drake, *Cornelius* (d. 1867), by Calandrelli, *G. W. von Knobelsdorff* (d. 1753), by Karl Begas the Younger, *Schlüter* (d. 1714), by Wiese, and *Winckelmann* (d. 1768), by Wichmann, to the left those of *Schinkel* (d. 1841), by Tieck (replica), *Otfried Müller* (d. 1840), by Tondeur, *Chodowiecki* (d. 1801), by Otto, *Carstens* (d. 1798), by Janensch, and *G. Schadow* (d. 1850), by Hagen. The frescoes, designed by *Schinkel*, and executed under the direction of *Cornelius*, represent (on the left) the development of the world from chaos, and (on the right) the progress of human culture. (The original designs, in the Schinkel Museum p. 180, with a key attached, afford more satisfaction. From the vestibule, a door leads to the first floor of the Museum, see p. 72.

The Upper Vestibule, to which a double staircase ascends, is adorned with a copy of the celebrated antique Warwick Vase in England. The frescoes, also designed by *Schinkel*, represent the struggle of civilised mankind against barbarians and the elements. A fine view of the Lustgarten with its fountains, the cathedral, the Schloss, etc., is obtained hence from between the columns.

The Old Museum contains exclusively antique works of art and examples of applied art dating from the Græco-Roman period.

First Floor.

The domed and vaulted *Rotunda, which we first enter, is distinguished by the harmony and effectiveness of its proportions. It contains the first part of the *Gallery of Sculptures, which is chiefly indebted for its origin to Frederick the Great, who purchased at Rome the collection of Cardinal Polignac. Most of its contents were formerly of mediocre merit, dating from the later Roman Empire and freely restored, but the purchase of the Saburow collection of Attic sculptures in 1884 and other acquisitions have placed the gallery upon quite a different footing. The sculptures mentioned in the following description are of marble when nothing is said to the contrary. *Large Illustrated Catalogue of the Antique Sculptures,* 1891 (25 *M*); *Kekule von Stradonitz,* the Greek Sculpture, 1906 (with illustrations; 5 *M*)

In the middle of the Rotunda: 1452. Lion in Pentelic marble (4th cent. B.C.). Between the columns are decorative sculptures by Roman artists, some freely restored. To the left: 178. Goddess restored as Hera; 278. Satyr, after Praxiteles; 583. Hellenistic draped statue, 215. Meleager, after a Greek work in the manner of Scopas. To the right: 496. Roman woman praying; 587. Noble Roman lady as Fortuna. — The Rotunda is adjoined by the North Room (p. 73), which we traverse to the left to Room 1. (inscriptions and architectural fragments). Then follows the —

II. Archaic Room, with Greek sculptures of the 6th century B.C. On the left: 1555 Torso of Apollo from Naxos; 1574, 1575 (and 1576, on the right), Seated female figures from Miletus, 1577. Torso of a large female figure (standing). — On the right: *308. Bearded head from Ægina, an admirable Attic work; 1614 Portion of a parapet with sphinxes, from Miletus; modern coloured reproductions of Poros sculptures (three-bodied demon and bulls' heads) from the Acropolis at Athens, 734. Fragment of a painted stele; 1531. Fragment of the sepulchral stele of a girl, with traces of colouring, from Attica. In a wall-cabinet: 1474. Graceful small female head from Selinus (1st half of 5th cent.: 732, 731. Early Spartan reliefs (hero-worship. In the middle, volutes from the corner of an ancient building at Miletus.

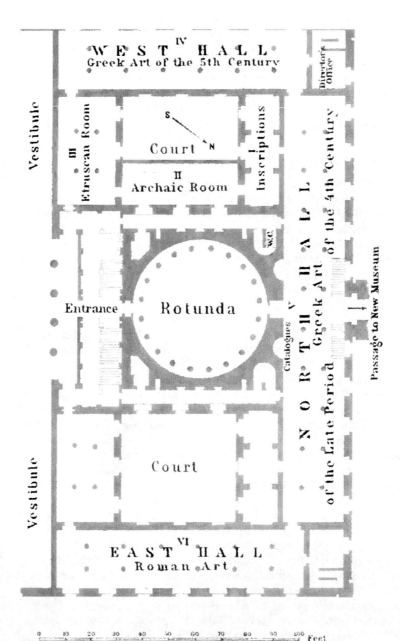

WEST HALL ^{IV}
Greek Art of the 5th Century

Vestibule

Director's Office

III
Etruscan Room

Court

S

N

II
Archaic Room

I
Inscriptions

W.C.

Entrance

Rotunda

Catalogues V

NORTH HALL Greek Art of the Late Period of the 4th Century

Passage to New Museum

Court

Vestibule

EAST HALL ^{VI}
Roman Art

0 10 20 30 40 50 60 70 80 90 100 Feet

Old Museum, First Floor
Gallery of Antique Sculptures

III. ETRUSCAN ROOM: Reliefs: sarcophagi and cinerary urns with high reliefs, partly of mythological scenes (3rd and 2nd cent.); in the middle an ancient sarcophagus in peperino, with well-preserved painting. The following rooms are divided into sections by columns.

IV. WEST ROOM, with Greek sculptures of the 5th and 4th centuries. Beginning at the back: 1494. Female draped figure in a severe style with a late Roman portrait-head, and 605. Head originally belonging to the figure; 83. Goddess (Demeter?), dating from the time of Phidias; 1459. Headless draped figure of a goddess, an excellent work resembling the figures in the pediment of the Parthenon; 1483. Relief with abduction of women; 229. Torso of a girl in a short garment (runner?), a work in the severe style — 1545. Votive relief from Rhodes, an exquisite Greek work of the time of the Parthenon frieze; 725. Votive relief of a victorious charioteer, from Oropos. — 1456, 1457. Reliefs with graceful dancers; 1530. Head of Pericles, from Mytilene; 608. Head of a goddess, a good ancient copy of an Attic work of the end of the 5th cent.; 735. Fragment of a sepulchral stele of a youth; 925. Relief. Medea and the daughters of Pelias, an antique copy, freely retouched, of an original of the time of the Parthenon frieze — *1482. Sepulchral stele of a girl, an excellent work in a severe style; *1455. Bust of Anacreon, the poet, 1504. Sepulchral stele of Polyxena, from Bœotia; 59. Artemis Colonna, Roman copy of a Greek work. — 736. Tomb-stone from Karystos; 76a. Head of Athena after the Parthenos of Phidias, with well-preserved painting; 1502. Bust of Zeus. — Attic tomb-reliefs of the end of the 5th and of the 4th cent. (No. 755 the best). — 498, 499. Statues of two mourning maidservants, from an Attic tomb; 1643. Palmette acroterium of a sepulchral stele, from S. Russia, Votive reliefs (No 805 from Cumæ).

V. NORTH ROOM. Western Section. In the foreground, works still belonging to the art of the 5th cent.. 179. Replica of the Farnese head of Hercules; ¯7. Amazon, after Polycletus; 79. Replica of the head of Athena of Velletri, ¯193. Hermaphrodite (4th cent.). 223. Statue of a youth. — School of *Skopas:* 610, 1558. Female heads. 482 Youthful Hercules — School of *Praxiteles:* 259. Satyr reposing; 28. Venus in the attitude of the Medici Venus. — Portrait-busts by the rear-wall. 296 Sophocles, ¯297 Euripides, 298. Socrates, 300. Plato. — Eastern Section. School of *Lysippus.* 469. Youthful pugilist (restored as an archer); 471. Athlete. — Hellenistic works (3rd-1st cent.): 150 Group of children; 316, 317. Greek portrait-heads; 505. Girl with a duck, ¯208 Dancing mænad (torso); 205. Head of a centaur; 495. Girl with Cupids; 262. Dancing Satyr; 213. Torso of Marsyas, 766a. Tombstone of Metrodorus from Chios , . : . n h . f m . mb d Tarentum; 2 ¯ 221 222. Mn .

VI. Roman Room. Beginning at the farther end: 354. Seated statue of an emperor with head of Trajan; 343 Statue of Augustus, freely restored; 332, 335, 336. Portrait busts of the Republican period; 391. Double bust of Socrates and Seneca 399 b. Bust of a boy, of the early Imperial period; 344 (between the windows), Head of Augustus; 157 (by the back-wall), Genius of an emperor of the Julian family. — 843 a. Sarcophagus of the time of Augustus; *1467. Bust of a noble Roman boy of the early Imperial period; 348 Head of Vespasian; *342. Bust of Caesar, in basalt; 840. Tombstone of a Roman married couple, of the Republican period. — 960. Head of a warrior, from a relief of the time of the Antonines· 345. Head of Tiberius; 921. Archaistic votive-relief for a poetical victory; 1527. Head of Jupiter — 922. Top of a large circular tomb from Falerii (1st cent. B.C.), 162, 463 (by the foremost columns), Heads of barbarians (Germans?). — 363. Head of Antinous; 358 Head of Hadrian (basalt); 843 b. Sarcophagus with scenes from the legend of Medea; 955. Fragment of a large relief from the Esquiline, of the Antonine period. — 494. Girl playing with astragali, *1503. Head of a negro; *384. Head of Caracalla; 958. Relief with weapons of Trajan's time; 903. Relief of Cupid from the Forum of Trajan; 902. Frieze (Cupids with garlands). — 447 Characteristic head of an aged woman; 385. Bust of Gordian III.; 461. Head of a barbarian.

Upper Floor.

The double staircase in the North Room ascends to the passage connecting the Old and New Museums (p. 78) and farther up to the upper floor of the Old Museum, with the —

⁺Antiquarium, a collection of small antique works of both ornamental and industrial art. Rooms 5-10, 13, 16, and 17 are being rearranged and are closed at present.

Entrance Room I. Nike on a globe, bronze-gilt (2nd cent. A. D.); figures of dead bodies from Pompeii (reductions of casts obtained by filling up the holes in the consolidated ashes).

Room II. ⁺Collection of Antique Helmets. Most of them were deposited on permanent loan by Baron Franz v. Lipperheide (d. 1906). Among the Greek helmets those of the so-called Corinthian shape (with visor resembling a face; 7-4th cent.) may be noticed. On the exit-wall, helmet with half-length figure of Athena, from Melos (3rd-2nd cent.). Among the Italic helmets that in the shape of a pointed hat, with engraved designs, and the sumptuous Roman helmets with embossed reliefs are remarkable. Here also are a bell-shaped helmet of the Hungarian bronze-period, and a Celtic iron helmet with ornamented bronze bands (another at the exit-wall). In the middle, a gladiator's helmet inlaid with silver; be-

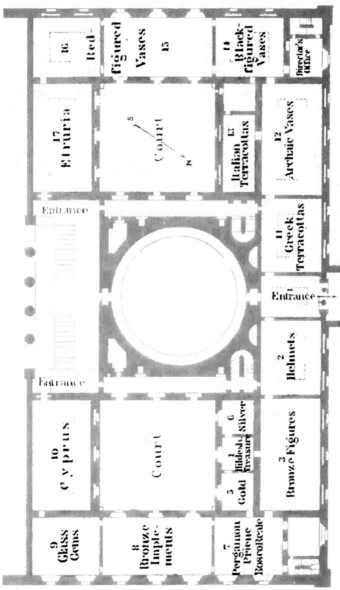

16 Red-

Figured Vases 15

14 Black-figured Vases

Director's Office

17 Etruria

Court

S

N

13 Italian Terracottas

12 Archaic Vases

Entrance

11 Greek Terracottas

Passage to New Museum

Entrance

2 Helmets

Entrance

10 Cyprus

Court

6 Silver Treasury

1 Hildesheim

5 Gold

3 Bronze Figures

9 Glass Gems

8 Bronze Implements

7 Pergamon Priene Boscoreale

0 10 20 30 40 50 60 70 80 90 100 Feet

Old Museum, Upper Floor
Antiquarium

tween the windows, half of a colossal helmet in the shape of a
Phrygian cap, from a trophy found in the Lake of Nemi near Rome.

Room III. BRONZE FIGURES. Larger works: ¹Torso of a youth
(Apollo?), of the end of the 5th cent. B.C., found near Salamis;
*Boy praying, the arms restored (the 'intention' therefore uncertain),
purchased by Frederick the Great and formerly in the palace of
Sanssouci (p 194); *Torso of a draped female figure, early Hellenistic,
found at Cyzicus (4th cent), Figure of Hypnos (god of sleep), an
excellent replica of a work of the 4th cent. B.C; Running boy
wearing a wreath, of the early Imperial period, found in the Rhine
near Xanten. — Small bronzes: in the first isolated cabinet, *Objects
from the celebrated sanctuary of Zeus at Dodona, comprising an
archaic statuette of a youth (6th cent.), two figures of warriors,
Zeus as thunderer, with green patina resembling enamel (ca 500 B.C.),
a seated mænad (end of 5th cent. B C.), and a statuette of Zeus (4th
cent.). — By the entrance-wall are works of archaic Greek art Aphrodite with flower, from Sparta; Dancers on a dining-table; Youth
(Hermes?) with ram, from Crete; small Arcadian figures. Statuettes
of the 5th cent.: Goat-headed Pan; Aphrodite with a dove; Girls'
figures as the handles of hand-mirrors; Two heads of youths; Hercules, recalling the Farnese statue. — Statuettes of the 4th - 1st
cent and of the early Roman period: between the windows Theseus
with the Minotaur; by the exit-wall: Satyr from Pergamon; slaves,
negroes, caricatures in the style of Alexandrian art; Mercury from
Lyons. — By the back-wall statuettes found to the N. of the Alps:
Dionysos, silvered, from Pomerania. — Utensils decorated with
figures; tripods, vessels, folding mirror.

Room IV. The chief object here is the **Hildesheim Silver
Treasure,* found in 1868 on the Galgenberg near Hildesheim, consisting of Roman plate of the time of Augustus. Some of the objects possess great artistic merit, particularly the round dish with a
relief of Athena, the large cratera (vessel for mixing), the cups
with masks, and the laurel cup

Room V. GREEK, ETRUSCAN, AND ROMAN GOLD AND SILVER
ORNAMENTS. Small golden plates with archaic designs, probably
made in Crete. *Gold treasure found at Vettersfelde in Lower
Lusatia. Objects from a Celtic tomb near Birkenfeld. Fragments
of a silver vessel with embossed ornaments and rich gilding, a Greek
work revealing the influence of Persian art (ca. 400 B.C.). *Treasure of the early Imperial period found at Pedescia in the Sabine
Mts.: gold bracelets in the shape of snakes, rings, etc.

Room VI. Silver ornaments from Luxor (2nd cent. A.D.): large
silver dish with hunting-scene in the middle and a frieze of masks
and animals on the margin. Decorations (phaleræ) of a Roman
officer, found at Lauersfort. We now return to Room III and
proceed to

Room VII. Objects from Pergamon, Priene, and Bosco Reale. Small objects from Pergamon and Priene (comp. p. 83), mostly of the Hellenistic period: bronzes, terracottas, coal-pans, etc. Bronze utensils and vessels from the dining-room and the kitchen of a villa at Bosco Reale near Pompeii, etc. Dining-couch with inlaid ornaments in silver and copper. Fragments of wall-paintings and reliefs in stucco from Rome and Pompeii. Mosaics: Centaur protecting the body of his wife, from the villa of Hadrian at Tivoli; Festival at the rising of the Nile, from Palestrina.

Room VIII. Bronze Vessels. Greek, Etruscan, and Roman vessels. Domestic utensils, lamps, and candelabra. Weapons, except helmets (see Room II). Articles used in the palaestra (strigils, oil-bottles, etc.; engraved discus). Ornamental pins in chronological order Rings, armlets, and other bronze ornaments. Etruscan cists and hand-glasses (4th-3rd cent.: notice the Semele mirror). Amulets. — Inscriptions on bronze and lead; the earliest known Greek letter (4th cent.), on lead, from Attica.

Room IX. Glass and Cut Stones. Small bottles, vases, etc., in opaque, generally dark-blue glass, with yellow and white stripes, from Oriental or Oriental-Greek factories Larger polychrome glass-vessels of the 1st cent. B.C. and the 1st cent A.D. Monochrome or colourless, glass vessels, mostly from the Rhine district. So-called Diatretum, a glass vessel enveloped in a raised network of glass. — Chains of beads in glass, stone, and fayence. — Intaglios from the Cretan-Mycenæan epoch down to the latest period of Greek art; large rock-crystal with bust of Athena, signed by Eutyches. — Cameos: Gorgon's head of the Ptolemæic period, Hercules with Cerberus, by Dioscurides, of the time of Augustus; large onyx cameo with the apotheosis of an emperor (Septimius Severus?). — Carvings in amber, ivory, and bone.

Room X. Cyprus Vessels from the earliest period, recalling the early Trojan pottery, down to the Hellenistic epoch. Fine sepulchral figure of a woman seated on a throne (4th cent. B.C.). Statuettes and fragments of archaic statues in terracotta and stone; the faces of the men and the gorgeous semi-barbaric ornaments of the women should be noticed. Archaic bronze carriage, as support for a kettle. Objects from Gordion in Phrygia, comprising a bowl with the signature of the Attic painter Klitias. — Prehistoric antiquities from the Greek islands. — Cretan-Mycenæan art (ca. 1500-1000 B.C.): bronzes (praying woman, figure of a youth), terracottas (bull. idols), copies. — We return to Room 1 and proceed straight on to —

Room XI. Greek Terracottas Between the windows, Archaic figures from Tanagra: women baking, washing, with a pan; barber, cook Severe style 1st half of 5th cent. , in the central cabinets: Youths and girls, sometimes with attributes of deities; charming small temple with Hermes and two goddesses By the entrance-wall (2nd half of 5th cent. and 4th cent): Girl with a duck, from Corinth; anointing vessels in the shape of figures or groups, from Attica; graceful figures of girls from Tanagra (4th cent.). — By the other walls: Figures of girls, Cupids and characteristic popular types, those at the exit-wall from Asia Minor (3rd-2nd cent. B.C.). — In the window-cases: Reliefs of the first half of the 5th cent. (Ulysses and Penelope from Rhodes, Calydonian hunt from Melos), figures from a vessel, representing an abduction, from Tanagra. — Traversing the adjacent R. XII, we next enter —

Room XIII Italian Terracottas. Fine works from Tarentum: head of a youth from a sepulchral statue (4th cent.). Large portrait-busts of a man and a woman, of the early Imperial epoch. Terracottas from Pæstum and Campania. Archaic Etruscan antefixæ and slabs from the facing of entablatures, with reliefs. Terracotta reliefs with various representations, orginally painted (end of the Republic and early Imperial epoch).

Room XII. Archaic Vases. Greek and Roman lamps. Vessels with geometrical ornamentation (ca 1000-800 B.C.), figures begin to appear on the later ones, *e. g* the large amphora from Hymettus (left, No. 56). — Bœotian bowls, with birds — Small 'Proto-Corinthian' vases, with friezes of pygmy figures. — Corinthian 'Pinakes' (votive tablets of potters), with scenes in potteries. — Corinthian black-figured vessels 1655 Large cratera with the expedition of Amphiaraos and the funeral games for Pelias; 1652 Amphora with the deliverance of Andromeda — Black-figured vases from Ionian, Ionian-Italic, and early Attic workshops — Panathenaean prize-amphorae with Athena (at the end of main passage). — By the long wall, terracotta sarcophagi from Klazomenæ, two of them in the manner of the red-figured vases

Room XIV. Black-figured and Earlier Red-figured Attic Vases (the former till the end of the 6th, the latter of the 6th and early 5th cent.). In the middle handsome large amphorae. a black-figured one with horsemen, found near Athens; 2159 Large amphora from the workshop of Andokides (theft of the tripod and scene from the palaestra), one of the earliest works in the red-figured style; red-figured amphora with Hermes and Silenus At the back, amphorae from Nola. To the left, red-figured lecythi

Room XV. Red-figured Attic Vases. Earlier period 2248, 2279 Bowls of Sosias and of Peithinos, both revealing most careful drawing; 2285. Bowl of Duris with teaching-scene; 2294 Bowl with brass-founder's workshop. — Middle of 5th cent.: large cratera with Orpheus and the Thracians, at the entrance-wall. — Second half of the 5th cent (period of the beautiful style): 2531. Bowl of the painter Aristophanes, with Battle of the Giants. 2633, 2631. Two hydriae companion pieces Cadmus slaying the dragon Judgment of Paris; graceful ointment-vessel), decorated with gold and colours. — Vases with polychrome painting on a white ground; lecythi with funeral designs. — Vases from workshops in Lucania and Campania (4th and end of 5th cent.).

Room XVI. Red-figured vases of Italian workmanship: Hellenistic and Roman pottey — Black vessels with striated patterns. — Large and excellently preserved black hydria of Attic workmanship. — Vases with reliefs; cups with designs from Greek poems. — Red Sigillata vessels from Arezzo and other places (1st cent B.C. and 1st cent. A.D.) — Fragments of moulds used in making vases with reliefs.

Room XVII. Italic - Etruscan Art. Vases of black clay ('Bucchero nero') with plastic ornamentation, imitations of metal vessels (7-5th cent.) — Early Italic bronze vessels, weapons and utensils. — Objects found in tombs. Tomb from Chiusi, Tomba del Guerriero (tomb of the warrior) from Corneto-Tarquinii (7th cent.); large family tomb from the environs of Volterra (3rd cent.). — Vases with vivaciously painted heads, recalling popular types. — Roman vases from the Rhenish provinces. — Mycenæan vessels.

b. The New Museum.

Admission, see p. 38. Official printed *Guide*, see p 71. Lift from Room XI of the groundfloor to Room IX of the middle story and to the last exhibition-room of the cabinet of engravings (10 pf.).

The *New Museum was erected by *Stüler* in the Renaissance style in 1843-55 (length 344 ft., depth 130 ft.; height of the central part, with the grand staircase, 102 ft.). The exterior of this edifice is comparatively insignificant, but its internal decorations are rich and artistic.

The main entrance is on the E. side, opposite the National Gallery. — The Passage (p. 74) connecting the Old and New Museums leads to the first floor of the latter. The visitor is recommended to traverse Rooms X, XI, and XII and enter the imposing *Staircase (Pl. II), 125 ft. in length, 50 ft in width, and 65 ft. in height, which occupies the centre of the building. A broad flight of steps leads from the groundfloor (see p. 79) to the first story, and two narrower ones from the first to the second (p. 82).

Six colossal *Mural Paintings by *W. von Kaulbach*, executed in 1847-66, representing important epochs in the history of mankind, adorn the upper walls of the staircase: 1. *Building of the Tower of Babel* (division of nations); 2. *Golden Age of Greece* (Homer and the Greeks); 3. *Destruction of Jerusalem by Titus* (rise of Christianity); 4. *Battle of the Huns* (wandering of the nations); 5. *The Crusaders before Jerusalem under Godfrey de Bouillon* (middle ages): 6. *The Reformation.* — Over the doors are figures of Tradition and History, Science and Poetry. Between the large pictures

appear the law-givers Moses, Solon, Charlemagne, and Frederick the
Great; above them, Egypt, Greece, Italy, Germany. On the window-
walls are allegorical figures of Sculpture, Painting, Architecture, and
Engraving. Around the entire hall, beneath the richly-decorated
open ceiling, runs a *Frieze*, bearing a humorous representation
(in grisaille) of the history of the development of mankind, termin-
ating with Humboldt leaning on his Cosmos, the whole hardly
intelligible without a detailed explanation.

First Floor.

The first floor of the New Museum and the passage leading to the
Old Museum are occupied by the very extensive and valuable **Collection of Casts** from the antique. Scientific catalogue by Friede-
richs (2nd edit. by Wolters, 1885; 12 *M*). Room III contains also
Greek landscapes, and Room X mural paintings from the Greek
heroic myths — Rooms XI and XII contain the casts of the sculptures discovered during the excavations carried on by Ernst Curtius
(d. 1896) in 1876-81 at *Olympia* at the expense of the German
Empire, and the duplicates of original sculptures found on the same
occasion.

The originals of the first-named sculptures remain at Olympia. The
chief objects here are the two *Pediment Groups from the Temple of
Zeus*, by an unknown sculptor of the beginning of the 5th cent. B C
The *E. Pediment* represents the preparations for the chariot race between
Pelops and Oenomaos, which Curtius describes as follows. In the centre
stands Zeus, with Pelops and Hippodamia on his right, and King Oenomaos and his wife Sterope on his left, to the right and left of these
appear the two four-horse chariots, held by kneeling charioteers, beyond
which, on the left, are a seated man, a kneeling girl, and finally the
recumbent figure of the river-god Alpheus, and, on the right, a bald-
headed old man, a boy seated on the ground, and the river-god Cla-
deus. On the *W. Pediment* the struggle between the Lapithæ and the
Centaurs at the marriage of Pirithous is depicted. In the middle is
Apollo extending his right hand in a commanding gesture, while on each
side are groups of combatants; to the left a Centaur abducting a woman
and attacked by Pirithous; to the right, Theseus protecting a woman
against her abductors, to the left again, a Centaur carrying off a boy,
and to the right, a kneeling Lapith strangling a Centaur, the succeeding
groups on each side resemble the first groups, but with the figures in a
kneeling position, the composition finally terminates with a recumbent
female form at each end.

The chief single figures are those of the Hermes of *Praxiteles*, the
only authenticated and at the same time well preserved masterpiece of
the greatest Greek sculptor of the 4th cent, and of the Nike of *Pæonios*,
erected at the beginning of the Peloponnesian War, in which the sculptor
has most admirably succeeded in representing the goddess of Victory in
the act of flying

From the staircase (see above) we descend to the —

Ground Floor.

Direct entrance see p. 78.

The ground floor is occupied by the **Egyptian Museum**, one
of the most important collections of the kind, founded by *Passal-*

acqua, and greatly extended by *Lepsius* in 1842-46. The acquisitions of more recent times have crowded the available space to such an extent that some of the rooms are not accessible at present. Illustrated Catalogue, 2nd edit., 1899 (3 *M*).

The Vestibule contains, on the N. side, an obelisk of Ramses II., a head of King Har-em-heb, and sacred monkeys. S. side, see p. 82. — We pass through the anteroom beside the staircase and enter the—

Colonnade Court (Pl. IV), which, together with Room V, represents the main features of an Egyptian temple. On the side nearest the entrance: Statues of the lion-headed goddess Sekhmet. In the middle: *Small antiquities of the earliest period, from tombs at Abydos and Abusir, some with the hieroglyphic sign of King Menes (about 3500 B. C.); alabaster vessel on a support which has played an important part in the deciphering of Ethiopian inscriptions; two criosphinxes (that on the right a cast). In the back-ground are two large figures of kings in a sitting posture, in porphyry:

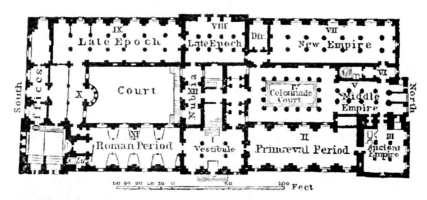

to the left Ramses II., to the right Usertesen I. (2100 B.C.), the upper part restored. Behind them are wooden coffins of Mentu-hotep (right) and Hennui (left), with the figures dedicated to the dead. On the walls are paintings of Egyptian landscapes, and papyrus MSS., protected by curtains. — We now pass through Room V and enter (to the right) Room III; the —

Room of the Primæval Period (Pl. II; before 2800 B.C.) is closed at present. Near the entrance are vessels, plants from tombs, bricks of Nile mud. In the middle, *Objects found in tombs of Upper Egypt (ca. 3000 B.C.); mummies. sewn up in leather coverings; fine stone vessels; stone knives and slates for pulverising pigments, some of them in the shape of animals. At the back, dating from the time of the Early Empire, the Tomb of Meten (ca. 2800 B.C.), rebuilt with the original slabs. Also, fine reliefs: boat among lotus and papyrus plants, flax harvest, boatmen, animals of the desert, fowling, *14,642. Fattening poultry.   The mural paintings represent sacri-

fices and the judgment of the dead; on the ceiling is a reproduction
of the Zodiac of Dendera.

Room of the Ancient Empire (after 2800 B.C.; Pl III). Wall I·
Walls of the tomb of Manofer, with admirable reliefs (the deceased at
table; his herds); sacrificial slabs and cups. Wall II· Tomb-chamber
of Prince Mer-eb (son of Cheops), who was buried beside the Great
Pyramid at Gizeh. This was reconstructed from fragments brought
home by Lepsius. — Window-wall: Family-groups; *10,858. Wooden
figure of Per-her-nofret. — Central passage. 15,701. Stone statue
of the major-domo Der-senez. — Wall XI: 1185. Pyramid-door with
fayence plaques; 1129. Relief with harvest-scenes.

Room of the Middle Empire (after 2200 B.C.; Pl V). In the
window-niches: fragments of *Scenes of animal life, from Abusir
(Early Empire); well-preserved mummy (about 2000 B C.). In front:
1121. Statue of Amen-em-het III. Between the columns: houses and
corn-magazines from tombs. To the right, by the vestibule: toilet
case of a queen. Wall VIII (on the left): 1160, 1161. Blocks of rock
with marks indicating the level of the Nile. At the end next the
Colonnade Court. Mural paintings of domestic scenes. — The —

Antiroom (Pl. VI) is devoted to the 18th Dynasty (1600-1400
B.C.). Heads of sphinxes, representing queens; 2296. Statue of
Sen-Mut, with a little princess in his lap.

Room of the New Empire (after 1600 B.C.; Pl. VII) Tombstones and coffins. Wall I· 2297. Statue of Ptahmai and his family.
Table-case B. Small household utensils and ornaments. — Case A.
Furniture and musical instruments. Case C. (Wall II): Funeral offerings from a tomb of the period of Ramses II. — Wall III: Case D.
Small statues, head-rests, draught-board. — Wall IV Case E. Figures buried with the dead. 2. Sarcophagus of a general called Meriti;
2058 Relief from the tomb of Seti I. — Wall V: 2079 An Egyptian
and an Asiatic. — Wall VIII: Case F. Weapons and baskets. —
Wall IX: 10,859 Wooden relief of Tamaket; 2060, 2061. Stucco paint-
ings from Thebes; Paintings on Nile mud. — Walls X and XI: Reliefs
of funeral feasts, particularly Nos. *12,411, 12,412, 2088, and 2089.
— *Libyan Epoch* (after 1100 B.C.). Wall XII: 2094. Relief from
Karnak of captive Jews, from the wars of Sheshonk (Shishak). —
Wall XIII: Case G. Sepulchral figures in dark blue fayence, 1480.
Door and wall of a chapel of the Ethiopian king Shabaco. — Time of
Amenophis IV. (ca 1400 B.C.), who tried to establish a new religion·
painted stucco slabs from El-Amarna (ducks among reeds); Wall
XV: 15,000. The king and his queen; 14,115 The king with his
family (reliefs); in the window case, *Head of his daughter — On
the walls are representations from Egyptian history.

The Rooms of the Late Period are closed at present. Room
VIII contains, among other objects, coffins of priests from Der-el-
Bahri; scarabs.   R. IX: Numerous coffins· figures of deities and

sacred animals, temple utensils, mummies of sacred animals. *12,500.
Head of an old man, in an unusual style; 10,114. Statuette of a
queen; 10,972. Statue of an old man; 14,463 Vessel with the name
of Artaxerxes in four languages; 2271. Statue of a general; 2123.
Head in the Phœnician style from a marble sarcophagus; 2115.
Relief with some of the Ptolemies. — In Passage X: 7733. Inscription of Zenobia, Queen of Palmyra, referring to a synagogue.

ROOM OF THE ROMAN PERIOD (Pl. XI). At the back (adjoining
the lift): 31. Wooden coffin in the form of the goddess Hathor; 17,039.
Coffin in the shape of a chapel. Terracotta figures of household gods,
etc.; stucco heads from mummies; 17,126. Chapel with coffin of a
child. — Mummies of the 2nd and 3rd cent. A.D. found in the Fayûm
(Central Egypt), with portraits on wood or linen. The portrait of
Aline and the gilded mask of her husband should be noticed. Palls
(13,277 that of Dion). — *Christian Period:* Greek and Coptic inscriptions, textiles, writing materials. Adjoining the vestibule is
the —

NUBIAN ROOM (Pl. XII; closed). Gold ornaments of a queen from
her pyramid at Meroe (her portrait is opposite on the rear-wall);
2268. Monument of victory erected by King Nastesen; by the rear-
wall, marks indicating the level of the Nile. — Other Nubian antiquities on the S. side of the vestibule (comp. p 79): 1157. Monument of victory of King Sen-wosret III. (1870 B.C.); 2261. Nubian
king adoring Isis, from a pyramid at Meroe.

SECOND FLOOR.

In the staircase of the New Museum (p. 78) the stairs below the
wall-paintings ascend to the second floor, which contains the engravings. Lift, see p. 78.

The *Cabinet of Engravings contains engravings, wood-
cuts, and lithographs (300,000 plates); drawings by artists who
died before 1800 (among which the German and Dutch schools are
especially well represented); illustrated MSS. of the 10-16th cent.;
old illustrated books; and lastly an extensive collection of photographs of paintings and drawings. Among the recent acquisitions
are the Posony *Dürer Collection*, the illustrated MSS. from the collection of the Duke of Hamilton, including 84 illustrations to Dante
by *Botticelli* (d. 1510), engravings by *Rembrandt* from various
private collections, including those presented by Baron von Lipperheide, the drawings by Italian masters (about 4000) of the *Beckerath
Collection*, and the engravings, etchings, and wood-cuts by modern
artists which are constantly augmented. Portfolios of engravings
are shown on application. — To the left (N.) the students' room for
ancient art. By the entrance, behind a curtain, is an excellent water-
colour portrait of Countess Potocka (d 1823), probably by *Kucharski*.

To the right (S.) are two rooms where a varying selection of the best drawings and engravings is exhibited, adjoined by the students' room for modern art.

c. Pergamon Museum. Antiquities from Western Asia.

ENTRANCE by the portal at the back of the National Gallery (see plan, p. 55). — ADMISSION to the Pergamon Museum, see p. 39. — Guide to the Pergamon Museum (1901), 30 pf.; Guide to the Ruins of Pergamon (4th ed , 1905; 50 pf.). Description of the Great Frieze (illustrated), 3rd ed , 1904; 1 *M.*

The **Pergamon Museum** (Pl. R, 23), an unpretending edifice by *F. Wolff,* opened in 1901, contains the larger objects found in the excavations undertaken by the Royal Museums in three Hellenistic towns of Asia Minor, viz. *Pergamon* (1878-86), *Magnesia* on the Mæander (1891-93), and *Priene* (1895-99). Its chief treasure is the great ** 'Frieze,* representing the contest of the gods and giants (Gigantomachia), which formed the artistic decoration of a huge marble altar to Zeus (and perhaps Athena) on the Acropolis of Pergamon, probably erected by King Eumenes II. about the year B.C. 180 in honour of his decisive victory over the Gauls of Asia Minor. The altar has been reconstructed so as to exhibit the sculptures in their original position. The engineer *Karl Humann* (d 1896) discovered several isolated reliefs in 1871 built into a mediæval fortification wall, and in 1878-80 succeeded in bringing to light the whole of this most valuable work of art, which is the largest existing monument of Greek sculpture and rivals in importance the Parthenon sculptures in the British Museum. The sculptures are characterized by strong dramatic feeling and great boldness in the representation of scenes of excitement; and at the same time reveal a knowledge of the human form, a richness of fancy, and a mastery of execution, such as are displayed in no other antique remains on so large a scale.

The ALTAR, reconstructed in its original size and shape, and surrounded by a broad gangway, occupies the centre of the museum. It has the form of a rectangular podium or platform, 30 ft. in height, and is 113 ft. broad and 124 ft. in length at its base. A flight of steps, 65 ft. broad (see below), let into the front, ascends to the top. The opening on the same side, with columns (a modern arrangement) and preceded by a fine *Mosaic Pavement* from Pergamon, forms the entrance to the inner court (see p. 84). Round the outside of the altar (including the side-walls of the flight of steps), above a kind of dado or pedestal, $7\frac{1}{2}$ ft. in height, runs the famous *Marble Frieze,* also $7\frac{1}{2}$ ft. high. The high reliefs have been in many cases reconstructed from numerous small fragments, but none has been restored. Above the frieze are the names of the Gods and Titans and of the Giants, many of whom are represented in half human half animal form.

The following are the more important groups and figures, beginning
at the steps and proceeding from left to right. *On the Front.* Dionysos
On the Right Side: Various deities, including Cybele mounted on a lion,
in combat with a monster in the form of a bull; Selene on horseback;
Helios in floating drapery in his chariot; Aurora riding through the
heavens; a lion-headed giant being strangled by a youth; Phœbe and
her opponents, Asteria supported by a dog. *On the Back.* Bearded giant
in combat with the triple-headed Hecate; Artemis and the youthful Otos;
Tityos hard pressed by the torch of Leto; magnificent torso of Apollo
in the background. Further towards the end are the main groups: Zeus
destroying three opponents with thunderbolts, and Athena grasping Alkyoneus (son of Gæa, the earth-goddess) by the hair (the Alkyoneus is
interesting on account of the resemblance to the Laocoon) *On the Left
Side:* Castor defending himself against Idas, Nyx hurling a vessel encircled by a serpent, a goddess, supposed to be Medusa, supported by a
lion. *On the Front* and on the adjacent side-wall of the staircase are marine
deities, including the fantastic form of Triton, and the mighty Oceanus.

On the platform at the top of the flight of steps stood the
sacrificial altar, which was surrounded by a low colonnade, with
elegant Ionic columns. The inner side of the rear-wall was decorated with the *Telephos Frieze*, 5 ft. in height, depicting the
history of Telephos, the mythical founder of Pergamon. The
numerous and in part uninterpreted fragments are exhibited on
the entrance-wall of the gangway (beginning beyond the corner to
the right of the entrance; inscriptions below the reliefs). — On the
other walls are other sculptures discovered at Pergamon, fragments of architecture and inscriptions. A series of large *Female
Figures* is noteworthy, and still more so a beautiful *× Female Head*
(opposite the E. wall of the altar, near the left corner), recalling
the Venus of Milo.

The INNER COURT (closed), within the reconstructed large altar,
contains architectural fragments illustrating the more important
buildings. By the entrance-wall and rear-wall are fragments from
Pergamon (by the entrance-wall a fragment of the sacrificial altar
also); to the left, fragments from Magnesia; and to the right those
from Priene. Here too, opposite the entrance, is a large marble
copy from Pergamon of the statue of Athena Parthenos by Phidias.
— Outside the entrance to the Museum is a semicircular marble
bench from Pergamon.

The **Collection of Antiquities from Western Asia** is
exhibited in a separate building near the Pergamon Museum. Admission on week-days 11-1.30, by application to the Director.

GROUND FLOOR (mostly originals). To the left are *Assyrian Alabaster
Stabs* from the palaces of King Assur-Nasir-Pal (885-860 B.C.) and Sennacherib (705-681 B.C.) at Kalah and Nineveh (the modern Nimroud and
Konyunjik), with reliefs of winged deities, kings, hunting and battle scenes,
and processions. Niche A: Early Babylonian inscriptions (ca. 3000 B.C.)
and statuettes, objects from S. Babylonian crematoria. Niche B. Babylonian, Assyrian, and Persian stone seals (the earliest in the shape of
cylinders; including some of the Babylonian King Merodachbaladan
(714). Niche C. Assyrian bull-monument to King Sargon (722-705),
from Cyprus. Niche D. in a case. Relief of Sennacherib and his favourite

NATIONAL GALLERY

First Floor

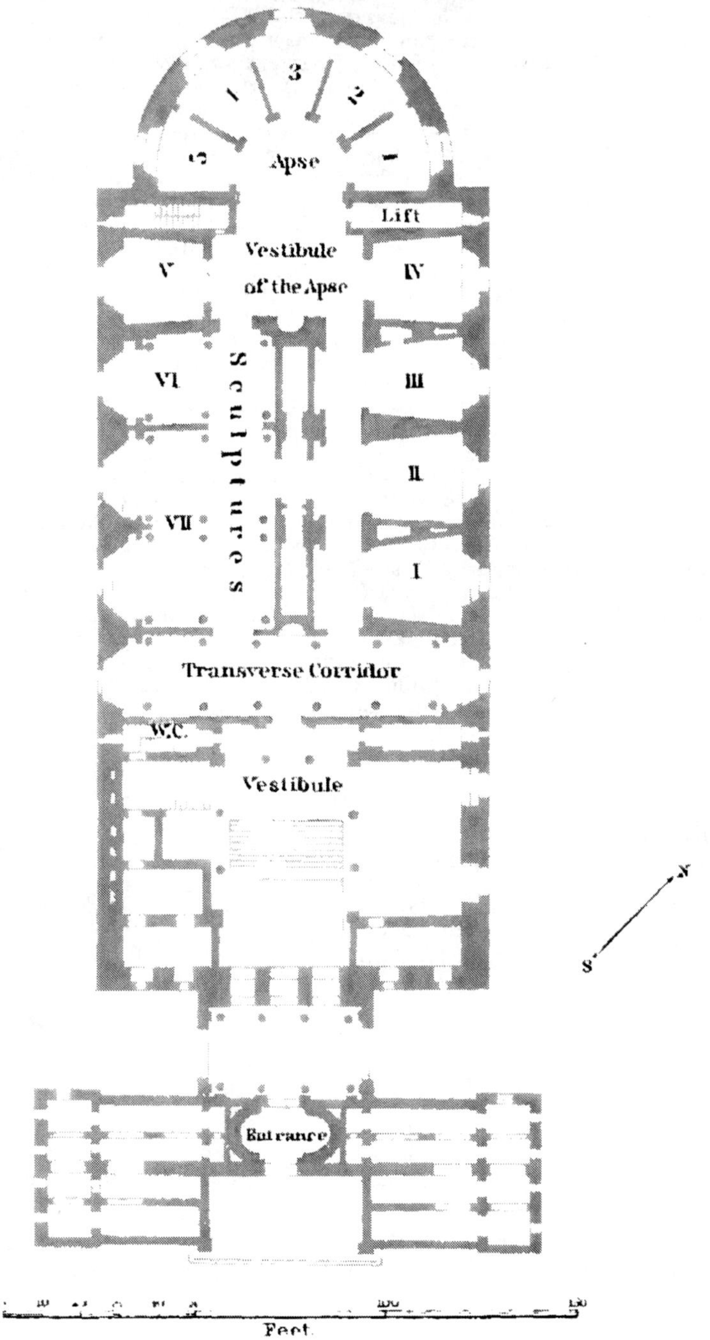

Apse

3

1   2

9   1

Vestibule
of the Apse

Lift

V   IV

Sculptures

VI   III

II

VII   I

Transverse Corridor

W.C.

Vestibule

N

S

Entrance

Feet

horse. Before the partition-walls: fragment of an ancient Babylonian memorial stone with a relief of the primæval king Gudea, Babylonian tiles (from Tello) with cuneiform inscriptions dating back to 3000 B.C.; tile with the stamp of Nebuchadnezzar (604-561) — At the end of Room I.: Punic tomb-stone, with Latin and Punic inscriptions, two colossal lions from Sendjeih (see below); in front, fragment of a colossal statue of King Panammu from N Syria (ca 720 B C.); statue of the God Hadad, with ancient Aramaic inscription, to the right, memorial stone of the Armenian King Rusas I (ca 720) — On the right side of the room are the so-called *Hittite Sculptures*, discovered in 1888-91 in N Syria (Sendjerli) and Asia Minor, some dating from between 1000 and 2000 B C. These are mainly mural reliefs (lion-hunt; deities with animals' heads), several bear ancient Aramaic inscriptions (King Barrakub with attendants), wine vessel, double sphinx as base of a column. — In the middle: cast of a diorite slab found in 1901 at Susa, with the laws of King Hammurabi (ca. 2500 B C.), the oldest existing civil code (original in the Louvre), eight enamelled slabs of brick with animals, from a triumphal avenue at Babylon Monument of victory of the Assyrian king Asarhaddon (681-668) — On the STAIRCASE are casts of Assyrian monuments, chiefly from Nimroud.

FIRST FLOOR To the left, casts of antiquities from Assyria, Phœnicia, and S. Arabia; to the right, casts from Cyprus, Persia, and Kommagene in Syria, and also of Hittite sculptures (see above). Among the most valuable originals are (in Niche Γ, to the left) the terracotta tablets found at El-Amarna in Central Egypt, consisting of letters addressed by Asiatic princes (one being from Jerusalem) and Egyptian vassals to the Pharaohs Amenophis III and IV. (ca 1400 B C) Niche G: Babylonian terracotta tablets (commercial documents, list of words, ground-plan of a palace). Niche H: Antiquities from Palmyra (3rd cent. A D); seals from N. Syria, Cyprus, and Chaldæa. Niche J: Leaden coffin from Jerusalem; Armenian bronzes To the right (Niches K and L) Sculptures (and casts) from the tomb of King Antiochus I. of Kommagene (69-34 B.C.). In the centre, Babylonian inscribed cylinders, particularly cylinders commemorating the buildings of Nebuchadnezzar (604-562) and Nabonedus (555-538): terracotta dishes with magic spells.

d The National Gallery.

ADMISSION, see p 38 Lift to the upper stories see p 87 — The official *Catalogue* (1908, 1¼ *M*) includes also works which are not exhibited. The large edition (2½ *M*) also contains short biographical and other notices and 300 illustrations The names of the artists and the subjects represented are given on each work

To the E. of the New Museum, in the centre of a square surrounded with Doric colonnades and embellished with flower-beds, rises the *National Gallery* (Pl. R. 26), designed by *Staler* in accordance with a plan of Frederick William IV., and built by *Strack* in 1866-76. The building is of red sandstone, and erected in the form of a Corinthian temple, 206 ft. long and 102 ft. wide, elevated on a basement 39 ft. in height. At the S. end is a portico of eight columns, and at the N. a semicircular apse. The sculptures are by *M. Schulz*, *Calandrelli*, and *Moser*. At the top of the imposing flight of steps in front of the S façade is an *Equestrian Statue of Frederick William IV.*, by Calandrelli (1886), with allegorical a_ ı.   ʃ . ᴵ.   ı   ı'   the pedestal.   ˢ ʸ.   ᵖ .   ..   ı   .   .ᵘ   aced in the gardens near the Museum. In front, by the fountain: *Max Kruse*, Messenger bringing the news of the victory of Marathon. To the left: +*Louis Tuaillon*, Amazon on horseback, *Heinrich Baucke*, Victorious barbarian; *Karl Janssen*, Woman breaking stone, *Louis Sussmann-Hellborn*, Drunken Faun. To the right: *Max Klein*, Fountain-group (marble); *August Kraus*, Ball-thrower, *Nikolaus Friedrich*, Archer; *Erich Hosel*, Hun on horseback: *Adolf Brütt*, Saved.

The collection in the National Gallery, the nucleus of which was formed by 262 pictures bequeathed by Consul J. H. Wagener (d. 1861), now contains more than 1100 paintings and cartoons, 233 sculptures, and 30,000 drawings and water-colours: all by masters, chiefly German, of the 19th and 20th centuries.

The entrance is under the outside flight of steps.

First Floor.

Vestibule. Marble sculptures: 46. *Albert Wolff*, Dionysos and Cupid: 111. *Tieck* and *Wittig*, Schinkel, 49. *E. Herter*, Dying Achilles Paintings (to the right) 272 *Gustav Richter*, The daughter of Jairus; 24. *Bendemann*, Babylonian Captivity. — To the left is the staircase to the second floor (p. 89); the door in the middle leads to the —

Transverse Corridor Paintings: to the right, 667. *Bruno Piglhein*, Moritur in Deo, 520. *Karl Becker*, Carnival in the Doge's Palace at Venice; 485 *Eduard von Gebhardt*, Ascension.

Bronze Sculptures, beginning to the left of the entrance to Room VII · 67. *Johannes Götz*, Boy balancing himself; 35. *Robert Toberentz*, Shepherd reposing: *108. *Adolf v. Hildebrand*, Arnold Böcklin, the painter; 8. *August Kiss*, Return from the hunt (high relief); 107. *A. v. Hildebrand*, General Bœyer; 119. *Fritz Klimsch*, Dancing girl: 221. *Ludwig Vordermeyer*, Cock. — In the middle. 37. *Leopold Rau*, Youth and sphinx, *152. *Hugo Lederer*, Bowl with centaurs; 38. *Leopold Rau*, Nature giving and refusing; 121. *August Gaul*, Two pelicans; 225. *Wilhelm Zügel*, Pelican; above, 117 *Theodor von Gosen*, Violin-player, 141. *Gustav Blaeser*, Statuette of K. Fr. Lessing, the painter. 122. *Ernst Moritz Geyger*, Youth with mirror, *82. *Franz Stuck*, Athlete. — 126 *Nicolaus Geyger*, Head of an old woman; 88. *Rudolf Maison*, Roman augur (painted terracotta); 84. *Georg Busch*, Girl praying (wood), 217. *Ignatius Taschner*, Parsifal; 51. *Karl Schlüter*, Portrait-bust of his wife; 166. *E. M. Geyger*, Ideal bust: 145. *Hermann Prell*, Prometheus — In the middle: 30. *Theodor Kalide*, Bacchante on a panther (marble); — 179. *Christian Rauch*, Bust of Staegemann, 25. *Reinhold Begas*, Mercury and Psyche (marble); 65. *Rauch*, P. C. W. Beuth. The rooms to the left of this hall contain the sculptures in marble (p. 88), those to the right the paintings.

Room I. *Arnold Böcklin*, 831. Portrait of a lady, 523. Hermit, 881. Descent from the Cross (1876), *772. Portrait of himself, with Death playing the violin. — *Bocklin*, ¯747. Spring, *448. Fields of the Blessed, *746. Billows. — *Bocklin*, *883. J. von Kopf, the sculptor, 635. Pietà; *828. *Hans von Marées*, Heger, the painter (1860); *882. *Bocklin*, Centaur and nymph.

Room II. To the right, *H. von Marées*, 955. St. Martin, 957. Roman vigna; above. *Anselm Feuerbach*, *473 Medea (sketch for the painting at Munich), *905. The artist's stepmother, 904. Spring (1878), ¯474. Battle of Amazons (sketch for the picture at Nuremberg); *Victor Müller*, 849. Little Snow-white and the seven dwarfs, 999. Salome with the head of John the Baptist; *903 *A. Feuerbach*, Mountain-scene near Castel Toblino. — 776. *H. von Marees*, St George; 773. *Hugo Habermann*, A child of sorrows; *775. *A. Feuerbach*, Portrait of himself.

Room III. To the right, 658. *Olaf Jernberg*, Harvest time; above, 750. *Max Koner*, Ernst Curtius, the philologist; *87. *Eduard von Gebhardt*, Last Supper: — 447. *Gregor von Bochmann*, Dutch ship-yard: 784. *Karl Bantzer*, Celebration of the Lord's Supper in Hesse: 639. *Richard Friese*, Elks fighting; — 779. *Eugen Kampf*, Village in the Eifel; above, 714 *Hans von Volkmann*, Vernal airs; 1034 *Karl Vinnen*, Evening; 1004. *Peter Philippi*, The visit; above 524 *Ludwig von Gleichen-Russwurm*, Idyl

Room IV. To the right, 678. *Gustav Schönleber*, Autumnal storms near Rapallo; *472. *Franz von Lenbach*, Bismarck. — 841. *H. Herrmann*, Fishing village: *F. von Lenbach*, 836. R. Begas the sculptor, 455 Marshal Moltke.

Vestibule of the Apse. Sculptures: 57 *Julius Moser*, Cupid disarmed; 56. *Rudolf Schweinitz*, Cupid in danger; 40. *Karl Cauer*, The witch: 24. *Edvard Mayer*, Mercury and Argus. — In the Apse are five radiating cabinets (to the right by the first is the lift, p. 93).

Cab 1. To the right, 843. *P. Burnitz*, Landscape in the Taunus; 631. *T. Schmitson*, Marble quarries of Carrara; 783. *E Jettel*, Hungarian landscape with bathing children; 728. *T. Schmitson*, Horses in the Puszta; *Karl Schuch*, 1069. Landscape, 1071. Still-life. — 718. *H. Darnaut*, Landscape in Lower Austria; 612 *Marie von Parmentier*, Dieppe.

Cab. 2. To the right, 1031. *H. Thoma*, The Rhine near Sackingen: ¯545. *Fritz von Uhde*, Saying grace ('Komm, Herr Jesu, sei unser Gast'); 1108. *Ed. von Gebhardt*, Burgomaster Woitmann; 896. *W. von Diez*, Dead roe; ¯1110. *Fr. Boehle*, Portrait. — 489. *W. von Diez*, Sylvan festivity.

Cab. 3 735. *H. Linku....He r.. t.a u.n..... ..l..... 755. Karl Stauffer-b.....t..ssa.. t. .t.a.. th. .author. 787 G.....l Max,*

The sisters; *848. *W. Trübner*, Karl Schuch the painter; 879. *G von Bochmann*, Reapers, 799. *Joh Sperl*, Spring; 1105. *F. von Lenbach*, Bismarck (crayon). — 655. *Ludwig Dill*, Dutch canal; above, 749 *Franz von Lenbach*, Prince Hohenlohe. 796. *L. Eysen*, The artist's mother, 916. *Karl Haider*, Schliersee; above, 770. *Hans Thoma*, Scene in the Black Forest with herd of goats; 782. *W. Trübner*, On the sofa; 722. *Gustav Schönleber*, Weir on the Enz near Besigheim; *790. *F. von Lenbach*, Theodor Mommsen; *1003. *Bernhard Pankok*, Portrait; above, 1078. *W von Diez*, St. George (sketch).

Cab. 4. *Wilhelm Leibl*, *945. Girl's head, 831. Peasant boy; above, 1021. *Karl Schuch*, Still-life; *W. Leibl*, *745. Women of Dachau, *946. Burgomaster Klein; above, 1020 *Schuch*, Still-life; 949. *F. von Lenbach*, Temple of Vesta at Rome; — *800. *Sperl*, Rustic interior; 852 *Theodor Alt*, Rudolph Huth in his studio; *Leibl*, *771. Hunter, *947. Woman of Dachau with her child; 1070. *Schuch*, Still-life; 798. *Sperl*, Farmhouse; 788. *Leibl*, Portrait (1870)

Cab. 5. 723. *Dora Hitz*, Portrait of a little girl; above, 768. *Skarbina*, Evening in the village; *592. *Max Liebermann*, Flax-barn in Laren (Holland); 833. *Reinhold Lepsius*, Prof. von Gneist, the jurist. — 1103 *M. Liebermann*, Eduard Grisebach, the poet (crayon); above, 938 *Friedrich Kallmorgen*, St Michael's Church at Hamburg; *Liebermann*, *781 Shoemaker's workshop, 668. Girls plucking geese; 839. *F Kallmorgen*, Going to work

Room V. To the right, *754. *Walter Leistikow*, Lake in the Grunewald; above, 1052. *H Zügel*, Cattle on a sunny pasture; — 840. *Robert Weise*, Lady in an autumnal landscape.

The next two rooms contain sculptures and a few paintings.

Room VI. Marble sculptures: 23. *Chr. Rauch*, Female bust; *Johann von Kopf*, 62. Emperor William I, 104. Empress Augusta; *11. *Rauch*, Frederick Tieck, the sculptor; 19. *Ludwig Wichmann*, T. Chr. Feilner, the manufacturer; 10. *August Kiss*, Bust of himself; 18. *Gustav Blaser*, Hospitality; 72. *Karl Begas*, Faun with the infant Bacchus.

Room VII. Northern Section. To the right: *475. *A. Feuerbach*, Concert. Sculptures: *A Hildebrandt*, *168. Werner von Siemens, *146. M. Pettenkofer, the chemist, 45. Young man; 79. *A. Brütt*, Eve with her children; *169. *Hildebrandt*, Theod. Heyse, the philologist; 132. *G. Lund*, Psyche lamenting; *155. *C. A. Bermann*, Franz von Lenbach, the painter, 54. *K. Begas*, Hans von Marées, the painter. — Southern Section. 808. *Count L von Kalckreuth*, The Château of Klein-Oels in Silesia Sculptures: *Reinhold Begas*, *154. Frau Augusta Hopten 76. Bismarck, 39. Moltke, *171. *H Kaufmann*, St. George.

We now return to the vestibule, and ascend the staircase to the second floor. — On the STAIRCASE is a frieze in stucco by *Otto Geyer*, representing the growth of German civilisation from the time of Arminius the Cheruscan down to the Franco-Prussian war in a series of portrait-groups. On the walls are hung: *207. *K. F Lessing*, Huss before the stake; *452 *A Feuerbach*, Plato's banquet; 537. *K von Piloty*, Death of Alexander the Great (unfinished)

SECOND FLOOR.

VESTIBULE. Paintings: 514. *Gabriel Max*, Christ healing a sick child; *343. *Moritz von Schwind*, The rose; 835. *A. Feuerbach*, Reminiscence of Tivoli — Sculptures: 158. *A. Brütt*, Diana; *Aug. Gaul*, *165. Lion (bronze), 231. Sheep reposing (limestone); 234. *Aug. Hudler*, The dreamer (bronze)

CUPOLA SALOON. In the middle: *73. *Gottfried Schadow*, Crown Princess Luise and her sister Frederica (plaster model for the marble group in the Royal Palace, p 68) 247, 248. *Bernhard Plockhorst*, Portraits of Emperor William 1. and Empress Augusta; *Werner Schuch*, 550. General Zieten in the battle at Katholisch-Hennersdorf, 551. Seydlitz at Rossbach. — The frieze in the vaulting, by *August von Heyden*, represents the signs of the zodiac. The four lunettes above the doors, scenes from the history of German art, are by the same artist: Emp Henry II. laying the foundation-stone of the cathedral of Bamberg; Dürer painting a portrait of Emp Maximilian, while Kunz von der Rosen entertains the emperor with a song; Contest of the singers at the Wartburg in Thuringia; Adam Krafft, the sculptor, in his workshop.

We begin to the right, postponing the inspection of the Menzel and Cornelius Saloons to the end.

SIDE ROOM I. This room contains almost exclusively gouaches, water-colours, and drawings by *Adolf von Menzel*, comprising those of the 'Children's Album'. We may also notice two studies of hands, a church-interior (sermon), and the view of the Hildebrand-Strasse from Menzel's studio

CORRIDOR (chiefly masters of the Dusseldorf School of the middle of the 19th cent.). To the left: 518. *Claus Meyer*, Dice-players; opposite, 664. *Chr. L Bokelmann*, Alone, to the left 392. *K. Fr. Lessing*, Landscape in the Eifel; *500 *Franz Defregger*, Borrowed plumes (der 'Salon-Tiroler'); 506. *Andreas Achenbach*, Dutch harbour; to the right 155 *Rudolph Jordan*, The widow's consolation; *Benjamin Vautier*, 565. On the sick-bed, 358 The first dancing lesson

SIDE ROOM II. First Section (Munich School). To the left, 1030. *A Teichler* Forest of Fontainebleau 315 *Fr Schlich* Evening scene, above *Fran Adam*, Retreat of the French army from Russia; 400. *Defregger*, Return of the Tyrolese landsturm in 1809; 897. *Otto Dörr*, The Elbe near Bethin; 1075. *A. von Ramberg*, Werther and Lotte; 465 *Ad Lier*, Evening on the Isar — Second Section (Düsseldorf School)· to the left, 334. *A. Schrödter*, Don Quixote; 399. *Oswald Achenbach*, Market-place at Amalfi; *Julius Hubner*, 530 Gottfr. Schadow, 932 Lessing, Sohn, and Hildebrand, the painters; *3. *Andr. Achenbach*, Evening at Scheveningen; *J P Hasenclever*, 108 Reading-room, 109 Wine-tasting in the cellar; *287 *W. von Schadow*, Half-length portrait of a lady; 118. *Rud Henneberg*, The pursuit of fortune (on the wall) — Third Section (Frankfort and Weimar Schools): 406. *Heinr. Dreber*, Landscape with hunt of Diana; 571. *K. Hausmann*, Pilgrims in the Campagna, above, 760. *Hausmann*, Galileo before the Council at Rome, 1633 (sketch); 1014 *H. Schillbach*, Landscape near the Wetterhorn, *K. Buchholz*, *886. Spring, 885. Scene in the Harz Mts., 1054. *Peter Janssen*, Portrait

CAB 1 (Dresden School, beginning and middle of 19th cent.)· 907 *K. D. Friedrich*, Landscape in the Giant Mts.; above, *1005. *Ferd. von Rayski*, Count H Einsiedel (1855). — 939 *G. Kersting*, The painter K D Friedrich in his studio; 997. *Paul Mohn*, Sunday morning in spring, near Dresden; above, 1068 *Theod. Grosse*, Portrait of a lady; *K F. Friedrich*, 906. Woman at the window, 78. (above) Moonrise on the sea, 480 *Leon Pohle*, Ludwig Richter, the painter; *1015. *Unknown Master*, Wilh and Rud. Schadow about 1810 in the garden of San Francesco near Naples.

CAB. 2 (Munich School, beginning and middle of 19th cent.): 1055 *W. von Kobell*, Portrait of himself; 17. *H. Burkel*, Kermess in Tyrol; 123 *Peter Hess*, Feast of St Leonard on the Schliersee; 230 *H. Monten*, Finis Poloniae — 48. *H. Burkel*, Landscape near Velletri. — *K Spitzweg*, 847. Street in Venice, 1025 Women's bathing-place at Dieppe *846. His reverence (sketch), no number, The poor poet: above, 282 *K. Rottmann*, Battlefield of Marathon

CAB 3 (Vienna School, beginning and middle of 19th cent.). *Moritz von Schwind*, 794. Adventure of Binder, the painter, 793 Farewell at day-break, 795. The Duchess of Orleans visiting the artist, 1072 The watchman· *1028 *Ed von Steinle*, The artist's daughter; *900. *Erasmus Engert*, Garden in a Vienna suburb — 682 *Aug. von Pettenkofen*, Gipsies; *Ferd. Waldmüller*, *1040. View of Ischl (1838), 1042. The artist's aunt, 1043. Early spring in the Forest of Vienna, 733 Return from the kermess, 1039. Mother and child, *1041. Scene from the Prater at Vienna

CAB. 4. Almost exclusively works by the Berlin painter *Karl Blechen:* 1066. Ruined tower with dragon: above, 877. Park with girls bathing, *765 View of houses and gardens, above, 865. Castle by the sea 878. Portrait of himself· 616. 618. Campagna landscapes 859 Faun sleeping; 615 Camp of the Semnones on the

NATIONAL GALLERY
Second Floor

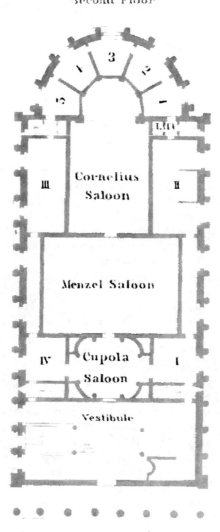

Cornelius Saloon

Menzel Saloon

Cupola Saloon

Vestibule

Müggel-See; 763 Forge near Eberswalde; '752 Palm-house on the Pfauen-Insel; 857. Lightning. Also, 28. 29. *Ed. Biermann*, Tyrolese landscapes.

Cab. 5 (Berlin School, beginning and middle of 19th cent.): to the right, 22. *K. Begas the Elder*, Useless labour; to the left, *Franz Krüger*, 724. Ride of Prince Wilhelm accompanied by the painter, 609. Prince Augustus of Prussia, 190. Emp. Nicholas of Russia, above, 574. *K. F. Schinkel*, Gothic cathedral — 741. *Ed. Meyerheim*, Skittle-players; above, 189. *F. Krüger*, Horses in the stable; 933 *J. E. Hummel*. The cutting of the granite basin in the Lustgarten at Berlin; 224 *Ed. Meyerheim*, Champion-shot, — 910 *Ed. Gaertner*, The Berlin Guard-House with the statue of Scharnhorst, 935. *J. E. Hummel*, Chess-players.

Side Room III (Berlin School). First Section: to the left, 736 *Alb Brendel*, Sheep in a stable; 330. *Jul. Schrader*, Consul Wagener (p. 86); 136. *Ed Hildebrandt*, The castle of Kronborg near Helsingor; 884. *Ad Brendel*, Summer landscape; above, 855. *Bennewitz v. Loefen*, Woodland scene, 457 *Ed Meyerheim*, Story-teller on the bleaching-ground· 851 *K Begas the Elder*, The artist's parents; 42. *A. Brendel*, Return to the village; 425 *Ed. Magnus*, Jenny Lind. — Second Section: to the left, 531. *Paul Meyerheim*, Menagerie; above, 453 *Alb Hertel*, Sea-shore near Genoa; *1047. Fritz Werner*, The librarian, 546. *Count F von Harrach*, Fallen, above, 96. *H. F. Gude*, Norwegian coast; 1048. *F. Werner*, The taxidermist; 649 *E Henseler*, Hoffmann von Fallersleben, the poet. — Third Section: *Ludwig Knaus*, *488. Herm. von Helmholtz, the physiologist. 941 The sharpers, 940 (above), Solomonic wisdom, *487. Theodor Mommsen, the historian, 1016 *Herm. Schnee*, Stol-berg in the Harz. *420. *G. Spangenberg*, Procession of death, 629. *Gust. Richter*, Portrait of himself; *169. *L Knaus*, Children's festival; above, 547. *Louis Douzette*, Alt-Prerow; 913. *Karl Gussow*, Portrait.

Corridor to the left, 1010 *Jos. Scheurenberg*, Rustic merry-making in the 18th cent.; 91. *Karl Grueb*, Rood-loft of Halberstadt Cathedral; to the right, 628 *Ed. Magnus*, Portrait; 466 *J Scheu-renberg*, Lord's Day; to the left, 670 *Ant von Werner*, Military quarters before Paris in 1871; 937. *Jul. Jacob the Younger*, Old cemetery in Berlin.

Side Room IV contains paintings by *Adolf von Menzel* (p 92), chiefly of the years 1840-60, comprising several of his best works. To the left, *845 The balcony room (1845); *984. Théâtre du Gym-nase (1856); '977. The artist's bedroom (1847), ¯976. Evening party; above, *989. Portrait of a lady. — 988. Back premises and court; above, 978 Man resting, '985. The ball supper (1878); above, 993. Horse's head; 986. Building round with willows. 1845 — ¯780 The Potsdam Railw   abou 970 Head in profile 982 study of clouds; *1107. Palace garden of Prince Albert (1846); above, 981. Falcon pursuing a dove (prize shield for a shooting competition); 987. Wall of a studio; 991. Torch-light procession of students, above, 980. Portrait of C. H. Arnold. — 995. *Ed. Meyerheim*, Portrait of Menzel when a youth

Returning to the Cupola Room, we now enter the —

MENZEL SALOON. The upper parts of the walls are decorated by *Ed. Bendemann* with allegorical figures symbolizing the creation of a work art. The room contains chiefly battlepieces and portraits Much the finest are those by *A von Menzel:* to the right, *218. Frederick II.'s round table at Sanssouci (1850); '219. Flute-concert at Sanssouci (1852); ¯975. Frederick addressing his generals before the battle of Leuthen (unfinished); 220. Rolling-mill (1875); on stands in the middle· to the left, ¯490. Departure of King William I. for the army in 1870; to the right, *481. Coronation of King William I. at Königsberg in 1861 (sketch for the painting p 68) and studies and sketches for it. *20. *Reinh. Begas*, Bust of Menzel. — To the left: 52. *W Camphausen*, Duppel after its taking in 1864, 552. *J Scheurenberg*, Zeller the philosopher, 600. *Werner Schuch*, Equestrian portrait of Emp. William II.; 567. *Franz Adam*, Cavalry attack at Mars-la-Tour (1870); above, 527. *Fritz Werner*, Vivandière in the Seven Years' War; 446. *F. Adam*, Cavalry attack at Sedan (1870); 602. *Heinrich von Angeli*, Emp. William I.

CORNELIUS SALOON The wall-paintings, by *Peter Janssen*, depict the Sway of Cupid, the Seasons and the Periods of the Day; in the spandrels, Olympus, the realms of Neptune and Hades. This room contains *Cartoons by *Peter v. Cornelius* for the Campo Santo, a royal burial-place planned by Frederick William IV. (see p. 63). Soon after his removal to Berlin (1841) Cornelius commenced this work, and he was engaged upon it down to the day of his death (1867). The scenes were intended to represent in connection with the Apocalypse, the Redemption of Man, the Incarnation, the Sway of the Church, and Last Judgment. Above each painting is a lunette, and below is a narrow painting in which the chief subject is illustrated and explained, while between the principal paintings were to be placed eight small groups, typifying the Beatitudes of the Sermon on the Mount. The finest of the principal paintings are the *Apocalyptical Riders (to the right, No. 6; one of the most remarkable creations of the artist), the Resurrection of the Body, and the Descent of the Holy Ghost. While in these we admire the richness of conception, the dramatic life, and the boldness of the drawing, the groups of the Beatitudes appeal to us by the beauty and compactness of their outlines, no less than by the expressiveness of their figures. On the S. wall are ¯Five cartoons for the frescoes in the town-hall at Aix-la-Chapelle by *Alfred Rethel* ·scenes from the life of Charlemagne . On the walls of the apse are five decorative biblical landscapes by *Joh. Wilh. Schirmer;* in front (No. 15) a colossal bust of Cornelius by *Wittig;* to the right and left, marble busts of Emp. William I. by *Jos. von Kopf* (103) and of Empress Augusta by *Bernh. Römer* (70).

The third floor is reached by a marble staircase, on the walls of which are: *84. *Louis Gallait.* The last hour of Count Egmont; 661. *Luis Alvarez,* Philip II. on his rock-seat near the Escorial; *443. *H. Makart,* Venice doing homage to Catharine Cornaro, Queen of Cyprus; 996. *Francesco Paolo Michetti,* The daughter of Jorio.

THIRD FLOOR. (Lift, see p. 87.)

The ANTEROOM (I) is decorated with good mural paintings by *Paul Meyerheim,* representing nature at the different seasons (covered at present). This room contains chiefly paintings and sculptures of the early 19th century. Paintings: to the left, *898. *J. G. v. Edlinger,* Count Preysing; 605. *Joh. Heinr. Tischbein,* Family group; *568. *Anton Graff,* Portrait of himself; 606. *J. H. Tischbein,* Councillor Ch. Fr. Robert; *218. *Tassaert,* General Zieten (bronze bust). — *561. *A. Graff,* Portrait of himself; *503. *Friedr. Tischbein,* Lute-player; 484. *A. Graff,* Female portrait; 197, 198. *Gottfr. Schadow,* Frederick William III. and Queen Luise (bronze busts); 551. *J. A. Koch,* Sabine landscape; 1060. *J. Schnorr von Carolsfeld,* Annunciation; above, *498. *Wilh. Schadow,* Thorvaldsen, Wilhelm, and Rudolph Schadow; *856. *Joh. Jac. Biedermann,* Landscape near Partenkirchen; 413. *J. A. Koch,* The convent of San Francesco di Civitella in the Sabine Mts. — *144. *G. Schadow,* Princess Frederica of Prussia (terracotta bust); *593. *A. Graff,* Henriette Herz; 908. *Heinrich Füger,* Princess Galizin; 577. *Anna Dor. Therbusch,* Henriette Herz as Hebe; *196. *G. Schadow,* Bust of Crown Princess Luise (plaster). — 1081. *Rafael Mengs,* Portrait of himself; 380.

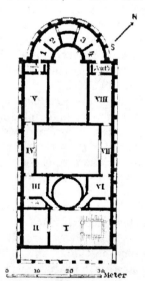

Fr. G. Weitsch, Alexander von Humboldt; 525. *Ed. von Heuss,* Peter von Cornelius; 366. *K. Chr. Vogel von Vogelstein,* Ludwig Tieck, the poet; 525b. *Ed. von Heuss,* Friedr. Overbeck, the painter. — 201, 202. *Gottfr. Schadow,* Designs for monuments to Prince Leopold of Dessau and Zieten. — Smaller sculptures by *G. Schadow* and others.

Room II, to the left, contains Frescoes from the history of

Joseph, which were skilfully transferred hither from Rome in 1888. They were executed in 1816-18 for the Prussian consul general Bartholdy in Rome, by the most eminent German artists then resident in that city, and formerly adorned a room in his house, the Casa Zuccari (since also called Casa Bartholdy). They are interesting as being the first important creation of modern German painting. The Interpretation of Pharaoh's dream (No. 587) and the *Recognition of the brothers (585) are by *Peter von Cornelius:* the Selling of Joseph (581), and the Seven Years of Famine (588), by *Fried. Overbeck;* Joseph and Potiphar's wife (583), and the Seven Years of Plenty (586), by *Philipp Veit;* Joseph interpreting dreams in prison (584), and the Brothers bringing the bloody coat to Jacob (582), by *Wilh. von Schadow.* — Sculptures: *Gottfr. Schadow,* '99 Countess Lichtenau (marble bust), 212 Girl sleeping (plaster), 12. Girl resting, *47. Goethe (marble bust), 26. *Ant. Canova,* Hebe; *219. *Tassaert,* Moses Mendelssohn, the philosopher (bronze bust); 167. *Friedr. Hagemann,* Kant, the philosopher (bronze bust)

A passage (in which is No. *109. The return of the miners, a bronze relief by *C. Meunier*) leads to the left from the anteroom to —

Room III. containing works by pre-impressionistic foreign artists. Paintings: to the left, *912. *Francisco Goya,* Bull-fight; above, 892 *Thomas Couture,* Female head; 891 *Gustave Courbet,* The wave (1870); 690 *John Constable,* Village on the Stour; above, 751. *R. P. Bonington,* Fishing boats — 150 *Jul. Lagae,* Léon Lequim (bronze bust), 737. *Narc. Diaz,* Sylvan scene, 692. *Courbet,* Mill-dam; *807. *Ch. Daubigny,* Spring: *Constable,* 691. Mill on the Stour, *889 (above), The artist's house on Hampstead Heath; 173 *Jul. Lagae,* Juliaan Dillens the sculptor (bronze bust). — 901 *H. Fantin-Latour,* Portrait of himself; *732. *J. F. Millet,* November evening, 705 *H. Fantin-Latour,* The artist's wife; — *911. *Fr. Goya,* Maypole; *890. *G. Courbet,* Eagle-owl tearing a roe; *893. *H. Daumier,* Don Quixote and Sancho Panza. In the middle, *183. *Aug. Rodin,* The thinker (bronze, a colossal replica stands before the Pantheon at Paris). — The adjoining —

Corridor (IV) also contains works by foreign artists. Paintings: to the left, 702 *Gugl. Ciardi,* Canal Grande at Venice; 684. *Gari Melchers,* The family. 711. *E. Farasyn,* The widow; 709 *H. W. Mesdag,* Summer evening at Scheveningen; 1051. *Félix Ziem,* View of Venice — To the right, earlier works, mostly Belgian, of the middle of 19th cent.: 742. *François Bossuet,* Before the walls of the Alhambra; *H. Leys,* 210. Dutch party in the 17th cent., 211. Durer drawing Erasmus: 39 *Ferd. de Braekeleer,* Quarrel after the meal. — In the glass-cases, small sculptures by *Dillens. Charpentier, Troubetzkoy, Carriès, Bourdelle, Falguière, Steinlen, Bugatti, Maillol.* At the exit 95. *Thomas Vinçotte,* Catiline (bronze bust)

Room V contains chiefly impressionist French masters and the Felix Konigs collection. To the left: *821. *Anders Zorn*, Maja; *819 *Hans Olde*, Winter sun; *820 *Giovanni Segantini*, Home-coming, 811. *Daubigny*, Landscape; above, 817. *Chr. Landenberger*, Boy bathing; 810 *Emil Claus*, Morning in February, 814. *Adolf Holzel*, Before sunset; 818. *Wilh. Leibl*, The bailiff. — 140 *Charles van der Stappen*, Girl from Zealand (bronze); 1038. *Ed. Vuillard*, View from the window; 738. *Ch. Cazin*, Landscape with Mary Magdalen; *Vuillard*. 1037 The model, 1036. View from the window. — 116. *Aug. Rodin*, Falguière, the sculptor (bronze bust); *998. *Claude Monet*, The church of St. Germain-l'Auxerrois at Paris (1866). *744. *Aug. Sisley*, Snow in spring. *Ed. Manet*, *693. Hot-house, 952. Country-house at Rueil. *Aug. Renoir*, 1073 In summer (girl), 1008. Children's afternoon at Vargemont; 748 *Cam. Pissarro*, Villas near Paris; 694 *Cl. Monet*, Vétheuil-sur-Seine. — *91. *Rodin*, Dalou, the sculptor (bronze bust); *777. *Monet*, Argenteuil; above, *887. *Paul Cézanne*, Still-life; 1095. *E. Degas*, Conversation. In the middle, *Rodin*, 135 Man and his thought (marble), *182. The iron age (bronze).

Cab 1 To the left: 137. *Prince Troubetzkoy*, Bust of Segantini, the painter (bronze) · 809 *Böcklin*, Portrait of Wallenreiter, the singer — 826 a-g *Max Klinger*, Decorative paintings for a villa at Steglitz. — *134. *M. Klinger*, Amphitrite (marble).

Cab 2 Works by foreign masters. To the left, 1085. *Buchan Nisbet*, Autumnal scene; 850. *J. Sorolla y Bastida*, Shore of Valencia. — 829. *R. M. Stevenson*, Jairus Pond; 707. *John Lochhead*, Village in Fifeshire; 1053. *Ign. Zuloaga*, Spanish peasants, *917. *Vilh. Hammershöi*, Sunny room, above, *701. *Giov. Boldini*, Adolf von Menzel. — 94. *Aug. Rivalta*, Hercules conquering the centaur (bronze); *696. *G. Segantini*, Gloomy hours, 93. *Const. Meunier*, The prodigal son (bronze); — 700. *J. Maris*, Dutch canal; above, 699. *Fritz Thaulow*, November in Normandy; *698. *Anders Zorn*, Girl bathing; above, 695 *John Lavery*, Lady in black; 961. *Anton Mauve*, Landscape with cattle.

The *Collection of Drawings, in Cab. 3 and 4, Room VIII, Corridor VII, and Room VI, consists of about 30,000 sketches and water-colours by German, and several hundred by foreign artists of the 19th cent., among whom we may specify *Bellermann, Blechen, Böcklin, Carstens, J. Constable. H. E. Cross, F. Dreber, Feuerbach, Friedrich, Genelli, Greiner, Guys, Knaus, W. v. Kobell, F. Krüger, C. Larsson, Leibl. Liebermann, Menzel, Pfannschmidt, Preller, Rethel, L. Richter, Rodin, Runge, Schnorr von Carolsfeld, Schwind, P. Signac, Const. Somoff, E. von Steinle, A. Th. Steinlen. J. M. Swan. J. Toorop,* etc. Catalogue 2 M. Some of the finest specimens are exhibited

e. The Emperor Frederick Museum.

This museum, situated to the N W of the last-mentioned, is not directly accessible thence, but must be reached by a circuit viâ the Iron Bridge and the Kupfergraben (8 min. from the Old Museum; comp. Plan, p. 55) — Tramways through the Charlotten-Str. (W.) see p 145, through the Museum-Str and from the Kupfergraben see p 70

Admission, see p. 37. — Official Guide (3rd ed , 1905) ¹/₂ *M* Detailed 'Descriptive Catalogue of the Paintings' (6th ed , 1906) 1 *M*, with 81 photographs 10 *M*.

The * ***Emperor Frederick Museum** (Pl. R, 23), situated at the N.W. end of the 'museum island', beyond the Stadtbahn, was built by *Ihne* in 1898-1903 and opened in 1904. Two bridges, from the Monbijou-Strasse (p. 145) and from the street Am Kupfergraben, lead to the entrance, at the N.W. angle, opposite which rises the equestrian *Statue of Emperor Frederick III.*, by Maison. The Italian baroque style has been adopted for the building, the two chief façades of which rise directly from the Spree and the Kupfergraben, while the third is turned towards the Stadtbahn. The corner with the entrance is rounded off into a semicircle; six massive columns support its upper story, which is crowned by the main dome. A smaller dome, above the rear staircase, rises over the centre of the façade towards the Stadtbahn. On the attic are ten statues by *A. Vogel* and *Widemann*, six of which represent the Arts and four the most prominent Art Cities.

The museum contains the sculptures of the Christian epoch, the picture-gallery, and the cabinet of coins, hitherto exhibited in the Old and New Museums. To these have been added collections of early-Christian, Byzantine, Coptic, and Persian-Mohammedan art. The collections are not strictly divided from each other. The 27 rooms and cabinets on the ground floor contain, on the N. side, the early-Christian, Byzantine, Coptic, Romanesque, and Gothic Monuments, on the S. side the German and Italian Sculptures, and the Cabinet of Coins But among the German sculptures a certain number of easel-pictures are exhibited, while all the bronze and most of the marble Italian sculptures are to be found on the first floor In the chief room on the ground floor, moreover, are collected the largest altar-pieces, both plastic and painted. The 45 rooms and cabinets on the first floor are occupied by the picture-gallery: on the N. side the Latin Schools (Italian, French, Spanish), on the S. side the Germanic Schools (Dutch, German, Flemish). Along with the former are exhibited the Italian bronzes, marble sculptures, and glazed terracotta works (Della Robbia); while with the others are shown the collections of James Simon (presented in 1904), Adolph Thiem (acquired in 1904), Wesendonk, and Carstanjen (both on loan).

Ground Floor

The chief entrance admits us to the Great Staircase (Pl. 1), decorated in the style of the time of the Great Elector. In the

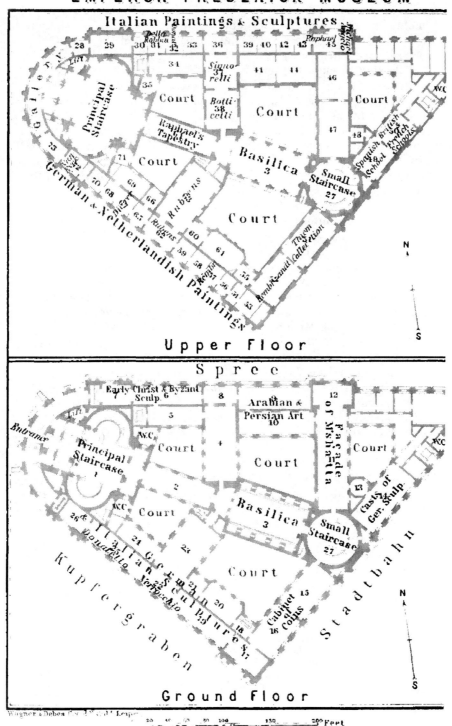

EMPEROR FREDERICK MUSEUM

Italian Paintings & Sculptures

Upper Floor

Ground Floor

middle is a bronze cast of the Statue of the Great Elector by Schluter (see p. 70), on the original pedestal. The stairs and the lift (10 pl., opposite the cloak-room) lead to the picture-gallery (p. 104).

Passing through the corridor (Pl 2), we enter the —

BASILICA (Pl. 3), designed in the style of a Florentine church of the early 16th century. In the centre of the spacious hall stand two ancient columns, one bearing the 'Marzocco', or heraldic lion of Florence, the other the she-wolf of Siena. Beyond them is a lectern with intarsia work (1531), between 'Choir-stalls with intarsia work by *Pantaleone de Marchis* (ca. 1495). On the pillars and in the stained-glass windows are coats of arms of Florentine families (15th and 16th cent.).

The large niches in the walls are occupied by a series of large altar-pieces, painted and carved. To the right. 259. *Begarelli*, Crucifixion, from Modena (ca. 1530); 287. *Giac.* and *Giulio Francia*, Assumption; 130. Ascension, glazed terracotta relief from the studio of the *Della Robbia; 249. Fra Bartolomeo*, Madonna enthroned with saints; 192. Processional Madonna, from the Mark of Ancona (ca. 1500); above, 171. Venetian sepulchral monument (ca. 1530). — To the right and left of the exit, two Venetian sacristy fonts; in the lunette above the door, 205. Bust of Pope Alexander VI (ca. 1500); on the balcony above it, 165. *Tullio* or *Antonio Lombardi*, Two shield-bearers (from the Vendramin tomb in the Frari at Venice). — In the niches of the left side-wall, beginning at the exit: 128a *Giovanni della Robbia*, Pieta, in coloured terracotta; 191. *Paris Bordone*, Madonna enthroned with saints; 118. *Andrea della Robbia*, Madonna enthroned with saints, a glazed altar-piece, dating from the artist's middle period; 1165. *Luigi Vivarini*, Madonna enthroned with saints (1503), *Andrea della Robbia*, Stone altar from Brescia with St. Dorothea. — The door to the left of this niche leads to —

ROOM 4, which contains three Venetian fountains and a prayer-niche from Damascus. To the left are Coptic textiles from Egypt (4-8th cent.), to the right Arabian textiles from Egypt (8-13th cent.). The walls are hung with Oriental tapestry. — The door on the left leads into the —

COPTIC ROOM (5), in which is exhibited a remarkable collection of examples of the art of the Christian inhabitants of Egypt. Most of the work and at the same time the best of it belongs to the early-Christian epoch (3rd-8th cent.).

The wall-cabinet to the right of the entrance contains wood-carvings, paintings on wood, glass vessels, and leather-work. — On the principal wall, to the left, is a beam-head with a carving of Daniel in the lions' den; farther on, Stone head of an emperor, from Keneh (4-5th cent. A D), between terracotta supports for vessels. Then follow numerous examples of Coptic sculpture chiefly sepulchral stelae, to the left of the next pillar, Relief of Christ on horseback between angels. In the course of the room are frames with columns and beams, with chiselled ornaments.

Near the door, fragment of a group of Orpheus; above the door, tutelary goddess of a town (high relief; 6-7th cent.) — The case at the end of the room contains painted terracotta vessels, bronze utensils, ampullæ (several of them representing St Menas between two camels), and terracotta lamps with Christian emblems. — In the first case on the window wall, Carvings on bone (to the left pagan, and to the right Christian subjects), in the second case. Small bronzes (engraved mirrors, engraved silver cross, etc.) — The glass-cases in the middle contain carvings (*e. g.* a battle before a besieged town) and bronze utensils, comprising lamps in the shape of animals. Round the upper part of the walls are hung frames with embroideries (some with representations copied from the antique).

We pass through the door under the tutelary-goddess (see above) into the —

EARLY-CHRISTIAN AND BYZANTINE ROOMS (6 and 7). In the apse, at the extreme end to the left, is a *Mosaic from the Church of *San Michele in Affricisco in Ravenna*, dating from 545 A.D., acquired by King Frederick William IV in 1843

The mosaic represents the youthful Christ, adored by the archangels In the surrounding frieze are the Lamb of God and doves, the symbols of Christ and the apostles. On the triumphal arch, Christ as Judge of the World, surrounded by angels bearing the instruments of the Passion and trumpets Below, SS. Cosmas and Damianus.

In the same room (7) are several early-Christian sarcophagi and fragments of others By the left wall, near the entrance, Sarcophagus with the story of Jonah (3rd-4th cent.); above, Fragments with pastoral scenes. By the window wall, Colossal capital from Constantinople (5th cent.). — Along the side-wall of Room 6, as far as the green pillar of verde antico, is arranged an important collection of early Byzantine sculptures. On the pillars are characteristic Byzantine capitals.

In the first section, End of a sarcophagus from Constantinople, representing Christ between two apostles (4-5th cent.), above, ornamental slab with vase, vine, and drinking peacocks (Syrian, 6th cent.); to the right, below, a game of balls in the shape of a staircase with scenes from the circus. Round the door of Room 5 are grouped several ornamental slabs and architectural fragments; in the pediment a mosaic picture of Christ the Merciful (12th cent.) Beyond the door are various representations of the Madonna in relief, the largest (headless) from Constantinople (10-11th cent.); beside it a smaller Madonna adoring the Child and, as a pendant, the Archangel Michael wearing the imperial insignia. — Farther on, beyond the verde antico column, Mediæval Italian sculptures showing the Oriental-Byzantine influence, mostly of an ornamental character The large, painted Madonna is by Presbyter Martinus (Tuscan; 1199)

The glass-cases contain smaller Byzantine works of art. In the first case (near Room 7) are noteworthy ivory carvings: diptych with Christ between Peter and Paul, and the Virgin between angels (Syro-Egyptian, 6th cent.); scenes from the life of Christ (Roman, 4th cent.); also ornaments, terracotta lamps, and bronze utensils. In the large glass-case are small bronzes and ivory carvings: in the middle, *Pyx with Christ and the apostles (4th cent.), below it, Bronze statuette of St. Peter (Roman, 4th cent.), and numerous lamps with Christian emblems (some in the form of doves), etc. In the middle of the second case is a wax mosaic of the Crucifixion (12th cent), to the left of it, ivory carvings of the 10-12th cent No. 19. Crucifixion. No. 110 Death of the forty martyrs); to the right, Italian ivory carvings in a style resembling the Byzantine, grouped round a large late Byzantine diptych in soapstone.

Room 8; Italian Sculptures of the 13-14th Centuries. Between the windows, a late Gothic chimney-piece from Venice. To the left of the entrance: 28a Head of a bearded prince, one of the rare busts of the Hohenstaufen period; to the right, 28. Bust of a lady, from Scala near Ravello (second half of the 13th cent.). In the corner, *Nicolò Pisano*, Angel of the Annunciation (much injured); to the left of it, 22. *Nicolò Pisano*. St Buonacorso between two angels; above, 24. *Giov. Pisano*, Pietà (lectern; from the pulpit of Pisa cathedral). — Between the doors are several statuettes by *Giov. Pisano:* Madonna, two sibyls (from the pulpit of Pisa cathedral), four prophets (studio works). 25 *Andrea Pisano*, Christ on the cross (litesize): *Pisan School* (about 1380), Annunciation, group with well-preserved old painting. — In the left corner, *Pisan Master of the 14th cent.*, Madonna, painted wooden statue. Near the window, Relief of the Madonna and two mourning figures from Neapolitan tombs of the 14th cent. (Nos. 29, 30): Madonna in alabaster (Sicilian; ca. 1500) — In the glass-cabinet, Gothic ivory carvings (chiefly French): 26 *Nino Pisano*, Alabaster statuette of the Madonna; 80. Madonna of the end of the 13th cent. (French); on the side next the window, three Diptychs with Passion-scenes (14th cent.), on the right side, chiefly non-religious works (mirror-cases, book-covers with love-scenes, etc.). — The door in the Venetian 15th cent. portal leads into —

Room 9, containing Works of Arabian and Persian Art.

On the entrance-wall are inscriptions; in the corner an alabaster wall-fountain with coloured tiles. On the other walls, Carpets of the 14-16th cent., conspicuous among which, in the centre of the long wall, is one with the heraldic dragon of the Ming dynasty of China; on the end-wall, Persian carpet of the early 16th cent. (betraying Chinese influence). In the show-cases are examples of Arabian and Persian industrial art. By the long wall is a large bronze casket inlaid with gold and silver for the preservation of the Koran; in the case to the right, Cover of a similar casket, and numerous book-bindings, two splendid examples of which are in the case on the left. In the other cases are glazed terracotta vessels and fragments of vessels found in Egypt and Asia Minor; in the middle, so-called 'Mosul' vessels of bronze inlaid with gold and silver, at the end, glass vessels, chiefly from Syria.

The door in the long wall leads into —

Room 10, containing the Islamic Collection of F. Sarre (on loan). Guide, with a survey of the Persian-Islamic art. 1 M.

To the left on the principal wall: Oriental metal works for Christian churches, above, Persian embroidery with portrait of a prince (ca. 1700), fine Persian carpet with figures of animals (16th cent.), Mosul bronzes (comp. above); ancient Arabian glass; tomb relief from Palmyra (2nd-3rd cent.) — By the exit-wall: Egyptian prayer-niche in wood with stucco mouldings, potsherds from Fostat (Old Cairo). — Window-wall: Lustred paving-tiles from Persian mosques, fayence and porcelain (partly from China or in the Chinese manner), Mosul bronzes, a large Venetian basin with Arabic inscription; miniature manuscripts and a magnificently bound Koran; on the adjoining screen sketches by the Persian Riza Abassi (17th cent.). — N . . . . osque lamps, mo . .

7

The door in the end-wall leads into —

Rooms 11 and 12, in which the *Façade of the Palace of M'shatta* has been erected, a gift of Sultan Abdul Hamid to Emperor William II. M'shatta ('winter-camp') lies about 30 M. to the E. of the influx of the Jordan into the Dead Sea. The palace was originally a desert-palace of Ghassanide Bedouins and dates from the 4-6th cent. A.D. The smooth upper wall and part of the right side of the chief portal are wanting (comp. the plans and models exhibited in this room). The part of the façade which has been brought to Berlin is completely covered with beautiful ornamentation in pierced work: from vases, beside which stand animals or fabulous beings, spring vines with birds in the branches. The larger left half shows an affinity with antique and Byzantine forms, while the right half, on which are no animals, recalls the Persian art of the Sassanide period — Similar ornamentation appears in the casts from the portals of ecclesiastical buildings in N. Syria, exhibited beside the door to the small staircase (see below).

The door in the end-wall opens upon the Small Staircase (Pl. 27), from which doors lead into the Basilica and the Cabinet of Coins. At the sides of the staircase ascending to the picture-gallery (p 101) are marble statues of Venus and Mercury by *Jean-Baptiste Pigalle*, from Sanssouci (p. 193).

We pass through the door straight opposite into the show-rooms of the ˣCabinet of Coins (Pl. 15, 16). The collection itself, the students' room, and the technical library are accommodated on the sunk-floor. Interested visitors may have access to particular sections of the collection by personal application to the director. The collection contains 300,000 coins, comprising 135,000 antique (100,000 Greek and 35,000 Roman) pieces.

The first room (15) affords a survey of the development of coining. Near the entrance is a large glass-case containing money-ingots, the preliminary stage before coined money; to the left, by the wall, are specimens of the earliest Greek coins, and further on is a collection of Roman coins from the earliest heavy cast bronze ingots to the late imperial epoch. Other sections comprise mediæval and modern European coins, German, Brandenburg, and Prussian coins, Oriental coins, and coins now current.

Room 16 Medals. Nearest the door are Italian medals of the 15th century. In the show-case in the centre are medals of the Hohenzollern family; further on come those of the other German princes and of private persons, with numerous matrices in box and pearwood, lithographic stone, and slate. Among the medals of other countries, the modern French specimens are most worthy of note. In the small case by the window to the left are five *Gold medals (rewards of victory, 3rd cent. A.D.) found in Egypt, with portraits of Alexander the Great, his mother Olympias, and the Emp. Caracalla.

The door straight in front leads from Room 16 to the last room of Italian sculpture (Pl. 17, see p. 104), and the door to the right into the German section. The latter gives upon Antroom 18, containing a wall-cabinet in which are various smaller works of art. — Proceeding straight on we enter —

Room 20: German Renaissance Sculptures. The windows contain admirable ⁓Stained Glass from designs by *Hans Baldung Grien* (from a church near Freiburg). By the entrance-wall· *Tyrolese Master* (ca. 1480), Large altar of the Virgin. In the case by the window: Small carvings in mother-of-pearl and wood, *e. g. Swabian School*, Madonna (end of 15th cent). — On the long wall: No. 1222. *Meister von Schoppingen* (School of Soest), Winged altar with the Crucifixion and Passion; to the left, 1235a. *Master of the Glorification of Mary*, Adoration of the Child; to the right, 1235. *Master of the Life of the Virgin*, Virgin with the Holy Women in a garden. Numerous sculptures from the Lower Rhine. On the end-walls: 1205, 1206 *Middle Rhenish Master*, Two large altar panels (ca. 1440); below them to the left, *Lower Rhenish Master*, Madonna and Child. In the case by the window: Ivory carvings in the baroque style and mother-of-pearl carvings. — In the middle of the room, Bronze fountain from the workshop of *Peter Vischer*. The adjoining glass-cabinets contain plaquettes by *Peter Vischer the Younger* and others, and statuettes (632. *Leygebe*, The Great Elector as Bellerophon).

Room 21: German Sculptures of the Renaissance, Baroque, and Rococo Periods. Entrance-wall: 341. *Hans Daucher*, Altar with the Passion, in limestone, 405a. *Peter Flötner* (?), Painted wooden statuette of a boy-musician. — On the rear-wall: Nos. 418, 419 *Jan de Zar*, Painted terracotta busts of Willibald and Anna Imhof (Nuremberg, ca. 1570). At the window, 404. *Georg Labenwolf*, Bust of Frederick II. of Denmark (?). By the exit-wall, *Franconian Master* (ca. 1500-20), Madonna, terracotta statuette (after Cranach); 364a. *Jodocus Vredis* (Westphalian School, ca. 1500), Madonna adored by angels. — In the glass-cabinet in the middle: above, 608. *Konrad Meit* of Worms (ca. 1525), Boxwood bust of a young man; 400a. *Netherlandish Master* (period of Jan van Eyck), Virgin and Child. 588. *Heinrich Hufnagel* (Augsburg, 1432), Silver-gilt figure of the Madonna; 370. *Lower Rhenish Master* (ca. 1430), Madonna with the grapes; below (under No 588). *Ratisbon Master* (ca. 1525), St. Sebastian; reliefs in limestone, alabaster, and soapstone by *Hans Daucher*, *Peter Flötner*, and *Ludwig Krug*

Rooms 23-24: German Sculptures of the Romanesque and Gothic Periods. The chronological arrangement begins at the end of Room 24, where the west gallery from the church of Kloster-Gröningen is built into the wall: Christ among the Apostles (stucco reliefs, 12th cent.) Below, 1216a. *Westphalian School* (ca. 1225), Triptych representing Christ before Caiphas, the Crucifixion, and the Holy Women at the Sepulchre. On the long wall: at the top, 1216b. *Westphalian School* (ca. 1250) Triptych with the Trinity between the Virgin and St John. Lower down, brought from the Schone Brunnen at Nuremberg (end of 14th cent.); 1627. Diptych from Cologne (ca. 1350), Madonna and Crucifixion. In the middle of the long wall: no number, Altar-top in the shape of a clover leaf, with scenes from the Passion, from Quedlinburg; below, no number, Mary with the body of Christ (Austrian, ca. 1420), in limestone, and several terracotta works. Further to the left, *1624. *Bohemian School* (ca. 1350), Madonna enthroned, from Glatz. Beside it on the right, 287. *Nuremberg Master* (end of the 14th cent.), Emp. Charles IV., in sandstone. To the left, 290b. St. Catharine (end of the 14th cent.); 291. *Brandenburg Master*, Statuette of the Madonna.—In the central stained-glass window (French, 13th cent.), Female saint; to the left and right, German medallions of the 12th cent., Expulsion from the Temple, and Mary Magdalen anointing the feet of Christ. In front of the middle window, Processional ass (South-German, 13th cent.; the oldest example known of these figures) The glass-case by the window contains mostly Romanesque ivory carvings, those on the right dating from the Carolingian period and the time of the Saxon emperors, those on the left French-Romanesque works; above, 42. Reliquary (beginning of the 11th cent.)

Room 23 contains sculptures and pictures mostly of the early 15th century. In the middle, Shrine of St. Patroclus, by *Meister Sigefrid* (1313), from Soest. To the left, 1207-1210. *Meister Berthold*, Four pictures from the altar of the Deichsler family at Nuremberg (SS. Elizabeth, Mary, Peter Martyr, and John the Baptist). Between them, 290d. Wooden statue of the Madonna *(South German)*. To the left, below, 1238. *Cologne School* (manner of Meister Wilhelm), Virgin surrounded by female saints. — On the other partition wall, 562. *School of Martin Schongauer*, Winged altar with the Crucifixion.

In the portion of Room 23 leading to the Basilica, the arrangement begins beside the marble portal. To the left and right of it, *School of Michael Pacher*, Statues of saints, richly gilded; *1621-1621c *Hans Multscher*, Eight altar-panels with scenes from the life of the Virgin and the Passion (1437). On the partition walls opposite, to the right, *Bavarian Master* (1516), Winged altar with the Adoration of the Magi; to the left, *333a. *Daniel Mauch* (?), Painted high-relief of the family of Christ; adjoining, *Bavarian Master* (ca. 1530), SS. George and Peter; above, 348 and farther on 342-356 *Adolf Daucher*, Wooden busts from the Fugger Chapel at Augsburg (ca. 1510). — In the second compartment, back-wall to the right: no number, *Veit Stoss*, Coronation of the Virgin; 301-306. Six high reliefs from the Rosary by the same master in the Germanic Museum at Nuremberg: front wall: 563b. 563c. *Bernhard Strigel*, Four saints. Left front wall: *330. *Swabian School* (ca. 1500), Madonna della Misericordia, remarkable for its spiritual and chaste expression. Beside it, 563 d. and 563 a. *Strigel*, Four saints. Back wall, Coronation of the Virgin (*Swabian School;* ca. 1500), 358 Birth of the Virgin (*Swabian School;* ca. 1510). — In the third compartment, right back-wall: 331 *Swabian School* (ca. 1500), Winged altar with the Adoration of the Magi On the right front wall, works by *Tilman Riemenschneider:* No 325 f. Christ appearing to Mary Magdalen (early work); 325 e. Trinity; 325 a. Angels' concert; 321-324. Four saints; on the left wall: 318. Madonna; 313-316. The four Evangelists; 320. Mourning women (from a Passion scene), 325 d. Pietà. On the left back-wall in the style of Riemenschneider: 319. Virgin handing the bottle to the Child.

The two doors at the end of the room lead into the section of *ITALIAN RENAISSANCE SCULPTURE, containing mainly works in painted terracotta and stucco, the works in marble and in glazed terracotta being on the upper floor The arrangement begins at the right end of the suite of rooms with —

ROOM 26: FLORENTINE TERRACOTTAS OF THE EARLY 15TH CENTURY. On the wall opposite the entrance. no number, *Florentine Master* (ca. 1450), Crucifixion; beside it, 151, 152. *School of Siena* (ca. 1440), Annunciation, a group in wood. — On the long wall various works by the so-called *Master of the Pellegrini Chapel* (Verona): Nos. 108, 108a, and 107 (at the window), also (no number) *Jacopo della Quercia,* Madonna and Child.

Room 25 contains chiefly works by DONATELLO and LUCA DELLA ROBBIA and their pupils On a buffet: No. 141. Painted terracotta bust of Giov. Rucellai, on the walls, numerous Madonnas by *Donatello.* In the middle, Chimney-piece by *Francesco di Simone;* to the left of it, 148 Terracotta bust of Lorenzo de' Medici, surnamed il Magnifico. Above the chimney-piece, ˜39 a. *Donatello,* Madonna and Child, painted and gilded, in an old frame. — Towards the exit are works by *Luca della Robbia* and his pupils: 115, 113 Lunettes, Madonna between angels; 114. Madonna with angels and saints. — In the centre, before the window, glass-case with small sculptures: 94 *Andrea Verrocchio,* Model of a kneeling Mary Magdalen· 639i. *Venetian School,* St. Sebastian in boxwood; 648. *Giovanni della Robbia,* Savonarola.

Room 22, chiefly works by VERROCCHIO. Above a chest: *97 a. Model of a relief of the Entombment; 103. Bust of a youth; 96, 97. Recumbent nude boys. To the right of the door: ^93 Sleeping youth; 150f. *Matteo Civitale,* Model of a small altar.

ROOM 19: FLORENTINE AND PADUAN TERRACOTTA WORKS OF THE LATE 15TH CENTURY To the left of the entrance· *Desiderio da Settignano,* Virgin and Child. On the long wall, no number, *Benedetto da Maiano,* Vision of Innocent III · 149, 85 Busts of St. Catharine of Siena and of Filippo Strozzi Between these, 61 *Antonio Rossellino* Adoration of the Child, unpainted terracotta relief, and several reliefs of the Madonna. — 191 d. *Sperandio*, Bust of a Bolognese jurist Farther on· 191. *Franc. Francia*, Portrait; above, 156 b. *School of Donatello*, Madonna. — 192 b *Guido Mazzoni*, Portrait; 199. *Lombard School* (ca. 1500), SS. Francis and Dominic.

Room 17 contains Sculptures of the Renaissance at its Zenith, and also a series of frescoes by *B. Luini* from the myth of Europa. To the left of the entrance, No. 218 *Baccio Bandinelli*, Model of a portrait of himself. On the wall opposite the window chiefly works by *Jacopo Sansovino·* to the left, 231. Madonna enthroned with saints; to the right, 232. Madonna and Child *Spanish Masters* (17th cent), 276. Mater Dolorosa, Angels playing music. In front of the curtain, *86 *Benedetto da Maiano*, Madonna and Child, life-size painted terracotta group By the window: 225. *Cristoforo Romano* (?), Bust of Teodorina Cibo.

B. Upper Floor.

Returning to the entrance hall (p. 96), we ascend the stairs or take the lift (10 pf.) to the upper floor, which contains the picture gallery and most of the Italian Renaissance sculptures. In the corridor adjoining the landing are busts of Voltaire and Gluck by *Houdon*, etc.

The nucleus of the ⁺*Picture Gallery consists of the pictures of the *Giustiniani Collection* purchased in 1815 at Paris, of the collection of *Mr. Solly*, an Englishman, purchased in 1821, and of a selection made in 1829 of *Pictures from the Royal Palaces*. The present importance, however, of the Berlin Gallery is due to the acquisitions of the last few decades. The purchase of the celebrated *Suermondt Collection* in 1874 (for about 50,000 *l*), particularly rich in excellent Dutch works, was followed by numerous single acquisitions in Italy, England (from the Blenheim and Dudley galleries, etc.), France, and Germany, by which many prominent works were brought to Berlin Though it has fewer masterpieces by the great painters than the collections of Florence, Paris, Dresden, and Madrid, the Berlin Gallery is rivalled by the National Gallery at London alone in the historical completeness with which the artists of the various schools and periods are represented

The Early Italian Masters are particularly well represented in the Berlin Gallery. Among the painters of the 14th century we meet *Duccio, Giotto,* the *Gaddi,* and others. The Last Judgment by *Fra Angelico*, the Madonna with the two SS. John by *Sandro Botticelli*, the Madonna enthroned and Saints by *Cosimo Tura* and *Carlo Crivelli*, the Portrait of a Woman by *Domenico Veneziano*, Pan among the Shepherds and Nymphs and also the Portrait of an Old Man by *Luca Signorelli*, the large altar-piece by *L. Vivarini*, the Adoration of the Magi by *A. Vivarini*, and the small portrait by *Antonello da Messina* rank among the finest creations of these leading masters of the 15th century. The Annunciation of *Piero Pollaiuolo*, the two allegorical pieces by *Melozzo da Forli*, three small panels by *Masaccio*, and the Adoration of the Magi by *Vittore Pisano* are among the greatest rarities in the Gallery. — The GOLDEN PERIOD OF ITALIAN ART is neither so fully nor so well illustrated. Of the four works by *Raphael* three belong to his earliest period, and the fourth, the Madonna della Casa Colonna. is unfinished. The rare *Sebastiano del Piombo* is represented by several works, one of which is the so-called 'Fornarina' from the Blenheim collection. Among the works of Raphael's Florentine contemporaries, the admirable altar-piece by *Andrea del Sarto* is a masterpiece. The Assumption of *Fra Bartolomeo* belongs to the period of his co-operation with *Albertinelli*. *Angelo Bronzino*, the best-known portrait-painter of Florence, is illustrated by a masterly portrait of Ugolino Martelli. — Among the MASTERS OF CHIAR-OSCURO *Leonardo da Vinci* is represented by a highly interesting altar-piece of the Ascension, and *Correggio* by the Leda, a work which, in spite of varied fortunes, still retains its attractiveness. — *Titian*, the chief of the VENETIAN SCHOOL, is represented by a few portraits only, among which are the unfinished portrait of himself, the Lavinia, and the delightful little daughter of Roberto Strozzi; *Giorgione* by an attractive portrait. The Gallery also contains altar-pieces and ceiling-paintings by *Bordone, Francesco Vecellio, Tintoretto, Paolo Veronese*, and *Lor. Lotto*, all of which, however, are excelled by several admirable portraits by Lotto. — The BRES-CIAN SCHOOL is well represented by works of *Savoldo, Moroni*, and *Moretto*.

ITALIAN ART IN THE 17TH CENTURY is abundantly and well exemplified by a number of the naturalistic works in which it was most successful. *Caravaggio*, in particular, is represented by works of every size and description, while *Guido Reni* is seen to advantage in a fine altar-piece of his early period. *Carlo Maratti* contributes an admirable Portrait of a Young Man, which was formerly in the Snermondt Collection. — The second short revival of the Venetian school is represented by good works by *Tiepolo* and several town views by *Belotto*.

Among works of the EARLY NETHERLANDISH SCHOOL the Gal-lery possesses the wings of the large altar-piece at Ghent by the brothers *Hubert* and *Jan van Eyck*, the finest work of the school, and six small pictures by *Jan van Eyck*, including his finest por-trait. *Rogier van der Weyden*, the best of the followers of the Van Eycks, is represented by two admirable altar-pieces. *Petrus Cristus, Dierick Bouts, Hugo van der Goes*, and the *Master of Flémalle* are also well represented, the last by a Crucifixion and two portraits by *Hans Memling*, two Memlings and an excellent portrait. The Virgin and Child of *Quinten Matsys*, who forms a

link between the early-Flemish school and the Renaissance, is one
of that master's best efforts. — The contemporary OLD FRENCH
SCHOOL is represented by an admirable devotional portrait by *Jean
Fouquet* and the Bertinus Altar by *Simon Marmion.*

The gem of the EARLY GERMAN SCHOOL is *Holbein's* portrait of
the merchant Gisze, which formed part of the Solly collection, and
is justly regarded as one of the very finest works by this master.
Two other admirable portraits by Holbein belonged to the Suermondt Cabinet, a third, superior to both, belonged to the late Sir
John Millais. The gallery has recently been enriched by seven genuine specimens of *Albrecht Durer:* a portrait of Elector Frederick
the Wise (of his early period), the admirable portrait of Muffel (1526),
the celebrated Holzschuher portrait, considered the finest he ever
painted (1526; bought in 1884 for 17,500*l.*), the Madonna with the
siskin, two portraits of ladies (both painted in Venice), and lastly a
Mater Dolorosa. The collection also contains masterpieces of two
of his best pupils, *Hans von Kulmbach* and *Albrecht Altdorfer:*
a large Adoration of the Magi by the former. the Rest on the Flight
into Egypt by the latter. The examples of *Lucas Cranach the
Elder* are numerous *Georg Pencz, Christoph Amberger*, and
Bartholomaeus Bruyn are represented by characteristic examples.

The NETHERLANDISH ART OF THE 16-17TH CENTURIES, the period
of the development of the two great national schools of the Flemings
and the Dutch, and the gradual development of the arts of painting
in miniature. landscape and genre painting. and painting from still
life, may be studied here to great advantage in numerous works by
the leading masters. Of the works of *Peter Paul Rubens*, the ver-
satile chief of the FLEMISH SCHOOL, the gallery possesses a small
collection only compared with those of Munich, St. Petersburg,
Paris, Vienna. and Madrid, but on the other hand its specimens
were nearly all executed without the co-operation of pupils. The
Raising of Lazarus is one of his best altar-pieces, the Rescue of
Andromeda, the Bacchanal, and Diana at the Chase are charming
examples of his mythological style, the St. Cecilia and the larger
Andromeda are delightful in their bloom of colour. The Portrait of
his first wife delights by its unusual colour harmony. The unfinished
Capture of Tunis affords an instructive insight into the technical
method pursued by the great master. The St. Sebastian and the
Neptune and Amphitrite are characteristic specimens of his early
period. The talents of *Van Dyck* are exhibited in a Mocking of
Christ, bearing the stamp of Rubens' influence, and perfect in its
colouring and treatment, two admirable portraits of the Genoese
period, and finally a Pietà from the period of his return from Italy.
The collection also contains good examples of *Snyders* and *Fyt.*
The best works by *Teniers the Younger* are the Backgammon
Players, the Temptation of St. Anthony and a Rural Feast. A large

landscape by *Adriaen Brouwer* is remarkable for its idealised fidelity to nature.

The DUTCH SCHOOL is also well represented. *Frans Hals*, the chief master of the earlier period, is nowhere else studied to so great advantage, except in the museum of his native town of Haarlem, the best examples of his skill being the Nurse and the Hille Bobbe. The collection of paintings by *Rembrandt* is one of the finest of its kind and includes characteristic specimens in both his earlier and later manner. The two small Biblical scenes, the large painting of Pastor Anslo (acquired in 1894), the Preaching of John the Baptist, the portraits of his wife Saskia and of his servant Hendrickje Stoffels, the Vision of Daniel, the Joseph and Potiphar, and the Susannah are in his most mature style. Among the ten landscapes by *Jacob van Ruysdael* are two Views of the Dunes near Overveen, the great Oak Forest and a large sea-piece. The Violoncello Player of *Terburg* is perhaps his most finished work; his so-called Paternal Admonition is mentioned by Goethe. Among the genre-painters of Rembrandt's time, *Pieter de Hooch* contributes an excellent interior, *Nicolaus Maes* a portrait of an Old Woman, and *Jan van der Meer of Delft* two works, while *Ph. de Koninck, A. van de Velde,* and *Ph. Wouverman* are also admirably represented. The gallery contains excellent examples of *De Heem, Huysum, Hondecoeter, Weenix, Kalf,* and other depictors of still-life.

The pictures are hung in historical order (but comp. p. 96), the Netherlandish and German schools occupying the S.W. side of the building (to the left), the Italian schools the N. and N.E. sides (to the right). We begin our enumeration of the most important works with the small Room 73, entered from the landing to the left.

ROOM 73. WESENDONK COLLECTION (on loan). To the left: at the entrance, 251. *Jac. van Ruysdael,* Landscape with ruins; 223 *Adriaen van Ostade,* Married couple in a village street; above, 87. *Francisco Zurbaran,* Monk praying — To the right, 10. *Moretto (Aless. Bonvicino),* Virgin and Child (fragment); 243. *Sir Joshua Reynolds,* Portrait of a lady; 230 *Joachim Patinir,* Landscape; 15. *Lorenzo Costa,* Madonna and saints.

CABINET 72. The main wall is occupied by six **Panels (Nos. 512-523) of the famous Altar-piece of the Lamb, by *Hubert* and *Jan van Eyck,* painted for the church of St. Bavon at Ghent and finished in 1432, the first painting executed wholly in oils. The central portion of the altar-piece, representing the Adoration of the Mystic Lamb, surmounted by figures of God the Father, the Virgin Mary, and John the Baptist, is still in St. Bavon; two other panels (Adam and Eve) are in the Museum at Brussels. The remaining six panels were purchased by Mr. Solly in 1800. The pictures are oil paintings on both sides of the panels the painted panels which are now exhibited side by side; comp. the survey at the entrance. The four lower panels (at the back, 512, 513, 516, 517) depict judges, crusaders, hermits, and pilgrims moving in procession to the Fountain of Life (central panel, a copy by Coxie, No. 524); the former backs of these panels (left wall) bear portraits of Jodocus Vydts and his wife (519, 522) and their patron saints, SS. John the Evangelist and John the Baptist (518, 523; in stone colour). Two other panels (514, 515) represent respectively a group of singing angels and St. Cecilia attended by angelic musicians; on the former backs (right wall, 520, 521) the Archangel Gabriel and the Madonna.

'There is not to be found', say Crowe and Cavalcaselle, 'in the whole Flemish school a picture in which human figures are grouped, designed, or painted with so much perfection as in this of the mystic Lamb. Nor is it possible to find a more complete or better distributed composition, more natural attitudes, or more dignified expression'. The beholder is charmed both by the naive and careful realism and by the brilliancy of the colouring. A photographic reproduction of the whole altar in its original condition is exhibited on the window wall

CABINET 70. EARLY NETHERLANDISH SCHOOLS OF THE 15TH CENTURY. To the left: *Dierick Bouts*, *533. Elijah in the desert, *539. Feast of the Passover. These with two other panels in the Munich Gallery form the inner wings of an altar-piece, the central part of which, representing the Last Supper, is in St. Peter's at Louvain. 532a. *Aelbert van Ouwater*, Raising of Lazarus (the only authenticated work by this founder of the Dutch school). — Rear-wall: left and right, *1645, 1645a *Simon Marmion*, two altar-wings with the exploits of St. Bertinus, from the convent of St. Omer; *Jan van Eyck*, *-523a. Portrait of Giovanni Arnolfini, *525f. Crucifixion, with the Madonna and St. John, 525g. Knight of the Golden Fleece; 532. *Petrus Cristus*, Half-length portrait of a woman; -538a. *Master of Flémalle*, Crucifixion; 529. *Hans Memling*, Virgin and Child. — 538b. *Flemish Master* (about 1480), Death of Mary. — Right wall. 523b. *Jan van Eyck (Petrus Cristus?)*, Madonna with a Carthusian; below, 529c. *Hans Memling*, Portrait of an old man; 526a *Flemish Master* (about 1450), Pietà, *545d. *Rogier van der Weyden*, Portrait of a lady; 1631. *Geertgen tot Sint Jans*, St. John the Baptist; *Jan van Eyck*, -*525a Man with carnations, a fine work, showing on a smaller scale much of the finished execution and powerful general effect of the Ghent altar-piece (see above), *525c. Virgin and Child in a church: above, 537. *Master of Flémalle*, Portrait of a young man; 519a. *Rogier van der Weyden*, Madonna; -1617. *Jean Fouquet*, Estienne Chevalier with his patron St. Stephen (the other wing of the altar-piece is in the Antwerp Gallery); 528b. *Hans Memling*, Madonna; 537a *Master of Flémalle*, Portrait.

CABINET 68. NETHERLANDISH SCHOOLS OF THE 15TH and 16TH CENTURIES. To the left *Petrus Cristus*, 529a Altar-wing (above, Annunciation; below Nativity, 529b Last Judgment -535. *Rogier* *van der Weyden,* Winged altar-piece, presented by Peeter Bladelin to the church at Middelburg, with the Adoration of the Holy Child, the Tiburtine Sibyl before Augustus, and the Star in the East; a masterpiece, 'remarkable for the finish of the parts, the delicacy of the touch, and the gloss of the colours'. — Above the middle door: 719. *Pieter Aertsen,* Young woman and child (fragment of a picture of the Nativity). — To the right. *Jan van Scorel.* 644. Portrait of C A. van der Dussen, 644a. Madonna, 644b. Portrait; *Lucas van Leyden,* 574a. Chess-players, *584b. Madonna and Child; *Sir Anthony More,* 585a. Two clerics (1544; an early work), 585b. Margaret of Parma; beside the door. 574. Style of the *Cologne Master of the Death of Mary,* Portrait. — Passing through the central door, we now enter —

Room 69 Netherlandish Masters of the 15th and 16th Centuries. To the left, 648. *Jan Gossaert,* surnamed *Mabuse,* Neptune and Amphitrite; *Quinten Matsys,* *561. Madonna and Child (a masterpiece of colouring), 574c. Mourning woman, from a picture of the Passion; 570. *Maerten Heemskerck,* Portrait of a girl. — *534b. *Rogier van der Weyden,* Winged altar-piece with scenes from the life of St. John the Baptist (an early work); **1622a. *Hugo van der Goes,* Nativity of Christ (next to the Portinari altarpiece in the Uffizi at Florence the most important work of the artist); above, *Rogier van der Weyden,* 534. Descent from the Cross (copy of the original in the Escorial), 534a. Altar with scenes from the life of the Virgin (earliest work of the master, from the convent of Miraflores near Burgos). — *Joos van Clere,* 633a. Portrait of a young man, *633b. Portrait of a woman; *Mabuse,* 650. Virgin and Child, 586a. Portrait, 551a. Christ in Gethsemane (an early work); 611. *Jean Bellegambe,* Last Judgment. — 573. *Gerard David,* Crucifixion. — We return through Cabinet 68 and enter —

Cabinet 67. German Schools of the 15th and 16th Centuries. To the left, *586d. *Hans Holbein the Younger,* Portrait of an old man (a late work, of the master's English period); 638c *Albrecht Altdorfer,* Nativity; **586. *Holbein the Younger,* Jorg Gisze, a Bâle merchant in the Steelyard at London, one of the greatest triumphs of portrait-painting (1532); 1658. *Konrad Witz,* Christ on the Cross; 583. *Christoph Amberger,* Sebastian Munster, the geographer (1552). — Rear-wall: *1629. *Martin Schongauer,* Adoration of the Shepherds; *Albrecht Dürer,* 557c. Elector Frederick the Wise of Saxony (an early work, ca 1496), **557c. Hieronymus Holzschuher, patrician and senator of Nuremberg, the finest of Dürer's portraits, painted in 1526 (purchased in 1884 for 75,000 *l.*); *557f. Madonna with the siskin (painted at Venice in 1506); *557d. Portrait of Senator Muffel of Nuremberg (1526); above, 557j. Portrait of a girl. *564a *Lucas Cranach the Elder,* Rest on the Flight into Egypt (1504; the earliest authenticated work of the master; above, 556.

Amberger, Emperor Charles V. (1532). — On the right, 586 c. *Holbein the Younger*, Portrait; 638 c. *Altdorfer*, Haughtiness; *557 g. *Albrecht Dürer*, Portrait of a young woman (a vigorous work full of life, probably painted at Venice in 1506); *638 b. *Altdorfer*, Rest on the Flight into Egypt (1510); 586 b. *Holbein the Younger*, Portrait of a young merchant (1533); above, 603 a. *Hans Baldung Grien*, Winged altar-piece with the Adoration of the Magi (1507).

CABINET 65. GERMAN SCHOOLS OF THE 16TH CENTURY. To the left. *588. *Barth. Bruyn the Elder*, Portrait of the Cologne Burgomaster Ryht (1525); above, 563. *Cranach*, Winged altar with the Last Judgment (an early copy after Hieronymus Bosch). — Rear wall: 597 a. *G. Breu*, Madonna in a landscape; 603. *Hans Baldung Grien*, Crucifixion (1520), 631. *Master of Messkirch*, Christ on the Mount of Olives; 700 *Ludger tom Ring*, Portrait of a young man; 603 b. *Hans Baldung Grien*, Pietà — To the right: 582, 587. *Georg Pencz*, Portraits of the Nuremberg painter Erhard Schwetzer and his wife (1544); 638 a. *Altdorfer*, Landscape with satyrs (1507); no number, *M Schaffner*, Four saints; *L Cranach the Elder*, 593. Fountain of Youth (1546), 589. Archbishop Albert of Mayence as St Jerome. — By the door in the main wall, to the left, we now enter the small —

ROOM 66, containing chiefly works by LUCAS CRANACH and his school. To the left: 577. *Amberger* (?), Portrait of Georg von Frundsberg — 559. *Lucas Cranach the Elder*, Archbp. Albert of Mayence. — *596 a *Hans von Kulmbach*, Adoration of the Magi (1511); *Hans Burgkmair*, 569. St. Ulrich, 572. St. Barbara (altarwings). — 639 *Barth. Bruyn*, Virgin and Child. — Returning to Cabinet 65, we proceed to the left to —

ROOM 62, or SMALL RUBENS ROOM, with a Dutch chimney-piece and Dutch furniture. — To the left. *Peter Paul Rubens:* 776 c. Landscape with the shipwreck of Æneas, *763. Boy with a bird, 798 g Conquest of Tunis by Emp. Charles V. — Rear wall: above the chimney-piece, 831. *Cornelis de Vos*, Married couple; beside the chimney-piece, 678. *Jan Brueghel the Elder*, Forge of Vulcan. — To the right, 782. *A van Dyck*, Prince Thomas of Savoy; *Rubens*, *785 Perseus delivering Andromeda (early work, about 1615), *762 a. Portrait of Isabella Brant, his first wife (begun in 1615, subsequently enlarged); above, 878. *Snyders*, Cockfight. — The doors in the main wall give access to the Large Rubens Room (p. 113); we proceed straight on to —

CABINET 59. Works by FRANS HALS and his contemporaries. — To the left: 853 h. *A. Brouwer*, Landscape with sheep; *801 h. *Frans Hals*, Tyman Oosdorp (1656); 901 c. *Sal. van Ruysdael*, Dutch landscape. — *Frans Hals*, *800. Portrait of a young man, *801 c. Hille Bobbe, the sailors' Venus; 808 a. *H. Seghers*, Dutch landscape near the town of Rhenen; *801. *Frans Hals*, Portrait of a young woman. — *Gerhard Terburg*, *793. Knife-grinder with his family, *791. Paternal admonition (described by Goethe in his Elective Affinities); *Fr. Huls*, *801 g. Nurse and child, 801 a. Singing boy.

CABINET 58. DUTCH PAINTINGS OF THE EARLY 16TH CENTURY. To the left, *A. Palamedesz*, 711 Portrait of a girl, 758 a. Party, 758 b. Portrait of a boy; 865 d. *Jan van Goyen*, View of Arnhem. — 753. *P. Moreelse*, Young lady; 750. *Thomas de Keyser*, Family portraits; 806 b. *Seghers*, Landscape; 743 *J G. Cuyp*, Portrait of an old woman. — 865 e. *Van Goyen*, View of Nymwegen; 750 b. and c. *Th de Keyser*, Two altar-wings with donors.

CABINET 57. Works by REMBRANDT: 812 b. The good Samaritan (sketch); *811 a Rembrandt's brother, with a helmet on his head (ca. 1650); **828 f. Vision of Daniel, a work of exceptional delicacy of execution (ca 1650); 805. Tobias; 828 i. Old man in a red cap (ca. 1654); *812. Saskia, the painter's first wife (1643; painted after her death). — Rear-wall· 808 Portrait of himself (1634); **828 e. Susannah at the bath, one of the master's finest and most mature productions (1647). — Main wall: *826 a. *Phil. Koninck*, Large landscape; *Rembrandt*, 810. Portrait of himself; 828 k. Preaching of John the Baptist, a vigorous sketch with numerous figures (ca 1635), *828 h. Joseph and Potiphar's wife, a masterpiece of his later period (1655); *828 b Hendrickje Stoffels, Rembrandt's servant, at a window (ca. 1659). — Other works of Rembrandt in Room 52 (p. 112).

CABINET 56. SMALL DUTCH WORKS OF THE 17TH CENTURY. To the left: 810 d. *Jan van der Meer van Haarlem*, Landscape; *885 g. *J van Ruysdael*, Oak-forest; *861 b. *A. Cuyp*, Cows at the river. — Rear-wall: 886. *M Hobbema*, Landscape, 792 a. *G. Metsu*, Cook; *922 c. *Adriaen van de Velde*, Farm (the artist's most finished production). — To the right, *Jan Steen*, *795. Tavern-garden, above, 795 b. The quarrel; 792 c. *G. Metsu*, Sick woman. — Traversing the corridor (54), we enter —

CABINET 53 DUTCH MASTERS OF THE 17TH CENTURY To the right: 791 a and b. *G. Terburg*, Portraits of Herr von Marienburg and his wife. — To the left: *819 c *Nich. Maes*, Old woman peeling apples; 885 f. *J van Ruysdael*, Village on a wooded slope; *912 c. *J. van der Meer van Delft*, Cavalier and girl drinking wine (acquired from Lord F. Pelham Clinton Hope in 1901); above, 809 *F Bol*, Old woman — 796. *Q. Brekelenkam*, Young woman with her servant; *820 b. *Pieter de Hooch*, Mother and child; *885 e. *J. van Ruysdael*, View from the dunes near Overveen; *922 b. *A. van de Velde*, River scene; 791. *Terburg*, Girl and cavalier; 872 a. *Paulus Potter*, The 'Bosch' near the Hague, with Prince Frederick Henry's hounds; *875 a. *Jan van de Cappelle*, Sunny beach — *791 g. *Terburg*, Lady playing violoncello a masterpiece 1623 *Jan van der Heyde*, Street in Amsterdam 795 d. *Jan Steen*, Christening;

*912b *J van der Meer van Delft*, Girl with a necklace of beads.
— We return to the corridor (54) and enter, to the right, —

CABINET 55 SMALL DUTCH PICTURES OF THE 16TH AND 17TH
CENTURIES. To the left: 848. *C. Netscher*, Kitchen; 792. *Metsu*,
A merchant's family — To the right: 796e *D J. van de Laen*,
Country-house; 850a. *M. van Musscher*, Portrait — Adjacent to
the right is —

ROOM 52 LARGER DUTCH WORKS, particularly by Rembrandt.
To the left: *Rembrandt*, 811. Moses destroying the Tables of the
Law (1659). **828l. Pastor Anslo and an aged woman, a large and
vigorous work of the same period as the Night Watch at Amsterdam (1641), acquired from Lord Ashburnham in 1894; 828 Jacob
wrestling with the angel (ca 1660); 823 Rape of Proserpine (early
work, ca. 1632); *812a. Capture of Samson (1628); 828d. Money-
changer (one of the earliest pictures, 1627); +802 Samson threaten-
ing his wife's father. — '812a *Aert van der Neer*, Moonlight
landscape; 826. *Salomon Koninck*, Crœsus exhibiting his treasures to Solon; 753a, 753b *Nic Elias*, Cornelis de Graef, burgomaster of Amsterdam, and his wife; *884 *Jac van Ruysdael*,
Stormy sea; 824. *G. Horst*, Magnanimity of Scipio; 830. *P. Verelst*,
Old woman — 861g. *A Cuyp*, Landscape in spring; *840, *840e.
A van der Neer, Conflagration, Landscape in winter; 858. *Abr
van den Tempel*, Nobleman and his wife in their park; 899 *Phil.
Wouverman*, Ridingschool

ROOM 51 FLEMISH MASTERS AND ADOLF THIEM COLLECTION.
To the left: *David Teniers the Younger*, 857. The painter's family,
856 Backgammon, 866f. Guard-room with gambling soldiers. 866d.
Dives in purgatory; 742. *Jan Breughel the Elder*, Paradise; 763b
Rubens, Venus and Adonis (ca 1615); 879. *Jac. Jordaens*, Merry
company, no number. *Teniers*, Landscape. — *Dierick Bouts*, *533a.
Christ in the house of Simon, 533a. Crucifixion; above, an Italian
tapestry (ca. 1480). — 112e. *Ercole de' Roberti*, St. Jerome, 1642.
Mignon, Dead birds; 1640. *Backer*, Old woman; 787a. *A van Dyck*,
Marchesa Spinola, 774c. *Snyders*, Dead poultry; 1401a *Pieter de
Hooch*, Dutch interior; 883c. *Fyt*, Still-life. — We return through
Rooms 52 and 55 to —

ROOM 61, containing the CARSTANJEN COLLECTION (on loan). To
the left: ¯14. *A. van Dyck*. Portrait of a lady (Italian period),
*37. *Jac. van Ruysdael*, Torrent; 23. *Quinten Matsys*, Two altar-
wings with St. John the Evangelist and St. Agnes, 9. *A Cuyp*, Landscape with cattle; below, *32. *Rembrandt*, Scourging of Christ,
an impressive little work, 16. *Frans Hals*, Portrait, no number,
Murillo, Beggar-woman and boy. — To the right: 26. *Murillo*,
Mary Magdalen 17. *Frans Hals*. Portrait· 19. *M. Hobbema*, Farm
near a wood; 33 *Rembrandt*. Portrait of himself at an advanced
age; 31. *Potter*, Boar-hunt; 8 *A. Cuyp*, Moonlight landscape;

18. *Fr Hals*, Fisher-girl, no number, *Rembrandt, Portrait of a scholar (1645); 6. *Antonio Canale*, Canal Grande at Venice.

CABINET 60 SMALL FLEMISH PICTURES AND MINIATURES. To the left: 776d. *Rubens*, Sunset. — 866 e. *Teniers*, Neptune and Amphitrite; *Elsheimer*, 664a. Nymph bathing, 664c. Arcadian landscape, 664d. Mercury and Argus, 664e Sylvan landscape with the death of Argus. — *Rubens*, 780. Madonna and saints, 798k. Pietà.

ROOM 63 LARGE RUBENS SALOON — To the left: 782a. *A. van Dyck*, Satyrs and nymphs; *Rubens*, ¯762b Conversion of St. Paul, a most animated composition, painted about 1617, *762c. Diana and nymphs surprised by satyrs, a masterpiece of his latest period, 762. Coronation of the Virgin. *A van Dyck*, ¯782b, ¯782c. Portraits of a Genoese nobleman and his wife, masterpieces of the master's Genoese period (formerly in the collection of Sir Robert Peel). ¯778. Pietà (ca. 1627); 771. *Rubens* and *Snyders*, Diana at the chase; *Rubens*, 783 Raising of Lazarus (partially by A. van Dyck), 763a. Repentant Magdalen (a late work); *776a. Neptune and Amphitrite, a characteristic and well-composed work of his early period; 776b. Bacchanal (partially painted by A. van Dyck). — 790f. *A. van Dyck*, Apostle's head; 798h. *Rubens*, St. Sebastian (painted in Italy); 770. *A. van Dyck*, Mocking of Christ; *781. *Rubens*, St. Cecilia, a masterpiece of his last period; 799 *A. van Dyck*, St. John the Baptist and St. John the Evangelist; *776c. *Rubens*, Andromeda (with the features of Helena Fourment, the painter's second wife), a late work (from Blenheim); ¯832. *C. de Vos*, The painter's daughters.

To maintain the historical sequence, we now return through Rooms 62-73 to the landing of the staircase in the vestibule and by the door to the right enter the N. wing, containing the Italian pictures and sculptures.

CABINET 28. Recent acquisitions from the Kann collection at Paris: *Aert van der Neer*, Skaters; *Ph. Wouverman*, Winter landscape; *Rembrandt*, Christ and the Samaritan woman (1655). Head of Christ; *J. van Ruysdael*, Windmills near the water: *Gonzales Coques*, Patrician family; *Jan Fyt*, Dead birds and melon. — ROOM 29. EARLY ITALIAN SCHOOLS (14th and 15th cent.). To the left: 1130 *Gentile da Fabriano*, Madonna and saints; 1071a *Giotto*, Crucifixion; 1079-81. *Taddeo Gaddi*, Winged altar (in the middle, Madonna and Child with saints); 1635. *Ugolino da Siena*, Three lifesize half-figures of saints, from the old high-altar of Santa Croce at Florence; *1070a. *Simone Martini*, Entombment, *Pietro Lorenzetti*, 1077 St Humilitas healing a sick nun, 1077a. Death of St Humilitas (wings of an altar at Florence); ¯1062a. *Duccio*, Nativity; 1072. *Lippo Memmi*, Madonna. — End wall: 1122. *Girolamo di Benvenuto*, Assumption 1081 *Lippo Memmi*, Madonna. — Right wall Lorenzo Lorenzetti Adoration by Masi 95a.

BAEDEKER   Berlin   14th

Vittore Pisano, Adoration of the Magi; 95. *Fra Filippo Lippi*, Madonna della Misericordia; 60. *School of Fra Angelico*, Madonna enthroned.

CABINET 30. FLORENTINE SCHOOL OF THE 16TH CENTURY. Right wall: *1614. *Domenico Veneziano*, Portrait of a girl: *73a. *Antonio Pollaiuolo*, David; 100. *Lorenzo di Credi*, Adoration of the Holy Child; 21 *Dom. Ghirlandaio*, Judith. — Rear-wall. Intarsia door with Annunciation by *Benedetto da Maiano;* above, 119. *Andrea della Robbia*, Madonna with angels; 338b *A. Bronzino*, Eleonora of Toledo, wife of Cosimo I. — On the left: *90 *Raffaellino del Garbo*, Madonna and Child with two angelic musicians; *104a. *Andrea Verrocchio*, Madonna and Child.

CABINET 31. Glazed and painted terracotta works by the DELLA ROBBIA family. To the right, *116p, *116n, *116r. *Luca della Robbia*, Madonnas; rear-wall, 119d. *L. della Robbia*, Head of a youth; above the door, 123. *Style of Andrea della Robbia*, Annunciation; to the left, *119c. *Andrea della Robbia*, *116a *Luca della Robbia*, Madonnas; *119a *Andrea della Robbia*, Annunciation.

CABINET 32. Works by DONATELLO and his contemporaries. To the right *62 *Desiderio da Settignano*, Bust of Marietta Strozzi; *Masaccio*, 58a. Adoration of the Magi, 58d Four saints from the Pisan altar (1426), *58b. Martyrdom of SS. Peter and John, *Donatello*, *39 'Madonna Pazzi', *38a. Bust of the youthful St. John, 42. 'Madonna Orlandini'. — Rear-wall: 99. *Andrea Verrocchio*, Relief portrait of Matthias Corvinus, King of Hungary, *60a. *Fra Angelico*, Last Judgment, a masterpiece, eminent for its deep religious feeling and charming expression; 98. *Verrocchio*, Beatrix of Aragon; 95b. *Fra Filippo Lippi*, St. Ambrose in the cradle (predella); no number, *Antonio di Banco*, David. On the left: *69 *Fra Filippo Lippi*, Madonna adoring the Child; *39b. *Donatello*, Scourging of Christ; 62a. *Desiderio da Settignano*, Portrait of a princess of Urbino.

CABINET 33. ITALIAN PLAQUETTES (small bronze reliefs employed for the decoration of utensils and furniture) The Berlin collection is the richest of its kind The works of the more important artists are exhibited in glass-cases on the walls. In the cabinet: *Benvenuto Cellini*, Six gold reliefs with mythological scenes. — Rooms 34 and 35, see pp 115, 116.

ROOM 36, with a Venetian painted ceiling and a chimney-piece in the manner of *Jacopo Sansovino* The Berlin collection of Italian bronze and marble sculptures exhibited here ranks among the finest out of Italy. Descriptive catalogue, with 81 heliogravures (Berlin, 1904), 25 *M*.

To the right: 236. *Donatello* (?) Nude woman with cornucopia; 222 *Antonio Rossellino*. Bust of a child: above 223. *Civalli* (?), Bust of Spagnuoli, general of the Carmelite order: *234. *Donatello*,

Putto with tambourine, from the Baptistery at Siena; *220. *Donatello*, Bust of Lodovico III Gonzaga. — By the chimney-piece: 225. *Italian Master* (ca. 1580), Bust of Pope Gregory XIII., 224. *Florentine Master* (ca. 1550), Bust of Marchese del Nero. To the left, 291 *Giovanni da Bologna*, Rape of Dejaneira. In the glass-case to the right, no number, *Ant Pollaiuolo*, Hercules; 235. *Donatello*, David; 232. *Lorenzo Ghiberti*, Caryatid. Also works by *Bertoldo*, *Riccio*, and others In the middle, **233 *Donatello*, John the Baptist (1423). The glass-case on the left contains bronze works of the 16th cent., by *Benvenuto Cellini*, *Giov. da Bologna*, *Francesco da Sant' Agata*, etc. — By one of the doors in the rear-wall we enter —

Room 37. Signorelli Saloon Entrance wall: *79a *Luca Signorelli*, Pan with shepherds and nymphs, 'most poetically conceived and beautifully arranged', and distinguished by the admirable drawing of the nude, here handled freely for the first time in Italian art (presented by the painter to Lorenzo de' Medici). To the left, *Signorelli*, 79, 79b Two wings of an altar with saints, Holy Family meeting the family of John the Baptist. To the right, 27a. *Fr. Squarcione*, Madonna; *79c. *Signorelli*, Portrait; *Andrea Mantegna*, 27. Madonna (early work), *29. Presentation in the Temple, 9. Portrait of Cardinal Mezzarota; above, *1170. *Marco Zoppo*, Madonna and saints.

Room 38. Botticelli Saloon. To the left of the entrance: *96 *Filippino Lippi*, Crucifixion, with the Virgin and St. Francis. Left wall. *Sandro Botticelli*, 1124 Venus (study), *106 Madonna enthroned with the two SS. John (a masterpiece of his middle period), 102 Madonna and Child with angels, 98 *Raffaellino del Garbo*, Madonna enthroned with two saints; 1128. *Botticelli*, St Sebastian. — Rear-wall (left), 107. *Piero di Cosimo*. Mars and Venus; (right) 1117. *Botticelli*, Annunciation (studio-piece). — Right wall, 106b, 106a *Botticelli*, Giuliano de' Medici and his mistress Simonetta; *73 *P. Pollaiuolo*, Annunciation, with a charming view of Florence and the valley of the Arno; **102a. *Botticelli*, Madonna and angelic musicians, an early masterpiece (on loan); 103 *Lorenzo di Credi*, Mary Magdalen (designed by *Verrocchio*); 204. *Piero di Cosimo*, Adoration of the Shepherds. — By the early-Florentine door (15th cent.) we now proceed to the tribune of the Basilica (p. 97), whence the central door leads to —

Room 64. The walls are hung with the celebrated **Tapestry, woven for Henry VIII. of England from designs (now in the South Kensington Museum) drawn by *Raphael* in 1515-16 for the Sistine Chapel of the Vatican. This tapestry, like the original set, of which it was the first repetition, was executed at Brussels in fine wools, silks, and gold thread, but like both the original and the later repetitions (Loreto, Dresden Paris has sadly faded. It was one in the possession of Charles I. then in that of the Dukes of Alva, and was purchased by Frederick William IV. in 1844. To the left: Paul preaching at Athens; Elymas the sorcerer struck with blindness; Paul and Barnabas at Lystra; Stoning of St. Stephen; rear-wall, Conversion of St. Paul; to the right, Death of Ananias; Peter and Paul healing the lame man; Christ giving Peter the keys of heaven; Miraculous draught of fishes.

The small door in the rear-wall opens upon the great staircase, whence the glass-door to the right leads to —

Cabinet 35. Lombard School. Exit-wall: 217. *Bernardino Luini*, Madonna and Child.

Room 34 Schools of Ferrara and Bologna. End wall: '111. *Cosimo Tura*, Madonna and Child enthroned, with saints, an excellent work of the earlier Ferrarese school; *115a *Francesco Cossa*, Autumn — Left wall: 122 *Fr. Francia*, Madonna enthroned, with saints. — Right wall: 266. *Lod. Mazzolini*, Christ teaching in the Temple; *Lorenzo Costa*, 112. Presentation in the Temple, 115 Pietà.

Cabinet 39 James Simon Collection. This rich collection of Renaissance works of art, chiefly Italian, was presented to the Museum in 1904 (Catalogue 50 pf., with 20 plates 5 *M*). — To the right *Barth. Bruyn*, 21. Portrait of a young woman, 20. Portrait of a young man; *2. *Angelo Bronzino*, Portrait of a youth. — Rear-wall. *Andrea della Robbia*, 26 Adoration of the Holy Child, 25. Madonna and Child with angels (both in glazed terracotta); 24. *Benedetto da Maiano*, Terracotta bust of a young cleric; 18. *Netherlandish Master* (ca 1515), Portrait of an ecclesiastic; 22. *Nino Pisano*, Madonna and Child (statuette); 32. *Italian Master of the 16th cent*, Mask of a buffoon. — To the left: 1 *Raffaellino del Garbo*, Adoration of the Child; *5. *Andrea Mantegna*, Virgin and Child. Numerous small bronzes and medals; the *Knockers deserve attention.

Cabinet 40 Florentine Marble Sculptures of the 15th Century. To the right: 82. *Filippino Lippi*, Madonna; 79. *Mino da Fiesole*, Bust of Niccolò Strozzi (1454); no number, *Antonio Rossellino*, *Stucco relief of the Madonna; *Mino da Fiesole*, 79a. Bust of Alexo di Luca, *80. Bust of a young woman; *Antonio Rossellino*, 65a Madonna, 67. Bust of a young man; 78. *Sandro Botticelli*, Portrait of a young man.

Cabinet 42. Venetian and Lombard Sculptures and Paintings. Mythological ceiling-paintings by *Paolo Veronese*. — To the right· 40. *Luigi Vivarini* (?), Madonna and angelic musicians; *61. *Francesco Laurana*, Bust of a Neapolitan princess; *28. *Giovanni Bellini*, Pietà, an early work. showing Mantegna's influence; no number *Tamagnini* Bust of the Genoese banker Acellino Salvago 1500 : 17. *Cima da Conegliano*, Madonna and

Child. Rear-wall: ⁻20. *Pseudo-Basaiti*, Altar-piece, in four sections. To the left: *Giovanni Bellini*, *1177a. Resurrection of Christ, 10a. Madonna.

CABINET 43. SMALLER VENETIAN PAINTINGS — To the right: 18. *Antonello da Messina*, Portrait of a young man; *12a. *Giorgione*, Young man. — Rear-wall: t25. *Fr. Francia*, Holy Family; 1632 *G. F Maineri*, Madonna; 112d. *Ercole de' Roberti*, Madonna; 17a *Cima da Conegliano*, Landscape. — To the left. ˙˙259b. *Sebastiano del Piombo*, Portrait of a young Roman woman, grandly and freely handled, painted under the influence of Giorgione and apparently the model for the so-called 'Fornarina' (from Blenheim); 182, ⁻320. *Lorenzo Lotto*, Portraits of youths. — The door in the rear-wall gives access to Rooms 44 and 41, containing paintings of the Venetian and North Italian schools

Room 44 Genoese portal with the legend of St. George (15th cent.). End wall, to the left, above an Autependium by the *Master of San Trovaso* at Venice (ca. 1500): *38. *Luigi Vivarini*, Madonna enthroned. with saints; 46a. *Liberale da Verona*, St. Sebastian; 37. *M. Basaiti*, St Sebastian. — Long wall, to the right: *15. *Cima da Conegliano*, St. Mark healing Anianus; 23 *Vittore Carpaccio*, St Peter consecrating St Stephen as deacon; ⁻1156a *Carlo Crivelli*, Madonna with saints; 23a *Vittore Carpaccio*, Entombment; *2. *Cima da Conegliano*, Madonna and Child enthroned, with saints — End wall: 1156. *Crivelli*, Mary Magdalen: 46c. *Franc. Bonsignori*, St Sebastian

Room 41. To the left of the entrance. 51. *Ambrogio Borgognone*, Madonna with angels. — Left wall: 30. *Girolamo dai Libri*, Madonna and Child enthroned, with angels; *Bartolomeo Montagna*, *41b. Christ appearing to Mary Magdalen, 44. Madonna enthroned — Right wall: 133 *Vincenzo Foppa*, Pietà; 47. *Marcello Fogolino*, 52 *Ambr. Borgognone*, Madonnas. — Retracing our steps through Room 44 and Cabinet 43, we enter—

Room 45 WORKS OF THE BEST PERIOD OF ITALIAN ART IN THE EARLY 16TH CENTURY. To the left: *Michael Angelo Buonarroti*, Apollo (statuette, unfinished). ⁻90b. *Leonardo da Vinci*, The Risen Christ, between St. Leonard and St. Lucia Though finished by Leonardo's pupils, this picture produces a powerful impression by the beauty of the two saints, the brilliancy of colouring, and the charm of the landscape background 338 *Angelo Bronzino*, Portrait of a youth; *246. *Andrea del Sarto*, Madonna enthroned, with saints; 245a. *Fr. Franciabigio*, Portrait of a young man; two beautiful chests of the early 16th century. — End wall· 245. *Franciabigio*, Portrait; *209. *Michael Angelo*, Statuette of the youthful John t' Baptist a early and rpine 4495 *338 *Bronzino*, Ugol V li a l Ass Sansovino*, Mad l K gh s il u l t 213 Garofenzio

Ferrari, Annunciation; above, 207. *Giov Boltraffio*, St. Barbara: 222. *Francesco Melzi*, Vertumnus and Pomona; to the right: *Raphael (Raffaello Santi)*, *248. 'Madonna della Casa Colonna' (ca. 1507; unfinished); ~145. Madonna and Child, with St Jerome and St. Francis (ca. 1503); ~247a. 'Madonna del Duca di Terranuova' (ca. 1505); 141. 'Madonna Solly' (ca 1502); 147. 'Madonna della Casa Diotalevi' (ca. 1500).—End wall: ~218. *Correggio (Antonio Allegri)*, Leda.

Room 46. Venetian School of the 16th Century. To the left of the entrance: 197a. and b. *Palma Vecchio*, Ideal female portrait. — Left wall. 157. *Girolamo Romanino*, Beheading of John the Baptist, 190. *Johann von Calcar*, Portrait of a young man; ~153 *Lorenzo Lotto*, Portrait of an architect; 230. *Andrea Brescianino*, Madonna and Child with St. Anna, above, *197. *Moretto*, Fra Bart. Averoldo and his nephew adoring the Virgin and St. Elizabeth; 193a. *Giovanni B Moroni*, Portrait: 314 *Jacopo Bassano*, The good Samaritan; 298. *Tintoretto (Jac. Robusti)*, Portrait of a procurator of San Marco. — End wall: 299. *Tintoretto*, Portrait of a procurator; *160a. *Titian*, Daughter of Roberto Strozzi (1512); 259a. *Sebast. del Piombo*, Knight of Sant' Iago; 298a. *Tintoretto*, Annunciation — Right wall: *Titian*, 161. The Venetian admiral Giovanni Moro, *163. Portrait of himself at an advanced age, *166. Lavinia, daughter of the painter, *301 Portrait. 307. *G. Savoldo*, Venetian woman; above, 303, 304, 309, 311. *Paolo Veronese*, Allegorical paintings; 300 *Tintoretto*, Madonna and Child with two saints.

Room 47. Italian Schools of the 17th and 18th Centuries. Entrance-wall: 273. *Fr. Marath*, Bust of the painter Carlo Maratti; *413a. *Italian Master* (about 1650; not Velazquez), Condottiere Alessandro del Borro, as conqueror of Pope Urban VIII, trampling on the banner of the Barberini, an unusually effective work; to the right, ~*Alessandro Algardi*, Marble bust of Cardinal Zacchia. — Left wall 503b, 503c. *Bern. Belotto*, Views of Pirna; *G. B. Tiepolo*, 459c. Christ bearing the Cross (sketch), ~459b. Martyrdom of St. Agatha, *Fr. Guardi*, 501f Rising of a balloon above the Canal of the Giudecca at Venice (1784), ~501e View of the Giudecca at Venice: 1652. *Ant. Canale*, Piazza di San Marco, 426a. *C. Maratti*, Portrait of a youth; 363. *Guido Reni*, Mater Dolorosa; 408. *North Italian School*, Mary Magdalen; above, 237, *Sebast del Piombo*(?), Pietà — Narrow wall, to the left, 381. *M. Amerighi*, surnamed *Caravaggio*, Cupid vanquished; to the right, 500 a. *P. Rotari*, Portrait of J. Accoramboni, papal nuncio at Dresden; 369. *Caravaggio*, Cupid as conqueror. — Right wall: 353. *Caravaggio*. Entombment: 352. *G. B. Crespi*, Franciscans taking the vow; 372. *Annibale Caracci*, Landscape. 372a. *Agostino Caracci*, Portrait of a woman 111. *Luca Giordano*, Judgment of

Paris; 373. *Guido Reni*, SS Paul and Anthony in the desert;
Caravaggio, 356. Portrait of a young woman, ⁻365. St. Matthew.
— In the middle, several Italian bronzes, wood and ivory carvings
of the 17th and 18th cent. (on loan). — Adjoining Room 11 on the
left is the small —

Room 48, adorned with allegorical and mythological frescoes
in grisaille by *Tiepolo*, from a villa near Treviso (1754) These
are hung in their original arrangement, and the original stucco
frames are carefully reproduced.

Room 49. Spanish Masters. To the right: 413 c. *Velazquez*,
Maria Anna of Spain, consort of Emp Ferdinand III ; 404 c. *Zurbaran*, Portrait of a noble boy; 414 b. *Alonso Cano*, St. Agnes,
407. *Juan Carreño*, Charles II. of Spain (1673); 406 b. *Al. Sanchez-
Coello*, Philip II. of Spain. — *Murillo*, ⁻⁻114. St. Anthony of Padua
with the Holy Child, one of the artist's later masterpieces, 414 c.
Adoration of the Shepherds. ⁻413 e *Velazquez*, Portrait of a Spanish
lady. — 413 f. *Velazquez*, The three musicians; ⁻404 a. *Zurbaran*,
St. Bonaventura showing to St. Thomas Aquinas the source of his
wisdom in the Crucifix (1629). — *405 b. *Ribera*, St. Sebastian;
Francisco Goya, 1619. King Ferdinand VII presiding over a meeting of the Philippine Company (sketch), 1619 a. Portrait of an old
lady (the artist's mother?), 1619 b. Praying monk, *No number,
Spanish Master (17th cent), Books and writing materials.

Room 50 French and British Schools of the 17th and 18th
Centuries. To the right. *478 a. *Nicolas Poussin*, View of the
Acqua Acetosa near Rome, with St. Matthew in the foreground (a
good example of the master's colouring); 428 *Claude Lorrain*,
Heroic landscape; 471. *Ch. Le Brun*, Jabach of Cologne, Louis XIV.'s
banker, and his family; *Watteau*, ⁻474 a. Al fresco breakfast,
*474 b. Open-air party; ⁺465 *Mignard*, Portrait of Maria Man-
cini, niece of Cardinal Mazarin: *Pesne*, ⁻489. Frederick the Great
as crown-prince (1739), 496 b. Portrait of the painter with his two
daughters; 494 c *Greuze*, Head of a girl: no number, *R. Wilson*,
Landscape. — 1637. *Sir Joshua Reynolds*, Portrait of himself;
*1626. *Gaspar Dughet*, surnamed *Poussin*, Roman mountain landscape; no number, *H. Raeburn*, Portrait of an ecclesiastic; *Reynolds*, Mrs. Boone and her daughter; ⁺1638. *Thomas Gainsborough*,
Squire John Wilkinson; 1636. *Sir Thomas Lawrence*, Portrait of
Mr. William Linley; 448 b. *Claude Lorrain*, Italian coast-scene.
— 499 *Angelica Kauffmann*, Portrait of herself; *Chodowiecki*,
⁻491 c. Portrait of Dr. Herz, 500 b Farewell of Calas. — Two cabinets
with porcelain figures, mostly of South German manufacture. —
Returning through Room 48, we arrive at the —

Back Staircase (Pl. 27). In the recesses are statues of Frederick the Gr
Platz, whe

Cadet School at Gross-Lichterfelde) In the middle · *G. Schadow,*
Frederick the Great (1793: modern copy of the monument at Stettin).
To the left, *Schadow,* Prince Leopold of Dessau (1800; originally in
the Lustgarten); *Tassaert,* Keith (1786). To the right, *Schadow,*
Zieten (1791); *Tassaert,* Seydlitz (1781). In the rear, *F. G. Adam,*
Schwerin (1769) and Winterfeldt (1777)

4. Southern Friedrich-Strasse. Gendarmen-Markt. Wilhelm-Strasse. Leipziger-Strasse.

To the S of the Linden lies the FRIEDRICH-STADT (p. 47), the
most regularly built quarter of Berlin. It is intersected from N
to S by the *Friedrich-Strasse,* by the *Wilhelm-Strasse* farther
to the W., and by the *Charlotten-Strasse* and *Markgrafen-Strasse*
farther to the E

The **Friedrich-Strasse** (Pl. R, 24-22, G, 22) is the longest
street in the inner town Including the section to the N of the
Linden (p. 144), it measures 2 M. from the former Oranienburg Gate
to the former Halle Gate, which lies $1^1/_4$ M. to the S. of the Linden.
The central portion, near the Linden, is flanked on both sides with
handsome and substantial business-houses, including the retail premises of several important breweries (comp. p. 9)

At the corner of the Friedrich-Str. and the Behren-Str., and
opposite the S. entrance to the Kaiser-Galerie (p 56), is the building of the *Pschorr Brewery,* built by Kayser & Von Groszheim, and
decorated with paintings by M Koch and Flashar. On the upper floor
is *Castan's Panopticum* (p. 38).

The BEHREN-STRASSE (Pl. R, 22), the first cross-street (running
E. and W.), contains many handsome modern buildings, several of
which were erected by large banking houses To the E. of the
Friedrich-Strasse, on the S side, are Nos. 38-39, the *Dresdner
Bank* (p. 34), built by Heim; No. 32, the *Berliner Handels-Gesellschaft,* built by Messel, No 47, the *Haus Trarbach* (wine restaur-
ant, see p. 8), built by Walther in a modern Romanesque style.
On the opposite side are Nos. 43-44, the *Diskonto-Gesellschaft*
(comp. p. 34), built by Heim; and No. 46, the *Berliner Bank.* To
the W. of the Friedrich-Strasse, Nos. 55-57, on the N. side, is the
Metropol Theatre (p. 28), built by Fellner & Hellmer (passage to
the Linden, see p. 56). On the S. side are Nos. 13-8, the *Deutsche
Bank,* a huge building occupying an entire block; No. 7a, built by
Kayser & Von Groszheim, containing the premises of the *Nord-
deutsche Grund-Kredit-Bank;* and No. 2, the *Mitteldeutsche
Kredit-Bank,* built by Ende & Böckmann

Continuing to follow the Friedrich-str. we come (on the left)
to No. 80, the *Restaurant zum Rüdesheimer* p. 8 ; No. 79, at the

corner of the Franzosische-Str , a Renaissance building by Grisebach, the property of the *Baroness von Faber ;* and No. 78, the
office of the *Germania Life Insurance Co.,* designed by Kayser
& Von Groszheim On the opposite (right) side of the street is
No. 172, the retail premises of the *Munich Spaten Brewery*
(p. 9), built by G. von Seidl. The *Kaiser-Hotel,* Nos. 176-178, at
the corner of the Jager-Str , contains a café, the wine-rooms of the
Kaiser-Keller (p. 8), and the Weihenstephan Restaurant (p. 9).
Opposite, No 72, is *Stangen's Oriental Bazaar,* in the Moorish
style — At No. 180, on the right, at the corner of the Tauben-Str ,
the retail premises of the *Tucher Brewery* (p. 9), by Walther,
with mural paintings by Wanderer. Farther on we cross the
Mohren-Strasse (access to the Underground Railway, p. 14) and the
Leipziger-Strasse (p. 124).

To the W. of the Friedrich-Str , Tauben-Str. Nos 48-49, is the
Urania (Pl. R, 22), a popular scientific institution, opened on its
present site in 1896. It contains experimental laboratories, natural
history collections, and a lecture theatre (adm., see p. 42). Observatory, see p. 141

To the E. of the Friedrich-Strasse, a few hundred paces from
the square by the Opera House (p 58) and the Linden, is the
*Gendarmen-Markt (Pl. R, 22), with the Schauspielhaus, the
French Church, and the New Church. Though the general effect
of the square is somewhat marred by the height of some of the
more modern edifices, the three buildings just named form an
admirable architectural group, the outline of which is very effective
by moonlight.

TRAMWAYS (see p. 17-21) from the crossing of the Franzosische-Str. and
Charlotten-Str. (N W. corner of the square) to Alexander-Platz (Nos. 60,
61, 70, 73, 75), Friedrich-Str. Station and Gesundbrunnen (34, 13), Donhoff-Platz (83, 84), Hackescher Markt and Museum Island (33, 40, 53, 54,
55, 111), Halle Gate (31, 43, 53, 55, 73, 75, 96, 97), Kreuzberg (34, 43,
96, 97), Rathaus (60, 61, 70, 73, 75, 81), Rixdorf (53, 55), Silesian Station (80),
Schloss-Platz (60, 61, 70, 73, 75, 80, 81), Stettin Station (34, 43). — To
Charlottenburg, Nollendorf-Platz (and Lützow-Platz), Potsdam Station,
Schoneberg, Spittelmarkt, and Zoological Garden a shorter route will be
afforded by the new Underground Railway (entrance at the S.W. corner
of the square; comp. p 14)

The *Schauspielhaus,* or *Royal Theatre* (Pl R, 22), was
erected by *Schinkel* in 1819-21, to replace the original building
which was burned down in 1817. It has a central length of 250 ft.,
a breadth of 164 ft., and a height of 125 ft., and contains 1120 seats
The skilful application of Greek forms to a modern edifice of several
stories and the vigorous articulation render it one of Schinkel's
finest works; some defects (such as the entrance) are due to the
cramping nature of his instructions and to the necessity of using
the old walls between 1880 and 1884 the whole building was entirely restored and the interior and the walls of plaster was faced

with freestone. The E. or principal façade is embellished with a portico with six Ionian columns, approached by a prominent flight of steps, flanked by two groups in bronze by *F. Tieck*, representing genii riding on a panther and a lion. The tympanum of the portico contains a group of the Children of Niobe in sandstone, by the same sculptor The summit of the principal part of the building is crowned with an Apollo in a chariot drawn by two griffins, a group in bronze by *Rauch* and *Tieck,* in the tympanum beneath which are Melpomene and Polyhymnia. On the W. summit of the building, corresponding to the Apollo, is a Pegasus in copper. The large N. tympanum contains the *Triumphal Procession of Bacchus with Ariadne; in the S. tympanum, Orpheus bringing back Eurydice, both by *F. Tieck*. The interior was entirely remodelled in 1904-5, except the fine foyer, which serves also as a concert-room. The decorations of the auditory are by *Lessing,* the ceiling-paintings by *Koberstein* Performances, see p 27.

In front of the steps of the theatre a marble *Monument of Schiller, 19 ft. in height, by *R. Begas*, was unveiled in 1871. The pedestal is adorned with allegorical figures of lyric and dramatic poetry, history, and philosophy.

To the N. of the theatre is the **French Church**, or French Cathedral, in which a French sermon is still preached every second Sunday. Built between 1701 and 1705, it was restored in 1905, but still retains its original insignificant appearance The **New Church**, to the S., dating from the same period (1701-8), and restored in 1881-82, is interesting on account of its pentagonal form. The handsome detached towers covered with domes (230 ft. in height) were added in 1780-85 by *Gontard*, and still hold their place as one of the most effective architectural designs in the city.

Opposite the Schauspielhaus (to the E.), at No. 21 Jager-Str., is the new building (1901) of the *Königliche Seehandlung,* founded in 1772, and now carrying on a banking business. The building at the other corner of the Jager-Str (No. 47, Markgrafen-Str.), was built in 1781 (probably by Gontard) at the orders of Frederick the Great. — At the N.W corner, Charlotten-Str. 49, is the old wine-house of Lutter (p 9), with memorial-tablets to the actor L. Devrient (d. 1832) and the poet E. Th. A. Hoffmann (d. 1822), who resorted here. Hoffmann's and Heinrich Heine's (1823) residences, at Nos. 31 and 32 Tauben-Str., to the W. of the square, are marked by inscriptions and relief-portraits.

The **Wilhelm-Strasse** (Pl R, 19, 22, G, 22) forms the W. boundary of the Friedrich-Stadt, and is about 1¼ M. long. The N. half of this street is considered the most aristocratic quarter of the city. No. 70, on the right, close to the Linden, is the *British Embassy.* No 72, on the right, is the *Palace of the late Prince George of Prussia,* built by Gerlach in the reign of Frederick

William I, the new façade dating from 1852 Opposite, to the left, No 67, is *Herr Pringsheim's House*, built by Ebe & Benda in 1873, with a mosaic frieze from designs by Anton von Werner. No. 73, on the right, is the house of the *Minister of the Household*, erected in 1734-37 for Count Schwerin. No. 74 is the *Reichsamt des Innern*, or *Imperial Home Office*, where the German Federal Council meets (comp. p. 139). No. 65, opposite, to the left, is the office of the *Minister of Justice;* No. 64, the *Privy Office for Civil Affairs*, erected by Vohl; and No. 63, the *State Ministry*, the *Offices of the State Lottery*, and the *General-Ordens-Commission*. Then on the right, Nos. 75-76, the *Foreign Office.* No. 77 is the *Imperial Chancellery* and the *Residence of the Chancellor*, originally built about 1738, rebuilt in 1875-76, and occupied by Prince Bismarck till March, 1890. (The Congress of European Powers for the settlement of the Eastern Question in 1878 took place in the large hall in front.) No. 78 is the *Palace of Prince Pless*, designed by the French architect Destailleur in 1872-75 in the style of the period of Louis XIII.

The WILHELM-PLATZ (Pl. R, 19, 22) is adorned with flower-beds and with **Statues** of six heroes of the three Silesian wars of Frederick the Great: *Schwerin*, who fell, grasping the colours, at Prague in 1757; *Winterfeldt*, Frederick's favourite, who fell at Moys, near Gorlitz, in 1757, both by Kiss; *Seydlitz*, the hero of Rossbach, who died in 1773; *Keith*, who fell at Hochkirch in 1758, both by Tassaert (d. 1788); the gallant *Zieten*, who died in 1786; and *Prince Leopold of Anhalt-Dessau*, the victor at Kesselsdorf, who died in 1747, the last two by G Schadow.

The former marble statues were replaced in 1862 by bronze statues copied from the original figures, with the exception of those of Schwerin and Winterfeldt, who had been inappropriately represented in Roman costume, and are now in the Emperor Frederick Museum (p 120).

On the N. side of the Wilhelm-Platz, Nos. 8-9, is the *Palace of Prince Frederick Leopold*, erected in 1737 and remodelled by Schinkel in 1827-28. — On the E. side lie the *Kur & Neumärkische Haupt-Ritterschafts-Direktion (No. 6)* and the *Kaiserhof* (p. 3), built in 1873-75 by Von der Hude & Hennicke Behind the latter is the **Church of the Trinity** *(Dreifaltigkeits-Kirche)*, erected in 1737-39 and enlarged in 1885-86; opposite the door is a bust, by Schaper, of *Schleiermacher* (p. 171), the eminent preacher and theologian, who was pastor here from 1809 until his death in 1834. — On the S side of the Wilhelm-Platz (No 1) is the *Imperial Treasury* (Reichs-Schatzamt).

In the Wilhelm-Str., farther to the S, beyond the Leipziger-Str. (Nos. 92-93), is the *Architekten-Haus* ('Architects' Union'; Pl. R, G, 22), built by Ende & Böckmann in 1875-76, with frescoes by Prell in the central hall restaurant, see p. 10. Beyond the Prinz Albrecht-Str. p. 135 and separated from the street by an arcade, is the *Palace of Prince Frederik Henry of Prussia*, erected in 1737-39, and remodelled by Schinkel in 1833.

From the Wilhelm-Platz the Voss-Strasse (Pl. R, 19) diverges to the W. At the corner (No. 1) stands the *Preussische Pfandbrief-bank* ('mortgage bank'), a noble structure in the Italian style by Lucae, originally erected for Borsig, the manufacturer (p. 166). The statues on the exterior are by R. Begas, Encke, Hundrieser, and Lessing, and represent Beuth, Borsig, and Schinkel (on the Wilhelm-Str. side), Archimedes, Leonardo da Vinci, James Watt, and Stephenson (on the Voss-Str. side). The extensive block at the opposite corner (No. 35) is the *Ministry of Public Works*, including the *Imperial Office of Railways*. At Nos. 4 & 5 in the Voss-Str. is the *Reichs-Justizamt* ('Imperial Justice Office'), and there are also many handsome private residences in this street.

A little to the S. of the W. end of the Voss-Str. lies the Pots-damer-Platz (p. 127), adjoined on the E. by the site of the old Potsdam Gate and the octagonal Leipziger-Platz (Pl. R, 19), which is adorned with gardens and statues of *Count Brandenburg* (to the left; d. 1850). the general and statesman, by Hagen, and *Field-Marshal Count Wrangel* (to the right: d. 1877), by Keil. The former was erected in 1862, the latter in 1880. At Nos. 6-10 in this Platz is the *Ministry of Agriculture, Domains, and Forests;* No. 13, on the N. side, is the *Admiralty* (Reichs-Marine-Amt); No. 14 the offices of the *Berlin Tramway Co.* (p. 14); No. 15 *Herr Mosse's House*, built by Ebe and Benda, with a sandstone frieze by Max Klein representing the development of the German genius; and No. 16 the *House of the Imperial Automobile Club*, designed by Ihne.

From the Leipziger-Platz the busy *Leipziger-Strasse (Pl. R, 19, 22), about 1 M. in length, crosses the Friedrich-Str. and runs E. to the Spittel-Markt. It is perhaps the chief artery of traffic in Berlin (numerous tramways to the West End; see p. 126), and excels even the Friedrich-Str. in the number of its handsome commercial buildings, most of which are in the Renaissance style. The visitor is advised to inspect this street in the evening, when the shop-windows are brilliantly lighted.

No. 12, on the right, is the *Ministry of Commerce and Industry,* on the groundfloor of which is the attractive depôt of the Royal Porcelain Manufactory (p. 179), which may be visited at any hour.— Adjacent (Nos. 3-4) are the Herrenhaus and (No. 5) the *War Office*.

The **Herrenhaus**, or *Upper Chamber of the Prussian Diet,* a handsome edifice in the Italian style by *F. Schulze,* was opened in 1904. It is connected with the House of Representatives (p. 135; passage on the E. side), and encloses a spacious fore-court, on either side of which are dwellings for the presidents of the two chambers. The sandstone façade is decorated with sculptures, for which O.

lumns, contains a representation of Borussia with the various ministries, on the attic are figures of the working and military classes. The ten allegorical figures on the wings are from designs by *Pfannschmidt, Dennert, Meisen, Uechtritz,* and *Calandrelli.* The house has seats for 218 members Admission, see p. 38.

Nos. 132-135, on the left side of the street, is ' *Wertheim's Emporium,* erected by Messel in 1897-1904, an excellent type of the modern German warehouse (comp. p. 51). The façade of the building, which covers about 18,000 sq. yds., is 590 ft. long and consists of granite pillars ornamented with metal work, from which projects a limestone colonnade on the Leipziger-Platz, with the bear-fountain by Gaul. The interior well repays a visit; visitors need not make any purchase. The E. glass-covered hall contains a statue of Industry by Manzel. Refreshment Bar — At No. 124, at the corner of the Wilhelm-Str., is the office of the *New York Mutual Insurance Co.,* built in 1885-86 by Kayser & Von Groszheim, with mosaics of six great towns.

At the corner of the Mauer-Str. is the **Reichs-Postamt,** or Office of the Postmaster General (Pl. R, 22), a handsome edifice in the Italian style, erected in 1871-73 and enlarged in 1893-98. — In the corner-wing, above which rises a group of giants holding aloft the terrestrial globe, is the —

*Imperial Postal Museum, containing a collection of objects illustrating the development of postal and other means of communication. The various rooms open off an inner court, which is decorated with sculptures. Above the entrance is a bust of Emp William II., flanked by figures of Industry and Peace, by K. Begas. In side niches are figures of Science and Traffic, by Wenck. Above are six realistic bronze figures representing different methods of communication. In the centre is a marble statue of *H. von Stephan,* the postmaster-general (d. 1897; comp. p 171). Adm., see p. 39. A label is attached to each exhibit.

GROUND FLOOR In the rooms round the inner court are models of German *Post Offices.* Rooms 1 and 5, on the left, contain letter-boxes, signs, etc. Traversing these, we reach the **Historical Department,* containing pictures, casts, and models representing the systems of communication adopted by the ancients and in the middle ages, as well as the postal system of the 16-18th centuries The entrance wall of Room 6 is devoted to the ancients. Room 7 German and Scandinavian objects, including Germanic bronze chariots, reconstruction of a Scandinavian chariot copied from fragments found in the Dejberg morass, viking's ship, plank roads, etc. Model of the Santa Maria, the vessel in which Columbus made his voyage of 1492. On the walls are miniatures illustrating the methods of writing and forwarding messages and letters during the middle ages; by the window, writing materials, wax tablets, and 15th cent letters On the window-wall of Room 6 are letters, guidebooks, MS. newspapers of the 16th cent., and pictures of the 16-18th centuries, post____'s ____ of the time of the Thirty Years' War autograph postal decre | w | | | | dels of travellin | l | | th | | | nin *Postal Syst*   ___ ___ | | M | | __ | | the

staircase) model of the locomotive 'Feuer-Ross' of the Fürth-Nuremberg railway, the first opened (1835) in Germany, postman of the Spreewald, railway postal service. Room 14. Military post. Room 15. Selections from the collection of *Postage Stamps*, one of the largest in the world.

FIRST FLOOR. Adjoining the staircase are reminiscences of Stephan (see p. 125). To the left is the interesting series of exhibits illustrating *Foreign Postal Systems*. The following may be mentioned: apparatus for collecting the mail-bags in transit by English trains, models and figures from Russia. Beyond the central room (adorned with stained glass), to the right, models of steamboats; to the left, the very complete *Telegraphic Collection*, beginning with optical telegraphs.

SECOND FLOOR. To the left of the staircase: *Submarine Telegraphy* (cable-laying steamers), and finally the building of telegraph and telephone lines (destruction of the poles by animals; effect of lightning on the apparatus, etc.). In the *Record Office* copies and originals of old maps and atlases are at present on view. — We now return to the staircase, to the right of which is the *Telephonic Collection* (including various devices for changing or reversing the current). In the end room are exhibits connected with the pneumatic post, phonography, Röntgen rays, wireless telegraphy, etc.

The *Bethlehems-Kirche*, to the right in the Mauer-Str., was built in 1735-37 by order of Frederick William I. for exiled Bohemian Lutherans.

Continuing eastwards along the Leipziger-Str., we come to the office of the *New York Equitable Insurance Co.*, a building by Schäfer, standing at the corner of the Friedrich-Str. The traffic at this point is very great, especially from 5 to 8 p.m. — The intersection of the Leipziger-Str. and Charlotten-Str. is one of the centres of the tramway system.

TRAMWAYS (pp 15-21): Nos. 6, 9, 31, 43, 53, 54, 55, 66, 67, 69, 71-79, 83, 84, 87, 88, 91, 92, 95, 96, 97.

At No. 43, on the right side of the Leipziger-Str. and at the corner of the Markgrafen-Str., is the silk warehouse of *Michels & Co.*, a brick building by Grisebach, with ornaments on a gold ground. — Nos. 46-49 form *Tietz's Warehouse*, erected in 1900 from designs by Sehring and Lachmann, covering over 6500 sq. yds of ground, and extending to the Krausen-Str. (comp. p. 32). — Beyond the Jerusalemer-Str. the Leipziger-Str traverses the Donhoff-Platz and, passing through the *Leipziger Kolonnaden* (built in 1776 by Gontard), ends at the Spittel-Markt (p. 159).

In the grounds of the DONHOFF-PLATZ (Pl R, 22, 25) are the bronze statues of two statesmen: on the N. side *Baron vom Stein* (d. 1831), by Schievelbein and Hagen (1875); on the S. side *Prince Hardenberg* (d. 1822), by Götze (1907)

TRAMWAYS (pp 15-22) run from the Donhoff-Platz (94, P, R) to the Brandenburg Gate (6, 9, 13), the Lehrte Station, Moabit (9, 12, 13), the Friedrich-Str. Station (12, 13, 18), Gesundbrunnen (38, 39, 42), the Alexander-Platz (17, 59, 62, 63, 64, 66, 67, 69, 71, 72, 74), the Silesian Station (9, 78), the Görlitz Station (12, 13, 18, 91, 92, 94), Rixdorf (94), the Halle Gate (38, 39, 42, 64), the Kreuzberg (38), the Anhalt Station (17, 59, 62, 63), the Gendarmen-Markt (84, 84), the Hackescher Markt (38, 39, 42), the Museum Island (39, 42), the Opern-Platz (12, 13, 18, 39, 42), the Potsdam Station (6, 9, 66, 67, 69, 71, 72, 74, 76, 78, 79, 87, 88, 91, 92, P, R), the

Rathaus (17, 38, 39, 62, 63, 64, 66, 67, 69, 71, 72), and the Schloss-Platz (17, 63)   To Charlottenburg, Nollendorf-Platz (and Lützow-Platz), Schöneberg, and Zoological Garden a shorter route will soon be afforded by the Underground Railway (p 14); entrances to the E at the Spittelmarkt, to the N. on the Hausvogtei-Platz.

5. Ethnographical Museum and Museum of Industrial Art.

The somewhat contracted Potsdamer-Platz (Pl. R, 19; comp. p. 124) is apt to be congested by the enormously developed traffic to the S.W. quarters of the city.

Tramways (pp 14-23) run hence to the Brandenburg Gate (1, 6, 7, 9, 14, 15, 23, 24, 51, 52, 56, 57), Gesundbrunnen (23), the Hackescher Markt (33, 40, 52, 54, 56), the Neues Tor (51, 57), the Rathaus (60, 61, 66, 67, 69, 71, 72, 74, 81), the Schloss-Platz (60, 61, 80), Lehrte Station, Moabit (6, 7, 9, 14, 15, 23, 24), the Museum Island and the Opern-Platz (39, 40, 54, 111), the Alexander-Platz (60, 61, 66, 67, 69, 71, 72, 74, 81), the Silesian Station (1, 6, 9, 76, 78, 79, 80), Rixdorf (7, 15), and Schöneberg (23, 24, 40, 51, 56, 57, 60, 61, 68, 69, 71, 72, 74, 87, 88, III, B, C) — Charlottenburg, the Görlitz Station, Halle Gate, Nollendorf-Platz, Lützow-Platz and the Zoological Garden are more conveniently reached by the Elevated Railway (p. 13), and the Gendarmen-Markt and Spittel-Markt (Dönhoff-Platz) by the new Underground Railway (p. 14) — In the neighbouring Link-Str. (see below) is the terminus of the tramways to Friedenau, Grunewald, Schmargendorf, Steglitz, and Wilmersdorf (see p. 181).

The Potsdamer-Platz, on the right side of which rise the *Palast-Hotel* and the *Hôtel Bellevue*, and on the left the *Hôtel Fürstenhof* (p 3), is traversed by the Königgratzer-Strasse (see below). The shady Bellevue-Strasse (p. 143), leading off to the right to the Tiergarten, contains at No 3 the *Künstler-Haus* (Pl. R, 19), erected in 1898 by Hoffacker for the Society of Berlin Artists (exhibitions, see p. 37). Opposite, Nos 19-20, is the *Rheingold Restaurant* (p. 8), erected by Bruno Schmitz and gorgeously fitted up, adjoined by the new *Esplanade Hotel* (p. 3). For the Potsdamer-Strasse, see p. 173.

To the S in the Potsdamer-Platz is the **Potsdam Station** (Pl. G, 19), erected in 1870-72, combined with the *Ringbahn* and *Wannsee Stations* (comp. p. 185). Elevated Railway, see p. 13.

The district to the S.E. of the Potsdam Station, to the right of the Königgratzer-Strasse, which leads to the Halle Gate, was a favourite residential quarter, much affected by officials, about the middle of the 19th cent., when it was popularly known as the 'Privy Councillors' Quarter' Now, however, many of the houses are let out in furnished apartments. — At Nos. 4-5 in the Dessauer-Str. is the *Post-Zeitungs-Amt*. In the Bernburger-Str. (No. 22) is the *Philharmonie* (Pl. G, 19; p 29), rebuilt in 1888 by Schwechten. The *Beethoven-Saal*, in connection with the Philharmonie, is entered from No. 32 Köthener-Strasse. The office of the *Siemens-Schuckert Electric Co* is at Askanischer Plaz No

On the [illegible] the [illegible]
Berlin Raila [illegible] completed

in 1895; and, on the Tempelhofer Ufer, at the corner of the Trebbiner-Str., the *Central Junction of the Electric Elevated Railway* (p. 13), in which the transition from the lower to the upper level is made.

The **Anhalt Station** (Pl. G, 19), in the Askanischer-Platz, is a handsome brick building erected by *Schwechten* in 1875-80. The main hall is 115 ft. in height and as broad as the Linden (200 ft.).

Tramways (pp. 14-21): Nos. 1, 7, 14, 15, 17, 59, 62, 63, 93, 98; Omnibus No. 12 to Alexander-Platz Station.

At Königgrätzer-Str. 112-13, opposite the station, is the *Hôtel Excelsior* (p. 3), by Boswau & Knauer (1908); farther on, Nos. 57-58, is the *Hebbel Theatre* (p. 28), by O. Kaufmann (1908).

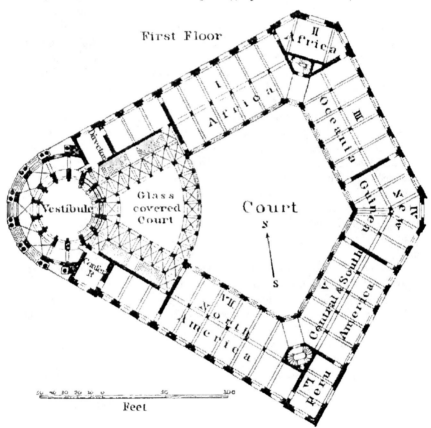

The Prinz-Albrecht-Strasse (Pl. G, 19, 22) diverges to the E. from the Königgrätzer-Str. between the Potsdam and Anhalt Stations. At the corner on the right is the —

*Ethnographical Museum (*Museum für Völkerkunde;* Pl. G, 19), designed by *Ende* and opened in 1886, the main entrance to which is in the semicircular structure on the E. side. On the ground-floor are the Prehistoric Collections (director, Prof. K. Schuchardt)

and Schliemann's Trojan Collections; the two upper floors are
devoted to the Ethnographical Collections, which rival in extent and
scientific value those in the British Museum — Adm see p. 37;
the official guide (1906; 50 pf.) is not clearly arranged. As the collections are constantly being added to and the arrangement of the
exhibits altered, visitors are referred to the directing arrows
and instructions on the door-posts of the rooms and to the labels
attached to the various objects.

Court. — The Vestibule, the ceiling of which is adorned with
a mosaic of the planets, and the adjoining glass-covered Court,
which is surrounded by galleries, contain the larger objects, notably numerous sculptures in stone from Mexico and Central
America In the vestibule is a colossal Buddha from Japan. In
the middle of the court, a large outrigged boat from the Bismarck
Archipelago; opposite the entrance, a plaster cast, 33 ft. in height,
of the E door of the great tope of Sanchi in Central India,
dating from the 3rd cent. B C, and adorned with reliefs from Indian
mythology and history; to the left and right are two Indian totem
poles from Canada, and on the right the chariot of a god from Orissa
in S. India, and a plaster cast of a monolithic gateway in Bolivia.
In the corridors at the sides are large dug-out canoes.

Ground Floor. — To the left of the vestibule are the *Prehistoric
Collections.* The ANTEROOM contains the European antiquities, with
the exception of those of German origin, which occupy Rooms I-IV.
The gold and silver objects in R. II, the tree-coffins and the skeleton-
tombs of the later stone age, found near Merseburg, in R. III, and
the objects taken from the burial-ground near Reichenhall (5-7th
cent. A.D.) in R. IV are of special interest.

Room V, partly belonging to the ethnographical department,
contains the *Peruvian Antiquities* collected by Prof. Bassler (see
also R. VI on the first floor; p 130). At the end of the room are
collections from *Persia, Turkestan, Siberia, Mongolia* and the
country of the *Ainos* (aboriginal inhabitants of Japan)

The Rooms to the right of the court contain the *Schliemann
Collections,* presented by the distinguished discoverer (d. 1890) to
the German Empire. Most of the objects were excavated in 1871-82
on the site of ancient Troy, including the famous series of gold
articles, formerly called the 'Treasure of Priam' (in the 2nd Room).
In 1909 this collection is to be transferred to the Antiquarium in
the Old Museum (p. 74).

First Floor. — The Corridor contains antiquities from *Southern Peru* and *Argentina* and life-size figures and other carvings
from *North Cameroon* — Proceeding to the left, we enter —

Room I. *Africa.* Close to the door is a '*Collection of Bronze
Objects from Benin,*' is.. ne of th se obtained by the British
in the West African expedition of 1897 heads of negroes, reliefs

of negroes in armour; chiefs with their retinues, and white warriors (probably dating from the 16th or 17th cent); animals of various kinds, etc. They should be compared with the ivory carvings in Cabinet 22 (to the left) and with the brass ornaments and painted wooden figures from the Slave Coast in Cabinet 263 (to the right of the entrance to R. III). In a case in front of the latter are gold ornaments brought by Wissmann from Kilwa.

Room II. Further collections from the *East Coast of Africa.*

Room III. *Oceania.* This collection is the most complete in existence, and contains objects from the time of Cook's (d. 1779) voyages onwards Near the entrance: *New Zealand;* on the back wall are old carvings. — To the right: *Polynesia* (Tahiti, Hawaii, Samoa, etc.). On these islands metal vessels, bows and arrows, woven cloth, and pottery are unknown, their place being taken by clubs, plaited mats and stuffs made from the fibres of the paper mulberry-tree, and wooden utensils and calabashes made from bottle-gourds — *Micronesia* (Caroline and Marshall Islands, etc.). The weapons studded with sharks' teeth (comp. R. IV) and the native armour of cocoanut fibre should be noticed. — To the left: *New Holland* and *Melanesia* (the chain of islands stretching from New Guinea to New Caledonia). In Cabs. 81, 55, and 53 are carved boards and masks, and costumes of the Duk-Duk secret society of the *Bismarck Archipelago,* made of tufts of leaves. Cabs. 70 & 71 contain carved clubs shaped like the old flint-muskets in use at the time of the discovery of the islands, glazed utensils (the only ones found in the South Sea), and objects used at cannibal feasts, from the *Fiji Islands.* — The following rooms are closed at present.

Room IV. *New Guinea,* especially *Kaiser Wilhelm's Land.*

Room V. *Central and South America.* To the right. *South American Indians,* including curiosities from *Gran Chaco* (feather ornaments) and the upper *Xingu,* in Central Brazil. — The rest of the room is devoted to antiquities and relics of the extinct civilised nations of America, from *Mexico, Yucatan,* and *Peru,* the last being especially valuable. The table-case near the exit contains Mexican turquoise mosaics and calendar-stones.

Room VI. Large collection of *Peruvian Antiquities* from the burial-ground of Ancon, to the N. of Lima; swathed mummies.

Room VII. *North America.* To the right are models of the fortress-like dwellings of the *Pueblo Indians.* To the left some more antiquities from *Central* and *South America* (see R. V). Then, objects from *North-West America,* collected in 1881-83 by Captain Jacobsen (including numerous dancing-masks and carved figures of the *Kwakiutl* tribe); below the windows to the left, paintings by *Sioux Indians.*

To the **Second Floor** we may ascend to the right or left of the court On the right staircase are Chinese state-halberds and a

Japanese standard in the shape of a carp On the wall of the left staircase and in the adjoining corridor are imitations of Siamese carving from the temple at Angkor. — Rooms I-IV (beginning on the left) are closed at present.

Room I. *Collections from Hindustan:* models of buildings and native types; technical groups. To the left, theatrical costumes, wood and ivory carvings (Cab. 12 and by Cab. 10a); to the right miniatures (in front of Cab 22), embroidery (Cab 24), Græco-Buddhist sculptures, paintings, and manuscripts from *Chinese Turkestan.* In an anteroom (adjacent to the left) are objects from *Bokhara* — Room II *Himalaya* and *Brahmapootra Districts.*

Room III. *Indo-China·* in front and to the right, *Burma,* to the right the *Nicobar* and *Andaman Islands,* at the back *Malacca,* and to the left, *Siam* and the *Eastern Islands.* Front wall: tiles with reliefs of mythological scenes, from Pagân, the capital of the early Burmese kings, destroyed in the 13th century. On the right, objects relating to the cult of Buddhism as practised in S. Asia. Behind, models of Malayan boats On the left by the windows, figures for shadow-pantomimes from Siam

Room IV. *Indonesia,* or *Malay Archipelago,* originally affected by the civilization of Hindustan To the left, *Sumatra* and *Borneo;* behind, *Java,* which was the chief centre of the Indian influence until 1500 when Islam was introduced To the right are the *E. Malay Islands.* — Costume-figures of head-hunters of Borneo (Cab. 69 & 71): old Javanese carvings; Javanese shadow-plays (scenes from the ancient heroic myths) and puppet shows. Tutelary deities of villages; ancestral figures, and matauka-figures or magic amulets against thieves (Cab. 88).

Room V. *Indonesia* (continued). Most of the exhibits here have been collected from *Timor,* the *Moluccas, Celebes,* the *Sulu Islands,* and the *Philippine Islands.* — In a space partitioned off, Lamaism as practised in *Tibet,* the chief seat of this N form of Buddhism At the back, Chinese shrine and altar of the goddess of small-pox and (in the passage to R. VII) model of the temple of a town-god.

Room VI. Fishing in *China* and *Japan.*

Room VII. *China* (in the first part of the room). Numerous model figures. Fine collection of objects illustrating the Chinese religion (Lamaism and Foism practised in the S. and centre of the country, but more especially Taoism, the religion of the people), figures of gods and genii (to the left, large Taoistic collection), paintings from temples, altar utensils, reliquaries. Wearing apparel, pottery and porcelain, and valuable carvings in jade, agate, etc. — *Japan* (second half of the room). Numerous idols To the right, gala-costumes interesting paintings those in Desk-Case 151 (by the window state eastern countries gigantic drum for religious dances. — Here is also an interesting collection of Chinese, Japanese, and Korean antiquities from the pre-Buddhistic and early Buddhistic periods.

Room VIII. *Japan* (continued). Objects in lacquer and instruments of war. Objects from the *Loo-Choo Islands* and *Korea.* — We return through R. VII to the staircase, where are Japanese porcelain and paintings on folding-screens.

Several rooms on the third floor (not yet open) contain objects from Africa, China (burial-customs), North America (negro races), and Graeco-Buddhist carvings from India.

In the Prinz Albrecht-Str., farther on, to the right, is the —

Museum of Industrial Art (Pl G, 19), founded in 1867, a very extensive and valuable collection of the products of many different countries, both ancient and modern. The handsome building was erected in 1877-81 in the Renaissance style by *Gropius & Schmieden*, with effective façades in hewn stone and terracotta. The mosaics below the cornice, executed in Venice from designs by *Ewald* and *Geselschap*, represent the epochs in the history of civilisation typified by single figures. At the sides of the flight of steps ascending to the door are sandstone statues of Peter Vischer and Holbein, by *Sussmann-Hellborn*. — Admission, see p. 38. Director, Prof. *von Falke*. Official catalogue (1907), 50 pf.

Ground Floor. — In the VESTIBULE (Pl 1) is a high-altar from a Mannheim church (ca. 1760), and the bow of a Venetian state-galley (16th cent.) — We pass hence through a second Hall (Pl. 2) and enter the glass-covered COURT (Pl. 3), which is used for exhibition purposes. Above, below the glass-roof, is a rich frieze by *Geyer* and *Hundrieser*, representing a procession of the nations most distinguished in industrial art, saluting Borussia. The lower arcade (Pl. 4-7) contains objects in wrought iron and Renaissance furniture (cabinets, chests, caskets, etc).

The rooms round the court contain furniture and domestic equipments arranged in chronological order. Nearly all the rooms contain fine stained-glass windows of the 13-16th centuries. Rooms 9 and 10 at the N.W corner are used for temporary exhibitions.

W. Side. Rooms 11-13: Domestic furniture in the Gothic style, chiefly cabinets and chests, adorned with carving and metal work. Room 12: Enamels from the Lower Rhine and Limoges (11-13th cent.). Works in metal (chiefly ecclesiastical), crosses, censers, and ewers *Flemish tapestry with gold threads (15th cent.). Room 13: *Collection of carved and painted caskets; ivory carvings. — Rooms 14-17: Italian and French Renaissance works. Musical instruments and backgammon boards; spinet of Duke Alfonso II. of Ferrara — Room 15. Italian stone carvings. Christ bearing the cross, German glass painting (ca 1510). Room 16: Fine coffered ceiling and leather

MUSEUM OF INDUSTRIAL ART

Ground Floor

First Floor

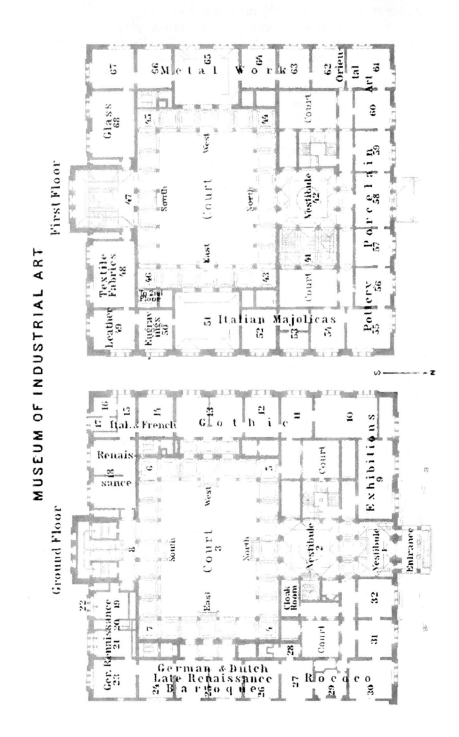

hangings from Florence (ca 1500). Room 17 Small Florentine chamber, painted about 1580 in the style of Poccetti

S. Side. Room 18: Large coffered ceiling of the 15th cent.; furniture, frames, candelabra of the Italian Renaissance. Seat from the synagogue of Siena Chests with representations of Neptune and the Niobides (Italian, 16th cent.); 'Bridal chest from the Palazzo Strozzi. — Rooms 19 and 21, beyond the staircase, contain the 'Panelling of two rooms of the 16th century (the original furniture was different). The richer of the two, elaborately adorned with intarsia and enclosing an old stove, is from the château of Haldenstein, near Coire, and dates from 1548 The other, from the château of Hollrich, near Würzburg, was made about 1570, and comprises a fine ceiling with armorial bearings. — Between these rooms is a space arranged as a chapel, with altar-screens dating from 1500 and glass-paintings of the 14th century. — R. 22 (above). Collection of mosaics, basket-work, etc. — Corner Room 23 Tapestry and furniture of the early Renaissance, mainly from Burgundy and the Lower Rhine Admirable collection of boxwood carvings, mostly goldsmiths' models. *Ribbon-weavers' loom carved in boxwood (Nuremberg; ca. 1550). *Chamber organ, beautifully carved (Flanders; ca 1530).

E. Side. Rooms 24-26: German and Dutch late-Renaissance works. Room 24: German furniture of the 17th cent : painted table by H. S. Beham, 1531 (replica of the original in the Louvre) carvings on amber (chiefly from Dantsic), cocoa-nuts, and ostrich eggs. Room 25: German baroque furniture of the 17th and 18th cent.; two 'Muscovite' cabinets; picture-frames Room 26: Dutch furniture; carvings on ivory, mother-of-pearl, and shells. — Rooms 27-29 · Rococo furniture. Room 27 Carved and gilded panels from the palace chapel at Versailles (ca. 1720); Clock and corner cabinet from Liège (ca. 1750); in the centre: French writing-table with bronze mounts. — Room 28: Chamber with carved panelling and paintings from Paris, ca. 1710; French pedestal table of boxwood, ca. 1720 — Room 29. 'Panelled reception-room from the Hôtel Sillery at Paris, ca. 1730. — Room 30: French works of the end of the 18th century: objects in the German rococo style. In glass-cases, **Furniture from the boudoir of Queen Marie Antoinette at Versailles, opposite, 'Commode by Riesener. Copies of the plate presented in 1772 by Frederick the Great to Empress Catherine of Russia. — Room 31: Furniture of the 18th and 19th cent.; in the middle two easy-chairs after Schinkel's designs.

The Staircase is adorned with stained glass windows representing the Emperor and Empress Frederick, who founded the museum, from designs by *E Ewald*. We ascend by the staircase on the N side

First Floor. Collection of glazed earthenware groups including pottery glass and needlework and others. The cases between the pilasters of the GALLERY contain modern French medallions and plaquettes by ˟*Roty* and others, New Year's cards of thin iron, etc.; then, small articles of domestic use, such as knives, forks, spoons, combs, fans, cake-moulds, and the like, many of them elaborately carved and ornamented. — On the W. side is a collection of ˟Ornaments, in geographical and chronological order: Cabinet 283, Eglomisé work (painting under glass); Cab 280, mediæval ornaments (ca. 1400), discovered near Pritzwalk in Brandenburg. On the N. and E. walls· Spanish, Italian, and Oriental tiles. — At the back (S. side): to the right German stoves and tiles; in the centre, modern porcelain; to the left, a selection of textile fabrics (stairs to the 2nd floor, see p. 135).

S. E. Corner. ROOM 48· Varying exhibition of textile fabrics. — ROOM 49 Bookbindings; leather-work, *e.g.* an octagonal box with love-scenes from Bâle, 14th cent. — ROOM 50: Drawings and engravings of ornaments.

E Side Here and on the N. side the highly important collection of artistic pottery is exhibited. LARGE CUPOLA ROOM 51 : *Collection of Italian majolica, one of the most extensive of the kind in the world. The art of majolica-painting enjoyed its highest development in 1480-1540, and also flourished at Urbino in the reign of Duke Guidobaldo II. (1538-74). Engravings and woodcuts were the favourite patterns of the painters. The chief manufactories were at Gubbio (celebrated for its gold and ruby tints: Cab. 321), Urbino (Cab 315, 316), Faenza and Caffagiolo near Florence. At a later period majolica was also made at Castelli, at Deruta in Umbria, with an opalescent sheen like mother-of-pearl (Cab. 314, 323), and in Northern Italy. — ROOMS 52-54: Oriental and Hispano-Moorish, ˥Delft, and German fayence.

N. Side. ROOM 55: German stoneware. Palissy and 'Hirsvogel' ware; Franconian, Rhenish, Nassau, and ˥Siegburg stoneware. — ROOM 56: French (Moustiers, Rouen, Strassburg, etc.), Spanish and Italian fayence; Wedgwood ware. — ROOMS 57-59 European porcelain. ROOM 57: Berlin; R 58: Dresden (to the left, specimens of Bottger's first efforts in 1710); pieces of the celebrated Swan service of Count Bruhl; three monuments to Gellert (Cab. 427). Room 59 contains examples of other German and foreign fabrics.

North West Corner. ROOMS 60-63. Porcelain, lacquer work, and metal-works from China, Japan, Persia, and India.

West Side. Works in metal ROOM 64: Clocks and scientific instruments. — CENTRAL CUPOLA ROOM 65: **˟Objects in the precious metals. German silver ware of the 17-18th centuries. ˟Church-plate from St. Dionysius at Enger, the earliest pieces dating from the time of Duke Wittekind. **˟·Luneburger Ratssilberzeug', a fine service of 36 pieces of plate of the 15-16th cent, purchased in 1874 for 33,000*l*. Adjoining is the ·Pommersche Kunstschrank', an ex-

quisite cabinet made in 1617 for Philip II, Duke of Pomerania.
*German silver ware of the Renaissance, including specimens by the
celebrated goldsmiths Chr Jamnitzer, J. Silber, H. Petzold, and
P. Gottich Reproductions of German plate, especially of the work
of Eisenhoit. The windows contain stained glass from Switzerland
— Room 66. Magnificent carved wood ceiling (ca. 1560), from a palace
in Fano. Italian bronze-works. *Door-knockers 'Painted enamels
from Limoges (15-17th cent.), including several specimens of great
beauty and rarity — Corner Room 67: Works in copper, tin, and
brass; German plaquettes in lead and bronze Pewter platters by
Briot and Enderlein. *Stained-glass window from Nuremberg, probably designed by Albrecht Durer (1508) — Room 68: Collection of
glass, one of the most complete departments in the museum. Venetian
glass Cab. 626 *Two enamelled glasses of the end of the 15th cent.
(Venice). Among the German glass may be specified the so-called
*'Schaper Glasses', with black enamel paintings. Bohemian glass;
Ruby and spun glass *Chinese glass. Antique Roman glass; Persian
glass; German glass vessels with enamel painting.

Second Floor. access in the S.E. corner of the gallery (p. 131).
— Rooms 72-76: *Collection of Textile Fabrics, the most complete
in existence, especially as regards the extremely rare mediæval
fabrics, which, however, are only of technical interest. Needlework
of every kind, period, and country is here represented, as also
tapestry and wallpapers. — The adjoining Gallery contains a collection of Italian, Spanish and Netherlandish leather hangings. —
Collection of decorative plaster-casts, extending from antiquity to
the 18th century.

Adjoining the Museum, an *Art-Industrial School* (director,
Prof. Bruno Paul) was erected in 1901-5

The Museum possesses a *Library and Collection of Ornamental Engravings* (director, Dr Jessen), of which special catalogues are issued. —
In the basement is the valuable *Library of Costumes* (30,000 plates and
10,000 vols.), collected by *Baron von Lipperheide* (p. 71) and presented
to the state in 1898 (varying exhibitions).

Opposite the Museum on the left side of the Prinz-Albrecht-
Strasse rises the —

Abgeordnetenhaus, or *Prussian Chamber of Deputies*
(Pl. G, 19), a handsome Renaissance edifice by *F Schulze,* erected in
1893-98, with allegorical statues on the exterior by *O. Lessing.* In
the entrance hall are four bronze figures by *Stark.* The large session
hall, the walls of which are adorned with views of twelve towns by
M. Koch, K. Lessing, Gunther-Naumburg, and *Schirm,* contains
seats for 433 deputies. Adm., see p 36 — The building is connected
with the Herrenhaus or Upper Chamber of the Diet (see p. 124) by
means of a passage at the back, which leads through an intermediate
building for _____ handsome
chamber for cabinet meetings M ___

6. Königs-Platz.   Ausstellungs-Park.   Sieges-Allée.

The Platz vor dem Brandenburger Tor (Pl. R, 20, 19) was transformed in 1903 after *Ihne's* designs. It is bounded by semi-circular marble walls and balustrades, in the middle of which are marble statues, on the right, of *Emperor Frederick III.,* with the busts of Helmholtz, the physicist, and General Blumenthal, by Brütt; on the left, that of *Empress Victoria,* with busts of Zeller, the philosopher, and W. von Hofmann, the chemist, by Gerth. Beyond these, on each side of the Charlottenburg road, are fountains. — Tiergarten, see p. 175; Königgratzer-Strasse, p. 127.

The *Friedens-Allée* leads to the right to the *Königs-Platz (Pl. R, 20), which with its environs forms one of the most imposing parts of the city. Originally laid out as a drill-ground by Frederick William I., it received its present name in 1864.

The 'Column of Victory (*Sieges-Säule; Pl R, 20), 200 ft. in height, designed by *Strack,* and inaugurated on 2nd Sept., 1873, rises in the centre of the Platz, on a circular terrace approached by eight steps of granite. This massive column, built of dark red granite, sandstone, and bronze, is perhaps the most imposing of its kind in existence. The square pedestal, 22 ft. in height, is adorned with reliefs in bronze: on the E. side is the Danish War of 1864, by *A. Calandrelli;* on the N. the Battle of Königgratz, 1866, by *M Schultz;* on the W. the Battle of Sedan, 1870, and the Entry into Paris, 1871, by *K. Keil;* on the S. the Return of the troops to Berlin, 1871, by *A. Wolff.* The base of the column is surrounded by an open colonnade, and embellished with Venetian mosaics designed by *Anton von Werner,* illustrating the war of 1870 and the restoration of the German empire. Above, in the flutings of the column, are placed three rows of captured Danish, Austrian, and French cannon (60 in all). The capital, formed of eagles, is crowned with a gilded figure of Victory (by *Drake*), holding a laurel-wreath in the right hand and an ensign with the iron cross in the left. The proportions of the monument are so calculated that this surmounting figure, 48 ft in height, bulks as the principal feature. Fine view from the platform of the capital, 151 ft. high (adm., see p. 37).

The Königs-Platz is bounded on the E. by the *Reichstags-Gebäude (*Hall of the Imperial Diet; Pl. R, 20), built in 1884-94 from the designs of *Paul Wallot.* The building, in the florid Italian Renaissance style, which cost 22,000,000 marks (1,100,000 *l*), is 430 ft. in length, 290 ft. in breadth, 88 ft. in height to the main cornice and 225 ft to the imperial crown. The external material is Silesian sandstone. Rising above a square central structure is a huge glass dome girt with highly gilded copper bands and bearing

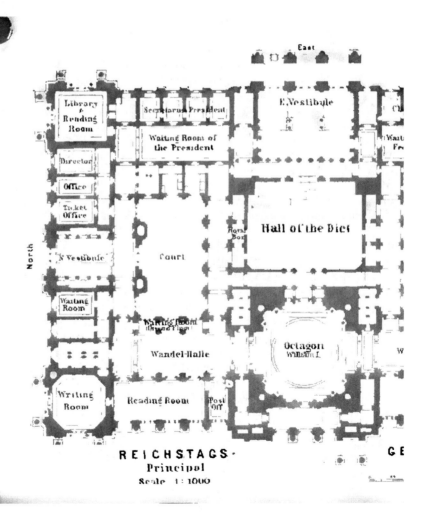

East

Library & Reading Room

Secretaries President

E. Vestibule

Ch

Waiting Room of the President

Wait Pre

Director

Office

Ticket Office

Hall of the Diet

Hors Box

North

N Vestibule

Court

Waiting Room

Waiting Room (Ground Floor)

Octagon William I.

W

Wandel-Halle

Writing Room

Reading Room

Post Off

GE

REICHSTAGS-
Principal
Scale 1:1000

a lantern encircled with columns, which is in turn surmounted by
an imperial crown. At the corners are four boldly designed towers,
195 ft. high.

The chief (W.) FAÇADE, turned towards the Königs-Platz, with a
portico borne by six columns, is the richest in plastic adornment.
To the right and left of the door are reliefs, by *O. Lessing*, of the
Rhine and the Vistula, leaning respectively against an oak-tree and
a pine-tree, in the branches of which hang the arms of the German
states; above the door is a figure of St. George (with the features
of Bismarck), bearing the imperial banner, designed by *Siemering;*
in the pediment is a relief by *Schaper*, representing Art and Industry protected by Germanic warriors; on the apex of the pediment is a colossal Germania on horseback, bearing shield and
banner and escorted by two genii, by *R. Begas* (in copper). — Over
the S. door is a lion guarding the regalia, by *Klein;* over the N.
door a figure of Truth, by *Brütt.* — On the E. façade is a portico,
beneath which is a covered carriage-way. At the sides are huge
representations of the imperial coat-of-arms protected by two
knights, and at the foot of the approach on each side are bronze
candelabra, surmounted by figures of Victory dispensing laurels,
by *A. Vogel.* Above are two mounted heralds (in copper), by *Maison.*

The exterior of the corner-towers also deserves notice. Above
the architrave supported by columns rising from the basement story
are 16 figures typifying the different industries and occupations of
the German people, by *Behrens, Diez, Eberle, Eberlein, Lessing,
Maison, Schlierholz,* and *Volz.* Between these are the names of
the German princes reigning in 1871. — The windows of the principal floor show the arms of the federal states and free cities

The INTERIOR (adm., see p. 39), the decoration of which is still
incomplete, is entered by Portal V, on the N. The N. Vestibule is
adjoined to the right by a Waiting Room, whence we ascend to the
principal floor. Here we enter the *WANDEL-HALLE, or Promenade
Hall,* which rises through two stories and runs N and S for the
length of 315 ft. The floor is inlaid with coloured marble. At
the sides, above, are galleries. The central portion consists of an
octagon (82 ft high, and 75 ft in diameter), surmounted by a dome
and separated from the side-halls by galleries and rows of columns.
In the centre is a marble monument to Emp. William I. by *Pfuhl*
(1905). Above hangs a huge bronze chandelier (25 ft. in diameter)
by *Riedinger* of Augsburg. The decorative figures above the four
angle-recesses of the dome are by *O Lessing.* The doors on the E.
of the octagon lead into the Hall of the Diet (see p. 138), while to
the W. is the main entrance (from the Königs-Platz), which is used
on ceremonial occasions only. The general effect of this hall will
be greatly enhanced when its columns are completed by
ceiling-paintings and stained-glass windows

To the W. of the Wandel-Halle is the READING ROOM, with panelled walls and ceiling. About 400 newspapers are laid out here. The frieze of putti is by *M Koch;* the wall-paintings, representing the Marienburg, the Wartburg, the Harbour of Hamburg, Arcona, the Frauen-Kirche at Dresden, Speyer Cathedral, and Tangermünde, are by *Ludwig, Kuhl, Prell, Dill, Hertel,* and *Bracht.* — The adjacent WRITING ROOM, in the N.W. tower, is also finished throughout in wood. In the corners are wooden statues of Vulcan, Neptune, Mercury, and Ceres. The wall-paintings (Strassburg, the Wendelstein, the Teufels-Schlucht, the Chiemsee, and the Bastei) are by *Schönleber, Ludwig, Bracht,* and *Raupp.*

The central space beneath the great glass dome is occupied by the *HALL OF THE DIET, 95 ft. long, 69 ft wide, and 43 ft. high. The walls are panelled in light oak and adorned with ornamental designs, coats-of-arms, and figures. Beneath the glass roof runs a circular vaulting, embellished with coats-of-arms. In the middle of the E. side is the seat of the president, beside which is the secretaries' desk. In front is the tribune, whence members address the house, flanked by the places for the ministers and members of the Federal Council. Immediately in front of the tribune are the seats of the shorthand-writers and beyond these, the table of the house. The seats for the 397 deputies are arranged amphitheatrically, facing the president, to whose 'right' and 'left' sit the political parties grouped under these names. The doors on the N. and S., leading to the division lobbies, are embellished with intarsia designs representing Ulysses escaping from Polyphemus and Rübezahl ('Number Nip'). — The hall is surrounded by a broad panelled corridor, the beams of which are supported by small half-figures, each bearing a gilded letter of the motto 'Erst das Vaterland, dann die Partei' ('country before party').

To the W. of the S. end of the Wandel-Halle are the REFRESHMENT ROOMS. The main room has a barrel-vault, embellished by *Hupp* with coats-of-arms and festoons of thistles, amid which are sportive putti with the imperial insignia. — The ceiling of the corner-room displays the phases of the moon in metal; in the angles of the vaulting are low reliefs of the four elements.

We now descend to the S. VESTIBULE, with rich Renaissance portals in sandstone, by *Vogel.* Above that to the E. are the arms of Prussia supported by Wisdom and Strength; above that to the W. the arms of Bavaria, with Justice and Unity. The stained-glass windows are both by *Linnemann:* to the N. is seen the imperial eagle, bearing the arms of the federal states on its wings; over the S. portal is Germania — In front of the columns are eight colossal bronze statues of early emperors, *viz.* Charlemagne, by *Breuer,* Henry I. by *Brütt,* Otho I., by *Maison,* Henry III., by *Manzel,* Frederick Barbarossa by *Baumbach,* Rudolf of Hapsburg, by *Vogel*, Charles IV., by *Diez*, and Maximilian I., by *Widemann*.

The S.E. part of the main floor contains the rooms of the Government and of the Federal Council. The VORSAAL DES BUNDES-RATS, or *Waiting Room of the Federal Council*, is adorned with sculpture in Istrian limestone, with which also the walls are lined. The pillars dividing off the rear part of the hall are adorned with beautiful bas-reliefs by *O. Lessing*. Along the walls run carved benches, upholstered in stamped leather. A hermes-bust of *Bismarck*, by Rumann, was placed here in 1903 — The HALL OF THE FEDERAL COUNCIL, in the S.E. tower, contains seats for the 50 members round a table. The gilded wooden ceiling is adorned with allegorical paintings by *Schuster-Woldan*. The huge chimney-piece, reaching to the ceiling, is adorned with a relief of Emp. William I. by *Vogel*. — After inspecting the *Royal Box*, the anteroom of which is adorned with stucco and bronze, we finally enter the E. VESTIBULE, with portals by *O. Lessing*. In the spandrels of the staircase are tasteful ornamentations, by *Widemann*, representing warlike trophies on the left, and peaceful tools on the right.

The N.E. part of the main floor is occupied by the rooms of the President of the Reichstag and by a Reference Library In the antechamber of the former is a bust of Moltke, by *Rumann*. — On the second floor are the assembly-rooms of the various 'fractions' or parties, and the large library.

At the corner of the Sommer-Str. and Reichstags-Ufer is the official residence of the President of the Reichstag, erected after Wallot's designs.

Opposite the W. façade of the Reichstags-Gebäude rises the ʳ**National Monument to Bismarck**, by *Reinhold Begas*, erected in 1901 The principal figure is impressive and the general effect is fine; but the somewhat unintelligible allegorical details, and the sketchy and uninteresting reliefs have been unfavourably criticised. The monument proper, 80 ft in height, rises from a sandstone platform, bounded at each end by a spacious fountain-basin. By the basin to the right is a graceful sandstone group of two fishermen with a mermaid in their net; by that to the left are a triton and nymph feeding a seal. The base and pedestal of the monument are of red granite. The figure of Bismarck, 20 ft. in height, expresses by attitude and gesture a proud self-reliance; the left hand holds the sword firmly against his side, while the right hand is spread upon the charter of the foundation of the empire. The chancellor is represented in the uniform usually worn by him in the old Reichstag (he never entered the new building) The reliefs on the pedestal represent, on the right, ravens hovering round an owl, and, on the left, genii beside a hermes of Bismarck. Four groups surround the base of the pedestal: in front Atlas bearing the globe; behind, Siegfried forging the imperial sword; to the right, an armed woman treading a panther under foot (Constitutional Power suppressing Revolt?), to the left, a sphinx supporting a woman engrossed in a document (Statecraft?) The front and rear of the base each bear three reliefs: in front, the German Michael in leading-strings, stirred up to fight, and victorious in combat; behind, Germania in the chariot of victory, the ally of Labour and Art, and hailed as the Bringer of Peace.

On the W. side of the Konigs-Platz is *Kroll's Establishment,* founded in 1842, built in 1852 by Titz, and now leased by the management of the royal theatres and used as the **New Opera Theatre** (p. 27; garden-concerts see p. 30).

In front of it, as a counterpart to the Bismarck Monument, a **Monument to Moltke** (Pl. R, 17, 20), by *Uphues,* was erected in 1905. On a large platform enclosed by a parapet rises a pedestal 20 ft. in height, bearing the marble statue (18 ft. high) of the field-marshal, 'the right man in the right war', in a slightly leaning position.

————————

To the N. of the Königs-Platz lies the ALSEN-PLATZ, adorned in 1904 with a bronze statue of *Field-Marshal Count Roon* (d. 1879), by Magnussen, on a granite pedestal. To the W. are the premises of the *General Staff* (Pl. R, 20), where Moltke worked and died in 1891. Opposite its N E. side, Moltke Str. 3, is the *Austrian Embassy.* — From the Kronprinzen-Ufer, on the Spree, the *Moltke-Brücke* leads to the N W. to the street known as ALT-MOABIT, to the left in which, close to the Spree, is the *Provinzial-Steuergebäude* (Pl. R, 17), or Office of the Local Tax Commissioners, with bronze statues of the finance-ministers *Motz* (d. 1830) and *Maassen* (d. 1834), who took an active part in the foundation of the German Zollverein or Customs Union, by Herter and Hundrieser. — Opposite, at a little distance, rises the handsome **Lehrte Station** (Pl. R, 18, 21), connected with a station of the *Stadtbahn* and a postal station (both in the Invaliden-Str., p. 141); tramways see p 141, at the Exhibition Park.

Opposite the Lehrte Station is the **German Colonial Museum** (Pl. R, 17; adm., see p. 37). Besides ethnographic collections and specimens of produce, it contains a number of dioramic views from the German colonies, reproductions of the dwellings and types of the natives, etc.

Five paintings, by *Hellgrewe,* in the restaurant, illustrate the occupation of German colonies To the right is a lecture-room. Below are dioramas of the Cameroons and the Naukluft (S.W. Africa); native huts from the Cameroons and Togo; a camp of Hereros; Chinese tavern. — Above (to the left)· Ivory-traders on the Victoria Nyanza; Arab dwelling at Dar-es-Salàm, with diorama of the harbour; Hindoo shop; street and temple in Kiowchow, with diorama of the bay; panorama of Blanche Bay in the Bismarck Archipelago, native huts from the Bismarck Archipelago, houses from New Guinea with a diorama of Stephansort.

Beyond the Museum in Alt-Moabit lies the **Ausstellungs-**

Park (Pl. R, 17). or *Exhibition Park*, which is intersected by the Stadtbahn. It is accessible also from the Invaliden-Str. and from the Lehrte Station of the Stadtbahn (tramways, see below). An annual exhibition called the *Grosse Berliner Kunstausstellung* is held here in summer (adm., see p. 37; catalogue 1 *M*, with illustrations 2 *M*; concerts, see p. 30). The *Domed Hall* in which the exhibitions take place is a sumptuous baroque erection, with sculptured groups at the corners, by Hundrieser, Eberlein, Geiger, and Kaßsack. The ceiling-paintings are by W. Friedrich. — In the W. part of the park (main entrance at Invaliden-Str. 57) is a restaurant and the *Urania Observatory* (adm., see p. 42; comp. p. 121).

Tramways (pp. 15-23): Nos 4. 6, 7, 9, 12-15, 18. 23, 24 (Alt-Moabit), and Nos 2, 10. 11, 16. 19. Q, V (Invaliden-Str).

To the S. of the Königs-Platz the broad *Sieges-Allée (Pl. R, 20, 19), or *Avenue of Victory*, runs through the E. part of the Tiergarten, adorned in 1898-1901, at the expense of the Emperor, with 32 marble **Statues of Prussian Rulers**. Behind each monarch is a semicircular marble bench, adorned in the style prevalent during his reign, and bearing hermes-busts of two eminent contemporaries. The statues of the E. row only are portraits.

Konigs-Platz.

West Row.	East Row.
Margrave Albert the Bear (d. 1170), with Bishop Otho of Bamberg and Bishop Wigger of Brandenburg; by Schott	*Emperor William I.* (1861-88), with Moltke and Bismarck; by R. Begas
Margrave Otho I. (d. 1184), with the Wendish prince Pribislaw and Abbot Sibold of Lehnin; by Unger.	*King Frederick William IV.* (1840-61), as a young man, with Rauch and Alexander von Humboldt; by K. Begas.
Margrave Otho II. (d. 1205), with Henry of Antwerp, the chronicler, and the knight John Gans von Putlitz; by Uphues.	*King Frederick William III.* (1797-1840), as a young man, with Baron vom Stein and Blucher; by Eberlein.
Margrave Albrecht II. (d. 1220), with Hermann von Salza, Grand Master of the Teutonic Order and Eike von Repkow, author of the Sachsenspiegel; by Bros.	*King Frederick William II.* (1786-97), with Immanuel Kant and Chancellor Count v. r. Carmer; by Brütt

Charlottenburger Chaussée (p. 176).

West Row.	East Row

Margraves John I. (d 1266) and *Otho III.* (d. 1267), with the Berlin magistrate Marsilius, and Provost Simeon of Berlin; by Baumbach.

Margrave John II. (d. 1281), with Conrad Belitz, councillor of Berlin, and Count Gunther I. of Lindow; by Felderhoff.

Margrave Otho IV. with the Arrow (d. 1308), with his confidants Droiseke von Krocher and Johann von Buch; by K. Begas.

Margrave Waldemar (d. 1319), with Heinrich Frauenlob, the minnesinger, and Siegfried von Feuchtwangen, Grandmaster of the Teutonic Order; by R. Begas.

Margrave Henry the Child (d. 1320), with the knight Wedigo von Plotho and Wratislaw IV., Duke of Pomerania; by Kraus. — Approach to the Haydn - Mozart - Beethoven monument behind.

Margrave Lewis I., the Elder (abdicated in 1351), with Chancellor Johann von Buch the Younger and Johann II., Burggrave of Nuremberg; by Herter.

Margrave Lewis II., the Roman (d. 1365), with the knights Friedrich von Lochen and Hasso the Red of Wedel; by Count Görtz

Margrave Otho the Lazy (deposed in 1373), with Burgomaster Thilo von Wardenberg and Thilo of Bruges, master of the mint; by Brütt

Frederick the Great (1740-86), as a young man, with John Sebastian Bach and Marshal Schwerin; by Uphues; and —

King Frederick William I. (1713-40), with his minister Von Ilgen and Prince Leopold of Dessau; by Siemering.

King Frederick I. (1688-1713), with Baron Eberhard von Danckelmann and Andreas Schlüter, the architect; by Eberlein.

Elector Frederick William the Great (1640-88), with Baron Otto von Schwerin and Marshal Derfflinger; by Schaper.

Elector George William (1619-40), with Count Adam of Schwarzenberg and Konrad von Burgsdorff, by K. von Uechtritz

Elector John Sigismund (1608-19), with the Governor Thomas von dem Knesebeck and the Oberburggrave Fabian of Dohna, by Breuer.

Elector Joachim Frederick (1598-1608), with Count Hieronymus Schlick and Chancellor Johann von Löben; by Pfretzschner.

Elector John George (1571-98), with Count Rochus von Lynar, the architect, and Chancellor Lampert Distelmeier; by M. Wolff.

West Row.

Emperor *Charles IV.* (d 1378), with Chamberlain Klaus von Bismarck and Dietrich Portitz, Archbishop of Magdeburg; by Cauer.

Emperor *Sigismund* (d. 1437), with Bernd Ryke, patrician of Berlin, and the Provincial Governor Lippold von Bredow; by Bormel.

Elector *Frederick I.* (1415-40), with the knight Wend von Ileburg and Count Hans of Hohenlohe; by Manzel.

Elector *Frederick II., the Iron* (1440-70), with Burgomaster WilkeBlankenfelde and Friedrich Sesselmann, Bishop of Lebus; by Calandrelli.

East Row.

Elector *Joachim II. Hector* (1535-71), with BishopMathias of Brandenburg and Margrave George of Ansbach; by Magnussen. Behind is a bronze medallion of Luther.

Elector *Joachim I. Nestor* (1499-1535), with Dietrich von Bulow, Bishop of Lebus, and Cardinal Albert of Brandenburg, archbishop of Mayence; by Götz

Elector *John Cicero* (1486-99), with his advisers Eitelwolf von Stein and Busso von Alvensleben; by Manthe

Elector *Albrecht Achilles* (1470-86), with Ludwig von Eyb, the historian, and Captain Werner von der Schulenburg; by Lessing.

We have now reached the KEMPER-PLATZ (Pl. R. 19), in which a Gothic fountain (36 ft high) in granite of different colours with a figure of *Roland,* by O. Lessing, was erected in 1902. On the main basin are coats-of-arms of Berlin families; and on the pedestal are representatives of the different classes and (in front) the sister-towns Berlin and Kolln quarrelling.— The Bellevue-Str. (see p. 127) leads hence to the Potsdamer-Platz, while the Viktoria-Str. runs to the Potsdamer-Brucke (p. 173).

Beside the *Goldfisch-Teich* (Pl. R, 19), behind the W row of statues, a marble Monument to *Haydn, Mozart, and Beethoven,* by Siemering, was erected in 1901. The triangular baroque edifice shows half-length figures of the composers in niches, with symbols of their art below and genii bearing garlands above — On the neighbouring Flora-Platz, to the W, stands an enlarged replica of the Amazon by Tuaillon (p 86).

The E. side of the Tiergarten is skirted by the Königgratzer-Strasse (p. 127), leading from the Brandenburg Gate to the Potsdamer-Platz (p. 127) on the S. At the entrance to the Lenné-Str, near the Koniggratzer-Str., is the **Monument to Lessing** (Pl. R, 19), by *O. Lessing* (1890); on the granite pedestal are portraits of Moses Mendelssohn, Ewald von Kleist, and Friedr. Nicolai (p. 157), and at the base are allegorical figures of Humanity and Criticism. — At the corner of the streets mentioned above a marble *Statue of the Great Elector* when a youth (after his statue by Jonnsch at Kustrin) was erected in 1901. In the Koniggratzer-Str is the

*Monument to Goethe (Pl. R, 19), by *F. Schaper* (1880); the marble figure of the poet stands on a pedestal on the base of which are figures of Lyric and Tragic Poetry and Scientific Research. Near it to the S W. of the Brandenburg Gate is a *Group of Lions*, by A Wolff. — Southern margin of the Tiergarten see p. 177.

7. Northern Friedrich-Strasse. Oceanographical Museum. Hohenzollern Museum.

The Friedrich-Strasse (p 120) runs in a straight direction towards the N. from the Linden (Pl R, 23) across the Weidendamm Bridge to the former Oranienburg Gate Its second cross-street is the Dorotheen-Strasse (for its E. part see p. 57). In the portion to the W. of the Friedrich-Str. stands the **Dorotheenstadt Church** (Pl. R, 23), built in 1678 and remodelled in 1861, containing the Monument of Count von der Mark (d. 1787), a natural son of Frederick William II, *Schadow's* first important work (sacristan, Mittel-Str. 28). — Opposite (Dorotheen-Str. 27) is the *Royal York Masonic Lodge*, built in 1881-83 as an addition to a house erected by Schluter in 1712. Farther to the W. we reach the Neue Wilhelm-Strasse (p. 161).

The third cross-street of the Friedrich-Str. is the Georgen-Strasse. Here, to the right (Nos. 34-36), is the —

*Oceanographical Museum (Pl. R, 23), opened in 1906 in connection with the University *Oceanographic Institute* Adm., see p. 38; illustrated guide, 50 pf.

The Groundfloor contains the *Imperial Naval Collection.* I. Historic Room: Models of ships (vikings' boat, Hansa vessel, etc); fragments of the frigate Gefion, taken in 1849 near Eckernforde; reminiscences of Admiral Brommy (1804-60), of the gun-boat Iltis, lost in 1896 on the coast of Shantung, of the fight of the new Iltis with the Taku forts in 1900, etc.; 20 pictures by Petersen (glorious days of the German fleet). — We descend to the Covered Court (II): Emp. William II. as admiral, bust by Pfannschmidt (1899); models of all types of German ships of war, model of a division of ships of the line in port; to the right of the entrance a column with coats-of-arms, erected by John II of Portugal in 1485 on Cape Cross (S.W. Afrika). — To the right of the covered court through Room III to the Court; among the larger objects placed here is a submarine boat constructed in 1851, sunk at the trial-trip in Kiel harbour, and recovered in 1887 — Room IV., to the left of the court and a few steps lower, contains reproductions of the cabins on board the former school-ship Niobe. — Behind the covered court is the Armoury (V), containing marine artillery and torpedos (to the left, model of a division of torpedo-boats). In the rooms adjoining to the right (VI-VIII) Signalling apparatus, rescue machines, uniformed figures. — The gallery to the left of the covered court (R. IX and X) contains models for ship-building, equipment of ships, and marine engines.

On the First Floor the Central Room (1) contains sailing ships and life-saving service. — To the left in Anteroom 2: Construction of harbours (portions of Hamburg harbour), fuelling and marking of the water-highways beacons etc — Rooms 5-10, to the left, *Oceanological Collection:* Nautical instruments comprising those for deep sea research; in

Room 9, diagrams showing the saltness of the sea; samples of the sea bottom; paintings referring to the second German polar expedition in 1869-70, by Wensel, in Room 10, models of Swinemünde and Heligoland.

The following rooms contain the *Biological and Fisheries Collection* Room 11. Sponge-fisheries of the Ægean See; animal life near the South Pole, guillemots' rock at Heligoland; animals living on reefs (coral reef from the Red Sea). Rooms 12, 13. Animal life in the North Sea. Room 11· Capture of marine animals and use of marine products (whale-bone, guano, mother-of-pearl, pearls, amber, etc.); three paintings by Salzmann (Whale-fishing, Pelicans breeding on the coast of Peru, Crab-fishing on the Oldenburg coast) Room 15: German deep-sea and longshore fishing. In the passage to the central room (see p. 144): Models of fishermen's huts in Finkenwerder and Rügen.

The **Bahnhof Friedrich-Strasse** (Pl. R, 23), at the corner of the Friedrich-Str and Georgen-Str., is the main station of the Stadtbahn (pp. 1 and 12). On the S. side is a bronze bust, by Brunow, of *Dircksen,* the builder of the Stadtbahn (1902).

Tramways (pp. 15-22) viâ the Dorotheen-Str (Nos. 13, N, O, S, and T) and the Charlotten-Str. (Nos. 12, 18, 25, 32, 34, 43) to the Brandenburg Gate (13, N, O, S, T), Donhoff-Platz (12 13, 18), Gendarmen-Markt (34, 43), Gesundbrunnen (34, 43. a) Görlitz Station (12, 13, 18), Halle Gate and Kreuzberg (34, 13), Moabit (12, 13), and Stettin Station (25, 32, 105)

Beyond the station, on the left (Nos. 139-141), is the *Kaiser Wilhelm Academy,* founded in 1795 for the training of army doctors (new building in the Invaliden-Park under construction; see p. 164).

The Friedrich-Strasse beyond the station crosses the Spree by means of the *Weidendamm Bridge* (Pl. R, 23) Before the bridge, to the right, at the corner of the Weidendamm, is the *Komische Oper* (p. 28), built in 1905 by Lachmann and Zauber in a modern baroque style. In the Weidendamm and Kupfergraben are the *Barracks of the Emperor Alexander Guards Regiment,* opposite which rises the Emperor Frederick Museum (p. 96).

Beyond the Weidendamm Bridge, to the right of the Friedrich-Str., Nos. 5-11 Ziegel-Str, are the *United Clinical Institutes* of the University (for surgery and for diseases of the eye and ear; visitors admitted on Wed., Frid, & Sun. 12-1 30), connected with the *Langenbeck-Haus,* the meeting-house of the German Surgical Society. Farther on, at Artillerie-Str. 20, is the *Midwifery Institute,* and beyond it, in the Monbijou-Str., the building of the *Policlinic Institute for Internal Diseases.*

The Monbijou-Strasse, beginning at the Emp. Frederick Museum (p. 96), leads to the N. to the ORANIENBURGER-STRASSE, in which to the left (No. 30) is the **New Synagogue** (Pl. R, 24), one of the finest modern buildings in Berlin, begun in 1859 in a modified Oriental style from designs by *Knoblauch,* and completed in 1866 under the superintendence of *Stüler.* The façade, which is constructed of brick, with details in granite and moulstone is very effective in spite of its lack of width The gilded dome stands a

height of 158 ft. The *Interior (adm., see p. 39) is still finer.
Passing through a vestibule, we first enter the *Small Synagogue*,
used for the daily services, beyond which is the *Chief Synagogue*,
130 ft. long (not including the apse), 79 ft broad, and $78^1/_2$ ft. high,
with 3000 seats. The iron vaulted roof is supported by slender
iron pillars During the evening-service (Fridays at dusk) the 'dim
religious light' from the stained glass and the cupolas produces a
remarkably fine effect. The places for men are on the groundfloor,
those for women in the galleries.

Near the E. end of the Oranienburger-Str. is the Monbijou-
Platz, embellished with a marble bust of *Chamisso* (p. 171), by
Mosen. Tramways see p 166 (Hackescher Markt). In this Platz is
the entrance to the royal —

Château of Monbijou (Pl R, 23). The nucleus of the edifice
consists of a villa erected by *Eosander von Goethe* in 1706 for
Countess Wartenberg; the two detached buildings facing the Monbijou-Platz were added by *Unger* in 1789-90. In the Monbijou
garden is the tasteful little **English Church** *(St. George's)*,
erected in 1884-85 by Baschdorff (services, see p 36).

The Château has since 1877 contained the *Hohenzollern
Museum**, a collection of personal reminiscences of the Prussian
rulers from the time of the Great Elector down to the present day.
It includes a large number of objects of genuine artistic interest,
and affords an excellent survey of the progress of industrial art in
the last two centuries. Director, *Prof. Seidel*. Adm., see p. 38.
Catalogue (1906), 30 pf, with illustrations 2 *M.*

Rooms 1-3 (comp. Plan, p 147) are devoted to *Emperor William II*. Memorials of his visit to Palestine (1898), including paintings by Ism. Gentz and a mother-of-pearl model of the Mosque of
Omar at Jerusalem. Original drawings and engravings of published
drawings by the emperor. Cavalry charge under the emperor's command, by Kossak. — R. 2. In the first cabinet to the left, Reminiscences of the wedding (1881) and silver-wedding (1906) of the emperor. Paintings: the emperor when a prince, two drawings by Menzel (1873); obsequies of Menzel (1905), by Pape; Baptism of the
present Crown Prince Frederick William (1882), by A. von Werner.
— R 3. Portrait of the emperor by Noster; paintings of state
ceremonials, by Pape (Audience of Prince Chung in 1901, etc.). In
the centre, Wedding gift from the 'Borussia' student-corps at Bonn.

Room 4: *Emperor Frederick* (1831-88) *and Empress Victoria*
(1840-1901). Memorials of the emperor at school and college; his
first uniform; marriage garments of the emperor and empress (1858);
address, painted by Menzel, on the emperor's 18th birthday; replica
of his monument at Bremen by Tuaillon. Painting, by E Hildebrand, of the royal family in front of the New Palace (p. 188);
above the chimney-piece, Portrait of the emperor, by G Richter;

Obsequies of Empress Victoria at Cronberg, by F. Brütt (1901).

Rooms 5-8: *Emperor William I.* (1797-1888). R. 5 contains M. Lock's marble *Group, 'No time to be tired', the marble angels from the mansoleum of Emp. Frederick, and the bust of the latter, by Schuler. — R. 6. Addresses, the most interesting designed by Menzel after the attempt on the emperor's life in 1878 (in the right corner). By the rear-wall are the emperor's coronation-robes (1861) and uniforms appropriate to his various orders. By the window-wall is Moltke's study-table, with a cast of his death-mask and his hands. Silver Hall of Fame by Friedeberg Sons. — R. 7. By the N. wall, costumes and uniforms; sabretache (to the left of the swords) on which the emperor wrote his letter to Napoleon III. at Sedan. In the centre is the table at which Napoleon III. signed the declaration of war at St. Cloud in 1870. On the window-wall are memorials of the emperor's youth, comprising a letter from Queen Luise to her son (1806). Portraits of Bismarck and numerous generals. — R. 8. Bust of Prince William by Rauch (1853). Paintings: Unter den Linden, March 22nd; 1887, by Geissler; the emperor on his death-bed, drawing by A. von Werner; the emperor in his private room, by Bülow (1888); *Address from the city of Berlin after the campaign of 1866, by Menzel.

Rooms 9 & 10: *Empress*

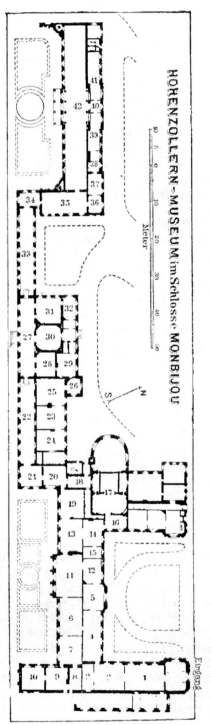

Augusta (1811-90). R. 9. To the right, Christening-robe of Emp.
Frederick — R. 10 Bridal-train (1829) and coronation-robe of the
empress; coronation-canopy; ornaments worn at her golden wedding; to the right her widow's dress Two portraits of the empress
by Plockhorst.

Room 11: *Frederick William IV.* (1795-1861). In the corner,
to the left, robes of the Order of the Garter. In the centre, table
with drawings by the king. By the central window, jewels of Queen
Elizabeth. On the walls are portraits of the king by Krüger and
Otto, and portraits of contemporary savants and artists, mostly
by K Begas the Elder.

Room 12 *Queen Elizabeth* (1801-73). Portraits of the queen
by Stieler and by Bülow; homage at the castle of Hohenzollern,
by Burde.

Room 13: *Frederick William III.* (1770-1840). Portraits of
generals Entrance-wall, Napoleon's table-service captured at Waterloo; memorials of 1813, including ornaments made of iron. By the
window-wall are memorials of Prince Louis Ferdinand, who fell at
Saalfeld (1806); paper money from Colberg (1807), robes of various
orders. Rear wall: portrait of Princess Liegnitz, the second wife
of the king (d. 1873); sketch of the king, by Th. Lawrence.

Rooms 14-17: *Queen Luise* (1776-1810). Numerous portraits
and busts of the queen, memorials of her childhood, articles used
by her, clothes, work done by her, and musical instruments. In R.14
is her death-mask, adjoined by a view of the château of Hohen-
Zieritz, where she died. — R. 15, fitted up in the style of Queen
Luise's bedroom at Potsdam, contains the cradle of her youngest
children and her painted wax-portrait after Rauch — R. 16. Urania
with the features of the queen by Wiedemann; view of the château
of Paretz (with the royal couple). — 17 Memorial Hall. *Marble
monument to the queen, a repetition (not a copy) of the monument
in the Charlottenburg Mausoleum (p. 183), executed in 1818-27 by
Rauch and purchased in 1834 by Frederick William III.; +Marble
portrait of her son Prince Ferdinand (d. 1804), by G Schadow.
In the vestibule: Marble busts of the king, with a figure of victory
on the pedestal (1815; left), and of the queen (1804-10: right), both
by Rauch, designs for the sarcophagus of the queen, by G. Schadow
and Rauch, and her portrait by Grassi — R 18 contains wall-decor-
ations brought from the Royal Palace

Room 19: *Frederick William II.* (1744-97). Cabinet with coloured marquetry made at Neuwied (1791); clock of 1793

Room 20: *Queen Frederica Louisa* (1751-1805), second wife of
Frederick William II. Portraits of the queen and the king, by Graff.

Rooms 21-26· *Frederick the Great* (1712-86), with furniture
from the New Palace. RR 21, 22 Porcelain collection; the service
dates from the original equipment of the palace. Fine rococo con-

sole; below, large Chinese vases. In R. 21, table with small articles used by the king: snuff-box hit by a bullet at Kunersdorf in 1759; snuff-box held by the king in his hand when he died. In the middle of R. 22, *Cabinet containing jewels, e. g.* thirteen snuff-boxes set with precious stones, watches and sticks of the king; plate remaining from his golden service melted down in 1808; ornaments found in tombs of Hohenzollern princes; chain of the Order of the Swan (unique original). Adjacent a case containing snuff-boxes in chrysoprase and jasper. — R. 23. *Cedar Room.* The king's piano; portrait of the king when crown-prince, by Knobelsdorff; large collection of snuff-boxes with portraits of the king, battle-scenes, etc.; specimens of the king's handwriting — R. 24. Alcove Room. Chinese cabinet that formerly contained the king's collection of maps, his writing-table. Terracotta bust of Prince Henry, his brother. By the windows the king with his greyhounds, statuette by G. Schadow; a volume of the Oeuvres du philosophe de Sanssouci, with annotations by Voltaire and the king; the king's first essays in writing and drawing. In the alcove (to the right of the entrance): Frederick's drawing of the Town Palace at Potsdam; ribbons recording victories; clothes and uniforms of the king from his childhood till his death, his first dress, his gala-uniform as colonel of the life-guards (when crown-prince); table-top with views of Rheinsberg; his death-mask. — R. 25. Throne Room, with upholstered furniture from the New Palace. By the rear-wall are Frederick's cradle and the chair in which he died; effigies of his favourite dogs. In the centre is his pianoforte. — R. 26: The king's flutes; the bullet by which he was wounded in 1760 at Torgau; Knobelsdorff's sketch-book, two tin cups engraved by Baron Trenck during his imprisonment at Magdeburg; porcelain group of the king and his grandson Frederick William playing shuttle-cock; porcelain bust of Voltaire ('immortalis'), presented in 1775 to the latter by the king.

Room 27: *Red Gallery.* Busts of members of the Hohenzollern family. On the walls are the remains of a table-service made in China as a gift for Frederick from the Frisian Trading Co, but lost in a shipwreck on the way to Europe; also an admirable rococo service from the Berlin porcelain factory.

Room 28. *Queen Elizabeth Christina* (1715-97), consort of Frederick the Great. Portrait of the queen in widow's weeds, by Graff.

Room 29, called the soapstone room, in the Chinese style.

Room 30: *Memorial Room.* Coloured wooden figure of the Great Elector; King Frederick I., a cast of Schluter's statue at Konigsberg; model for a statue of Frederick William I., by Bettkober. On the walls, portraits of the children of Frederick William I.

Room 31. *Queen Sophia Dorothea* (1687-1757), wife of Frederick William I. On the walls are portraits of their children.

Upholstered furniture from the New Palace. — Room 32 contains views of the château of Monbijou.

Room 33: *Green Gallery.* Busts of generals, statesmen, and savants (comprising six after Rauch). Views of Old Berlin; table-services; in the first cabinet, cups in memory of Queen Louise and of the year 1813; in the fifth, specimens of a fine table-service of Frederick the Great. Valuable collection of glass, including glasses ridiculing Gundling, the court-jester, from the 'Tobacco Parliament' (see below), and ruby-coloured glass made by Kunkel, the alchemist.

Room 34: Engravings. Frames with miniatures, including Frederick the Great (in 3, 4, and 5), Queen Luise (7), Blücher and Schill (9).

Room 35: *Frederick William I. (1688-1740).* By the rear-wall are portraits of the king's family, the chair in which he died, and his turning-lathe. By the windows: arm-chair made for Peter the Great; pulpit from Königs-Wusterhausen (p. 202); specimens of the king's handwriting; memorials of Lieutenant Katte, who was executed in 1730 for complicity in Frederick the Great's attempted flight (when crown-prince). In the centre are the table, chairs, and pipes used at the 'Tobacco Parliaments'.

Rooms 36-38: *Frederick I. (1657-1713) and Queen Sophia Charlotte (1668-1705).* — The ceiling of R. 36 is a reproduction of a contemporaneous one in the Palace at Berlin; to the right, portrait of the king, by Weidemann; in the glass-case to the left, statuette of the Great Elector as Bellerophon. — R. 37. Portrait of the queen, by Weidemann; her pianoforte; bust of the king (after Schlüter); reliefs of the royal couple from Schlüter's sarcophagi (p. 64). — R. 38, with Renaissance panelling, is a reproduction of the room in the Palace of Königsberg in which Frederick I. was born. Wax figures of the King, the Great Elector, and Frederick the Great.

Room 39: *Frederick William, the Great Elector (1620-88).* Felt hat and iron helmet, worn by the Great Elector at the battle of Fehrbellin; casque and boots. Tapestry representing the elector's military achievements. Ivory ornaments of the latter half of the 17th century.

Room 41: *The Early Electors.* Triptych (1417) from the church of Kadolzburg, with portraits of Elector Frederick I. and his wife; vestment worn by Cardinal Albrecht of Brandenburg. By the window: Model of the new castle of Hohenzollern.

Room 42: *Large Saloon.* By the rear-wall: Map of Berlin in 1685; views of old Berlin; casts from the tomb of John Cicero, by Peter and Johannes Vischer (comp. p. 64). Paintings: Frederick William III., and Frederick William IV. receiving homage, by Krüger; Queen Luise visiting an orphanage, by Schrader; Battle of Königgrätz, by Sohn(?); Moltke's 90th Birthday, by A. von Werner. — By the window are three colossal busts in plaster: Frederick the

Great, after Rauch; the Great Elector, after Schluter; and Emp. William I., after R. Begas. Cast of Blaser's statue of Frederick William IV at the castle of Hohenzollern. Models of the castle of Nuremberg, the Mausoleum at Charlottenburg (p. 183), and the Palace at Berlin as it was in the time of Joachim II.

8. Old Berlin.

Rathaus. Markisches Provinzial-Museum. Museum of German Costumes and Industries. Ravene's Picture Gallery.

From the Kurfursten-Brucke (p. 70) the KONIG-STRASSE leads to the N.E through Old Berlin (in the narrower sense, comp p 47) to the Alexander-Platz (p. 153). In this street to the left, between the Heilige-Geist-Str. and Spandauer-Str., is the **Central Post Office** (Pl. R, 26; comp. p. 25), built in 1874-84, and officially called 'Hofpostamt' and 'Briefpostamt' (letter post office), the latter is a brick-building in the Brandenburg Gothic style, erected in 1901 in the Heilige-Geist-Str.

In the Konig-Strasse to the right, at the corner of the Spandauer-Str., is *N. Israel's* large drapery establishment (p 33). Opposite, with its façade towards the Konig-Str., stands the —

*Rathaus, or *Town Hall* (Pl. R, 26), an imposing brick edifice with tasteful terracotta embellishments and granite facings, erected in 1861-69 from the plans of *Waesemann* on the site of the old Rathaus to which the Gerichtslaube (p. 198) belonged The structure is 325 ft. long, 288 ft. deep, and 88 ft. high to the top of the attic stage above the third story, while the tall tower rises to a height of 243 ft. (to the top of the flag-staff 318 ft). The dial-plates of the clock measure $15\frac{1}{2}$ ft. in diameter. Like many of the other modern buildings of Berlin, the Rathaus exhibits a union of a mediæval structural system (round-arched) with Renaissance details, and resembles the edifices of North Italy. The open-work projections at the angles of the tower recall the Cathedral of Laon. — The bronze statues of Emp William I. and Elector Frederick I, in the niches by the portal, were executed by *Keil* and *Encke*; the reliefs of the balconies represent scenes from the life in Old and New Berlin.

The architectural decoration of the principal rooms on the FIRST FLOOR (adm., see p. 39), which gave a new impetus to industrial art in Berlin, is due to *Kolscher*.

On the left side of the staircase, next the Konig-Str, is the VESTIBULE OF THE MAGISTRATES' ROOM. This contains a marble figure of the Spree, by *Christensen*, and a series of historical paintings: 1. (beginning on the E) The Great Elector receiving the refugees (p. 47); 2 ... all ... in both taking the sacrament (1539), b ... Cranach; 3 ... of the ... rooms by

Elector Frederick I.; 4. The Council of Berlin-Kölln sitting in judgment on Tyle Wardenberg (ca 1380), both by *Schenrenberg;* 5. Frederick William I inspecting the buildings in the Friedrich-stadt (p. 47), by *Vogel;* 6 Frederick the Great riding in Unter den Linden; 7 Return of Frederick William III. and Queen Luise in 1809, both by *Simmler;* 8. The Berliners on the battlefield of Grossbeeren (1813), by *Bleibtreu;* 9. Frederick William IV. at the unveiling of the statue of Frederick the Great (1851), by *Simmler.* — The MAGISTRATES' ROOM contains fine panelling and portraits of the Great Elector and the nine kings of Prussia

On the right side, next the König-Str , we first enter the LIBRARY. — The MÄRCHENSAAL ('hall of legends'), the ceiling of which is adorned with figures from German legends, by *L. Burger,* contains the silver-plate for festivals and marble busts of honorary citizens: Bismarck, Moltke, Ranke, and Schliemann. — The large FESTSAAL, 103 ft. in length and 57 in width, is 49 ft. high, extending through three stories. The pictures of the months in the lunettes are by *O Begas* This hall also contains statues of Frederick the Great and Frederick William III., by *Sussmann-Hellborn,* a bust of William II , by *Schott,* and *A. von Werner's* well-known picture of the Berlin Congress of 1878 — Hence we pass through the TOWN COUNCIL CHAMBER and its vestibule, with pictures in the lunettes by *Hertel* (Works of charity, in a landscape setting), and regain the staircase.

Three walls of the staircase on the UPPER FLOOR are adorned with large paintings by *Mühlenbruch:* to the left, The German States before the Temple of Concord; in the centre, Germania bearing the imperial crown in triumph to William I.; to the right, Meritorius citizens of Berlin (75 portraits). — On the upper floor is the BÜRGER-SAAL, with a frieze by *A. von Heyden* representing scenes of Berlin life from the earliest times to the present day.

On the groundfloor is the *Ratskeller* (p 10). — The Tower commands the best **Panoramic View of Berlin* (405 steps; adm., see p. 39).

Tramways (pp. 15-21) to: Anhalt Station (17, 59, 62, 63), Dönhoff-Platz (17, 38, 59, 62, 63, 64, 66, 67, 69, 71, 72, 74), Gendarmen-Markt (60, 61, 70, 73, 75, 81), Gesundbrunnen (38), Hackescher Markt (16, 19, 28, 29, 30, 38, 47, 48), Halle Gate (38, 64, 73, 75), Kreuzberg (38), Lehrte Station and Moabit (16), Lützow-Platz (17, 63, 66, 67, 81), Neues Tor (16, 19), Nollen-dorf-Platz (60, 61, 64, 75), Potsdam Station (60, 61, 66, 67, 69, 71, 72, 74, 81), Rixdorf (28, 29, 47, 48, 49, 58), Silesian Station (16), Schöneberg (59 60, 61, 69, 71, 72, 71), Spittelmarkt (38, 47, 48, 58, 62, 64-67, 69, 70, 72), Stettin Station (16, 19, 28, 29, 68), Zoological Garden (61, 75, 81)

The E. end of the König-Strasse, beyond the crossing of the Kloster-Strasse and Neue Friedrich-Strasse (p. 154), is flanked by colonnades *(Königs-Kolonnaden),* built by Gontard in 1777 to form the approach to the former Königs-Brücke, which spanned the city-moat. Both bridge and moat were removed on the construction of the Stadtbahn. The name commemorates the formal entry of the

first king of Prussia after his coronation at Königsberg in 1701.
— Through the left colonnade the Gontard-Strasse leads to the
Central Market. Behind the colonnade, to the N.W., is the
Alexander-Platz Station (Pl R, 26; see pp 1, 12

Tramways (pp. 15-21) from the station and from the Alexander-Platz
(on the E ; Nos 3, 5, 11, 22 31, 35, 36, 37, 41, 49) to · Anhalt Station
(17, 59, 62, 63), Donhoff-Platz (17, 59, 62, 63, 64, 66, 67, 69, 71, 72, 74),
Gendarmen-Markt (60, 61, 70, 73, 75, 81), Gesundbrunnen (35, 36, 41),
Gorlitz Station (11, 22, 46), Hackescher Markt (16, 19), Halle Gate (64,
73, 75), Kreuzberg (35, 36, 37, 41), Moabit (5, 11, 16, 19), Lützow-Platz
(3, 17, 63, 66, 67, 81), Neues Tor (11, 16, 19), Nollendorf-Platz (3, 60, 61,
61, 75), Potsdam Station (60, 61, 66, 67, 69, 71, 72, 74, 81), Rixdorf (22,
16, 19, 58), Schloss-Platz (17, 60, 61, 63, 70, 73, 75, 81), Schöneberg (3, 5,
11, 59, 60, 61, 62, 69, 71, 72, 74), Spittelmarkt (58, 59, 62, 64-67, 69-72,
74), Stettin Station (11, 16, 19, 68).

The König-Strasse passes under the Stadtbahn and ends at the
spacious ALEXANDER-PLATZ (Pl R, 29). The N.W. side of the Platz
is bounded by one of *Tietz's Stores* (comp. p. 31), built by Cremer
& Wolffenstein. In front of it stands a colossal copper figure of
Berolina, by *Hundrieser* (1895: statue and pedestal each 25 ft
high). To the S. are the **Police Headquarters** (Pl. R, 29), a huge
pile covering an area of about 18,870 sq. yds., erected in 1885-90.
The niches at the N.E. corner contain bronze statues of the Great
Elector, King Frederick I, Emperor William I, and Emperor
Frederick III On the E side of the Platz, Alexander-Str. 41, is the
office of the *Berliner Lehrerverein*, with an educational museum.
— At No. 10 in the street 'Am Königsgraben', diverging from the
Alexander-Platz to the N., are a bust and tablet commemorating
the fact that *Lessing* completed 'Minna von Barnhelm' here in 1765.

To the N.E. of the Alexander-Platz, between the Landsberger-
Str. and the Neue König-Str., is the **Church of St. George**
(Pl. R, 29), built in a Transition style by *Otzen* in 1895-98. The
principal tower (340 ft.), rising high above the surrounding houses,
admirably fills in the vista along the König-Strasse.

To the N of the König-Strasse in the NEUE MARKT (Pl. R. 26)
rises the *Luther Monument, begun by *Otto* (d. 1893) and
completed by *Toberentz* in the year of his death (1895). The
figure of the great reformer, Bible in hand, stands upon a lofty
granite pedestal, at the foot of which are seated figures of Jonas and
Crueiger, Reuchlin and Spalatin, and standing figures of Melanchthon
and Bugenhagen, while at the sides of the steps are statues of Ulrich
von Hutten and Franz von Sickingen.

In the same square is the **Marien-Kirche** (Pl R, 26), built
in the 13th cent, rebuilt in the 14th, and restored in 1892-94 The
singular Gothic spire of the tower (295 ft.) was added in 1790. In
front of th W entrance are a space   th murder of a
Prior of Bernau 1325 The extend of the church plat, but

the interior (sacristan, Bischof-Str. 4-5) well repays a visit. In the hall below the tower is a *Dance of Death*, a mural painting of about 1470, with rhymes in Low German. In the choir is the *Monument of *Count Sparr* (d. 1668), a field-marshal under the Great Elector, an admirable work by A. Quellinus the Elder from Amsterdam The curious marble pulpit is by *Schlüter* (1703). Concerts see p. 30. — To the N.W. stretches the *Rosen-Strasse*, see p 51.

Along the N W side of the Neue Markt passes the Kaiser Wilhelm-Str., which leads to the left to the Lustgarten (p. 63) and to the right to the Central Market (p 153) Beyond it, Spandauer-Str. 1, stands the **Handels-Hochschule** ('commercial high-school'; Pl. R, 26), built in 1906 in the baroque style by Cremer & Wolffenstein and maintained by the Berlin merchants (director. Prof. Jastrow; 40 lecturers and 370 students). The old *Chapel of the Holy Ghost*, dating from the early 14th cent , is used as a lecture room.

The neighbouring Protestant **Garrison Church** (Pl. R, 26), in the Neue Friedrich-Str., erected by Gerlach in 1721-22, and rebuilt in 1900, was destroyed by fire in April, 1908. Of the French standards captured by Blücher and others, two only were saved; the vaults, in which *Marshal Keith* (d. 1758), *Kleist von Nollendorf* (d. 1823), and many other generals are buried, were not injured. — Not far off, to the W , the *Friedrichs-Brücke* crosses the Spree, beyond which to the left rises the Cathedral (p. 63), to the right the National Gallery (p 85). On this side of the river, in the Burg-Str , is the —

Börse, or **Exchange** (Pl. R, 26), erected in 1859-64 by *Hitzig*, and extended towards the S in 1884-85, the first modern building in Berlin executed in stone instead of brick. The chief façade is embellished with a double colonnade, above which, in the centre, is a group in sandstone by *R. Begas*, representing Borussia as the protectress of agriculture and commerce. In the vestibule is a seated marble figure of Emperor William I. as law-giver, by *Siemering*. The main hall is 110 yds. in length, 20 yds. in breadth, and 65 ft. in height, and is divided into three sections by two galleries supported by arches. During business-hours (12-2) more than 4000 merchants congregate here daily; best survey from the gallery (adm , see p. 37).

To the S. of the König-Strasse (p 151), at the corner of the Gruner-Str. and Neue Friedrich-Str , is the **District Court I.** (*Land- und Amtsgericht:* Pl R, 29), completed in 1904 from designs by *Schmal* in a free adaptation of the S. German baroque style, presenting its main façade, flanked by two lofty turrets, to the N. towards the Gruner Strasse The imposing pile contains upwards of 600 rooms; the façade towards the Neue Friedrich-Str. is 210 yds in length. Fine staircase.

The Neue Friedrich-Strasse ends to the S. at the *Waisen-Brücke,* which affords to the S a survey of the channels of the Spree encircling Alt-Kölln. Near it to the left is the pier of the steamboats on the Upper Spree (p. 24) and the *Jannowitz-Brucke Station* of the Stadtbahn (Pl. R, 28, p. 12). Beyond the Waisen-Brucke is the MÄRKISCHE PLATZ (Pl. R, 28), with a handsome *Fountain* by Brunow (1897), bearing the figure of a woman washing. On the S. side in the Wall-Str. (comp. p. 47) is the —

¨**Märkische Provinzial-Museum** of the city of Berlin, erected in 1901-7 by *L. Hoffmann.* Borrowing suggestions from various mediæval structures (both sacred and profane) in the Mark of Brandenburg, the architect has applied them to a number of different buildings, the whole forming an irregular but highly effective group, dominated by a tower of massive construction Adm., see p. 40. Guide (1908) 10 pf.

On the MAIN FLOOR is a large domed Gothic hall containing the larger antiquities, among which may be mentioned a wooden figure of a bishop, a Madonna in sandstone (both of the 14th cent.), and several altars with wood-carvings of the 15th and 16th centuries. The other rooms contain the *Natural History Collection* (including many biological groups), the library (also manuscripts and paintings) and a section for local statistics — The UPPER FLOOR contains a lecture room and the collections relating to the *History of Civilization,* in 14 sections: weapons, history of the town and the province, old maps and views of Berlin, trade and industry, ornaments and fashions, domestic and agricultural implements, chamber of torture, ecclesiastical antiquities, etc. — The SUNK FLOOR contains the *Prehistoric Collection* (king's tomb from Seddin in the Prignitz) and the *Göritz-Lubeck Library* of 40,000 vols. comprising numerous original editions of German poems and books relating to Berlin, engravings, etc.

Beyond are the last two relics of the old fortified town of Berlin (comp. p 47), *viz.* a part of the town wall, and the 'Wusterhausener Bär' (comp. the inscription), which was removed hither from its original site Opposite the Museum to the E rises the *Landes-Versicherungs-Anstalt* ('insurance office'), by Messel. — To the S. of the Museum, at the beginning of the Köpenicker-Str. (Pl. R, 28), a marble statue of *Schulze-Delitzsch* (d. 1883), founder of the co-operative system in Germany, by Arnoldt, was unveiled in 1899 The bronze groups on the pedestal represent the alliance of industrial and field labour, and a woman of the working-class teaching her son.

In the S. part of the Kloster-Strasse (Pl R, 26), which still preserves its quaint appearance, on the right (No 36), is the —

Museum of German National Costumes and Domestic Industries (Pl. R, 26), an extensive and valuable collection founded in 1889 by private munificence and handed over to the government in 1901 The different sections are not adequately commodation. Adm. see Cent 1908 at p.

The rooms surround a court Everywhere are lifesize costume figures. — To the right in Room 1: Eastern Prussia (Lithuania), Silesia, Pomerania (objects from Monchgut in the island of Rügen), Schleswig-Holstein, Vierlande near Hamburg Kitchen at the end of an E Frisian 'house-place' from the Leer district — Corridor 2 leads to the Virchow Room (3): Objects from the 'Old Country' near Hamburg, presented on the occasion of Virchow's 70th birthday (1891). — Room 4. Hanover, Lippe, Oldenburg, Brunswick, Hesse, Saxony — Room 5: Thüringen (Altenburg costumes), Prussian Saxony (Halloren costume), Mark Brandenburg, Lusatia.—Room 6: Peasant's room in the Spreewald, Alsatian peasant's room — Through Corridor 7 to Room 9 Swiss room with panelling (1644), fayence stove from Winterthur Baden (funeral cross from the Black Forest), Württemberg

Room 10: Bavaria. — Room 11: Chamber, kitchen, and larder from Upper Austria. — Room 12 Austria, Tyrol — Room 13: Tyrol (Sterzing cabinet of 1478), Salzburg. — Room 14 Models of houses: Upper Bavarian house near Berchtesgaden, farm-houses from Hesse, the Kinzig valley (Black Forest), the Spreewald, the Husum district, Westphalia (Osnabrück), etc. German costumes Salzburg and Swiss masks: rider on a white horse. Ceramic collection. Women's caps and hats. Funeral objects (funeral boards and painted skulls from Salzburg), ecclesiastical utensils, offerings, festive utensils and pastry, superstition, peasants' medicine, peasant s ornaments. Neapolitan 'Presepe' (18th cent).

Building in the Court (apply to the attendant) Vestibule. Gothic stove from Sterzing (Tyrol) Hindeloopen room from Dutch Friesland, walls lined with Delft tiles; carved cabinets. At the back, so-called Besemer (fast) carriage. Room from Lüneburg, with handsome panelling of 1570

Opposite, at Kloster-Strasse 76, is the *Lagerhaus*, used for different purposes, built in 1706 on the site of the so-called 'Hohe Haus', the Berlin residence of the margraves and early electors before the palace was built (p. 47) Elector Frederick I. received the homage of his subjects here in 1415 Behind rises the *Royal Privy Record Office* (Geheime Staats-Archiv). — Adjacent (No 75) is the *School of Art* ('Kunstschule', director, Prof. Mohn), erected in 1877-80 by Gropius & Schmieden. Behind this, in the rooms once used by Rauch as a studio, is the **Rauch Museum** (director, Prof. E. Hundrieser), a collection of casts and models of the works of the master, and the Rauch Archives. Adm., see p 39; catalogue, 1 *M*

Adjoining the School of Art is the *Gymnasium zum Grauen Kloster*, a grammar-school founded in 1574 and containing the conventual and chapter-rooms (the latter dating from 1471) of the old Franciscan monastery, in good preservation. A tablet on the outer wall recalls the fact that *Bismarck* was a pupil here in 1830-32. — The early-Gothic **Kloster-Kirche** (Pl. R, 29), erected at the end of the 13th cent., is, in virtue of its fine choir, the most interesting mediæval building in Berlin. The interior (sacristan, Propst-Str. 14-16) contains a painting in memory of Count Johann von Hohenlohe (d 1412), a memorial stone of the poet Sam. Rodegast (d 1708), once rector of the 'Grey Convent', a large triumphal cross (late-Gothic wood-carving), etc. The choir-stalls date from about 1500. The church was restored in 1842-44, when the vestibule, staircase-towers, and ridge-turret were added

Farther on in the Kloster-Str. to the left is the *Parochial Church* (Pl. R, 29), erected in 1695-1714 from Nering's design; the tower, containing a peal of bells, was added in 1715, the interior restored in 1881. — To the right, on the area bounded by the Kloster-Str., Parochial-Str., Juden-Str., and Stralauer-Str., the **Stadthaus**, a large municipal building with a massive tower in the Juden-Str., was erected in 1908 from *L. Hoffmann's* designs

To the S. of the Rathaus is the MOLKEN-MARKT (Pl. R, 26, 25), the nucleus of the earliest settlement on this side of the Spree. To the S.W. of it the Mühlendamm leads to Alt-Kölln (comp. below). Before reaching it, we pass the palatial *Ephraim House* (to the right, at the corner of the Post-Str.), built in 1765 by Ephraim the Jew, known for his dealings with Frederick the Great. The building is now municipal property, and is occupied by administrative offices. — To the N., in the Post-Str., is the —

Church of St. Nicholas (Pl. R, 26), the parish church of the Old Town and the oldest church in Berlin, restored in 1877-80 by *Blankenstein*, who added the N. tower. The lower parts of the towers, consisting of square blocks of granite, date from the beginning of the 13th cent., the choir from the 14th, and the nave from the 15th century. The interior (sacristan, Propst-Str. 14-16) deserves a visit for the sake of the picturesque general effect of its brick nave and aisles, and also for the numerous monuments, tablets, paintings, etc., in which every artistic style, from the end of the Gothic period down to the rococo era, is represented. The figure of Death, by *Schlüter*, at the Mannlich family vault (1700, under the organ), is especially worthy of attention. The Kotteritz Chapel (under the organ-loft to the right) is a well preserved example of late-Renaissance work. To the left in the choir is the tomb of *Pufendorf*, the celebrated jurist (d. 1694). *Paul Gerhardt*, the hymn-writer (p. 207), was pastor of this church from 1657 to 1666

In ALT-KÖLLN (p. 15) the Brüder-Strasse and the Breite-Strasse run from the Schloss-Platz towards the S. The house No. 13 Brüder Str. (on the right), once the property of *Friedrich Nicolai*, the bookseller and friend of Lessing (d. 1811; comp. p. 143), was the temporary abode of *Theodore Körner* in 1811 and 1813 (tablets in memory of both). Breite-Str. 8-9, opposite the Royal Stables (p. 70), is the office of the *Vossische Zeitung*, the oldest newspaper in Berlin, founded under licence by Rüdiger in 1722, and carried on by Voss after 1751. The more eminent contributors to the paper, including Lessing, are represented in medallions on the façade. Almost the entire block between this point and the Brüder-Str. and Scharren Str. belongs to the firm of *Rudolf Hertzog* (p. 83) The composer *Lortzing* 1801-51 was born at No. 12 together with

portrait, above, to the right) Opposite the end of the Breite-Str.,
in the KÖLLNISCHE FISCHMARKT (Pl. R, 25), stands a house (No. 4)
with a bust of *Field-Marshal Derfflinger* (d 1695), its original
owner. The Rathaus of Kölln, which stood on the right, was pulled
down in 1899. -- The Fischer-Strasse, running hence to the S.E,
is considered to be the oldest existing part of Alt-Kölln. At its
beginning stands the municipal *Testing Office for Hygienic and
Industrial Purposes.*

To the left of the Köllnische Fischmarkt stretches the imposing
Mühlendamm-Brucke (Pl. R, 25), which was transformed in
1888-92, and fitted with new locks and flood-gates. To the left rises
the castellated **Dammmühlen-Gebäude** (including the municipal Savings-Bank, etc.), a reconstruction of the former royal mills,
from designs by Blankenstein (1892-93). Opposite, at the diver-
gence of the Fischer-Brucke, are bronze statues (1894) of the Margraves Albert the Bear (d 1170), by *Boese*, and Waldemar I. (d.
1319), by *Unger*

To the right of the Köllnische Fischmarkt the GERTRAUDTEN-
STRASSE runs towards the S.W., one of the chief thoroughfares of
the inner town. In a square on the W. side rises the *Church of
St Peter* (Pl. R, 25), a Gothic brick building erected in 1847-53 by
Strack, with a graceful tower 316 ft. in height. — The Gertraudten-
Str. ends at the *Gertraudten-Brucke,* which was rebuilt in 1894-95,
and embellished in 1896 with a bronze group by Siemering represent-
ing *St. Gertrude* (d. 659), abbess of the Franconian convent of Ni-
velles and patron saint of travellers, reviving an exhausted wanderer.
Beyond the bridge is the Spittel-Markt (p. 159).

In the FRIEDRICHS-WERDER (p. 47), opposite the W. front of the
Royal Palace (p. 65), on the other side of the Spree, extends the
SCHINKEL-PLATZ (Pl R, 26, 25), which is adorned with bronze statues of ·*Schinkel* (d. 1841; comp. p. 166), by Drake, erected in
1869; *Thaer* (d. 1828), the agriculturist. Rauch's last work, completed by Hagen in 1860; and *Beuth* (d 1853; comp. p 166), to
whose efforts Prussia has been much indebted for her advance in
industrial pursuits, designed by Kiss, with reliefs by Drake (1861).
— Nos. 1-2 are the *Bank fur Handel und Industrie* (Darmstadter
Bank), by Ende & Bockmann, with a façade of red sandstone. On
the S. side is the old **Bau-Akademie,** or *Academy of Architecture* (Pl. R, 25), a lofty square edifice erected by *Schinkel* in
1832-35, 150 ft in length, with handsome details in terracotta. The
successful union of mediæval structural forms with Greek details
stamps this as one of Schinkel's most interesting creations It contains the *Royal Meteorological Institute* (director, Prof. Hellmann),
founded by Alex von Humboldt in 1818 and entrusted with the

elaboration of the materials obtained by observations from the astronomical stations of N. Germany (comp. p. 199), and the *Royal Photometric Institute,* with a collection of about 12,600 views of interesting buildings and monuments; the plates (on sale) may be seen on Tues and Frid. 5-7 p.m

To the S. of the Bau-Akademie, beyond the Werder-Str , whence the Schleusen-Brücke leads to the E. to the Schloss-Platz (p. 69), lies the Unterwasser-Str., which contains the *(First) Gerson Bazaar* and (Nos 2-4) the **Royal Mint** (Pl. R, 25; no admission). The sandstone frieze of the latter, executed by *Schadow* in 1798 from designs by *Gilly,* represents the processes of obtaining and treating the metals, and was enlarged in 1871 by Siemering and Hagen.

The WERDER'SCHE MARKT, to the W. of the Bau-Akademie, contains numerous shops, including (Nos. 5-6) the *(Second) Gerson Bazaar.* On the N. side is the **Friedrichs - Werder Church** (Pl R, 22), a brick structure erected by *Schinkel* in 1824-30. The exterior, in modified Gothic, is not happy, but the vaulted interior is more pleasing. (Sacristan, Oberwall-Str. 21)

In the JAGER-STRASSE, to the S. of the Werder'sche Markt, rises (No 34) the **Deutsche Reichsbank,** or *Bank of the German Empire* (Pl R, 22, 25), a noble brick and sandstone edifice, built by *Hitzig* in 1869-76 The bank, which has been enlarged several times, now occupies an entire block, the office for securities in the Hausvogtei-Platz (S.W.; see below) was built in 1894 from designs by *Emmerich* and *Hasak* — At the corner of the Jager-Str. and Oberwall-Str. is the large *Central Telegraph and Telephone Office* (Pl R. 22; p. 26)

The HAUSVOGTEI-PLATZ (Pl. R, 25) takes its name from the 'Hausvogtei', an old house of detention which in its time held many political prisoners and has since been replaced by the Reichsbank (see above). The remaining three sides of the 'Platz', which is a centre of the dress-making trade, are occupied by large business-houses. Underground Railway approaching completion (see p. 14). — From the Hausvogtei-Platz we may proceed either to the W. by the Mohren-Str. to the Gendarmen-Markt (p 121) and Wilhelm-Platz (p 123), or to the S by the Jerusalemer-Str to the Dönhoff-Platz (p. 126), or to the S.E. by the Niederwall-Str. to the SPITTEL-MARKT (Pl. R, 25), a small but very busy square, surrounded by large business-houses In the centre of the Spittel-Markt rises the *Spindler-Brunnen,* a fountain of red and grey granite Near it to the N.E. is the Gertraudten-Brucke (p. 128).

TRAMWAYS (pp 15-22) run from the Spittel-Markt to the Alexander-Platz (50, 59, 62, 64-72, 74), Anhalt Station (59, 62), Brandenburg Gate (6, 9), Gesundbrunnen (38), Gorlitz Station (91, 92), Hackescher-Markt (38, 17, 18), Hall G. . . Krei . . Läd Stati . M. bit (6, 9), Rathaus . . . . 98), Silesian Stati . . . . to the Gendarmen Markt S. Hundorf-

Platz (and Lützow-Platz), Potsdam Station, Schoneberg, and Zoological Garden a shorter route will soon be offered by the Underground Railway (p. 14)

In the Wall-Str. (Nos 5-8), to the E. of the Spittel-Markt, are the business premises of *Jacques Ravené Sons*, wholesale metal-merchants (founded 1775), erected in 1895-96 On the third floor (entrance, Wall-Str. 7) is —

*Ravené's Picture Gallery (Pl. R, 25), a collection of about 200 works by modern German and French masters, including several choice examples of the older Berlin and Dusseldorf schools (adm, see p. 39).

Room I To the left: *Knaus*, Mouse-trap, Woman and cats; *K. Becker*, Family portraits, Morning after the ball, Jeweller and senator; *Tidemand*, Sunday in Norway; *E. Hildebrandt*, Santa Gloria near Rio de Janeiro; *Saltzmann*, Cape of Good Hope; *Graeb*, Fontana Medina in Naples; *Knaus*, P. L Ravené; *E. Hildebrandt*, Winter pleasures; *Körner*, Nile landscape; *Graeb*, Near Florence, *Schrödter*, Eulenspiegel as baker's apprentice; *P Meyerheim*, Trophies of the chase. Water-colours by *Hilgers*, *Hosemann*, *Hoguet*, etc

Room II *Hasenclever*, Jobs (a dunce) undergoing examination, Jobs as schoolmaster; *Fleury*, Massacre of Jews in London, 1307.

Room III., with busts of the founder of the collection, *Peter Louis Ravené* (d. 1861), and of his son, *Louis Ravené* (d 1879) by Hoffmeister. *Jordan*, Child's funeral in Heligoland; *Leu*, Landslip in Norway; *Stevens*, Mourners; *Gallait*, Bohemian musicians; *Henry Ritter*, Drowned fisher-boy — *Hasenclever*, Portrait of himself; *Couture*, Page; *Schrader*, Death of Leonardo da Vinci, *Graeb*, Halberstadt Cathedral, *Hasenclever*, Hilgers the painter, *E Hildebrandt*, Leisure hours; *A. Achenbach*, Ostend harbour; *Flamm*, Italian scene; *Menzel*, Frederick the Great, *Scheuren*, Landscape in storm, *Lessing*, Huntsmen. — *Hasenclever*, Jobs as night-watchman, *Tidemand*, The old wolf-hunter; *Biard*, French custom-house; *Schreyer*, Hussars attacking; *Tidemand*, Funeral in Norway; *Hasenclever*, Scene in a cellar; *Troyon*, Cattle, Hounds, *Schmitson*, Hungarian brood-mares; *F. Kruger*, Stable; *K. Begas*, Useless labour, *C. Hubner*, Game-law; *Hoguet*, Landscape.

Room IV. *Gudin*, Storm at sea; *Leu*, Norwegian landscape; *Hilgers*, Winter landscape, *Willems*, Picture-sale; *A. Achenbach*, Norwegian coast; *Hoguet*, Silvan scene; *Hasenclever*, Preyer the painter; *E. Hildebrandt*, Boa Viagem near Rio de Janeiro.

Room V. To the left: *Waldmüller*, Carnival scene; *Jernberg*, Return home. — *Zugel*, Cattle watering, Evening at the pasture; *Kameke*, Alpine landscape — *A. Kampf*, The sisters, *Sorolla y Bastida*, Mother and child; *Klaus Meyer*, Card-players; *Bokelmann*, Klaus Groth; *G Melchers*, By the fire; *Munthe*, Autumn. — On a stand, *Emp. William II.*, Men of war (water-colour drawing). — *Gude*, Fishing off Rügen

Cabinet 1 (apply to the custodian). *E. Hildebrandt*, Street scenes from Rouen and Lyons; *Andr. Achenbach*, Landscape; *Preyer*, Sparrows' breakfast; *Lessing*, Westphalian landscape; *Hilgers*, Winter landscape; *Knaus*, Girl gathering flowers. — Cabinet II. *F. E Meyerheim*, Woman and girl of the Harz, The youngest born, Going to church, Morning hours; *P. Meyerheim*, E Meyerheim; *Dupre*, Landscape; *F Kruger*, Frederick William IV., *E. Hildebrandt*, Fisher-girl, Children on the beach; *Fleury*, The report. — Cabinet III. *Graeb*, Cloisters; *Hilgers*, Fishermen's huts; *Horace Vernet*, Zouave acting as a nurse ('Le soldat nourrice'); *Roux*, Linnæus as a youth; *E. Hildebrandt*, Irish hut, *Brendel*, Sheep, *Hosemann*, Genre scene, *Meissonier*, Genre scene.

To the left of Ravené's, at Wall-Strasse 9 13, are a series of courts and buildings occupied by Spindler's dye-works (p. 201),

known as the *Spindlershof*. In front is a large warehouse in the
Romanesque style built by Kayser & Von Groszheim — The Wall-
Str. ends to the E. at the Markische Provinzial-Museum (p. 153).

9. Northern and Eastern Quarters.
Natural History Museums

The Wilhelm-Str. (p. 122) is continued to the N. of the Linden
by the NEUE WILHELM-STRASSE (Pl R, 20). In the latter, at the
corner of the Dorotheen-Str. (p. 144), is the *Military Academy*,
founded by Scharnhorst in 1810 for German officers The present
building, by Bernhardt & Schwechten, dates from 1882. Farther to
the N. are the *Physiological, Second Chemical,* and *Physical
Institutes* of the University.

Beyond the *Marschalls-Brücke* the LUISEN-STRASSE (Pl. R, 21,
20) runs parallel with the Friedrich-Strasse to the Neue Tor. Near
by to the left, Schiffbauer-Damm 25, is the *Neue Operetten-
Theater*, by W. Hentschel (1908). At Luisen-Str. 32 is an annexe
of the *Imperial Home Office* (comp. p. 123). A tablet on No 24a,
opposite, marks the house where the historian *Ranke* died in 1886
(comp. p. 167). No. 35 is the office of the *Berlin Electricity Works*,
which produce the force for the electric tramways, the lighting of
streets, etc.

Farther on, at the corner of the Schumann-Str. and the Luisen-
Str., is a monument to *Albrecht von Graefe*, the oculist (d. 1870),
with excellent reliefs in terracotta, by Siemering. Near this point
is the **Charité** (Pl. R, 21), a large hospital founded in 1710, now
being rebuilt. The Charité serves also as a teaching institution in
connection with the University (11 clinics), and is united with the
Pathological Institute, which reached its present importance under
the management of Prof. Virchow (d. 1902). Visitors are admitted
to the hospital on Wed , Sat., & Sun., 2-3 p m

At No. 56 Luisen-Str. is the *Veterinary College* (Pl. R, 21;
400 students), opened in 1790 In front of the main building is a
bronze statue of *A. C. Gerlach* (d 1877), a former rector, by Panzner.
In the garden is the *Anatomie*, or *University Dissecting Room*,
built by Cremer in 1863-65 (main entrance, Karl-Str. 23a). — In
the Luisen-Platz, to the left (Nos. 2-4), is the *Kaiserin-Friedrich-
Haus* for medical instruction, containing medical collections (adm.
to the collection of instruments Mon.-Frid. 10-3, free), etc. — To
the E of the Neue Tor, Hessische-Str. 1-3, is the *First Chemical
Institute* and (No. 4) the *Hygienic Institute* of the University.

Outside the Neue Tor (Pl. R, 21) the Luisen-Str. joins the long
INVALIDEN STRASSE which begins on the E by and the Stettin Station (p. 166 and ends on the W in Alt Moabit At the point of

11

junction (Pl R, 21) are three important scientific institution , in buildings by Tiede: *viz* the Agricultural Academy, to the E.; the Museum of Natural History, in the middle; and the School of Mines, to the W (p 164); comp the adjoining Plan

TRAMWAYS (see p. 14-22) from the Neue Tor: Nos. 2, 10, 11, 16, 19, 51, 57, Q, V, and (viâ the Chaussée-Str., to the E) Nos 25, 26, 28, 29, 32, 34, 43, and 68

The **Agricultural Academy** (950 students), founded in 1810 by A. Thaer (p 158) at Moglin near Wriezen, was removed to its present quarters in 1880. It contains the AGRICULTURAL MUSEUM (adm. see p. 36; official guide, 1908, 75 pf). In the vestibule are models by Rau, illustrating the history of manual tools and of the plough. In the covered court straight on is the *Machinery Department* (objects changed from time to time), including a collection of models. On the groundfloor also (in front and to the left) is the *Zoological Department*, with a large collection of the skulls and skeletons of domestic animals. — On the first floor, on the N. side, is the *Zootechnical Department*, illustrating the development of stock-farming and fisheries, with models of farm-cattle, etc The W wing contains the *Mineralogical and Geological Department:* specimens of rocks and soil; mineral fertilizers; geological map of Berlin (to the depth of 1250 ft.) under glass; representations of the salt industry in Stassfurt and of the saltpetre industry in Chili. The *Vegetable Department*, in the S. wing, illustrates the history of gardening, agriculture, and forestry; also the relative values of different foods, etc. On the side next the glass-covered court is a colonial section In the E. wing is a Technological Department; also collections illustrating the biology and pathology of plants

The ***Museum of Natural History** (Pl. R, 21), built in 1883-89, bears on its façade portraits in sandstone of L von Buch (d 1853), the geologist, and Joh. Muller (d. 1858), the physiologist. Adm , see p. 38 The building accommodates three separate institutions, each with its museum, *viz.* the *Geological & Palaeontological Institute*, the *Mineralogical & Petrographical Institute*, and the *Zoological Institute* — The 'Main Collections', on the first and second floors, are reserved for students. The 'Exhibition Collection', to which alone the public are admitted, occupies most of the groundfloor. All the objects are labelled. Numerous direction-boards assist the visitor to find his way.

To the right of the entrance are two rooms containing the GEOLOGICAL SECTION.

The PALÆONTOLOGICAL MUSEUM lies also to the right, adjoining the court It contains fossils of the chief types of antediluvian animals, the invertebrates (large ammonites) being to the right, the vertebrates to the left By the entrance-wall, Ichthyosauri

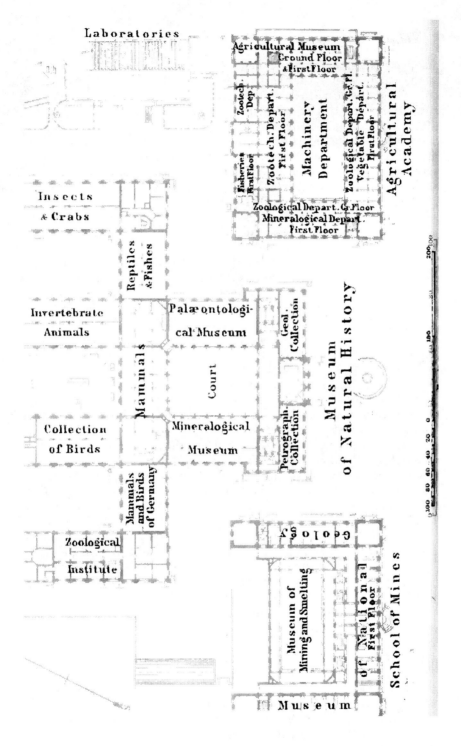

Laboratories

Agricultural Museum
Ground Floor
& First Floor

Zootech.
Dep.

Fisheries
First Floor

Zootech. Depart.
First Floor

Machinery
Department

Zoological Depart. Gr.Fl.
Vegetable Depart.
First Floor

Agricultural
Academy

Zoological Depart. G. Floor
Mineralogical Depart.
First Floor

Insects
& Crabs

Reptiles
& Fishes

Invertebrate
Animals

Palæontologi-
cal Museum

Geol.
Collection

Mammals

Court

Museum
of Natural History

Collection
of Birds

Mineralogical
Museum

Petrograph.
Collection

Mammals
and Birds
of Germany

Zoological

Institute

Geology

Museum of
Mining and Smelting

of National
First Floor

Museum

School of Mines

(one with traces of the skin, another with embryo) and foot-prints
of the Chirotherium; by the partition in front, to the left, marine
crocodiles (Steneosaurus); by the partition wall to the right, Ple-
siosaurians, at the back, a specimen in perfect preservation By the
fifth window to the left is a well-preserved Archæopteryx in Soln-
hofen slate, the oldest fossil bird as yet discovered, slightly im-
pressed on a slab of stone, the chief glory of the collection. (Another
specimen of the Archæopteryx is in the Natural History Museum at
London, and a cast of it is exhibited here) In the middle are skeletons of the extinct giant bird (Dinornis) of New Guinea. The last
section of the room contains a sea-cow (Halitherium Schinzi), remains of extinct quadrupeds, and the skin of a giant sloth from
Patagonia.

The MINERALOGICAL MUSEUM lies to the left of the entrance
The room next the street contains the petrographical collection. In
the principal room opposite is a series of table-cases containing
an unusually beautiful crystallographic collection, systematically
arranged. The stages in the upright cases illustrate the co-occur-
rence of minerals and their usual position in geological sequence
In the first cabinet on the right are large specimens of amber,
malachite, and topaz; in that to the left are rock-crystals and ame-
thysts. The table-case by the last window to the left contains
precious stones. The collection of meteorites in the centre of the
main corridor is one of the largest in existence. The Gothic cabinets
contain the finest specimens from the collection of Karl Rumpf.

The ZOOLOGICAL MUSEUM is an admirably selected collection,
illustrating all the important groups of the animal world, with the
fauna of Germany placed in the foreground (official guide 20 pf.).
The preparations of various parts of the body should be noticed.
The visitor should begin with the glass-covered court in which the
larger animals are exhibited, comprising the cast of the skeleton
of a Diplodocus 79 ft. in length, from N. America. Beyond, in the
central rooms of the transverse building, are the *Mammals.* — A
hall adjoining these on the W. is devoted to the most important
Mammals and Birds of Germany, of which the complete lists
number respectively 69 and 410 species. — Three wings project to
the N from the above-mentioned transverse building. In that to the
W. is the extensive *Systematic Collection of Birds.* — The second
contains the *Invertebrate Animals* (sponges, corals, shells, snails,
etc.). At the beginning, on the right, is a gigantic cuttle-fish, at
the end a coral-reef and an oyster-bed. — The E. portion of the
transverse building is devoted to *Reptiles, Amphibia,* and *Fishes.*
— The E. projecting wing, immediately adjoining, contains *Insects
and Crabs,* with illustrations in some cases of the animals' habits
and methods of life. To the left are butterflies and bees, notably
colonizing bees ; to the right, beetles and spiders.

11

The **Geological Institution and School of Mines** (Pl. R, 21, plan, p. 162) was built in 1874-78 The School of Mines, which was founded in 1860 and has now about 100 students, occupies the groundfloor. In the vestibule are two paintings by L. Spangenberg (the Kurische Nehrung, and the Papenkaul near Gerolstein). The glass-covered court and the gallery of the first floor are occupied by the *Museum of Mining and Smelting* (adm , see p. 38). The processes of extracting and working the ore are shown in the court. We may also notice here the gigantic fossil tree-trunks and the fine examples of artistic casting from the former royal foundry at Berlin. In the gallery of the first floor is a systematic collection of minerals obtained by mining; in the N.E. corner a room containing the mineralogical collection — The other rooms of the first floor are occupied by the Prussian *Museum of National Geology.* — On the second floor (no adm.) are the offices of the Geological Institute and a valuable collection of amber from Königsberg.

In the Invaliden-Str , to the W. of the School of Mines, rises the ⁺**Gnaden-Kirche** (Pl. R, 21; open daily, 12-1 and 5-7), a Romanesque sandstone building by *M. Spitta* (d. 1902), erected in 1891-95 to the memory of the Empress Augusta The elaborate choir has stained-glass windows by Linnemann and mosaics designed by Geselschap In front of the church stands an obelisk commemorating the loss of the corvette *Amazone* in 1861. — Farther on, to the W. of the Scharnhorst-Str . a new building for the Kaiser Wilhelm Academy is being erected (comp. p. 145).

The *Invalidenhaus* (Pl R, 21), on the W. side of the Scharnhorst-Str . erected by Frederick the Great in 1748 'læso et invicto militi', is devoid of architectural interest. Opposite, in the *Invaliden-Park*, is the *National Warriors' Monument*, a Corinthian column of iron, 145 ft. high, erected in 1854 to the memory of soldiers who fell in 1848-49 (view from the top; apply to porter of Invalidenhaus; adm. 10 pf.).

The INVALIDEN-KIRCHHOF, adjoining the Invalidenhaus on the N., is the burial-place of many distinguished officers, including *Scharnhorst* (d. 1813; monument by Schinkel, with reliefs by Tieck); *Boyen* (d. 1848), founder of the 'Landwehr', *Friesen* (d. 1814); *Winterfeldt* (d. 1757, transferred hither in 1857); and *Tauenzien von Wittenberg* (d. 1824).

To the W. of the Invaliden-Park the Invaliden-Strasse crosses the *Berlin and Spandau Canal*, which is connected with the Spree on the S. by means of the *Humboldt-Hafen* (Pl R, 21) and separates the Oranienburg suburb from the quarter of MOABIT (comp. p. 54) — In front of the old *Hamburg Station* is a bronze bust of *Fr. Neuhaus* (d 1876), founder of the railway from Berlin to Hamburg. Since 1906 the building has contained the **Royal Museum of Traffic and Engineering** (Pl. R, 21; adm., see p 38), demonstrating in a comprehensive manner the development of railway-matters by means of models and originals; smaller sections to the right are dedicated to structures above ground and in the water.

Farther on, to the left, are the *Lehrte Station* of the Stadtbahn (p. 12), connected with the main Lehrte Station (see p 140), and the Exhibition Park (p. 141). To the right, opposite the latter, are the *Zellengefängnis* or *Prison*, a model establishment for the reception of 565 inmates, built in 1842-49; the *Oberfeuerwerker-Schule*, founded in 1840 for training non-commissioned officers of artillery; and the *Barracks of the 2nd Uhlan Guards Regiment.*

Beyond the Exhibition Park, the Invaliden-Strasse joins the Alt-Moabit street (p. 140). From this point we may proceed by the Paul-Str. and across the Luther-Brücke near the château of Bellevue (p. 176) to the Tiergarten. — In Alt-Moabit, to the right, is the **Criminal Court** (Pl. R, 15, 18), built in 1877-81, with cells for prisoners on trial On the façade are statues of Prussian kings. The court sits almost daily from 9, in winter from 9.30 a.m.; visitors are admitted, but for trials exciting unusual public interest tickets of admission should be secured beforehand (at rooms 253, 439, and 565 respectively). In front of the building is a bronze group of a lion and a serpent, by A. Wolff.

Farther on in Alt-Moabit is the *Church of St John* (Pl. R, 15), by Schinkel, with a tower added by Stüler in 1835 connecting it in one block with the parsonage and school-house. The Kirch-Str., diverging here to the left, leads to the *Moabiter-Brucke*, rebuilt in 1893-94 and embellished with bronze bears. Beyond the bridge is the *Bellevue Station* of the Stadtbahn (p. 12). — Nos 99-103 Alt-Moabit accommodate *Bolle's* well-known dairy. — Alt-Moabit now skirts the S. side of a park known as the *Kleine Tiergarten.* Farther on, at the end of the Strom-Str., to the left, is the *Lessing-Brücke*, built in 1901-3 and adorned with four reliefs, by O. Lessing, of scenes from G. E. Lessing's dramas

In the W. part of Moabit, beside the Allgemeine Elektrizitats-Gesellschaft (p. 167), are several large manufactories. the *Berlin-Anhalter Maschinenbau-Aktien-Gesellschaft* (Pl. R, 9), Kaiserin-Augusta-Allée 27, the engine-tools factory of *Ludwig Löwe & Co., Ltd*, Hutten-Str. 17-20: the *Deutsche Waffen- und Munitions-Aktien-Gesellschaft*, Kaiserin-Augusta-Allée 30 (3500 hands), etc.

At **Plötzensee**, to the N of Moabit, and $\frac{1}{2}$ M. from the Beussel-Str. station of the Ringbahn (p 13; tramway No 12), is the *Penitentiary* (Pl B, 9), built in 1868-78, where executions take place.

— — —

At the N   nd on the Friedrich Strasse   th   ht the Oranienburger Strasse p 115   joined   the S t   nd the former Oranienburg Gate (Pl. R, 21) begins the CHAUSSEE-STRASSE, until 1880 the chief seat of the Berlin engine works

The OLD DOROTHEENSTADT CEMETERY (Pl. R, 21, 21), at the beginning of the Chaussée-Str. to the left, contains many handsome monuments and interesting graves. Near the E wall repose the philosophers *Fichte* (d. 1814) and *Hegel* (d. 1831); to the left of the main walk are the graves of *Schinkel* (d. 1811, monument designed by himself), *Rauch* (d. 1857), *Stüler* (d 1865; monument by Strack), *A. Borsig* (d 1854; monument by Schadow), and *G Schadow* (d. 1850); to the right of the main walk is the grave of *Beuth* (d. 1853).

No. 6 Chaussée-Str. is *Borsig's Office*, built by Renner & Körte; the Borsig Factory, formerly Chaussée-Str. 1, afterwards in Moabit, was in 1898 transferred to Tegel (p. 201). Farther on the Chaussée-Str. intersects the Invaliden-Str., leading to the left to the Scientific Museums mentioned on pp 162-64, and to the right to the **Stettin Railway Station** (Pl. R, 24; see p. 1), with a station for suburban traffic (p. 13) beside it on the W.

Tramways (pp 15-22): Nos 2, 10, 11, 51, 57, 68, Q, and V; also a (Garten-Str.) and Nos. 16, 19, 25, 26, 28, 29, 32, 34, and 43 (Chaussée-Str.). Omnibus 5 (at night see p. 23) to Friedrich-Strasse Station, Potsdam Station (also 13), and 7 to Alexander-Platz and Görlitz Stations.

The Chaussée-Strasse leads to the suburb of WEDDING (Pl B, 17; station of the Nord-Ring, see p. 13). In the N, to the E. of the Müller-Str. leading to Tegel (p. 201), a *Schiller-Park* is being laid out. To the W, near the Putlitz-Str Station of the Nord-Ring (p. 13), on the Spandau ship-canal, is the *Institute for Infectious Diseases* founded by Prof. Koch. — Here also is the municipal **Rudolf Virchow Hospital** (Pl. B, 14, 15; chief entrance in the Augustenburger-Platz), erected in 1899-1906 by *L. Hoffmann*, with 62 buildings, the tasteful simple architecture of which is admirably adapted to the surrounding gardens. It covers an area of 63 acres; the expense including the equipment amounted to 95,000 *l.* (2000 beds, 80 physicians; hours of adm. Sun, Wed., & Sat. 2-3 p.m). Tramways Nos 29, 12, 68 (See-Strasse), h (Augustenburger-Platz).

For the quarters of the town situated in the NORTHERN part of Old Berlin, the chief centre of traffic is the small *Hackesche Markt* (Pl. R, 26), situated near the Börse Station (p. 12) and the Monbijou-Platz (p. 146).

Tramways (pp. 15-21): Nos. 16, 19, 28, 29, 30, 33, 38, 39, 40, 42, 47, 48, 52-56, III

From the Hackesche Markt the Rosenthaler-Str. runs to the former Rosenthal Gate, passing (Nos. 23-31) a large store of *A. Wertheim* (p 125), built in a thoroughly modern style by Messel, and a *Wall Fountain*, with the figure of a girl drawing water, by K. von Uechtritz.

A little to the W of the Rosenthaler Str. rises the *Sophien-Kirche* (Pl R, 27), founded by Queen Sophia Louise in 1712 and rebuilt in 1892.

of *Leopold von Ranke*, the historian (d. 1886) — To the E in the Kleine Rosenthaler-Str. (Pl. R, 27) is the *Old Garrison Churchyard*, with the graves of *F. de la Motte-Fouqué*, the poet (d. 1843), and of *General von Lutzow* (d. 1831).

At Brunnen-Str. 107a is the *Allgemeine Elektrizitäts-Gesellschaft* (Pl. B, 23), founded in 1883 by E. Rathenau, one of the largest of its kind (share-capital 5,000,000 *l.*; 30,000 workmen and officials); comp. pp. 165, 201. — Beyond it is the —

Humboldthain (Pl B, 20, 23), a park 90 acres in area, laid out in 1869-76. Near the Brunnen-Str. are a group of large erratic boulders, dedicated to *Alexander von Humboldt*, and a marble bull by *M. Geyger*. The botanical section (adm. Wed. & Sat. 1-6; strangers at other times also) is on the S side, near the manager's office; it contains a department in which plants are grown to be used in object-lessons at schools. Here also is a *Geological Wall* (explanation 10 pf.). — Beyond the park is the *Gesundbrunnen Station* of the Nord-Ring, the Stettin line, the Nordbahn, and the Kremmen and Wittstock line (Pl. B, 23; comp. pp. 13, 201), which traverses to the E. the *Swinemünder-Brücke*, 250 yds. in length and borne by one pier only.

Beyond the station is the suburb of **Gesundbrunnen** (Pl. B, 19, 22), which has its name from a mineral spring discovered in 1701.

Outside the former Schönhausen Gate, in the Schönhauser Allée (Pl. R, 27, 30), is a marble monument to *A Senefelder*, the inventor of lithography (1771-1834), by Pohle (1892). At Schönhauser Allée Nos 36-39 is the large *Schultheiss Brewery* (Pl. B, 30), which produced 27 million gallons of beer in 1907.

About 3 M beyond the Schönhausen Gate (tramways Nos. 5, 47, 49, 51, 57) lies the village of **Pankow** (Pl. B, 25, 26, *Linder's Restaurant*), a favourite resort in summer (35,000 inhab), with a station on the Stettin railway and on the Nordbahn (pp. 201, 204). — About ³/₄ M. further on is the village (12,200 inhab) of **Nieder-Schönhausen** (*Rest Liedemit*), with a royal château built by Eosander von Goethe and long occupied by the wife of Frederick the Great — To the W of Pankow lies (1¹/₄ M.) **Schönholz**, a station on the Nordbahn (p 201), with a large park belonging to the Berlin riflemen's society and a frequented restaurant.

The E. and N.E. quarters of the old town of Berlin are of little interest to strangers The more important points are here mentioned in order from S. to N.; most of them are most conveniently reached by means of the tramway (p. 14)

Near the Spree lies the **Silesian Railway Station** (Pl R, 31), with which the Wriezen Station is connected on the E. side.

Tramways (pp. 14-22): Nos 9, 31, 80; also 1, 2, 3, 4, 6, 22 (Andreas-Str), 16, 78, and 79 (Grüner-Weg); d to Stralau and Treptow (p. 170).

In the *Andreas-Plat* Pl R 31 are two bronze groups Workman and his wife by Havenkamp and Woman of the working-class with her child by Germanski Near the beginning of the Grosse

Frankfurter-Str. stands the *Church of St. Mark* (Pl R, 32), built in the round-arched style by Stüler, in 1848-55

The Grosse Frankfurter-Str goes on to the **Städtische Zentral-Vieh- und Schlachthof** (Municipal Cattle Market and Slaughter Houses, Pl. R, 38, tramways Nos. 58, 65, 66, 67, 75, 81, c, g, and h). The market is busiest on Wed. & Sat. till 1 p.m. (adm. free), the slaughterhouses on Mon. & Thurs (adm by tickets obtained at the office in the Thaer-Str.). Good restaurant. The market has a special station on the 'Nord Ring' (p 13). — Near the market lies the town of **Lichtenberg**, with 70,000 inhab (Frankfurter Allée Station on the 'Nord Ring', tramways Nos 66, 68, 69, 70, & 71). A tramway (No. 71) runs to the N.E. from the Frankfurter Allée Station to the municipal lunatic asylum of *Herzberge*.

Outside the old Königs-Tor extends the **Friedrichshain** (Pl. R, 33, 36), a park laid out in 1845 and enlarged in 1874-76 (tramways Nos. 1, 2, 4, 17, 59, 62, 63, 64, 65, 74, 81, b, g, and h). The entrance near the Königs-Tor is to be embellished with a fountain with legendary figures by Taschner, Rauch, and Wrba. — The large municipal *Hospital (Krankenhaus) am Friedrichshain*, No. 159 Landsberger Allée, was erected in 1868-74 by Gropius & Schmieden. Visitors are admitted on Sun., Wed., & Sat. 2-3. By the W wall of the hospital, near the Landsberger Allée, is the cemetery of the insurgents who fell in March 1848 (Pl R, 32).

About 3 M to the N of the Königstor is the village of **Weissensee** (Pl B, 34, *Schloss-Restaurant*), with 10,000 inhab (Station of the Nord-Ring, see p. 13, tramways Nos 50-62) To the N W is the (1½ M) race-course for trotting-matches (p. 30).

10. Southern and South-Western Quarters.

Kreuzberg. Tiergarten Quarter. Schöneberg.

From the southern part of the Friedrich-Strasse (p. 120) the Koch-Strasse runs to the E. to the *Jerusalem Church* (Pl. G, 22, 25). Short of this, the Koch-Str. is crossed by the Charlotten-Strasse Near the S. end of the latter, in the Encke-Platz, is the *Royal Observatory* (Pl. G, 22), erected by Schinkel in 1832-35. In 1878 the mean altitude for the kingdom of Prussia (121 ft. above sea level) was marked on the N. façade of the building. The instruments are shown by the castellan on Wed. & Sat. 9-11 (in winter 10-11) Director, Prof. v. Struve. — At the corner of the Jerusalemer-Str. and Schützen-Str. is the house of *Mosse & Co* (Berliner Tageblatt)

Past the Jerusalem Church the LINDEN-STRASSE (Pl. G, 22) leads to the S to the Belle-Alliance-Platz (p. 170). — To the right of the church at Nos. 20-21 are the offices of the *Victoria Insurance Co.* No. 14 is the *Kammer-Gericht* (Royal Court of Appeal; Pl. G, 22), founded by the Elector Joachim I., built by Gerlach in 1734-35, and remodelled in 1880. Opposite (Markgrafen-Str. 104-107) is *Jordan's* establishment (p. 34)

The ORANIEN-STRASSE leads to the E. from the above-mentioned

Jerusalemer-Kirche into the heart of the industrial S E. quarter. At Nos. 90-91 (corner of the Alte Jacob-Str) is the **Reichs-Druckerei,** or *Government Printing Office* (Pl. G, 25; no adm.), an institution controlled by the Imperial Post Office The imposing building contains a model art-printing department in which the bank-notes and postage-stamps of the empire are produced. The façade with its round tower is by Busse. — In the Waldeck-Park, at the corner of the Kürassier-Str., a marble *Statue of Waldeck,* the liberal politician (d. 1870), by Walger, was unveiled in 1889.

Continuing along the Oranien-Str. we reach in turn the Moritz-Platz (Pl. G, 25) and the ORANIEN-PLATZ (Pl. G, 28), the latter intersected by the *Luisenstadt Canal.*

Tramways (pp 14-21), from the Moritz-Platz: Nos 1, 2, 4, 12, 18, 28, 29, 35, 36, 37, 41, 47, 48, 53, 65, 93, 95, 98; from the Oranien - Platz· Nos 11, 12, 18, 28, 29, 30, 47, 48, 53, 93, 95, 98

A little to the N of the Oranien-Platz, at the Engelbecken, rises the handsome **Church of St. Michael** (Pl. G, 28), designed by *Soller,* and erected in 1853-56 as the (first) Roman Catholic garrison-church. A walk of 5 min. to the S.E. takes us to the **Church of St. Thomas** (Pl. G, 31), built by *Adler* in 1864-69 Both churches are domed and exhibit a combination of Romanesque with Renaissance details. — Near the latter church, in the Mariannen-Platz, rises the large **Bethanien Hospital** (Pl. G, 28; adm. Tues., Frid., & Sun 2-3), managed by Protestant sisters of charity and opened in 1847. In front is a monument to the celebrated surgeon *Wilms* (d 1880), by Siemering, and to the S , in the Waldemar-Str., rises a marble monument erected in 1902 from designs by L. Hoffmann to the *Firemen of Berlin.* The latter consists of two pylons flanking reliefs, by A Vogel, of Athena directing the struggle with the monster Hydra and of suppliants seeking help.

At the end of the Oranien-Str. is a station of the Elevated Railway (p. 13). The Wiener-Str and the Skalitzer-Str stretch hence to the S E and E. Close by, in the Lausitzer-Platz, rises the **Emmaus Church** (Pl. G, 31), built by *Orth* in 1893, a handsome brick edifice in the Romanesque style. A glass mosaic over the porch, designed by Mohn, represents Christ with the two disciples. — To the S., in the Wiener-Str., is the **Görlitz Railway Station** (Pl. G, 32)

Tramways (pp. 15-22)· Nos 11, 12, 18, 22, 46, 91, 92, 93, 98, e; also 13, 82, 89, 90 (Skalitzer-Str.), and 94 (Reichenberger-Str). — Omnibus 7 to the Stettin Station.

The Elevated Railway (p. 13) passes eastwards down the centre of the Skalitzer-Str., which leads past the Emmaus Church to the site of the old SILESIAN GATE, or *Schlesische Tor,* now occupied by the handsomest of all the Elevated Railway Stations, a structure by Grisebach to the adjacent to the right on the river side is a landing-stage for the mail ... by 24 bronze figures in the German

and a *Boat-Builder*, by Janensch and Bernewitz (1896). — Farther
to the E. the river is spanned by the **Oberbaum-Brücke** (Pl.
G, 34), a massive brick structure 500 ft. long and 90 ft. broad, built
by *Stahn* in 1895-96. The E. side of the bridge, from the centre of
which rise two towers, is occupied by the arcades of the Electric
Railway, with numerous turrets and ornamental gables. — Beyond
the bridge we come to the Stralauer Tor Station (p. 13) of the
Electric Railway, followed by the terminus (Warschauer-Brücke,
p. 13), close to the *Warschauer-Strasse Station* of the 'Stadtbahn' (Pl. G, 34; p. 12).

A handsome avenue, running to the S.E. from the Silesian Gate, and
forming a continuation of the Köpenicker-Str., leads viâ the *Schlesische
Busch* to (25 min.) the *Treptow Station* (Pl. G, 38) of the 'Süd-Ring'
(p. 13). Beyond the station it passes through the *Treptower Park* (230
acres), which stretches to the left as far as the Upper Spree. The park
was laid out in 1876-87 by *G. Meyer*, of whom a statue, by Manthe,
stands to the right of the play-ground. — About 1 M. from the station lies
the village of **Treptow** (Pl. G, 42; 15,500 inhab.), containing several garden
restaurants on the river (*Regelin; Abtei*, on an island). Steamers see pp. 24
and 201; tramways (pp. 21-22): Nos. 83, 89, 102, 104. Near the village is
the *Treptow Observatory* (astronomical museum), containing Archenhold's
'Giant Telescope', which is interesting for the simplicity of its installation
(adm., see p. 37). Beyond Treptow lies the *Plänter-Wald* (220 acres),
another public park intersected with paths, in which the timber for the
city parks and grounds is grown. In the park itself, and on the bank of
the Spree (1 M. from the village) are the *Eier-Häuschen* (steamboat station), two restaurants much visited from Berlin. — On the right bank of
the Spree, opposite the point at which Treptow commences, lies the village of *Stralau* (Pl. G, 41), containing a picturesquely situated church.
The two villages are connected by a tramway tunnel (line d, p. 22) nearly
500 yds. in length.

In its less fashionable portion to the S. of the Leipziger-Str.
(p. 124) the Friedrich-Strasse crosses the Koch-Strasse at the *Café
Friedrichshof* (p. 11). Farther on, at Friedrich-Str. 18, is the municipal *Market II.*, with a flower-market.

In the centre of the circular BELLE-ALLIANCE-PLATZ (Pl. G, 23),
laid out by Frederick William I. at the end of the Friedrich-Str.,
rises the *Friedens-Säule*, or **Column of Peace,** 60 ft. in height,
erected by King Frederick William IV. in 1840 to commemorate the
25th anniversary of the peace of 1815. The granite column, rising
from a lofty pedestal, has a marble capital, crowned with a bronze
Victory by *Rauch*. The four surrounding groups in marble represent the principal powers that took part in the victory of Waterloo (England, Prussia, the Netherlands, and Hanover). On the S. side
of the Platz are marble figures of Peace, by *A. Wolff*, and Historio-
graphy, by *Hartzer*.

On the S. the square is bounded by the **Halle Gate** (Pl. G, 23),
a monumental edifice erected in 1879 by *Strack* on the site of the
old building. Outside the gate, to the right in the Königgrätzer-
Str., is a station of the Elevated Railway (p. 13). To the left in the

Gitschiner-Str. is the *Imperial Patent Office*, erected in 1905 from designs by Solf and Wichards, one of the largest buildings in Berlin (600 rooms).

Tramways (pp. 15-22) run from the Halle Gate and the Blücher-Platz (S. side; I, II, and IV from here) to the Lehrte Station, Moabit (4, 7, 11, 15), Gesundbrunnen (34, 38, 39, 42, 43), the Opern-Platz (34, 39, 42, 43, 53, 55), the Alexander-Platz (64, 73, 75), the Silesian Station (1, 4), Rixdorf (7, 15, 53, 55, I, II, V), Kreuzberg (34, 38, 43, 96, 97, I, II, V), Schöneberg (43, 82, 89, 90, I, II, V), the Anhalt Station and the Brandenburg Gate (1, 7, 11, 15), the Donhoff-Platz (38, 39, 42, 64), the Friedrich-Str. Station (34, 42), the Gendarmen-Markt (34, 43, 53, 55, 73, 75, 96, 97), the Hackescher Markt (38, 39, 53, 55), the Museum Island (39, 42, 53, 55), the Rathaus (38, 42, 64, 73, 75), the Schloss-Platz (73, 75), the Spittelmarkt (38, 64), and the Stettin Station (4, 34, 43). For the Görlitz Station, the Nollendorf-Platz the Potsdam Station, and the Zoological Garden Station the Elevated Railway (see p. 11) is quicker.

Opposite the Halle Gate the *Landwehr Canal* is crossed by the *Belle-Alliance Bridge,* 110 ft. wide, on the buttresses of which stand marble groups of Navigation, Fishing, Industry, and Trade. The canal is $6\frac{1}{2}$ M. in length, and stretches from the Silesian Gate to Charlottenburg, connecting the Upper and Lower Spree. — At the S. end of the bridge is the *Blücher-Platz* (Pl. G, 23), whence the Tempelhof Quarter stretches to the S.

Near the Blücher-Platz lie several old Cemeteries Those of the *Jerusalemer-Kirche,* the *Neue Kirche,* and the *Dreifaltigkeits-Kirche* are connected, and have entrances from the Blücher-Platz (to the left), and the Belle-Alliance-Str, the portion of the grounds lying along the Baruther-Str. (to the S.) being of particular interest. By the S. wall of the E. section is the grave of *Iffland* (d. 1814; comp. p. 48); close by, to the right of the main path in the central section, lies *F. Mendelssohn-Bartholdy* (d. 1847). Near the side-path to the left a handsome monument by Uphues marks the last resting-place of *H. von Stephan* (d. 1897; comp p 125). A gateway leads to the S W section, which contains the grave of *A von Chamisso* (d 1838), near the path along the S. wall, and that of *E Th. A. Hoffmann* (d 1822; comp. p. 122), near the junction of the central path and that leading off to the W.

The Blücher-Strasse (Pl G, 23, 26), which diverges from the Blücher-Platz to the S E., passes (to the left) the **Church of the Holy Rood** (*Zum Heiligen Kreuz;* Pl. G, 23), a Gothic brick structure erected in 1885-88 by *Otzen.* — The Blücher-Str. ends at the Kaiser-Friedrich-Platz, in which rises the *Second Protestant Garrison Church.*

Several cemeteries lie to the S W. of the Kaiser-Friedrich-Platz, in the Bergmann-Str. In the *Neue Dreifaltigkeits-Kirchhof,* which lies furthest to the W., are the graves of the poet *Ludwig Tieck* (d. 1853), the philologist *K. Lachmann* (d. 1851), the theologian *Schleiermacher* (d. 1834, comp. p. 123), the historian *Theod. Mommsen* (d. 1903), and, on the E. wall, *Ad. von Menzel* (d. 1905; bronze bust by R. Begas, p. 92)

To the E. extends the Hasenheide street (Pl. G, 27, 30), formerly, when the pine-grove situated to the right was still accessible, a favourite Sunday resort of the lower classes. Beer-gardens see p. 11. Near the end to the S., on a site within the district of Rixdorf is a gymnasium ground with a bronze statue of *F L. Jahn,* the German

'Turnvater' (father of gymnastics), by Encke (1872). The pedestal is formed of stones sent by German gymnastic societies in all parts of the world. The first gymnasium ground, founded by Jahn in 1811, was situated to the S. on the site of the present *Karlsgarten.*

Rixdorf (*Deutsches Wirtshaus,* Berg-Str 137; *Bergschloss,* see p. 11), a suburb which attained to the dignity of a town in 1899, now numbers upwards of 166,000 inhabitants. It is served by the stations of Rixdorf and Hermann-Strasse, on the Sud-Ring; and by tramways (pp 15-22) Nos. 7, 15, 22, 28, 29, 30, 46, 47, 48, 49, 53, 55, 58, 91, I, II, and V — An equestrian statue of *Emp William I.,* by M Wolff, was erected in 1902 on the Hohenzollern-Platz Remains of antediluvian animals have been discovered on the heights (Rollberge) of Rixdorf — To the S. Rixdorf is adjoined by the village of Britz (12,000 inhab), with extensive cultivation of roses; tramways Nos 29, 55, and I.

The BELLE-ALLIANCE-STRASSE (Pl G, 24, 23), which diverges from the Blucher-Platz to the S., passes farther on a little to the left of the *Kreuzberg* and ascends to the Tempelhofer Feld (see p 173).

The Kreuzberg may be reached direct by tramways Nos. 34-38; also by Nos 2, 41 43, 96 97, 1, 11, and V.

The **Kreuzberg** (Pl. G, 21, 24) is the highest eminence (203 ft.) in the S. portion of the Spree basin. The *Victoria Park,* laid out on the slope of the hill in 1888-94, contains a *Waterfall* in an artificial rocky ravine, which runs 8 hrs. daily from May 1st to Oct. 15th, and is illuminated for 2 hrs. every Wed. and Sat evening The falling waters are distinctly visible far down the Grossbeeren-Str. In the basin at the foot of the fall is a bronze group ('The strange fish') by *Herter,* and in the grounds are six marble hermæ of national poets (Korner, Rückert, Uhland, Schenkendorf, Kleist, Arndt).

The **National Monument of the War of Liberation**, on the top of the Kreuzberg, is an iron obelisk in the Gothic style, originally 65 ft high. designed by *Schinkel,* and inaugurated in 1821. In 1878 it was raised 24 ft and placed on a bastion-like substructure. In the niches of the monument are 12 figures, by *Rauch, Tieck,* and *Wichmann the Younger,* symbolising the chief victories. Most of these are portraits, the battle of Bar-sur-Aube, for instance, is represented by a symbolical figure bearing the features of the subsequent Emperor William I. — From this point a splendid ˚View of Berlin is obtained, especially on Sundays when the atmosphere is free from smoke. The Grossbeeren-Strasse stretches due N. from the foot of the hill; to the left of it is the central hall of the Anhalt Station, with the Gnaden-Kirche, the Reichstags-Gebände, and the Column of Victory in the distance: somewhat nearer we see the Central Station and triangle of lines of the Electric Elevated Railway, the Luther-Kirche, the Charlottenburg Rathaus, and the Emp. William Memorial Church; to the W lie the Grunewald and Steglitz. To the right of the Grossbeeren-Str rise the domed towers in the Gendarmen-Markt and the Hedwigs-Kirche, then the Cathedial and the cupola of the Royal Palace. Farther on, the Marien-Kirche, beyond the neighbouring Bonifazius-Kirche the Rathaus, the Nicolai-Kirche and Petri-Kirche, the Georgen-Kirche and the Märkische Museum are visible, with the Church of the Holy Rood in the foreground. To the E. are the Hasenheide and Rixdorf, and to the S. lie the Tempelhofer Feld and Tempelhof

In the *Tempelhofer Feld* the manœuvres and reviews of the Berlin garrison have taken place since the days of Frederick William I. (1721), as also the great reviews of the Guards in the spring and autumn (p. 31) — The village of **Tempelhof** (tramways Nos 96, 97, and I; station of the Sud Ring, p 13), with ca 8000 inhab, belonged to the Knights Templar down to 1319

From the Potsdam Station (p. 127) the bulk of the traffic to Schöneberg (comp p 174) runs to the E. through the POTSDAMER-STRASSE, formerly a centre of the fashionable West End quarter, but now a busy commercial thoroughfare. Among the monumental build-ings recently erected here, we may notice, on the right, Nos. 10-11, *Alt-Bayern* (p. 10), built of basaltic lava, and on the left, Nos. 127-128, the *Roland-Haus* (p. 9), in red sandstone, both built by Walther, with handsome courts and sculptural adornments.

In the Link-Str., which diverges to the S from the Potsdamer-Str. not far from the Potsdamer-Platz, a memorial tablet at No. 7, marks the house in which *Jacob* (1785-1863) and *Wilhelm* (1786-1859) *Grimm*, the founders of Germanic philology, lived and died.

At the point where the Potsdamer-Str. is joined by the Viktoria-Str leading from the Kemper-Platz (p. 143), the Landwehr-Canal (p 171) is spanned by the **Potsdamer und Viktoria Brücke** (Pl. G, 16), erected in 1897-98, on which are bronze seated statues of four eminent men of science· *Helmholtz* (by Klein), *Röntgen* (by Felderhof), *Siemens* (by Moser), and *Gauss* (by Janensch). — Along the canal we may proceed to the W. by pleasant streets past the Her-cules Bridge (p. 175) to the Zoological Garden. The TIERGARTEN QUARTER, between the canal and the Tiergarten, is the most fashion-able residential quarter in Berlin (comp. p. 54). Here, particularly in the vicinity of the Zoological Garden, are numerous examples of those self-contained houses standing in gardens of their own that may be regarded as the most attractive achievements of architec-ture in Berlin since the days of Schinkel Tiergarten-Str., see p. 176: Bellevue-Str., p. 127. On this side of the canal, to the N. of the bridge, are several public buildings of interest. No. 18 Viktoria-Str., is the *Teltow Court House*, by Schwechten (1891). In the Matthai-Kirch-Str. (20-21) is the *House of the Provincial Estates of Branden-burg*, by Ende & Böckmann — The *Hofmann Haus*, by March, at Sigismund-Str. 4. was erected by the German Chemical So-ciety in 1900 in memory of August Wilhelm von Hofmann (d. 1892), the first president. The large Renaissance building to the *Imper-*

ial Insurance Office (Reichs-Versicherungs-Amt; Pl. G, 16), by
Busse, is situated on the canal, at Königin Augusta-Str. 25-27. Its
vestibule contains a group of workmen, by Brütt. — Near the canal
(Regenten-Str. 15) is the *Spanish Embassy*, in a villa built in
1873-76 by Ende & Benda, and embellished with a frieze from Northern mythology by Engelhard.

Beyond the Potsdamer Brucke, at Potsdamer-Str. 120, is at present the *Academy of Science* (p. 57). The Potsdamer-Str. is then
crossed by the Lützow-Str., in which, to the right (Nos. 89-90) is the
German Colonial House (p. 32), with figures of negroes on the façade, and (No 76) the *Blüthner-Saal* (concerts, p. 30) — Farther on
in the Potsdamer-Str. is the *Bülow-Str Station* of the Elevated
Railway (p. 14), constructed above the promenade of the Bülow-Str.
Near by, to the left, is the **Luther-Kirche** (Pl. G, 17), a Gothic
brick structure by *Otzen* (1891-94). The Potsdamer-Str. terminates
near Schöneberg at the former Botanic Garden (comp. p 185), part
of which is being converted into a public park. A new building for
the Kammer-Gericht (p. 168) is to be erected here.

The town of **Schöneberg** (*Ratskeller Restaurant*, Kaiser-Wilhelm-
Platz; *Schloss-Brauerei*, Haupt-Str 112-114), although connected with
Berlin by unbroken rows of streets, enjoys independent administration
and numbers over 160,000 inhabitants. — It is served by the stations of
Schöneberg and Ebers-Strasse on the 'Süd-Ring', by the Grossgörschen-
Strasse station on the Wannsee Railway (p 185), and by a station on
the Military Railway (Pl G, 18, for the ranges at Kummersdorf and
Juterbog). Tramways (pp. 14-22): Nos. 2, 3, 5, 23, 24, 40, 41, 43, 51, 56,
57, 59, 60, 61, 62, 69, 71, 72, 74, 82, 87-90, I, II. III, V, B, D, E, and H.

In the N part, near the Nollendorf-Platz (Pl. G, 14), rises the Rom.
Cath. *St. Matthias-Kirche*, erected in the Gothic style by Seibertz. Not
far off, at Eisenacher-Str. 12, is the *Grand Lodge of German Freemasons*,
built by Lange (1900) The handsome *Victoria-Luise-Platz* and the
adjacent streets contain numerous interesting private residences in modern
style. — The Grunewald-Strasse, to the W., contains the *Apostel-Paulus
Kirche*, built by Schwechten, and the *Prinz Heinrich's Gymnasium*
(Pl. G, 15), built by F. Schulze, both fine specimens of the brick architecture of the Mark of Brandenburg. The *Hohenzollern-Schule* (Reform-
Gymnasium), a building by Egeling, is in the Belziger-Str. To the N.
of the Church of St. Paul, at Barbarossa-Str. 74a, is the *Pestalozzi-Fröbel
House*, in the hall of which is a marble statue of Queen Luise with
Prince William in her arms, by Schaper. — The main street contains a
bronze *Statue of Emp. William I.*, by Gerling, and the *Town Hall* (Ratskeller, see above)

St. Matthew's Cemetery (Pl. G, 18) lies close to the Grossgörschen-
Str. Station. It contains the graves of numerous scholars and artists.
L. von Sybel (d. 1895), the historian, is buried close to the E pathway;
F Drake (d 1882), the sculptor, to the right of the central path; *A. Kiss*
(d. 1865), the sculptor, at the end of the third intersecting path to the
right; the *Brothers Grimm* (d. 1859 and 1863; comp. p 173) near the path
running parallel to the central path on the S.; and *G. Kirchhoff* (d. 1887),
the physicist, close to the side pathway.

From the Potsdamer-Str. the Bülow-Strasse runs to the W. to
the Nollendorf-Platz (Pl. G, 13), in which stands the domed station
of the Elevated Railway p. 14). This square is situated on the
outskirts of Berlin, its S. side belonging to Schöneberg, and its

W. side to Charlottenburg (p. 179). At Motz-Str 6, to the S W. of
the Nollendorf-Platz, is the **American Church**, a tasteful sandstone building in the Gothic style by March, opened in 1903 (services, see p. 36). Near by is the *Neue Schauspielhaus and Mozart-
Saal*, by Boswau & Knaner (1906; comp. pp. 28, 29). — To the W.
the Kleist-Str. and Tauenzien-Str. lead to the Emperor William
Memorial Church viâ the Wittenberg-Platz (Pl. G, 13; station of
the Underground Railway, p 14), in which rises the *Kaufhaus des
Westens* (p 31), erected in a freely treated Renaissance style by
Staudt. with sculptures by Wrba.

TRAMWAYS (pp 14-22) from the Nollendorf-Platz: Nos. 2, 3, 51, 52,
53, 57, 60, 61, 64, 75, 91, 92, A, D, and H

The Nollendorf-Platz connects the Maassen-Str., which passes
to the N. near the *Headquarters of the Engineers* (Kurfürsten-Str.
63-69) with the LÜTZOW-PLATZ (Pl. G, 13), embellished in 1903 with
the **Hercules Fountain**, 46 ft. high, designed by *O. Lessing;* at
the top is Hercules as the deliverer of Promethens, below are four
groups typifying the power of water unfettered, tamed, refreshing,
and serviceable — The groups in sandstone by Schadow on the
Hercules Bridge, which here crosses the Landwehr Canal (p. 173),
were taken from another bridge near the Exchange.

TRAMWAYS from the Lützow-Platz (pp. 14-22): Nos. 2, 3, 17, 33, 54,
63, 66, 67, 78-81, 93, 98, P, and R

11. Tiergarten.   Zoological Garden.

The following DRIVE of 4½ M. (7½ kil., taximeter cab about 2½ ℳ)
includes the most interesting points in the Tiergarten — From the Bran-
denburg Gate by the Königgrätzer Str (Goethe Monument), Lenné-Str.
(Lessing Monument), Kemper-Platz (Sieges-Allée; View of the Column
of Victory), and Tiergarten-Str to the monuments of Richard Wagner,
Frederick William III, and Queen Luise, thence by the Grosse
Weg, passing the Rousseau Island and the Neue See, to the Tiergarten
Station by the Charlottenburger Chaussée to the Grosse Stern, by the
Spree-Weg, past the Zelten to the Königs-Platz, then the whole length
of the Sieges-Allée, and finally back to the Brandenburg Gate.

The **Tiergarten** (Pl. R, 10-19), the largest and most attractive park near the town, extends from the Brandenburg Gate to
Charlottenburg and covers about 630 acres. It is the private property of the crown, and until the reign of King Frederick I. it was
really a deer-park. In the 16th cent it extended as far as the
E. end of the present Jäger-Strasse, where a royal hunting-lodge
stood. Some portions, still laid out in the Versailles style, owe
their arrangement to Knobelsdorff, the architect of Frederick the
Great, while Frederick William III., assisted by his landscape-
gardener Lenné, did much to beautify the park in the 19th century.
Within rec . . . . . the . . . . its
former cha . . . . of

a public park. The Sieges-Allée and the roads skirting the Tiergarten on the E. and S. are fashionable promenades in the afternoon. — The remoter parts of the park should be avoided after dark.

From the Brandenburger Tor the Charlottenburg Chaussée runs through the middle of the Tiergarten to Charlottenburg, crossing the Sieges-Allée (p. 142) and the Grosse Stern. Beyond the Sieges-Allée to the right is a bronze figure of the *Victor*, by Wandschneider. The *Grosse Stern* (Pl. R, 13), a circular space whence roads radiate in all directions, was embellished in 1904 by order of Emp. William II. with five bronze groups of hunting-scenes, *viz.* the Hubertus fountain, by *K. von Uechtritz;* Ancient German buffalo-hunt, by *Schaper;* Mediæval boar-hunt, by *K. Begas;* Hare-hunt in the 18th century, by *Baumbach;* and Modern fox-hunt, by *Haverkamp.*

On the N. margin of the Tiergarten, about $1/2$ M. to the W. of the Alsen-Platz (p. 140), on the Spree, are the places of recreation known as the *Zelte* (*i. e.* tents, from their original construction). These are simply 'al fresco' restaurants and have been popular resorts ever since the reign of Frederick the Great. The *Kronprinzen-Zelt* is a handsome building by Grisebach (1888).

From the Kurfürsten-Platz (Pl. R, 17), at the W. end of the Zelte, shady walks traverse the N. part of the Tiergarten, running towards the S.E., the S., and the W. In the latter direction, towards the Spree, is the royal **Château of Bellevue** (Pl. R, 14), built in 1785 by Prince Ferdinand of Prussia, the youngest brother of Frederick the Great (adm., see p. 36). The park (open till dusk) contains a monument, by Zumbusch, to *Prince Augustus of Prussia* (d. 1843), reorganizer of the Prussian artillery.

The *Luther-Brücke* here crosses the Spree to Moabit (p. 165). Farther along the river are the *Bellevue Station* of the Stadtbahn (Pl. R, 14) and the fine residential quarter known as the Hansa Quarter (Pl. R. 14, 10, 11; comp. p. 54). In the centre, at Klopstock-Str. 19-20, is the *Imperial Public Health Office* (Pl R, 14), a Romanesque brick edifice by Busse (1896-97) To the S., on the edge of the Tiergarten, is the *Emperor Frederick Memorial Church* (Pl. R, 13), by Vollmer (1895). Adjoining is the popular *Charlottenhof Restaurant* (p. 10).

The S. margin of the Tiergarten is skirted by the Lenné-Strasse and the Tiergarten-Strasse, both with tasteful villas and mansions In the Tiergarten-Str., which begins at the Roland Fountain (p. 143), we may notice the *Staudt Mansion*, at the corner of the Regenten-Str., built by Rieth, with gorgeous plastic ornamentation by Vogel and Widemann.

In the park, to the N. of the Tiergarten-Str., is the *Luisen Island* (Pl. R, 16), in which a marble **Statue of Queen Luise**, by *Encke*, was erected in 1880; the reliefs on the pedestal represent woman's work in war. On the W. side of the island is a marble bench in memory of the victories of 1870-71; near it, a marble *Statue of Emp. William I.* when a youth, by Brutt, was erected in 1904. To the N. of the island rises the **Statue of Frederick William III.** (Pl. R, 16), by *Drake*, erected by the citizens of Berlin in 1849, the pedestal of which, 18 ft. in height, is adorned with *Reliefs representing the enjoyment of nature. Farther to the N., near the Bellevue Allée, is a graceful figure of a girl wreathed with vine-leaves, by *Drake*.

Farther on in the Tiergarten-Str. a marble **Monument to Richard Wagner** (Pl. R, 16), by *Eberlein*, was erected in 1903, showing the seated figure of the master upon a Romanesque pedestal adorned with scenes from his operas (Wolfram von Eschenbach; Tannhauser; Brunhilda and the dead Siegfried; Alberich and one of the Rhine Maidens) — The neighbouring *Rousseau Island* (Pl. R, 16) and its pretty environs were laid out in the latter half of the 18th century. Near it to the N. is a marble statue of *Albert Lortzing*, the musical composer (p. 157), by Eberlein (1906) — At the W end of the Tiergarten lies the *Seepark*, with the *Neue See* (Pl. R, 13; p. 30), where numerous skaters display their skill in winter. On the Schleusen-Insel (Lock Island) are the *Experimental Institutes for Hydraulic and Naval Architecture* and for *Water Motors* (connected with the Technische Hochschule, p. 179). A little to the N. is the *Tiergarten Station* of the Stadtbahn (p. 12)

On the S. bank of the Landwehr Canal, opposite the W. end of the Tiergarten and to the W. of the Lower Friedrichs-Vorstadt, lies the Zoological Garden.

Stadtbahn, see p. 12. — *Underground Railway*, see p. 14. — *Tram- ways* (pp. 15-22): Nos 4, 33, 64, 75, 78, 82, 93, 98, A, D, F, G, H, O, P, R, and S

The ***Zoological Garden** (Pl. G, 10, 13) was founded in 1841-44 as the third of the kind in Europe by a company to whom Frederick William IV. presented the small collection of animals previously kept on the Pfauen-Insel (p 186) The first director was the naturalist *Lichtenstein* (d 1857) Under *H. Bodinus* (d. 1884), who became director in 1869, the collection developed to greater importance The present director is *Prof. Heck* Adm., see p. 42 (usually overcrowded on Sun.); concerts, see p. 30. Restaurants: *Haupt-Restaurant (first class, see p. 8: D., 1-8 p m., 3½ or 5 *M*); the *Waldschenke* is cheaper; *Wiener Cafe*, open in summer only

From the entrance we follow the paved path, which leads to all the points of interest (illustrated description 25 pf). The present arrangemer t of th garden d t fr i 1898 Th arr a buildings are mostly in th s le f t i p t to *Van Fd nce Gate*, on t knd n Drn t *Off* nd th *W ding*

Birds' House are in the Japanese style. The new *Aviary* is in the Moorish style, as is also the *Antelope House,* which has a painting on majolica, by P Meyerheim. The group of centaurs in front of the latter is by R Begas. The *Elephant House* is in the form of an Indian pagoda; while an ancient Egyptian style has been adopted for the *Ostrich House,* and Russian, Siamese, and Alaskan buildings have served as models for the *Buffalo Houses.* The *View Tower* (ascent 10 pf.) may also be mentioned. — Exhibition Hall, see p 181.

The collection of animals embraces upwards of 1300 different kinds, several here shown for the first time in any zoological garden. Many interesting specimens have recently been brought from the German colonies. Among the beasts of prey mention may be made of the N. varieties of the tiger, leopard, and puma, which remain here in the open air even in winter. The completed wing of the great aviary contains 400 separate cages for foreign birds, among 130 varieties of parrots. 20 are green Amazon-parrots. Nearly every known variety of cranes and storks is represented. Many rarities are to be found also among the deer (50 varieties), horses, wild goats, wild sheep, and wild cattle. — The animals are usually fed between 6 and 7 p.m. from June to September. Wed. is a fast-day for the carnivora. Comp. the lists exhibited at various points in the garden.

Key to the Zoological Garden Map (red numbers)· 1. Ostriches, cassowaries, — 2. Poultry, — 3. Small carnivora house, — 4. Goats, — 5. Sheep;   6. Dogs; — 7. Hippopotamus, — 8. Pheasants, peacocks; — 9. View-tower; · 10. Chamois, lamas; · 11. Poultry; — 12. Camels; — 13. Giraffes, — 14. Antelopes; — 15. Chinese temple; — 16 Pelicans; — 17 Stags;   18 Reindeer; — 20. Buffaloes, — 21. Stags; — 22 Yak; — 23 Zebu, — 24 Beavers and seals, — 25. Otters; — 26. Prosimiæ and marsupials, — 27. Solipedes, · 28 Small birds of prey, — 29. Large birds of prey.   30 Bears' den; · 31. Large carnivora house; — 32 Cascade pond; — 33. Ducks;   34. Waldschenke Restaurant; — 35 Parrots; · 36. Large aviary, — 37 Ibis; — 38. Wading birds; — 39. Old bears' den, — 40. Mouflons' rock;   41. New monkey-house, — 42. Old aviary; · 43. Rodentia, — 44. Garden-ground; — 45. Exhibition ground, — 46. Elephants; — 47. Swine.

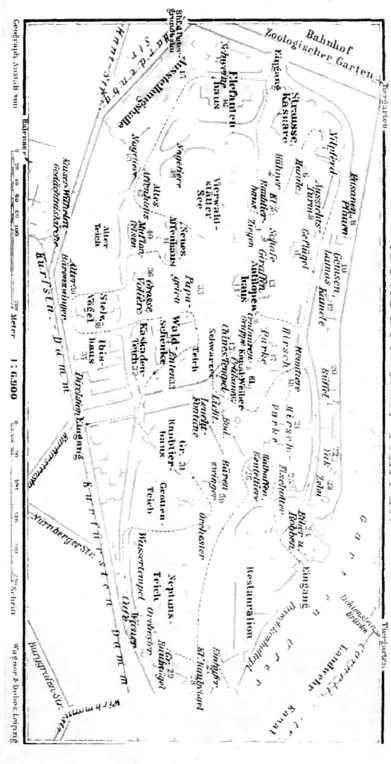

ZOOLOGISCHER GARTEN

II. ENVIRONS OF BERLIN.

12. Charlottenburg.

STADTBAHN STATIONS (named in order from Berlin, see p 12) *Tiergarten, Zoologischer Garten, Savigny-Platz, Charlottenburg, Westend,* and *Jungfernheide*. The Zoological Garden and Charlottenburg Stations are the only ones with luggage-offices or with connection with main-line trains. — STATIONS OF THE ELEVATED AND UNDERGROUND RAILWAY (pp. 13, 14): *Nollendorf-Platz* (p. 174), *Zoological Garden* (p 177), *Knie* (p. 181; 13 min.'s journey from the Potsdamer-Platz). — TRAMWAYS (pp 15-22): Nos. 5, 8, 18, 33, 54, 64, 76, 80, 81, 93, 98, H, N, P, R, T, V; from the Brandenburg Gate to Charlottenburg Palace 25 min, from the Kupfergraben (near the Museum Island) 35 minutes.

Hotels *PARK-HÔTEL (Pl q; G. 10), Hardenberg-Str. 29, at the Zoological Garden Station, 50 R. at 5-20, B. 1¼ *M*, FÜRST BISMARCK, at the Knie (p. 181), 60 R. at 2½-6, B 1 *M*, very fair; HIPPODROM, at the Knie; SCHLOSSPARK-HÔTEL, Luisen-Platz 1, 18 R. from 2, B.¾, D 1½ *M*; all with restaurant. — Pensions, see pp. 7, 8.

Restaurants. *Tiergartenhof*, near the Tiergarten Station; *Romanisches Café*, by the Emp William Memorial Church, *Josty* (confectioner), Hardenberg-Str. 27, *Hellwig & Sohn* (wine), Hardenberg-Str 15, *Mommhaus*, same street 6; *Falkenberg*, at the Knie, with garden; *Ratskeller*, in the Rathaus (p. 182); *Café Empire*, Theater-Platz 5; the restaurants of the *Theater des Westens* (p. 181), the *Schiller-Theater* p 182), etc

POST, TELEGRAPH, & TELEPHONE OFFICES, Berliner-Str. 62; also six branch offices

Charlottenburg, a town with 266,000 inhab. (in 1880 only 30,483), begins immediately to the W. of the Tiergarten, about 1¾ M. from the Brandenburg Gate. It is now practically part of Berlin, though it still retains an independent municipality, and its present size and prosperity is entirely owing to the recent rapid advance of its large neighbour. It lies on the site formerly occupied by the village of *Lietzow*, where Sophia Charlotte, wife of Frederick I., founded a country residence at the end of the 17th century.

Beyond the Tiergarten Station, to the right in the Wegely-Str., stands the **Royal Porcelain Factory** (Pl. R. 10); adm., see p. 39; see also pp. 33, 124. The factory, founded in Berlin in 1761 and acquired for the state by Frederick the Great in 1763, was removed to the present site in 1871

The Charlottenburger Chaussée (p 176) is continued through Charlottenburg by the BERLINER-STRASSE. Beyond the *Charlottenburger Brücke* over the Landwehr Canal, on the left, rises the —

*Technische Hochschule, T. . . . . . . Pl. R, 7, 10), erected in 1878-84 from d St . . L . . . Hitzig under the superintendence of Roscholtz . . . 83 . . th . . . building,

12*

750 ft. long and 295 ft. wide, is embellished with numerous sculptures. The balustrade in front of the aula is embellished with five
bronze busts by *K. Begas:* Gauss, the mathematician (d. 1855),
Eytelwein, the civil engineer (d. 1848), Schinkel, the architect (d.
1841), Redtenbacher, the mechanical engineer (d. 1863), and Liebig,
the chemist (d. 1873). The niches on the central building and the
projecting wings are filled with statues; *viz.* Erwin von Steinbach
and Bramante, by *Encke;* Andreas Schluter, by *Hundrieser;* Leonardo da Vinci, by *Eberlein;* James Watt and George Stephenson,
by *Keil.* In front of the building are bronze statues of Werner von
Siemens (d. 1892; by *Wandschneider*) and Alfred Krupp (d. 1887;
by *Herter*) — The Academy has a teaching-staff of 150 and is attended by 2300 students.

The Central Court, covered with a glazed roof, contains a bronze
statue of Frederick William III in classical costume by *Kiss*, the Genius
of Steam by *Rensch*, busts of eminent teachers, etc. In the corridor on the
first floor is a bronze group by *Herter*, representing Art paying homage
to Technical Science; at the sides are busts of Schinkel and Beuth.

On the second floor, to the left (E. & S. sides), is the Architectural
Museum (adm, see p. 42; director, Prof. Raschdorff), a large collection
of models and plans. Specially noteworthy are the Callenbach collection
of models of mediæval German buildings and the competing designs for
the Cathedral, the Reichstags-Gebaude, and the Monument of William I
In a separate room is the *Beuth-Schinkel Museum*, containing the collections of Beuth (p 158) and the *Works of Art* left behind by Schinkel
on his decease The latter include landscapes and architectural paintings,
architectural plans (*e. g* of the Château Oranda in the Crimea), the
original sketches for the frescoes in the Old Museum, and designs for
theatre-decorations.

To the S. of the Zoological Garden Station rises the ⁷ **Emperor
William Memorial Church** (Pl. G, 10), a late-Romanesque edifice
by *Schwechten*, erected in 1891-95. The main W tower, 370 ft. high,
is the loftiest building in or near Berlin. There are four smaller
towers at the angles. The choir is adorned with a dwarf arcade and
there are large rose-windows in the W., N, and S. façades. The
finely executed portals also merit notice. Admission, see p. 37.

Passing through the W door we first enter the Memorial Hall
(*Gedächtnis-Halle;* 69 ft long and 23 ft. wide), decorated with mosaics
by *Schaper*. On the ceiling are Reformers and Emperors of the first
German Empire The frieze on the E. wall represents princes and princesses of the Hohenzollern family, that on the W. wall depicts the heroes of the campaigns of 1813 and 1870-71. The marble reliefs on the
walls are by *Brütt;* four are scenes from the life of Emperor William I ;
beside the main door are the Productive Class and the Military Class;
over the other doors, Biblical scenes The centre of the mosaic pavement
is occupied by a figure of the Archangel Michael The apses at the sides
of the vestibule are decorated with stained-glass windows, representing
(right) scenes from the life of John the Baptist, and (left) scenes from
the history of the Prophet Elijah.

The Interior of the church, which produces a handsome and spacious effect has three galleries supported by columns of labradorite.
It is embellished with mosaics from designs by *Linnemann*. On the
choir-arch appear SS. Peter and Paul, by *Geselschap* above whom are
angelic musicians by *Queen* Above the triforium gallery are five

beautiful stained-glass windows by *Linnemann*, representing Moses and
the four major Prophets. In the choir are statues of the Evangelists
by *Janensch* and *Wenck*; of SS Peter and Paul, by *Haverkamp;* and
of Luther and Melanchthon, by *O. Lessing.* The altar, the pulpit, and the
font are elaborate works in Istrian limestone, marble, and bronze. Beneath
the altar-canopy is a figure of Christ in the attitude of blessing, by
Schaper. To the left of the altar is the richly decorated imperial pew,
with a Jerusalem cross in mosaic. The vaulting of the Crossing, which
is 69 ft. square and 82 ft. high, bears colossal figures (21 ft in height)
of four archangels and four fathers of the church. Beneath hangs a
handsome circular chandelier, 18 ft. in diameter, ornamented with apostles'
heads The rose-windows in the transepts, each framed in mosaic, are
filled with stained glass, by *Geiges*, representing the Presentation in
the Temple and the Resurrection, adjacent, the Last Supper and the
Entry into Jerusalem, mosaics after *Pfannschmidt* The windows in
the Nave are filled with scenes from the life of Christ (above) and the
Christian virtues (below). Below the Organ Gallery are mosaics after
Seliger, Mary and Martha, Christ and the centurion of Capernaum The
organ, with a case in forged copper, has 80 stops and 4800 pipes

The Tower has a peal of five bells cast from the metal of captured
cannon and worked by electricity. The belfry-stage commands a beautiful view of the W. environs of Berlin

The Romanesque houses opposite each end of the church are
also by Schwechten The neighbouring *Exhibition Hall* of the
Zoological Garden, 210 yds. in length, shows also Romanesque
forms (restaurant, see p. 177). Among the streets radiating from
the church, the Kurfürsten-Damm, an avenue leading to Halensee
(p. 184), is the most conspicuous for its many handsome structures.
At Nos 208-9 is the exhibition of the *Berliner Sezession* (Pl G, 7;
adm., see p. 37). — At Kant-Str. 12, near the Stadtbahn, is the
elegantly fitted up *Theater des Westens* (Pl G, 10; p. 28), built in
1896 by Sehring

A little to the S of the Emp. William Memorial Church begins
Wilmersdorf, a town with 84,000 inhab (incl Halensee). Station of
the Ringbahn, see p 13 *Tramways* (pp 18-22), Nos. 66, 67, 78, 82, 89-92,
B, F, G, O, S, and V.

In the Hardenberg-Strasse, which leads to the N W. from the
Zoological Garden Station to the bend ('Knie') of the Berliner-Str
(see p. 182), are the *Ober-Verwaltungs-Gericht* (Supreme Administrative Court), a baroque structure by Furstenau (1907; with
decorative paintings by F. W. Mayer), and the *Artillery and Engineering School* (Pl. R, 10). Farther on are the **Royal Academy
of Music** (director, Prof. Ad. Schulze), with a long façade towards
the Fasanen-Str. (Nos. 1-9), and the **Royal Academy of Art**
(director, Prof. Anton von Werner), arranged round a skilfully conceived court; in the wall of the façade are two fountains with Orpheus (by Herter, to the right) and Prometheus (by Hundrieser, to
the left): relief in the pediment by Manzel, the Arts under the pro-
tection of Peace.

The Academy of Music contains the **Collection of Musical Instruments** du p found d t d t in t by the
acquisitic f s t ti u a e N mprising
numerous i t o i t f i t i

Hardenberg-Str 36 is the *Royal Academic Institute for Sacred Music* (director, Prof. Kretschmar).

From the 'Knie' (Pl. R, 7), or bend, of the Berliner-Strasse (station of the Underground Railway, p. 14), beside the Hardenberg-Strasse, the March-Strasse (see below, tramway Q to Moabit) runs to the N.E., while the Bismarck-Strasse leads due W The latter is continued as a military road through the Grunewald to the manœuvring-ground at Döberitz (comp. margin of the map at p. 185) — In the Bismarck-Str., at the corner of the Grolmann-Str., is the *Schiller-Theater Charlottenburg* (comp. p. 28), built by Heilmann & Littmann (1906), with a room for popular lectures.

To the N. of the Knie, March-Str. 25, is the *Imperial Physico-Technical Institution* and to the W. of it, Fraunhofer-Str. 11-12, the *Workmen's Welfare Permanent Exhibition* (Pl. R, 7, 8, adm see p. 42), with fenced machinery in motion, etc

In the industrial district farther to the N (Pl R, 8) are two electric works in close connection: viz. the *Siemens-Schuckert Works Co. Ltd* , Franklin-Str 28 (capital 1,500,000 *l.*), and the *Siemens & Halske Co.* (capital 2,600,000 *l*), the latter founded in 1847 by Werner Siemens, the discoverer of the dynamic principle (1867) and inventor of electric tramways (1879) The office of the two societies, which employ 35,000 workmen and officials, is mentioned at p. 127

The Berliner-Strasse leads to the N W from the Knie to the Luisen-Platz. At Nos 72-73 in this street is the **Rathaus** (Pl. R, 5), an imposing building erected in 1899-1905 by *Reinhardt* and *Süssenguth*, with a richly ornamented façade and a tower 360 ft. in height (adm , see p. 39, Ratskeller, p. 179).

In front of the palace is the Luisen-Platz (Pl. R, 2), in which an **Equestrian Statue of Emp. Frederick III.**, by *Uphues*, was erected in 1905. The pedestal, with its garland of thorns, the massive substructure and the rear-wall with its two pylons (52 ft. high) are of granite; on the top of the pylons are two marble statues of Apollo and Athena; on the base are bronze-reliefs representing the emperor distributing decorations at Königgrätz and reviewing his army for the last time in Charlottenburg Park. — At the beginning of the Schloss-Str. (leading to the left) is a bronze statue of *Prince Albert of Prussia* (d 1872), by Börmel and Freyberg (1901) The street runs to the S. to the vicinity of the *Lietzen-See* (Pl R, 1, G, 1), which is surrounded with pleasant grounds

The ***Royal Palace** (Pl R, 2) consists of a large group of buildings, with a total length of 550 yds. The central portion, erected by *Schlüter* in 1695-99, was enlarged by *Eosander von Goethe* (p. 65) in 1701-7 and provided with its effective dome. The right wing ('Neues Schloss') was added by *Knobelsdorff* in 1741-42, while the theatre at the end of the left wing and the belvedere in the park were erected by *Langhans* in 1788. — Tickets of adm., and also tickets for the Mausoleum (p. 183) are obtained to the right, in the first court (marked 'K' on the Plan); comp. p. 37

INTERIOR. At present only the apartments formerly occupied by Frederick I., in the central part, next the garden, are shown. Emp. Frederick III. also spent ten weeks of his last illness here (March 11th to June 1st, 1888). The rococo decorations are well worthy of inspection. Visitors should note the *Porcelain Chamber*, with Chinese porcelain presented to Queen Sophia Charlotte by English merchants; and Wichmann's marble statue of the Empress Charlotte of Russia, in the round garden-saloon.

The entrance to the pleasant PALACE GARDEN, laid out by the eminent French landscape-gardener *Le Nôtre* in 1694, a favourite promenade for Berliners and Charlottenburgers, is near the small guard-room, adjoining the W wing. Crossing the orangery to the right, turning to the left and skirting it on the farther side, and then following an avenue of pines to the right, we reach (in 8 min. from the entrance) the **Mausoleum** (Pl. R, 2; tickets, see p. 182), erected by *Gentz* in the Doric style from Schinkel's designs and enlarged in 1888-90. Queen Luise (d. 1810) and her husband Frederick William III. (d. 1840) repose here, together with Princess Liegnitz (d. 1873), the second wife of Frederick William III., Emperor William I. (d. 1888), and Empress Augusta (d. 1890). The recumbent figures of the first-named pair, executed in marble by *Rauch's* masterly hand, are strikingly impressive. The beautiful figure of the queen, executed at Carrara and Rome in 1812-13, was placed here in 1815 and at once established the sculptor's fame. The monument of the king was finished at Berlin in 1846. The fine figures of the Emperor William and his wife, by *Encke*, were placed here in 1894. The mourning angel in the vestibule is also by Encke. The beautiful candelabrum on the right, with the three Fates, is by *Rauch*, that on the left, with the Horæ, by *Tieck*; the crucifix in the apse by *Achtermann*, the painting by *Pfannschmidt*.

From the Palace the Spandauer Str. leads to the W. to the *Westend Station* of the Ringbahn (p. 19); behind it, to the right, lies the extensive *Municipal Hospital.* Farther to the W. is the colony of villas known as **Westend** (*Westend Restaurant*). Beyond it, about 1½ M. from the station, on the Spandauer Chaussée (tramway R), is the *Spandauer Bock*, a popular beer-garden commanding a view towards Spandau. About 2½ M. to the S W of it is *Pichelsberg* (p. 184).

13. The Forest District between Charlottenburg and Potsdam.

An extensive wooded district extends to the S.W. from Charlottenburg and Spandau (p. 200) to Potsdam, lying on the E. bank of the *Havel*, which expands here to the proportions of a lake (steamer between Spandau and Potsdam, see p. 200). This district is divided into two unequal parts by the *Wannsee*, a bay-like indentation of the Havel; to the N.E. is the Grunewald, to the S.W. accessible from the station of Wannsee, is the Potsdam Forest. The land-

scape of mingled wood and water, to which the more favoured parts
of the Mark of Brandenburg owe their characteristic charm, may
here be enjoyed to special advantage.

a The Grunewald.

The Grunewald is reached from Berlin by various routes 1 Viâ the
STADTBAHN (p. 12) to *Grunewald Station*, by the suburban trains to Potsdam (p. 187) or to Nieder-Schoneweide-Grunewald (p. 203). — 2 Viâ the
RINGBAHN (p 13; 'Südring') to *Halensee* (see below), from any station. —
3. By TRAMWAY A (p 21) to *Hundekehle* (restaurant 4 min distant). —
4. The WANNSEE RAILWAY (p 185) touches the stations of *Zehlendorf-
Beerenstrasse* and *Nikolassee* (p. 186). — MOTOR OMNIBUS (p 23): from the
Brandenburger or Oranienburger Tor to Beelitzhof and Wannsee Station,
from the Nollendorf Platz to Onkel Tom's Hütte, from the Knie at Charlottenburg to Pichelsberg and Schildhorn; also circular trips (comp. the
advertisements). — STEAMBOATS between Spandau and Wannsee see p 200.
— For CYCLISTS (pp 13, 200) the best routes are viâ the Kurfürsten-Damm
and the Kaiser-Damm

The *Grunewald*, a royal forest of coniferous trees, about
11,350 acres in area, is a favourite resort of the Berliners, and
offers a refreshing change to the tourist when jaded with sight-
seeing and weary of the bustle of the city.

Near the station of *Halensee*, with its charming terraces and
villas, and within the precincts of the forest lies the fashionable
*Villa Colony of Grunewald, consisting chiefly of elegant
and comfortable residences grouped on the banks of a number of
little lakes, some of which are artificial Founded only in 1889, it
already numbers upwards of 4800 inhabitants. From the Bismarck-
Platz, embellished with a bronze *Statue of Bismarck* by M. Klein
(1897), we may proceed to the S. by the Hubertus-Allée to the
(1 M.) prettily situated *Hubertus Restaurant* and *Café Grunewald* (good cuisine), or to the S.W. by the Bismarck-Allée to the
(2 M.) *Hundekehle Restaurant* (D 3 ℳ). About 1 M. to the N.
of the latter, beyond the Hundekehlen Lake, is the *Grunewald
Station*.

From the Grunewald Station paths lead through the woods to
the W., in the direction of the Havel, to (3½ M.) the peninsula of
Schildhorn (restaurants; steamboat station), where a monument
commemorates the legendary escape of the Wendish prince Jaczo,
when fleeing from Albert the Bear. *Pichelsberg* (Seeschloss Restaurant) lies 1½ M. to the N., prettily situated on a bay opposite the
island of *Pichelswerder* (Königgratzer Garten Restaurant). Near
Pichelsberg passes the new military road from the Knie at Charlottenburg (4 M., see p. 181); beyond the island it is carried on from
Pichelsdorf (electric tramway to Spandau, p. 200) to the man-
oeuvring ground of Döberitz. Pleasant return-route to Grunewald
Station viâ the *Teufels-See*. — About 1½ M. to the S of Schildhorn, on the lofty bank of the Havel steamboat pier, rises the
Kaiser Wilhelm Turm, erected in 1897 and commanding one of

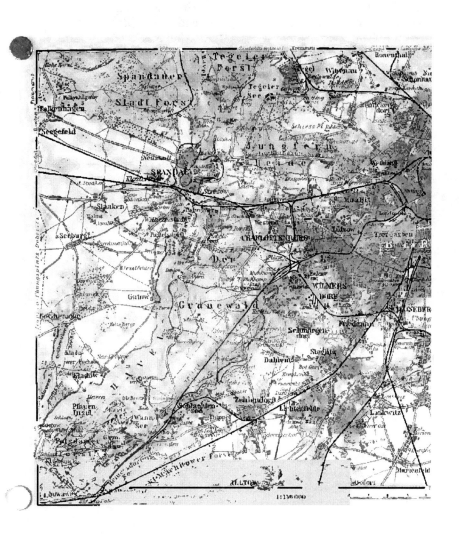

the finest views in the neighbourhood of Berlin. In the memorial hall are a marble statue of the emperor and bronze reliefs of Roon, Bismarck, Moltke, and Prince Frederick Charles, all by Manzel. We may return to the station of Grunewald past the forester's house of *Saubucht* (rfmts.).

To the S. of the Grunewald Station we may proceed viâ Hundekehle (p. 184) to the (2½ M.) S. end of the *Grunewald Lake*, on which lie (1 M.) the *Shooting Lodge of Grunewald*, built in 1542 by Kaspar Theyss (p. 65) for Elector Joachim II., and the *Paulsborn Restaurant*. To Steglitz, see below. — Farther on to the S.W. we pass Onkel Tom's Hutte, a restaurant on the *Riemeister-See*, then the *Krumme Lanke* (another lake), and the picturesque *Schlachten-See* (boats for hire; Alte and Neue Fischerhutte Restaurants), above the left bank of which we see the villa-colony of the same name (p. 186). The Grunewald comes to an end at *Beelitzhof* (restaurant), situated on the *Wannsee*, ½ M. to the N.W. of the station of Nikolassee (p. 186) and 1 M. to the N. of the station of Wannsee.

b. The Wannsee Railway and the Potsdam Forest.

Wannsee is served by the suburban trains to Potsdam viâ *Grunewald* (p. 184) on the STADTBAHN and by the trains of the WANNSEE RAILWAY (station, Pl. G, 19; pp 13, 186), which run to Zehlendorf (see p. 186) every 10 min. (during part of the day) and to Wannsee every 20 minutes.

The stations of the Wannsee Railway are as follows: 1¼ M. *Grossgörschen-Strasse.* — 3 M. *Friedenau* (Kaiser-Eiche Restaurant), a villa-colony with 23,000 inhab., with the optical institute of C. P. Görz, station on the Süd-Ring (p. 13).

4¼ M. **Steglitz** *(Ratskeller; Schloss-Restaurant)*, a village with 41,200 inhab. Below the *Fichtenberg* (view from the watertower) is the *Royal Blind Asylum*, with the Blind Museum, removed hither from Berlin in 1877. Tramways 59, V, D, E, and F (p. 21); also to Gross-Lichterfelde (two lines: Gross-Lichterfelde East Station and Cadet School) and to Sudende. — From Steglitz to the shooting-lodge of Grunewald and Paulsborn tramway to the end of *Dahlem*, then a walk of 25 min. In the district to the S.W. of the Fichtenberg, near the former estate of *Dahlem*, the new **Botanic Garden**, laid out by Prof. Engler, was opened in 1903 (adm., see p 36). It is inferior in size (1100 acres) to Kew Gardens near London, but surpasses them and all other institutions of a similar kind in its arrangement of plant-types from all parts of the world on the appropriate rock-formations. Entrances in the Potsdam road (S.) and the Dahlemer Chaussee (N.). In the latter also are the *Pharmaceutic Institute* of the University, the new building of the *Botanic Museum*, the *Royal Gardeners' Seminary*, and the biological station of the Imperial Health Office. 176

5½ M. **Gross-Lichterfelde** *Hans Sachs Restaurant*, at the W. Station· *Henning*, at the E. Station, a villa-settlement with about 38,500 inhab , extends from the Potsdam railway (Gross-Lichterfelde West Station) to beyond the Anhalt line (East Station; suburban trains, see p. 13). Tramways ply from one station to the other, passing the Cadet School, and also to Steglitz (p. 185) and Machnower Schleuse (p. 187). In the middle of the village, which is intersected by the Teltow Canal (p 187), is a *Monument to Emperor William I.*, by Wenck. Near the E. station, Wilhelm-Str. 36 a, is the large *Orthopaedic Sanatorium of Georg Hessing* — At the W. end of the village is the Royal *Central Cadet School* (1000 pupils; entr. on the N. side), which was founded in 1717 and transferred hither from Berlin in 1878. The 'Field-Marshals' Hall', in the school-building, contains the portraits of 61 Prussian marshals. The 'Flensburg Lion', originally erected by the Danes at Flensburg in 1862 in memory of the battle of Idstedt (1850), stands in the court.

At (7½ M) *Zehlendorf* (Burg Hotel), a village with 15,000 inhab., the Wannsee line diverges to the right from the main Potsdam railway. Beyond (8¾ M.) *Zehlendorf-Beerenstrasse* we pass (9¼ M.) *Schlachtensee* (Schloss-Restaurant) and (10½ M.) *Nikolassee*, two groups of villas situated in the Grunewald (p. 184).

12 M **Wannsee** (Restaurants *Kaiser-Pavillon, Schwedischer Pavillon*), in the Potsdam Forest, a fashionable villa-colony, the handsome and sometimes imposing houses of which are grouped in a wide curve on the elevated banks of the picturesque *Wannsee*. At the N E angle of the Little Wannsee, ¾ M. from the station, is the grave of the poet *Heinrich von Kleist*, who shot himself and his friend Henriette Vogel here in 1811.

STEAMER FROM WANNSEE TO POTSDAM, plying on week-days 13, on Sun 19 times; highly recommended Stations. *Schwedischer Pavillon* (see above), *Pfauen-Insel, Moorlake, Sakrow, Glienicke Bridge*, and *Potsdam* (p. 189) Fare to Pfauen-Insel 30, to Potsdam 55 pf. — Steamer to *Neu Babelsberg Station* see p. 187, to *Spandau* see p 201.

To the W. of Wannsee the main road traverses the Glienicker Werder and runs straight on to the Glienicke Bridge; by the road diverging to the N. after ¼ hr. we reach (1 hr from Wannsee) the ferry (and steamboat-station) for the *Pfauen-Insel, the favourite resort of Frederick William III. The pleasant park laid out by the king abounds in fine oaks. The *Royal Villa*, of the end of the 18th cent., presents the appearance of a ruined castle; the *Kavalier-Haus* is constructed of the materials of a late-Gothic house brought from Dantsic. — Above the road, which farther on skirts the Havel, rises the *Church of SS. Peter & Paul*, built in the Russian style by Schadow, containing the tombs of Prince and Princess Frederick Charles (d. 1885 and 1906). Beside it is the log-house of *Nikolskoë* (rfmts.; view). — About 1½ M. farther, beyond *Moorlake Restaurant* (steamboat pier, situated on a bay we ferry to *Sakrow* (restaurant on the river, steamboat pier, with the *Heilands-Kirche* (St Saviour's, built by Persius. A walk may be taken hence through the woods to the (3 M.) *Römer-Schanze,* an entrenchment opposite *Nedlitz* (p. 197). — The road ends at the Glienicke Bridge (p. 198), 1 M. from the Sakrow ferry.

Beyond Wannsee the railway crosses the *Teltow Canal,* which connects the Havel, via the *Griebnitz-See* (see below), with the Dahme (near Grünau, p. 203). — 14 M. **Neu-Babelsberg,** a cluster of villas on the W. bank of the Griebnitz-See. From the station to Klein-Glienicke and Babelsberg 1³/₄ M. (steamer see below, omnibus in winter).

STEAMBOATS from the Neu-Babelsberg station ply frequently across the Griebnitz-See to *Babelsberg* and *Klein-Glienicke* (to the Glienicke Bridge 20 pf.; junction for Potsdam. p. 198), whence certain steamers cross the Jungfern-See to *Moorlake* (Sakrow ferry, see above), *Meierei* (Neuer Garten. p. 197), and *Nedlitz* (p 197; 40 pf) Other steamboats ply on the *Prinz-Leopold Canal* to *Wannsee Station* (30 pf.), some of them going on to *Beelitzhof* and Moorlake (where visitors bound for Babelsberg change for the line mentioned above); and on the *Teltow Canal* to the Schleuse (30 pf, restaurant) near the charmingly situated estate of *Klein-Machnow;* tramway to Gross-Lichterfelde (p. 186)

16 M. *Nowawes,* a village established by Frederick the Great, with 22,200 inhabitants — 16¹/₂ M. *Potsdam*

14. Potsdam and its Environs.

A visit to Potsdam is highly recommended on account both of its natural beauties and its historical associations. The spacious parks with their rivers and fountains and the palaces with their well-preserved interiors and contemporary decorations and furniture present us with a better picture of a royal residence of the 18th century than can be seen even at the larger and more pretentious palace of Versailles, which was deprived of so much of its splendour by the Revolution. If Versailles has the advantages of a uniform scheme in its arrangement, Potsdam has the charm of variety.

Railways from Berlin to Potsdam.

1. POTSDAM MAIN LINE (station, Pl. G, 19: pp. 1, 127) The long distance trains stop at no intermediate station and have no reduced fares A suburban service, with its terminus at (18¹/₂ M) *Wildpark* (¹/₂ M. from the New Palace, p. 196) or (21¹/₂ M.) *Werder* (p 199), calls at (13¹/₂ M.) *Neu-Babelsberg,* (16 M.) *Potsdam,* and (17¹/₂ M.) *Charlottenhof* (10 min by the Waldemar-Str. from the S. entrance to the park of Sanssouci; p. 193).

2. WANNSEE RAILWAY (station, Pl. G, 19), trains to Potsdam every hour; comp. pp. 185-187.

3 STADTBAHN (N. platforms). Beyond *Charlottenburg* these trains call at *Grunewald* (6 M from Friedrich Strasse Station, p. 181), traverse the Grunewald, and beyond 11 M. *Nikolassee* follow the road described on pp. 186, 187

The journey to Potsdam occupies by Route No 1 ¹/₂ hr., by Nos. 2 and 3 1 hr. Fares by suburban trains from the Potsdam Station or the Friedrich-Strasse Station 85 or 50 pf., by long distance trains 1 ℳ 40 or 90 pf.

Excursion Trips see p. 23 — Circular Drives from the station at 11 a. m., 5 ℳ.

Potsdam.

Hotels Palast-Hôtel, Humboldt-Str 1, near the Town Palace, with restaurant and steamboat station, 12 R from 3, B. 1, D. 3 ℳ, Stadt Königsberg, Brauer-Str. 1, on the Havel, 22 R from 2¹/₂, B 1, D. 3 ℳ, both good; Hôt. zum Einsiedler, Schloss-Str. 8, Eisenbahn-Hôtel, at the station, with a garden on the Havel, R. 2 3, B. ³/₄, D. (12-4) 2 ℳ; Deutsches Haus, Schloss-Str. 6, R. 2¹/₂-4, B. 1, D 1¹/₄, pens. 6 ℳ; Zentral-Hôtel, Nauener-Str 29, in the Wilhelm-Platz, with restaurant; Hôt.-Restaurant zum Oberlissken, Hohenzollern-Str 27, near the Brandenburg Gate; New Hospice and Family Pension, Kaiser-Wilhelm-Str. 11, R. 2-6, B. ³/₄, déj. 1, D. 2, pens. 4-8 ℳ, with baths and garden, good.

Restaurants. *Railway Restaurant*, D. 3 ℳ — In the town: *Stadt Königsberg* (see above), *Zum Schultheiss*, at the Palast-Hôtel (see above), both with terraces on the Havel; *Dornuth*, at the Zentral-Hôtel (see above); *Residenz-Restaurant*, Nauener-Str 15, D. 1¹/₄ ℳ, *Hormess & Sons* (wine-room), *Kloster-Keller*, *Weiss* (confectioner), Nauener-Str, Nos 34a, 11-12, and 33-34; *Café Sanssouci*, outside the Brandenburg Gate; *Wackermann's Höhe*, on the Brauhausberg, with garden and viewtower, D. 2 ℳ. — In the environs· *Wildpark Station* (see p 187), D. 1¹/₂ ℳ, with garden; *Meierei* in the Neue Garten (p 197), *Hugahn*, Neue Königs-Str. 58, near the Glienicke bridge (p 198). — In Klein-Glienicke. *Glienicke Restaurant (Fernau)*, on the Berlin highroad, déj. 2¹/₂, D. from 3 ℳ; *Burgershof*, in the village (steamboat-pier), D from 1¹/₂ ℳ; *Babelsberg*, opposite the main entrance to the park, D 2¹/₂ ℳ, all with gardens

Post and Telegraph Office, at the corner of the Wilhelm-Platz

Cabs — a. Taximeter Cabs 1-2 pers 800 metres 50 pf., each additional 400 metres 10 pf., 3-5 pers. 600 metres 50 pf, each addit 300 m. 10 pf. At night (11-6.30, 10-7.30 in winter)· 1-2 pers. 600 m. 50 pf., each addit 300 m. 10 pf., 3-5 pers. 400 m. 50 pf., each addit. 300 m 10 pf. — *Outside the Town*, 1-5 pers 400 m. 50 pf., each addit. 300 m. 10 pf.

b. Other Cabs. *First Class* (for 2 persons only)· per drive within the town 75 pf., outside the town per ¹/₄ hr. 75 pf., ¹/₂ hr. 1¹/₄ ℳ, ³/₄ hr. 1¹/₂ ℳ, 1 hr. 2 ℳ, for each additional ¹/₄ hr 50 pf. more, a whole day 12 ℳ.

	1-2 pers	3 pers	4-5 pers.
Second Class: for ¹/₄ hr	— 50	— 75	1 25
¹/₂ hr.	— 75	1 —	1 50
³/₄ hr.	1 —	1 25	1 75
1 hr.	1 50	1 75	2 25
To Babelsberg, Sakrow ferry, Moorlake	1 50	1 75	2 —
To Pfauen-Insel, Templin, Baumgartenbrück	3 —	3 50	4 —

Luggage 25 pf.

Fares by time: 6 hrs. 12 ℳ, 12 hrs. 15 ℳ, for 1-5 persons. Double fares at night

Steamboats (in summer only; recommended). 1. From the Lange Brücke (Eisenbahn Hotel). *a.* At noon and hourly from 2 5 to *Glienicke* (p. 198; 20 pf), *Sakrow* (p 186), *Moorlake* (p. 186, 30 pf, return-fare on week-days 50 pf.), the *Pfauen-Insel* (p. 186, 40, 60 pf.), and *Wannsee* (p 186, 55, 80 pf) — *b* Twice or thrice every afternoon (on Sun every hr from 2 pm), to the *Glienicke Bridge* the *Meierei*, and *Nedlitz* (p 197, 30, 50 pf)·— *c* At 12 every aft on Sun to *Kl witt Tornow*, *Templin, Caputh, Baumgartenbrück* and *Werder* (p 190, 40 60 pf) or *Ferch* (several comfortaion aft noons appropriate trips to Werder, *Glindow,*

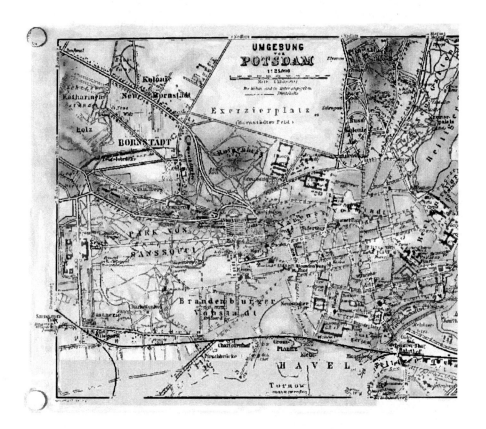

Phöben; also to *Schildhorn* and *Pichelswerder* (p. 184; there and back 60 pf.). — *d* On Mon a trip is generally made round the 'Island of Potsdam' ('Potsdamer Werder'), touching at *Glienicke* and the *Meierei* (1 hr.; 1 ℳ), starting at 3 p.m. Restaurant on board.

2. From the Lange Brücke (Schultheiss Restaurant) seven times daily to *Glienicke* (15 pf.), in connection with the steamers plying to *Neu-Babelsberg* station (30 pf., comp. p 187).

Tramways. From the Railway Station to the Kaiser-Brücke (Wilhelm-Platz) and thence: A. To the Brandenburg Gate (Sanssouci) and *Charlottenhof Station* (p 187). — B To the *Glienicke Bridge* (p. 198); — C To the *Allee-Str.*, near the New Garden (p. 197) Fares 10-15 pf., with change of carriage at the Kaiser-Brücke 20 pf.

The **Fountains** of Sanssouci usually play in summer on Sundays, from noon till 7 p.m. The great fountain also plays on Tuesday and Thursday, 3-7 p.m.

The **Royal Palaces** are usually open from 10 to 6 (Sun. 11-6) in summer, 10-4 in winter. Admission to the Town Palace (p 191), the Garrison Church (p. 192), the Mausoleum of Emp. Frederick III (p. 193), Sanssouci (p. 194), the Picture Gallery (p 194), the Orangery (p 195), the New Palace (p 196, from the middle of Jan to the end of April, or in the absence of the royal family), the Japanese House (in summer only, p 195), and Babelsberg (p 198) is granted by ticket (25 pf. each pers.).

Smoking is prohibited in the royal gardens, except at Babelsberg and near the Orangery.

Plan of Excursion. One day is insufficient for the excursion to Potsdam, unless only the chief points be visited and a free use of cabs etc. be made In any case visitors are recommended to be at the *Town Palace* (p. 191) punctually at 10 a.m. when the first party is admitted Thence take the tramway to the Brandenburg Gate (p 192), and walk to the *Friedens-Kirche, Sanssouci* (p 194), the *Orangery* (p 195), and the *New Palace* (p. 196). If the latter be closed to visitors, walk from the Orangery via Charlottenhof to the Viktoria-Strasse, and return by tramway to the town. In the afternoon by tramway or steamboat to the Glienicke Bridge, walk via *Glienicke* to *Babelsberg* (p. 198) and Neu-Babelsberg station (p 187); or from the tramway terminus to the *Pfingstberg* (p 197), thence to the Meierei in the *Neue Garten* (p. 197) and past the Jungfern See back to the Glienicke Bridge (steamboat to Neu Babelsberg Station, tramway to Potsdam Station).

An alternative plan for one day is as follows. Take the tram (p. 187) to *Neu-Babelsberg* and the steamboat (p 187) thence to *Klein-Glienicke* Walk to *Babelsberg Palace* and through the park, passing the *Flatow-Turm* (view) to the Havel. Cross by boat to *Potsdam* (Holzmarkt-Str.; see p. 188) and visit the *Town Palace* about midday Then take the tramway to the Brandenburg Gate; walk to *Sanssouci* and the *Orangery,* and proceed thence either to *Wildpark Station* or to the tramway in the Luisen-Strasse, which takes us to Potsdam station.

Cycling Route (comp p 199, cycles are not admitted to the royal parks). After visiting the *Town Palace* proceed via the *Altmarkt, Schloss-Str., Plantage, Bäcker-Str,* and *Charlotten-Str.,* to the *Café Sanssouci* outside the Brandenburg Gate, where cycles may be left. Visit the park of *Sanssouci.* Mounting once more, ride via the *Hohenzollern-Str., Kaiser-Wilhelm-Str., Jäger-Str,* and past the *Russian Chapel,* via the *Pfingstberg* to the *Dairy* in the New Garden (leave cycle). Visit the park on foot. Ride via the *Grosse Weinmeister-Strasse, Schul-Strasse, Jänger-Strasse,* and the *Neue Königs-Strasse* to the *Glienicke Bridge* (which must be crossed on foot) and to the *Burgershof Restaurant* in Klein-Glienicke (leave cycle). Visit *Babelsberg* on foot, and finally ride back to Potsdam Before recrossing the Glienicke Bridge a digression may be made to . . . .

Potsdam of 1000 inhab . . . . . garrison town the seat of . . . . government for the province of Brandenburg and the frequent residence of the imperial court, is charmingly situated on the *Potsdamer Werder,* an island in the *Havel,* which here expands into a series of lakes and is bounded by wooded hills. The town, first mentioned in the 10th cent., is of ancient Slavonic origin, but was of no importance until the *Great Elector* founded the original town-palace. It is indebted for its modern splendour to *Frederick William I.* and still more to *Frederick the Great,* who generally resided at Potsdam. From the reign of the latter date the present Town Palace and the Palace of Sanssouci, the interiors of which are among the finest examples of the then prevalent rococo style, and also the gorgeous New Palace and a large part of the royal parks. The Marble Palace, in the incipient 'classicist' style, was built by *Frederick William II.; Frederick William III.* began the Church of St. Nicholas and laid out the park on the Pfauen-Insel. *Frederick William IV.,* while still crown-prince, erected the Charlottenhof, a charming work in the developed classicist style, and after he came to the throne added, besides the Friedens-Kirche and the church of Sakrow, the Orangery and the building on the Pfingstberg, two highly effective examples of the Italian decorative style. In the Gothic palace of Babelsberg, built by *William I.* before he became king, we recognize the influence of Rhenish romanticism. The edifices at Glienicke, designed by Schinkel for Prince Charles, are of greater artistic importance. — The royal influence extended even to the private buildings. Frederick William I. erected a Dutch quarter, and Frederick the Great adorned the main streets with reproductions of the façades of Italian palazzi. On the whole, the older parts of Potsdam present as monotonous an appearance as Versailles.

Potsdam is the true cradle of the Prussian army. From Potsdam Frederick William I. issued the regulations for the promotion of uniformity of drill and discipline in the army, which he had previously tested on his gigantic grenadiers. Every regiment had annually to send a detachment of officers, non-commissioned officers, and men to Potsdam, where the king personally demonstrated to them the application of his regulations. To this day the numerous soldiers, especially the picked men of the regiments of guards†, form the most characteristic feature in the streets of the town.

---

† The garrison consists of the 1st regiment of Foot Guards, a battalion of Riflemen of the Guards, the Gardes du Corps, the Hussars of the Life Guards, the 1st and 3rd regiments of Lancer Guards (Uhlans), and the 2nd and 4th regiments of the Field Artillery Guards. The Infantry Instruction Battalion, to which officers, non-commissioned officers, and men from all regiments in the German army (with the exception of the Bavarian contingent, are temporarily attached from April 15th to Oct. 1st, serves the same purpose as the above-mentioned arrangement of Frederick William I.

The *Railway Station* is situated in the Teltow Suburb, on the left (E.) bank of the Havel. The *Lange Brücke*, which leads thence to the town, rests partly on the W. end of the 'Freundschafts-Insel' and is adorned with eight typical figures of soldiers since the time of the Great Elector, by Herter (1895). — On the island, close to the bridge, is an **Equestrian Statue of Emperor William I.**, by *Herter*, erected in 1900. A goddess of victory is seated in front of the pedestal, which is embellished with reliefs of Prince William as 'galloper' at Bar-sur-Aube in 1814 and of the Entry into Paris in 1871. From beside the monument we command a view, to the S., of the Brauhausberg, with the Military Academy, while from the bridge we have a view, to the E., of the Church of the Holy Ghost and Babelsberg.

On the right bank, in the middle of the street, stands the lime-tree where petitioners used to station themselves in order to attract the attention of Frederick the Great, when he was in residence at the Town Palace.

The ¬**Town Palace**, or *Stadt-Schloss*, originally erected about 1660, but dating in its present form from its reconstruction by Knobelsdorff in 1745-51, is a remarkable specimen of the dignified classic style, though built at the zenith of the rococo period. The excellent materials used and the admirable taste displayed in the execution of the interior place it on a very high level. Only the apartments on the groundfloor of the S. main building are shown (adm., see p. 191; tickets at the N.E. angle of the court).

In the S.E. corner Frederick the Great's richly decorated apartments, with sumptuous furniture and noteworthy pictures by Pater, Lancret, and Pesne, have been preserved in their original condition. Adjoining the *Library*, which is separated from the *Bedroom* by a massive silver balustrade only, is a *Cabinet* with double doors, from which the dining-table could be let down by means of a trap-door, and where the king occasionally dined with his friends without risk of being overheard by his attendants. The *Study* in the S.E. angle is noteworthy. (The library and bedroom are still frequently used for royal christenings.) — In the centre is the *Marble Saloon*, built by the Great Elector and richly decorated by Frederick the Great. It contains a ceiling-painting, four large allegorical paintings, and three bronze reliefs, referring to the achievements of the Great Elector. The adjoining *Bronze Saloon*, with its white panelled walls and mirrors adorned with charming bronze-gilt ornaments by J. M. Rambly and Schwitzer, is an admirable example of rococo decoration. Over the fireplace is a double portrait of King Frederick William I. and Augustus the Strong, by Silvestre. The handsome French clock opposite should be noticed. — Farther on are the *Reception Rooms*, containing paintings by Hasenpflug, Begas, Gudin, etc., and marble groups by F. Wolff and Moller. — In the S.W. corner is the so-called *Russian Suite*, used for distinguished guests.

In front of the palace, on the bank of the Havel, extends the **Lustgarten**, with a colonnade and fountain, decorated with statues of the early 18th century. Near the fountain are bronze busts of personages eminent at the period of the war of liberation, by *Rauch*. A bronze statue of Frederick William I., *Hilger's* replica of

that in the Berlin Arsenal) was erected here in 1885 on the side
next the parade-ground, where he used to drill his gigantic grenadiers. The spring review of the garrison still takes place here.

To the N. of the palace is the ALTMARKT, in which is an *Obelisk*,
75 ft. in height, embellished with medallion portraits of the Great
Elector and the first three kings of Prussia. On the E side of the
square is the *Rathaus*, built in 1753 in the Dutch style, with a
gilded figure of Atlas bearing the globe above the gable

The **Church of St. Nicholas**, in the Altmarkt, erected in
1830-37 from *Schinkel's* designs, a lofty edifice of cubical form
with a dome added in 1842-50, contains a large fresco in the apse
(Christ with the apostles and evangelists) by *Schinkel*, and four
prophets by *Cornelius* in the spandrels of the vaulting under the
dome. Fine view from the open colonnade of the dome. (Sacristan
at the parsonage, adjoining the church on the right.)

The **Garrison Church**, 5 min to the W. of the palace, was
built by *Gerlach* in 1731-35. Adm. (see p. 189) in summer 10-6 by
Portal B; in winter apply to the sacristan, Kiez-Str. 24 A vault
behind the marble pulpit contains the remains of Frederick the Great
and of his father Frederick William I., the founder of the church. In
this church Frederick William III and Alexander I. of Russia formed
their friendly alliance on Nov. 4th. 1805. The peal of bells in the
tower chimes at the quarters. — To the N., in the Plantage, is a
bronze replica of the statue of Frederick the Great, by Uphues
(p. 112). To the W. is the large *Military Orphanage*, founded by
Frederick William I. and rebuilt in 1771-78 by Gontard. Adjacent, in
the Waisen-Str , is the *Rechnungshof des Deutschen Reiches* (built
in 1904-7), where the budget of the German Empire is controlled.

The WILHELM-PLATZ, skirted by the tramway, is adorned with a
Statue of Frederick William III., by Kiss (1845). — To the N.E ,
in the BASSIN-PLATZ, are the *French Church*, built by Knobels-
dorff in 1752, and the *Roman Catholic Church* (1867-70) To the
N. and W. of the square is the *Dutch Quarter* mentioned on p. 190.
To the W., the Charlotten-Strasse, with numerous palatial buildings
erected by Frederick the Great (see p. 190), and the Brandenburger-
Strasse lead to the Brandenburg Gate; between these streets, in the
Waisen-Str , is the *Offizier-Casino*, built by Schinkel in 1823-24.

The **Brandenburg Gate** ($1^1/_2$ M. from the rail. station; tramway see p. 189) was erected by Unger in 1770 in the form of a Roman triumphal arch. Outside the gate, in the Luisen-Platz, is a
bronze *Statue of Emperor Frederick III.*, in bronze, by Börmel
(1903). To the S.W of the Luisen-Platz extends the Brandenburg
Suburb, with the station of *Charlottenhof* p. 196. The Hohenzollern-Str. leads to the N to the main entrance of the Park of
Sanssouci p. 193 beside the obelisk and to the so-called *Weinbergs-*

Tor, erected by Fred. William IV. in 1852 in honour of the return of his brother Prince William (afterwards Emp. William I.) from the campaign in Baden (1849). A few minutes farther a path diverging to the right from the Nauen road and passing through pretty grounds leads in $^1/_2$ hr. to the Neue Garten (p. 197).

The usual entrance, however, to the Park of Sanssouci is by the 'Green Railing', reached by an avenue bearing a little to the right from the Brandenburg Gate. On the right, before the gate-house (tickets for the Mausoleum, see below), rises the ¯**Friedens-Kirche**, or *Church of Peace*, in the early-Christian basilica style, designed by *Persius*, and completed in 1850, the favourite building of Fred. William IV. The detached campanile is 130 ft. in height. In the *Atrium* (the 'paradise' of the ancient basilicas), in front of the church, stand *Rauch's* ⁺Group of Moses, Aaron, and Hur, and (in the centre) a copy of *Thorvaldsen's* Risen Christ. To the S. of the atrium are cloisters, the entrance to which from the park is formed by a terracotta reproduction of the entrance to the abbey-church of Heilsbronn. In the cloisters are a few fragments of early-Christian sculptures

The somewhat bare INTERIOR of the basilica, borne by sixteen Ionic columns in black marble, contains, in front of the chancel, the burial-vaults of Frederick William IV. (d 1861) and his Queen Elizabeth (d. 1873). The apse is adorned with an old Venetian mosaic from the church of San Cipriano di Malamocco, representing Christ, Mary, and Peter on the right, and John the Baptist and St Cyprian on the left.

On the N. side of the atrium is the **Mausoleum of Emp. Frederick III.** (adm., see p. 189: tickets in the gate-house, to the right), erected by *Raschdorff* in 1890 in imitation of the chapel of Innichen in Tyrol The interior of the circular domed structure is supported by nine columns of labradorite. The marble *Sarcophagi of the emperor (d 1888) and of Empress Victoria (d. 1901) as well as those of their sons Waldemar and Sigismund are by *R Begas*. In the altar-niche is a ⁺Pietà by *Rietschel* (1845). The dome is embellished with mosaics of angels, after *Ewald's* designs.

Entering the ¯**Park of Sanssouci** by the green gate and bearing to the right round a corner we soon reach a reduced marble replica of Rauch's equestrian statue of Frederick the Great (p. 57). Beyond it is the *Great Fountain* (p 189), the water of which rises to a height of 130 ft. The twelve figures surrounding the basin are French works of the 18th century. The Mercury and the Venus (copies; originals see p. 100), by *Pigalle*, were presented by Louis XV.: the figures of Hunting and Fishing are by *Lambert Sigisbert Adam*, and most of the others are by his brother *François Gaspard Adam*. To the N., in front of the fountain, is the porphyry bust of Duke Paolo Jordanzio of Bracciano bought by Frederick the Great for 3000*l*. The first section is situated on the top of a terrace 1 M.

in length, which intersects the park from E. (Obelisk, p. 192) to W. (New Palace, p. 196).

A broad flight of steps, 66 ft. in height, intersected by six *Terraces,* ascends from the great fountain to the palace. On the highest terrace two elegant fountains project their water in the form of bells. Frederick the Great's greyhounds are buried at the E. end of this terrace. The king expressed a wish to be buried at the foot of the statue of Flora here ('Quand je serai là, je serai sans souci').

The **Palace of Sanssouci,* a building of one story, 320 ft. in length and 39 ft. high, erected by Knobelsdorff for Frederick the Great from the king's own sketches in 1745-47, and that monarch's almost constant residence, stands on an eminence above the town. The terrace on the N. side is enclosed by a semicircular Corinthian colonnade. Frederick's rooms are still preserved almost unaltered; they are interesting on account of their rococo decorations as well as for their historical associations (adm., see p. 189; tickets obtained at the rear of the palace).

The WEST WING contains *Voltaire's Room,* with interesting wood-carving and a porcelain bust of Voltaire ('immortalis'), and *Fred. William IV.'s Rooms,* in which he died in 1861. — In the CENTRAL BUILDING is the oval *Dining Room,* the S. side of which can be thrown open to the terrace. The figures of Apollo and Urania are by Fr. G. Adam (p. 193). The king's famous round table is well known from Menzel's painting (p. 92). — EAST WING. The *Audience Room* and the adjacent apartments are hung with admirable **Paintings* by *Watteau, Pater,* and *Lancret,* and contain handsome furniture. — The clock in the *Concert Saloon,* which Frederick was in the habit of winding up, is said to have stopped at the precise moment of his death (2.20 a.m., 17th Aug., 1786). The wall-paintings in this room are by *Pesne;* handsome ceiling. — *Frederick the Great's Apartment.* This room, in which he died, was reconstructed the same year by his successor. *Graff's* portrait of Frederick represents him at about the age of fifty-six. Marble **Statue* by *Magnussen* (1898), representing the 'last moments of Frederick the Great'. In the alcove is a portrait of the king's mother, Sophie Dorothea, by *Pesne.* — The **Library,* charmingly decorated in the rococo style in cedar-wood and gilt-bronze, contains a few antique busts, the best of which is one of Homer. Specimens of the king's handwriting and a drawing (design of the palace) by him. — The *Gallery,* with paintings by Watteau and his school, leads to the *Parole Room,* behind the dining-room, where our visit terminates.

The **Picture Gallery,** built in 1756, occupies a separate building to the E., the interior of which is lavishly decorated with stucco (adm., see p. 189; visitors are conducted by an attendant). It contains a few good works by *Rubens* (17. Holy Family), *Van Dyck* (8. Four Evangelists; 155. Cupid skating), *Cranach, Cornelis van Haarlem, Hans Baldung Grien,* and *P. Molenaer.* There are also several works by the two *Van der Werffs,* some good examples of *Jan Brueghel* (102. Vulcan's forge), and paintings by *Pesne, Graff* (53. Iffland the actor as Pygmalion), etc. A small room at the back contains a vase of bloodstone. The *Grotto of Neptune,* a little to the L., is a relic of the rich architectonic decoration of

the Park of Sanssouci in the reign of Frederick the Great (1761).
In front of it stands a reproduction of the statue of Frederick by
Uphues (p. 112).

From Sanssouci a path leads in ¼ hr. to the Ruinenberg, an eminence with artificial ruins (1748), beneath which is the reservoir for the
fountains of Sanssouci. The water is pumped into it from the Havel by
means of steam-engines. The tower (fee) commands a beautiful and extensive prospect. Rfmts. from the keeper

The way to the Orangery leads to the W. from Sanssouci past
the famous *Windmill*, the owner of which is said to have refused
to sell it to Frederick the Great (now royal property). Near it a
restaurant is under construction. To the right of the mill a path
ascends to the Orangery (see below); to the left the Maulbeer-Allée
runs to the New Palace (p. 196), dividing the *Nordische Garten*
(right) from the *Sizilianische Garten* (left). In the latter are figures
of a colossal archer, by Geyger, and of a Girl drawing water, by
E. Wolff. To the W., beyond the terraces ascending to the Orangery,
on the right of the Allée, is the *Paradies-Garten*, with a charming
atrium in the Greek style (see p. 196).

The *Orangery, an extensive structure in the Florentine style,
330 yds. in length, was completed in 1856 from plans by *Hesse*.
The façade is embellished with allegorical statues, and in front of
the central building is a marble statue of Fred. William IV., the
founder, by *Bläser* (1873). On the terrace is a copy of the Farnese
Bull, in bronzed zinc, and below are two ancient sarcophagi, used as
fountain-troughs. The astronomical instruments from the Imperial
Observatory at Pekin, brought to Europe by the German troops in
1901, are also placed on this terrace. These magnificent specimens
of Chinese bronze-casting are stated by the Jesuit Father Verbiest
to have been finished by Chinese artists in 1673. The towers of the
château command a wide *View.

The CENTRAL SALOON contains forty-eight *Copies from Raphael* and
numerous modern sculptures — MALACHITE SALOON: *Thorvaldsen*, Head
of Antinous and Head of a shepherd, *Troschel*, Bacchus; *Cauer*, Statuette of Fred. William IV. Paintings. *O. Achenbach*, Park near Frascati,
etc — AMBER ROOM: *Rauch*, *Danaïd, good Berlin and Dresden china —
TORTOISE SHELL ROOM: *E. Hildebrandt*, Views in Palestine. Adm. see p 189.

Behind the W. wing of the Orangery, to the left, we may descend
to the Paradies-Garten (shortest route to the New Palace, see p.
196). Straight on, beyond a ravine crossed by a bridge, are the
Drachen-Häuschen (1769; rfmts.) and a *Belvedere* erected in
1770-72 by Unger (no adm.).

To the S. of the main avenue (comp. p 193 and the Map, p. 188)
are the *Sea Horse Fountain*, by Kiss, and the *Japanese House*,
called the 'ape-saloon' by Frederick the Great (accessible in summer,
p. 189). Farther on (best route over the bridge at the beginning
of the Lennéstr. and past the water-tower) is a *Roman Bath
House* (fee, closed in winter, containing a double bath of jasper,

a copy of the antique mosaic of the Battle of Alexander, etc. — In 25 min. from the Orangery we reach the —

*Charlottenhof, originally an unpretending country-house, but tastefully transformed by *Schinkel* in 1826 into an Italian villa and surrounded by beautiful grounds. The vestibule contains reliefs by *Thorvaldsen*, a bust of Schinkel by *Rauch*, etc. In one of the rooms is a chair of steel and silver, made by *Peter the Great*. Two rooms contain memorials of A. von Humboldt (Castellan on the groundfloor; fee.) — The *Wildpark Station* (p. 187) is ³/₄ M. from here.

We now skirt the W. portion of the park of Sanssouci (generally closed to the public in summer and autumn) in order to visit the New Palace, which lies 1 M. from the Orangery, about 1¹/₄ M. from the Charlottenhof, and ¹/₂ M. from Wildpark Station. The —

*New Palace, the summer-residence of the Emperor, was planned by Frederick the Great during the Seven Years' War as a visible proof of his power and wealth and was built by him in 1763-69 at a cost of 150,000*l.* The plans were furnished by *J. G. Buring* of Hamburg, who followed Dutch and English models. The main building is 700 ft. in length, and the central portion, surmounted by a dome, has three stories. The chief façade is turned towards the E., overlooking the park. To the W., behind the palace, are the *Communs*, intended as quarters for the royal retinue, picturesquely designed buildings by *K. von Gontard*, united by a semicircular colonnade. The palace and the communs together form an imposing pile, though the execution of the details is sometimes careless. The sculptures are mediocre, but the effect of the weathered sandstone figures against the red brick background is very pleasing. Emperor Frederick III., who was born in the palace in 1831, resided in it for a considerable time as crown-prince, and died there in June 1888. William II. has thoroughly restored the building and has added a large terrace, with candelabra by Schott, on the side next the garden. Adm., see p. 189; entrance in the S. wing.

The INTERIOR contains about 200 rooms, the fanciful decoration of which speaks highly for the decorators employed by Frederick the Great, although the elegant execution of the rooms in the Town Palace is not equalled here. The rooms of the S. wing are shown; the N. wing contains the private rooms of the Emperor. — GROUND FLOOR. Among the *Apartments of Frederick the Great* the library contains a portrait of Voltaire drawn by the king, in the king's study is a good example by *Watteau* (Dance in the open air). The *Shell Saloon* is inlaid with shells, the friezes with minerals and precious stones. The tasteful *Theatre* has seats for 500 persons. — On the FIRST FLOOR are numerous old pictures. In the *Marble* or *Concert Room* (100 ft. long): *Van Loo*, Ganymede introduced to Olympus (ceiling-painting), Sacrifice of Iphigenia; *Pesne*, Rape of Helen — In the *Ball Room: G. Reni*, Lucretia, Diogenes, *L. Giordano*, Judgment of Paris, Rape of the Sabines.

In a garden to the N.E. of the New Palace (closed) stands a *Marble Statue of Empress Augusta Victoria by P. Breuer (1905)*.

To the E., on the left and right of the main avenue (p. 195), are the *Antiken-Tempel*, where Frederick the Great preserved antique works, and the *Temple of Friendship*, erected by Gontard for Frederick the Great in memory of his sister the Margravine of Bayreuth (d. 1758), with her statue

To the W. of Wildpark Station (p. 196) is the entrance to the pretty Wildpark, in which Frederick William IV erected the *Bayrische Häuschen* for his consort Elizabeth, a Bavarian princess (3 M. from the station, rfmts)

———

To the N. of Potsdam, about ½ M. from the Nauener Tor (tramway to the Allée-Strasse, p. 189), is the colony of *Alexandrowka*, consisting of fourteen log-houses and a Greek chapel, built in 1826 by Frederick William III. for the accommodation of the Russian musicians who were at that time attached to the 1st Regiment of Guards.

On the *Pfingstberg, which we reach in 20 min. from the tramway terminus, stands a handsome ornamental building, enclosing a reservoir. The two towers afford an extensive view of the environs, with Berlin, Spandau, Nauen, and Brandenburg in the distance, most striking by evening-light. A carriage road ascends to the summit of the hill. The castellan lives in the N.E. tower (fee). – To the N., about 2½ M. from the Pfingstberg, is the village of *Nedlitz* (several restaurants; steamboat, see p. 187), opposite which is the Römer-Schanze (p. 187; ferry); to the N.E. (direction-board) of the Pfingstberg the Meierei (see below) may be reached in ¼ hr.

To the E. of Alexandrowka (see above) lies the NEUE GARTEN, or New Garden, distinguished for its fine examples of foreign trees. In its E. part, on the *Heilige-See*, rises the graceful —

Marble Palace, begun in 1786 by *Gontard*, continued in 1788-96 by *K. G. Langhans*, and completed in 1845. Emp. William II. occupied this palace before his accession (1881-88); since 1905 it has been a summer residence of the Crown Prince and, along with its environs, is no longer accessible to the public

In the COURT, in front of the palace, Prometheus, by *E. Wolff*. In the ARCADES, scenes from the Niebelungenlied and views of the Rhine and the Danube by *Kolbe* and *Hesse*. The INTERIOR contains marble sculptures by *Rauch*, *Tassaert*, *E. Wolff*, and *Troschel*, and pictures by *Hackert* and others. In the Oriental Cabinet is a costly table, presented by Empress Catherine II. of Russia to Frederick the Great — In the Dining-Room are marble busts of Emp. William II. and the Empress Frederick, by *R. Begas*

In the N. angle of the park lies the *Meierei*, or dairy (rfmts.); ferry to the woods between Sakrow and the Römer-Schanze, see p. 187; steamboats, see p. 188. Attractive footpath hence, skirting the *Jungfern-See*, past *Krampnitz* . . . . built in the Norwegian style . . . *Glienicke Bridge* . . . . p. 198.

To the E. of Potsdam we ferry from the Holzmarkt-Str., outside the Berliner Tor, to Babelsberg (see below). The Neue Konigs-Strasse, which begins at the Berliner Tor, passes the *Barracks of the Hussar Guards* (right) and of the *Gardes du Corps* (left) to the *Glienicke Bridge* ('Kaiser-Friedrich-Brucke', rebuilt in 1907; tramway, see pp. 189, 199) The bronze groups in front of the latter barracks (soldiers of the regiment leading horses) are by Kiss.

At **Klein-Glienicko** (see p. 187), beyond the bridge to the left, is the *Palace of Prince Frederick Leopold*, built for Prince Charles (d. 1833), the prince's grandfather, by Schinkel. The park is not accessible; at the corner near the Glienicke Bridge is a rotunda, built by Schinkel in imitation of the Monument of Lysicrates at Athens.

Farther along the Babelsberg road, on the right, is the *Hunting Château of Glienicke*, originally built in 1678 by the Great Elector, restored and enlarged in 1856 by Prince Frederick Charles (d. 1885) and subsequently by his son, Prince Frederick Leopold (no admittance). — The bay of the Havel, on which the château lies, is connected by the Teltow Canal with the *Griebnitz-See*, to the E.; There are stations of the steamers to the Neu-Babelsberg station (p. 187) in the village near the Burgershof Restaurant and near the canal bridge.

To the S of the canal bridge is the principal entrance to the park and the palace of Babelsberg, a visit to which occupies 1½ hr. Numerous stones with way-marks.

The picturesque *Château of Babelsberg was erected in the English Gothic style by *Schinkel* in 1835, and extended in 1843-49 by *Strack*. It stands in a beautiful park, laid out by Prince Puckler. The interior of the château is simply but tastefully decorated in the unassuming style which prevailed in Germany about the middle of last century. Emp. William I invariably spent the latter half of summer here, and his study and bedroom as well as the reception rooms are shown to visitors. The walls are hung with numerous works of art, mainly of the early Berlin and Dusseldorf schools. Memorials of the campaigns of 1849, 1864, 1866, and 1870-71 are also preserved here. The N windows command charming views.

In front of the palace is the *Gerhard Fountain*, a present from the architects of Cologne Cathedral; and behind the palace is a monument with the Archangel Michael, by *Kiss*.

A walk through the park is recommended (guide-posts) To the S.W. stands the *Gerichts-Laube*, a Gothic portico originally attached to the old Rathaus in Berlin. To the S. rises the *Flatow-Turm*, a copy of the Eschenheimer Tor Turm at Frankfort, erected in 1856 and commanding a fine View of Potsdam and the environs, across the broad expanse of the Havel in the foreground (adm by the castellan) To the E of the tower is the *Kldtherru-*

Bank, with bronze busts of generals of 1870-71; a little higher up
is a *Column of Victory* (fine view). — Ferry to the Holzmarkt-
Str. from the S.W. corner of the park (15 min., 10 pf.).

To the S. of Potsdam rises the wooded **Brauhausberg**, which
may be easily ascended in $1/4$ hr. from the railway-station by
crossing the bridge over the line and skirting the Schutzen-Platz
to the right. On the Brauhausberg stand the *Military School* and,
to the W., a *Belvedere* (10 pf.; keeper in the tower in fine weather),
commanding a fine View. The *Wackermannshohe Restaurant,*
a little lower, also has a good view.

Farther to the S., on the *Telegraphenberg,* are three government scientific institutions, with conspicuous domes. The *Astro-
Physical Observatory,* usually known as the 'Sonnenwarte', is an
admirably-equipped institution, opened in 1878 (adm Frid., 3-6;
visitors are conducted by the castellan; director, Dr. Lohse). The
new double refracting telescope, with object glass 20 inches in diameter for ocular observations and $31^{1}/_{2}$ inches in diameter for photographic purposes, is the largest existing instrument of the kind but
two. The other institutions are the *Meteorological-Magnetic Observatory* (comp. p. 143: director, Prof. Sprung) and the *Geodetic
Institute* (director, Prof. Helmert) in which is the central office for
the international measurement of the earth.

Other pleasant points in the neighbourhood of Potsdam are the forester's house of *Templin* (restaurant), on the Havel, a drive of $1/2$ hr. or
walk of $1^{1}/_{2}$ hr. (steamer, see p. 188), and the village of *Caputh,* $3/4$ hr.
farther on, behind which rise the *Krähenberge* (views). We may cross
the Havel at Caputh and proceed to ($1/2$ hr.) *Baumgartenbrück* (restaurant),
at the point where the Havel emerges from the *Schwielow-See,* about
$5^{1}/_{2}$ M to the S.W. of Potsdam

The orchard-covered hills beside the little town of **Werder** (6900 inhab.)
afford charming views, especially when the fruit-trees are in blossom.
One of the best points of view is the *Bismarckhohe Restaurant.* The
town, which lies on a little island. $1/2$ hr. from the station (tramway), is
reached by the suburban trains from the Potsdam Station in Berlin;
steamers, see p 188. A bronze statue of Emp. Frederick III , by Arnold,
was erected here in 1904. A ferry plies to the opposite bank of the
Havel at a point within $1^{1}/_{4}$ hr.'s walk by a pleasant road from Wildpark Station.

Cycling Route. From Berlin to Potsdam, $18^{1}/_{2}$ M , by a good
and generally level road. Start from the Schloss-Platz (prohibited streets,
see p 13) — 4 M *Schoneberg* — 5 M. *Friedenau* — $6^{1}/_{4}$ M. *Steglitz* —
$9^{1}/_{2}$ M *Zehlendorf,* beyond which wood is traversed — 13 M. *Wannsee.*
— Beyond the kilometre stone 21 9 ($13^{1}/_{2}$ M.) we keep straight on via the
(16 M.) *Bottcher-Berg* to the ($16^{1}/_{4}$ M.) *Glienicke Bridge,* which must be
crossed on foot. — $18^{1}/_{2}$ M. *Potsdam* (Altmarkt), p. 192.

Return route (20 M.). — $1^{1}/_{4}$ M. *Glienicke Bridge* (dismount). — At
kilometre-stone 26 2 turn to the left and then skirt the Havel — At
kilometre ... '1' ... then turn ... to ... I ... M ... see. —
Turning ... th ... fil..m .. .. 's -line),
proceed th ... h b tr..... dd ... tt M th ... M H ... rekehle

(dismount). — 13¹/₄ M *Grunewald-Halensee.* — Thence viâ the Kurfürsten-Damm, past the Emp. William Memorial Church (keep to the right), across the Cornelius-Brücke, and viâ the Hitzig Str. and the Tiergarten-Str. to the (20 M.) Brandenburg Gate.

15. Spandau and Tegel.
The Upper Spree and Dahme.

SPANDAU AND TEGEL. — Spandau may be reached by the Nauen suburban trains from the Lehrte Station (7¹/₂ M.) or by the trains of the Stadtbahn (p. 12).

Spandau (*Friedrichshof*, R. 2¹/₂-3, B. ³/₄, D. 1¹/₄ ℳ, *Kaiser-hof*, similar charges, both near the station; *Restaurant Pohrt*, Breite-Str. 32; *Restaurant Havel-Terrassen*, at the Charlotten-Brücke), a formerly fortified town with 70,300 inhab., at the confluence of the *Spree* and the *Havel*, has large military factories. Beyond the Charlotten-Brücke is a bronze *Statue of Emp. Frederick III.*, by Manthe (1892); and in front of the *Nicolai-Kirche* is a bronze *Statue of Elector Joachim II.*, by Encke, unveiled in 1889, commemorating the elector's confession of Protestantism here in 1539. At the beginning of the Neustadt, beyond the *Garrison Church*, is a *Monument to Bismarck*, by G. Meyer (1901). The imperial military reserve fund of six millions sterling is kept in the *Julius-Turm* of the citadel, to the N.E. of the town.

TRAMWAYS: to the S. to *Pichelsdorf*, on the right bank of the Havel opposite the Grunewald (p. 184), to the N. to the *Stadtpark Restaurant* and to *Hakenfelde*, both on the margin of the pleasant Bürgerheide, to the E. to the *Spandauer Bock*, near the Grunewald (p. 183).

STEAMERS ON THE LOWER HAVEL, from the Charlotten-Brücke (¹/₂ M. from the station) on week-days 6 times, Sun. 12 times daily to *Pichels-werder* (p. 184; 20 pf.), *Schildhorn*, *Gatow*, *Kaiser Wilhelm-Turm* (30 pf.), *Lindwerder*, *Wannsee* (p. 186; 50 pf.), *Pfauen-Insel*, *Moorlake*, *Sakrow*, *Glienicke Bridge* (p. 198), and *Potsdam* (Lange-Brücke, 80 pf.), comp. p. 188.

The suburban trains on the Lehrte line go on beyond Spandau viâ *Seegefeld* to *Finkenkrug*. The popular Finkenkrug Restaurant, ³/₄ hr. from the station, is situated in the *Brieselang*, the only considerable forest of foliage-trees now left in the neighbourhood of Berlin.

CYCLING ROUTE. *From Berlin to Finkenkrug*, 25¹/₂ M., a pleasant excursion through wood; start from the Brandenburger Tor (prohibited streets, see p. 43). — 4¹/₂ M. *Schloss Charlottenburg*; ascent to Westend. — 6¹/₄ M. *Spandauer Bock*; rapid descent — 8³/₄ M. *Spandau* (from the market-place to the right, viâ Potsdamer-Str. and Schonwalder-Str.) — 10 M. *Fehrbelliner Tor* — 10⁴/₅ M. *Stadtpark Restaurant.* — 15 M. *Schwanenkrug.* — 20 M. *Pausin*, here to the left. — 22¹/₂ M. *Brieselang Colony* — 25 M. *Finkenkrug* — Thence to Falkenberg and (to the right) the station of Seegefeld (3³/₄ M.).

Steamers from Spandau to Tegel, starting near the Garrison Church (30 pf.), ply frequently across the broad Havel to the pleasure-resorts of *Tegelort* to the N. and *Saatwinkel*, and then cross the wood-girt *Tegeler See,* which branches off towards the N.E., to Tegel.

Tegel may be reached direct from Berlin by tramway (see p. 16; No. 25, 26, 31), or by railway (8 M.; suburban service on the Kremmen line, from the Stettin Station). Stations: 1¹/₄ M. *Gesundbrunnen* (p. 167); 3 M. *Pankow* (p. 167); 3³/₄ M. *Schönholz* (comp. p. 167); 5 M. *Reinickendorf* (26,000 inhab.), with numerous factories; 6¹/₄ M. *Wittenau* (Dalldorf, 7800 inhab.), with the large Berlin Lunatic and Idiot Asylum (tramway No. 28, p. 16); 8 M. *Tegel.*

Tegel (Restaurants: *Strandschloss, Kaiser-Pavillon,* both on the lake) is a village with 16,100 inhabitants To the S. are *Borsig's Engine Factory* (comp p. 166), the extensive *Berlin Gas Works,* and a penitentiary. To the N. (¹/₄ hr. from the station) is *Schloss Tegel* (Schloss Restaurant), rebuilt by Schinkel in 1822 in the style of a Roman villa Formerly in the possession of the *Humboldt* family, it now belongs to the allied family of *Heinz.* The house contains plaster casts and a number of original antique sculptures (adm. in the absence of the family; fee). In the park (adm. 25 pf.) are the graves of William (d. 1835) and Alexander (d. 1859) von Humboldt, marked by a replica of Thorvaldsen's statue of Hope (in the château). To the S. of the park, on the lake, is the *Kurhaus Schloss Tegel* Numerous pleasant walks in the woods of the vicinity.

After flowing through two lakes of some size, the *Spree* unites at Köpenick with the *Dahme,* the lower course of which is tolerably broad, and thence flows on towards the Oberbaum-Brucke (p. 170) as the *Upper Spree (Oberspree).* This reach is the chief resort of the boating circles of Berlin, and the settlements on its wooded banks are very popular (served by the suburban trains on the Silesian and Görlitz lines).

A STEAMBOAT TRIP ON THE UPPER SPREE is recommended (p. 21), especially as it affords also an opportunity of estimating Berlin's importance as an industrial centre. Beyond the Süd-Ring (p. 13) the steamer touches at *Stralau* (left) and *Treptow* (right; comp. p. 170), adjoined by the *Eierhäuschen.* Then, opposite each other, the manufacturing localities of *Ober-Schöneweide* (on the left; 18,000 inhab), with a cable factory of the Allgemeine Elektrizitats-Gesellschaft (p. 167), and *Nieder-Schöneweide* (on the right; 4200 inhab.). The stations mentioned on p. 24 are restaurants; railway-stations see p. 203. To the right, belonging to Köpenick, is *Spindlersfeld,* the large cleaning and dyeing establishment of Messrs. Spindler pp. 160, 202 The village and **Köpenick** (*Ratskeller Restaurant*, a thriving town of 27,700 inhab. and the château (now a normal school) in which Frederick the Great was tried by court-martial in 1730, when crown-prince. Tramway from the railway-station (see below) through the town to *Colony Wendenschloss* (opposite Grunau, p 203), a convenient approach to the Muggel-Berge (p. 203).

SILESIAN RAILWAY TO ERKNER (from the platform of the Stadt-bahn). — 1¹/₄ M. (from the Silesian Station) *Stralau-Rummels-burg.* Stralau, see p. 170; Rummelsburg, p. 202. — 4¹/₂ M. *Karls-horst*, a villa-colony, with a steeplechase course (p 30), 1¹/₂ M. to the S. is Ober-Schöneweide (p. 201). — 7¹/₂ M. *Kopenick*, see p. 201 — 9¹/₂ M. **Friedrichshagen** (*Ratskeller Restaurant*; steamer, see p. 24), a village with 13,200 inhab., founded by Frederick the Great, to whom a bronze statue, by Gerling, was erected here in 1904. On the N bank of the *Muggel-See*, where sailing regattas frequently take place, are the Berlin waterworks. A tramway runs from the station to the (1 M.) efflux of the Spree from the lake. On the other side is the *Muggel-Schlösschen Restaurant*, whence we may proceed, passing the *Teufels-See* (restaurant), to the (1 hr.) Müggel-Berge (p 203).

15 M. **Erkner** (*Railway Restaurant*) is a village situated between the Dämeritz-See and the Flaken-See. — Rüdersdorf is visited hence by steamer in ³/₄ hr (fare 35 pf) The steamer crosses the *Flaken-See* to the summer-resort of *Woltersdorfer Schleuse* (Hôt. zum Kranichsberg; steamer to Berlin, see p. 24), situated in the woods. View-tower on the Kranichsberg We change steamers here and proceed on the *Kalk-See* to **Kalkberge Rüdersdorf** (*Restaurant zur Traube*). The large limestone quarries here belong to government; one-sixth of the annual revenue is paid to the city of Berlin Pleasant walks in the grounds laid out on the heaps of débris; view-tower. — From the railway station of Ruders-dorf (³/₄ hr to the N.) a branch-line runs to (3 M) *Fredersdorf* (p. 208).

Another pleasant route from Erkner to the Kalkberge is as follows. We cross the *Flakensee* (Woltersdorf Loek) by motor boat (8 times daily) and then via the *Löcknitz* and the adjoining lakes (Werls-See, Peetz-See), between the pleasant colonies of the *Werlsee Gemeinde*, reach 1¹/₂ hr. Alt-Buchhorst (restaurant, the Fangschleuse Station, ³/₄ hr. to the S.W., is on the Silesian suburban railway). Thence on foot we traverse fine wood to the N via *Dorf Rüdersdorf* to (1¹/₂ hr.) Kalkberge Rüdersdorf.

Cycling Route. FROM BERLIN TO THE MÜGGELSEE AND BACK, a circular tour of 33¹/₂ M. Start from the Silesian Gate. — To (4¹/₂ M) *Nieder-Schöneweide*, see p 201 Turning to the left at the station, we proceed via *Spindlersfeld* to (7 M.) *Kopenick* Beyond the bridge over the Dahme at Kopenick turn to the left, then, beyond the bridge over the Spree, at kilomètric-stone 11 6, and again at kil stone 12, to the right. — 8¹/₄ M *Hirschgarten*, a group of villas. — 10 M. *Friedrichshagen*, where we keep to the right (2⁴/₄ M *Rahnsdorfer Mühle*, another group of villas. — At kil. stone 25 (14¹/₂ M.) to the right through *Erkner* and *Neu-Buch-horst*. — 18 M. *Neu Zittau:* here to the right Beyond (19²/₄ M. *Gosen*, the *Seddin-See* appears on the left — 22¹/₄ M. *Müggelheim* A road to the *Müggel-Berge* (see below) diverges to the left, 2 M. farther on. — 26¹/₁ M. *Kietz-Köpenick* — 29 M. *Nieder-Schöneweide*, see p. 201. — 33¹/₂ M. Berlin (Silesian Gate).

GÖRLITZ RAILWAY TO KÖNIGS-WUSTERHAUSEN (suburban service; to Nieder-Schöneweide or Grünau also from the local stations of the Staatsbahn, N platform) —3 M. (from the Silesian and Görlitz stations) *Baumschulenweg Späth's Nursery*, 1 M. to the S., is the largest in Europe. — 4¹/₂ M. *Nieder-Schöneweide* (p. 201); branchline to (2¹/₂ M.) Spindlersfeld (p. 201).

8¹/₂ M. **Grünau** (*Gesellschaftshaus Restaurant*: steamer to Schmöckwitz, see p 24) is a villa-colony, pleasantly situated on the Dahme, on which sailing and rowing regattas are held (comp. p 30). About ¹/₄ hr upstream is a monument to Emp. William I., beside a restaurant. Pleasant walks lead through the woods on the opposite bank (ferry from Colony Wendenschloss, p. 202) to the (³/₄ hr.) *Müggel-Berge* (several restaurants), ¹/₄ hr to the N. of the steamboat station. The 'Bismarck Tower' commands a wide view (to the N the Müggel-See and Friedrichshagen, p. 202) — 12 M. *Eichwalde* The village of *Schmöckwitz* (Palme Restaurant), ³/₄ hr. to the E., is prettily situated between the Lange-See, the Seddin-See, and the Zeuthener See. — 13¹/₂ M. *Zeuthen* (Seglerschloss Restaurant) is a colony of villas on the Zeuthener See, frequented by boating and sailing parties. — 15¹/₂ M *Wildau*

17¹/₂ M. **Königs-Wusterhausen** (*Hôtel Pfuhl*, at the station), a village on the *Notte*, with a *Royal Shooting Lodge*, famous as the meeting-place of King Frederick William I s 'Tobacco Parliament'. The house contains various memorials of that king (portraits of his gigantic grenadiers painted by himself, etc) and also of Emp William I. In 1730 Fred. William I here pronounced the final sentence on the crown-prince (afterwards Frederick the Great); comp. p 202. On the Dahme, 1¹/₂ M. to the E. of the station, is the pleasure resort of *Neue Mühle* (steamer, see p. 24).

Cycling Route. FROM BERLIN TO KÖNIGS-WUSTERHAUSEN, 18¹/₄ M. Beyond Nieder-Schöneweide the road is good and level, numerous woods Start from the Silesian Gate. — 1¹/₄ M *Treptow;* riders must dismount before the village. — 3¹/₂ M Paved road, where riding is prohibited. 4¹/₂ M *Nieder-Schöneweide.* To Köpenick, see p. 201. Our route lies straight on. 6¹/₄ M. *Adlershof.* — 8¹/₂ M. *Grünau.* — 15¹/₄ M. *Zeuthen.* — 18¹/₄ M *Königs-Wusterhausen*, whence a trip may be made to Neue Mühle (to the left before the station)

Return-route: 5¹/₂ M. *Waltersdorf.* — 10¹/₄ M. *Rudow* — 11¹/₄ M *Rixdorf* — 17¹/₂ M Berlin (Halle Gate).

16. Longer Excursions from Berlin.

The long distance trains call only at the termini of the suburban service, not at the intermediate stations, with the exception (for the routes described below) of *Gesundbrunnen, Spandau,* and *Nieder-Schöneweide.*

a. EBERSWALDE. CHORIN. FREIENWALDE. — Railway (Stettin line; suburban service to Bernau, comp. p 13) to Freienwalde, 40 M , in 2 hrs.; special trains on Sun. in summer. — 3 M. *Pankow-Schönhausen* (p 167). — 9¹/₂ M. *Buch,* with sewage-fields and a lunatic asylum of the city of Berlin. — 14¹/₄ M. **Bernau** *(Kaiserhof),* a town of 9500 inhab., with remains of a circular fortified wall, noted for its determined resistance to the Hussites in 1432. — 20¹/₂ M. *Biesenthal.* The little town (2800 inhab.) lies 2¹/₄ M to the W. of the station.

About 3 M. to the W of the town is *Lanke* (Hôtel-Restaurant Schlosspark), with a château and park of Count Redern. Thence we may go on through fine woods to (1¹/₂ M.) *Uetzdorf* (restaurant) and skirt the pretty *Liepnitz-See* to the (3 M.) restaurant at its W extremity. At *Wandlitz Station,* 1¹/₂ M from the restaurant, we may join the branchline of the Nord Bahn (p 203), beginning at Reinickendorf. Motor-car trips see p. 24; cycling route, p. 205.

28 M. **Eberswalde** *(Deutsches Haus,* R. 2-3, B. 1, D. 2 *M,* well spoken of; *Pinnow,* at the station; *Railway Restaurant),* a busy town with 23,850 inhab., situated on the *Finow Canal,* which here receives the *Schwärze,* is the seat of a school of forestry The well-wooded neighbourhood attracts numerous visitors in summer. — A pleasant walk leads to the S., vìa the *Schützenhaus* (restaurant and view-tower) and *Kurhaus* to the (2¹/₄ M.) *Zainhammer Restaurant,* whence we may go on to the *Wasserfall Restaurant,* to *Spechthausen* (restaurant), and the *Nonnenfliess* — Cycling route to Eberswalde, see p. 205.

The second, station beyond Eberswalde is (35¹/₂ M) *Chorinchen,* about ³/₄ M. to the E of which lies *Amt Chorin (Neue Klosterschenke),* a former Cistercian monastery, founded about 1258. The ruined abbeychurch, a brick basilica in the purest early-Gothic style, is the most interesting mediæval building in the Mark of Brandenburg The monastery is surrounded by fine woods.

FROM EBERSWALDE TO FÜRSTENBERG, 48¹/₂ M , branch-line in 3¹/₂ hrs. — 11 M. *Werbellinsee.* About 6 M to the S in the *Schorfheide,* near the Werbellin-See, lies the royal shooting lodge of *Hubertusstock.* — For details see *Baedeker's Northern Germany*

We leave the Stettin main line at Eberswalde and take the branch-line, vìa (36¹/₂ M.) *Falkenberg* (Hôtel Kettlitz), a favourite summer-resort, to —

40 M. **Freienwalde** *(Hôt. Schertz,* R 2-3, B. 1 *M,* well spoken of), a town with 8300 inhab., charmingly situated on the verge of the Oderbruch. The wooded hills which rise behind it dispute with those near Buckow p. 208 the title of the *"Markish Switzerland Märkische Schweiz).* The tower on the *Wilhelms-*

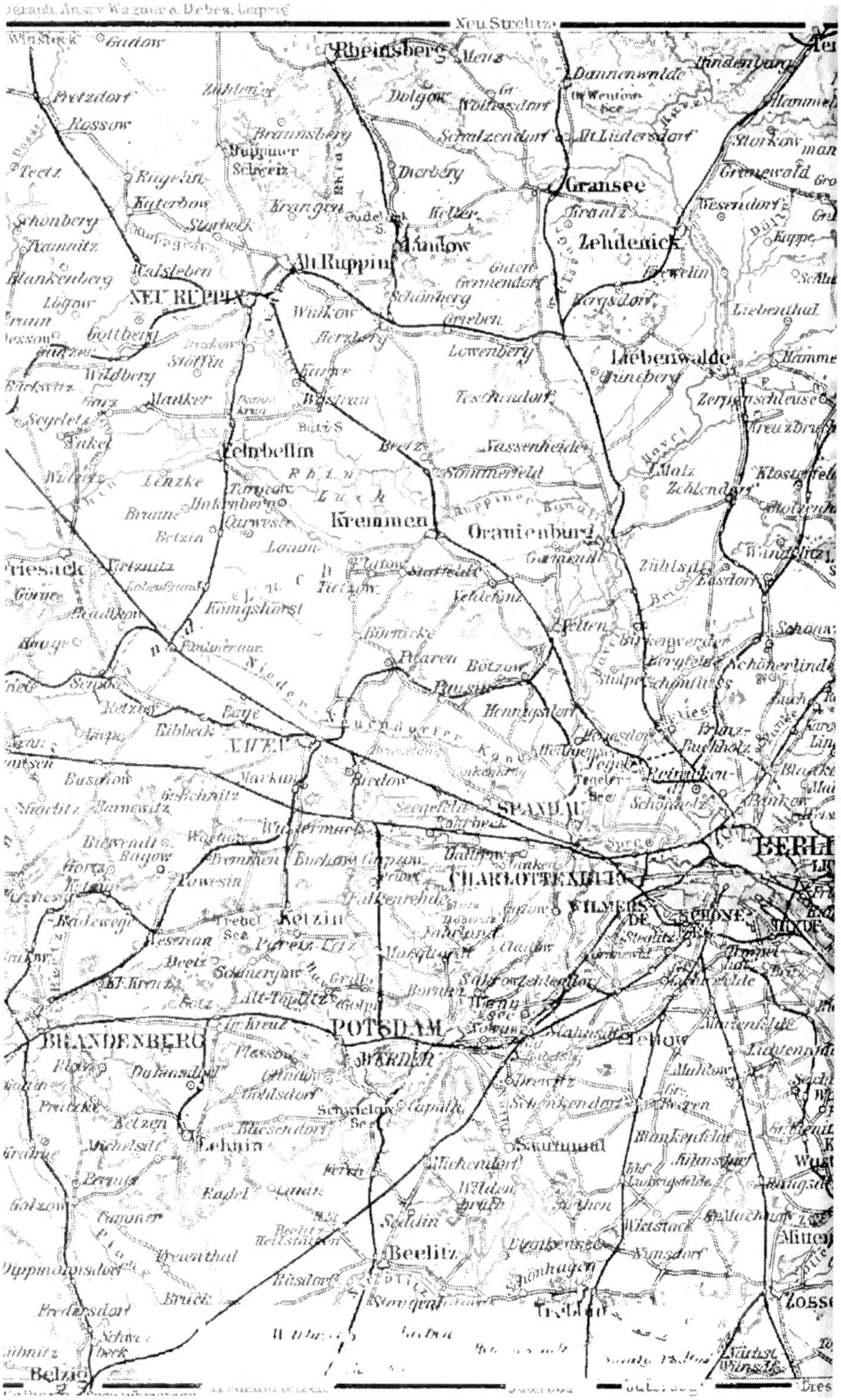

Wagner & Debes, Leipzig
Neu Strelitz
Rheinsberg
Gadow
Pretzdorf
Rossow
Dannenwalde
Dolgow
Braunsberg
Schulzendorf
Alt Lüdersdorf
Dierberg
Gransee
Storkow
Grüneweld
Teetz
Katerbow
Zernikow
Kranzin
Wesendorf
Zehdenick
Schönberg
Lindow
Walsleben
Alt Ruppin
NEU RUPPIN
Gutergermendorf
Bergsdorf
Wulkow
Grieben
Liebenthal
Gottberg
Herzberg
Löwenberg
Liebenwalde
Wildberg
Stöffin
Zernsschleuse
Segeletz
Teschendorf
Fehrbellin
Sommerfeld
Zehlendorf
Lenzke
Tarmow
Hakenberg
Kremmen
Oranienburg
Friesack
Königshorst
Velten
Paaren
Bötzow
Schönerlinde
Hennigsdorf
Ribbeck
NAUEN
Buchholz
Tegel
Seegefeld
SPANDAU
BERLIN
Bredow
Wustermark
Dallgow
CHARLOTTENBURG
Ketzin
Falkenrehde
WILMERSDORF
SCHÖNEBERG
Paretz
Marquardt
Fahrland
Gladow
Steglitz
Lichterfelde
Töplitz
Golm
Zehlendorf
POTSDAM
BRANDENBURG
WERDER
Teltow
Plessow
Glindow
Dreewitz
Lehnin
Saarmund
Blankenfelde
Kilmsdorf
Michendorf
Beelitz
Schönhagen
Trebbin
Zossen
Treuenbrietzen
Belzig
Dresden

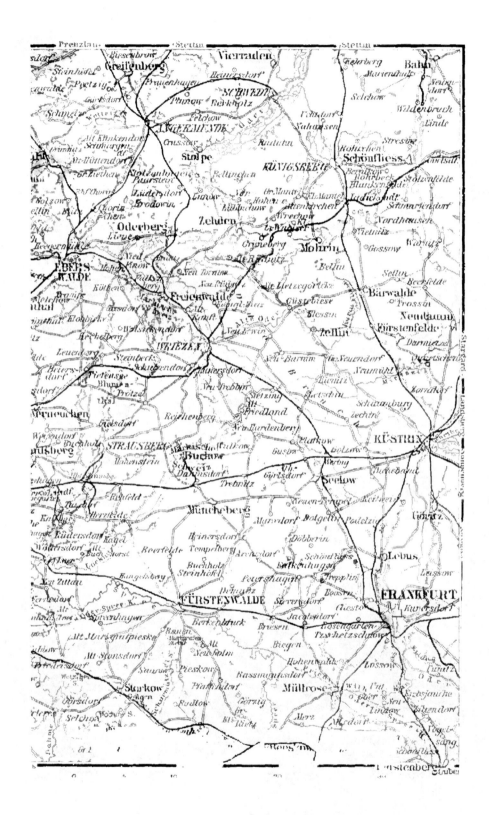

hohe and the *Ruinenberg* command beautiful views. A weak chaly-
beate spring, rising in the *Brunnental* (Brunnen-Hotel, Hôtel Bellevue), $^3/_4$ M. to the S of the town, was used by the Great Elector.
The *Restaurant zur Grünen Tanne*, a little farther to the S., is
the starting-point for pretty walks through the woods: to the *Baa-
See*, 1 hr.; to the *Bismarck-Turm* (Schweizerhaus Restaurant) and
Falkenberg (p. 204), $1^1/_4$ or 2 hrs.

CYCLING ROUTE. *From Bernau to Freienwalde* (viâ Liepnitz-See,
Biesenthal, Eberswalde), 36 M, a pleasant excursion through wood Start
from Bernau Station. — $^3/_1$ M from the *Mühlentor* (N), straight on. —
$2^1/_2$ M *Waldkater* (restaurant) — $6^1/_4$ M., at kilomètre-stone 32.1, digress-
ion to the right to Rest. Liepnitz — $7^1/_2$ M., near *Wandlitz Station*, to
the right, and at kilomètre-stone 30.7 again to the right. — $8^3/_4$ M.
Arendsee. — $11^1/_4$ M *Utzdorf.* — 13 M *Lanke.* — $15^1/_2$ M. *Biesenthal.* —
($17^1/_4$ M Biesenthal Station). To the left at kilomètre-stone 2.4. — $18^3/_4$ M.
Melchow — $22^1/_2$ M *Spechthausen* — $24^1/_4$ M *Gesundbrunnen.* — $25^1/_2$ M
Eberswalde (market-place), here to the right (Bicite-Str.). — 26 M., at
the crossing turn to the left. — $27^1/_2$ M. *Sommerfeld.* — $28^3/_4$ M. *Tornow.* —
$30^1/_2$ M. *Hohen-Finow.* — 32 M. *Falkenberg.* — 34 M. *Schweizerhaus*
(Bismarck-Turm). — 36 M. *Freienwalde.*

b BRANDENBURG Travellers who are interested in the mediæval
art of the Mark (of which there are comparatively few examples in
Berlin itself; comp. p. 52) should not fail to devote a day to Brandenburg. Railway in $1-1^1/_2$ hr. (fares 5 ℳ 30, 3 ℳ 50, 2 ℳ 20 pf., or
4 ℳ 80 pf., 3 ℳ, 1 ℳ 95 pf.) viâ *Potsdam* (p. 188), *Werder* (p 199),
and *Grosskreutz.* From the last a branch-line runs to (7 M.) *Lehnin*,
which has a monastic church of the 12-13th centuries (restored).

38 M. **Brandenburg** (*Schwarzer Bär*, Stein-Str., *Schwarzer
Adler*, St Annen-Str, both very fair; *Railway Restaurant*), a
town with 51,900 inhab., is divided by the Havel into an Old Town,
a New Town, and the Cathedral Island. Under the name of *Brenna-
bor* it was the chief town of the Slavonic Hevelli. It was captured
in 927 by King Henry I, and in 1150 by Albert the Bear, who
thenceforward styled himself Margrave of Brandenburg From 949
to 1544 the town was the seat of a bishop

From the railway-station (tramway) we proceed viâ the Schützen-
Str, the Annentor Bridge, and the St Annen-Str. to the ($^3/_4$ M.)
Rathaus, which dates from the 15th century. In front of the Rathaus stands a *Roland Column*, $16^1/_2$ ft. in height, the ancient
emblem among the Lower Saxons of free market rights — A little
to the W. is *St. CATHERINE's CHURCH, a handsome Gothic brick
edifice without transepts, of which the nave was built in 1381-1401,
the choir about 1410, and the W. tower in 1583-85. The carved
wooden altar (restored) dates from 1474; one of the N. chapels contains a brazen font of 1440 (sacristan, Katharinen-Kirch-Platz 4).
— From the Rathaus we proceed viâ the market-place and the
Mühlendamm to the —

*CATHEDRAL sacristan Zielgass og, on the S a Romanesque
columnar basilica of about 1200 converted in the 15th cent. into a

Gothic church with a vaulted roof, and frequently restored. On the walls of the interior are numerous tombstones. The choir contains an altar of 1518 and portions of another of 1375. The elaborately adorned columns and the excellent sculptures in the Romanesque crypt should be noticed. The S. transept contains a small museum.

We now cross the Grillendamm to the old town, in which the most interesting buildings are the *Gotthards-Kirche* (13-15th cent.) and the former *Altstadt Rathaus* (15th cent.).

The *Marienberg*, to the N.W. of the town, commands a good view (tower 98 ft. in height, erected in 1880 as a monument of victory from Stier's designs); tramway from the Rathaus to the Plauer Tor.

Amongst other towns of interest to the student of mediæval art in the Mark are *Stendal* and *Tangermünde*, *Chorin* (p. 204), *Königsberg in der Neumark*, and also *Havelberg* and *Lehnin* (p. 205). For details concerning these, and for farther details about Brandenburg see *Baedeker's Northern Germany*.

c. NEU-RUPPIN. — Railway in 3 hrs., either by the Hamburg line (17½ M.) or the Kremmen line (40½ M.). — By the Hamburg line to Spandau and (14 M.) *Finkenkrug*, see p. 206 (suburban service to Nauen, see p. 13). — 30½ M. *Paulinenaue*. A branch-line runs hence to Neu-Ruppin, via (40¼ M.) *Fehrbellin* (Deutsches Haus), 4½ M. to the N.W. of the village of *Hakenberg*, where the Great Elector defeated the Swedish in 1675. A column, 105 ft. in height, with a figure of Victory and a relief portrait of the Great Elector by A. Wolff, was erected here in 1879. View of the battlefield from the top. — 48 M. *Neu-Ruppin*, see below.

The Kremmen line starts from the Stettin Station (see p. 13). — As far as (8 M.) Tegel, see p. 204. — 15½ M. *Velten*, with numerous stove-factories. At (23 M.) *Kremmen* (2800 inhab.) we change carriages. — 33 M. *Radensleben* is the station for the village of *Wustrau*, situated 1¾ M. to the W., at the S.E. angle of the Ruppiner See (8 M. in length). *Hans Joachim von Zieten* (d. 1786), the well-known general of Frederick the Great, is buried in the church here. — The railway crosses the lake to —

40½ M. **Neu-Ruppin** (*Märkischer Hof*, R. 2-3, B. ³/₄, D. 1½ *M*; *Krone*, both in the Friedrich-Wilhelm-Strasse), a town with 18,600 inhabitants. About 4 min. from the station a statue of *Theodor Fontane*, the poet (1819-98), by Wiese, was unveiled in 1907. A *Monument to Fred. William II.*, by Tieck, commemorates that monarch's contribution towards rebuilding the town after a conflagration in 1787. Another monument, by Wiese, commemorates *Karl Fried. Schinkel* (1781-1841; p. 49), who was born here. On the lake stands the *Abbey Church*, a 13th cent. Gothic edifice of brick, restored by Schinkel. The so-called *Ruppin Switzerland*, a hilly district with beech-woods and several lakes, is one of the prettiest parts of the Mark. On sun. afternoons in summer (sometimes in the morning also) a steamboat plies to the forester's house of *Tornow* (rfmts.). Visits may be paid also to the forester's house of *Rottstiel*, to the *Bolten-Mühle* on the Tornow-See, and to *Binenwalde* on the Kalk-See

d. RHEINSBERG. Railway from the Stettin Station, 52 M. in 2½ hrs. (Nordbahn: suburban service as far as Oranienburg, comp. p. 13). — 4½ M *Reinickendorf-Rosenthal* Branch-line hence to Liebenwalde and Gross-Schönebeck (comp. Wandlitz, p. 204); Reinickendorf. see p. 201 — 8 M *Hermsdorf*, with 11,000 inhab. lies at the beginning of the wood which stretches hence far beyond Oranienburg and attracts many visitors. — 14 M. *Birkenwerder* (Boddensee Restaurant). About 1½ M. to the N E., near *Colony Briese* (restaurant) begins an imperial shooting-preserve.—18 M. **Oranienburg** (*Hôtel Eilers*, R from 2, B. ³/₄, D. 1½ ℳ), with 10,650 inhab., is situated on the *Havel*. A monument, by Fr. Wolff, in front of the château (now a normal school), commemorates *Princess Luise Henriette of Orange* (d. 1667), wife of the Great Elector, to whom the town owes its name. — From (28½ M.) *Löwenberg*, where we change carriages, we take a branch-line via (41½ M) *Lindow* to —

52 M. **Rheinsberg** (*Ratskeller: Kronprinz*, R 1½ ℳ), a town with 2600 inhab., situated at the efflux of the *Rhin* from the *Grinerick-See*. The château, purchased by Frederick William I in 1734, was the residence of Frederick the Great as crown-prince in 1736-40, a bronze statue of whom, by Elster, was erected here in 1903 From 1753 to 1802 it was occupied by Prince Henry, Frederick's brother. It has ceiling-paintings by Pesne and retains some memorials of its former owners: the sculptures in the park are in poor preservation. — The woods on the N , extending to the borders of Mecklenburg, include extensive stretches of deciduous trees and several large lakes Drives may be taken to the hamlets of *Zechlin*, *Zechliner Hütte*, and *Neu-Globsow*.

Cycling Routes. FROM BERLIN TO ORANIENBURG, 19½ M Rough paved road to Dalldorf; thence a mediocre road We start from the Schloss-Platz (prohibited streets, see p. 13) — 5¾ M. Lunatic asylum tof *Dalldorf* (p. 201). — 7 M. *Wittenau*. At kil. stone 11.8 (7¼ M), keep to he left — 9 M. *Hermsdorf* — 9¾ M *Glienicke*. — 13 M. *Stolpe-Hohen-Neuendorf* — 11¾ M. *Birkenwerder*. — 17 M *Havelhausen* — 19½ M. *Oranienburg*

FROM BERLIN TO RHEINSBERG, 52 M The road is good almost throughout. We start from the Schloss-Platz (prohibited streets, see p 13). — 4½ M *Tegeler Chaussée-Haus*, beyond which we keep straight on. - 7½ M *Tegel* — 9½ M. *Schulzendorf* — 12½ M. *Hennigsdorf* — 13¼ M. Cross the railway to the left — 17 M. *Marwitz*. — 19 M. *Eichstädt*. - 21 M. *Vehlefanz*. — 21¾ M *Schwante*. 25½ M *Kremmen* Turn to the right at the Rathaus. — 28¼ M *Sommerfeld*. — 29¾ M *Beetz*. — 31½ M. *Ruthenick* — 37 M. *Herzberg* — Beyond the village, at kil. stone 13 7, M M *Lindow* Here keep to tl M ½ M. *Heinrichs* M

e. Buckow. — Railway to (28¹/₂ M.) Dahmsdorf-Muncheberg in 1¹/₂ hr. from the Silesian Station (Ostbahn; suburban service as far as Strausberg, comp. p. 13). — 3 M. *Lichtenberg - Friedrichs-felde.* For Lichtenberg see p 168 Friedrichsfelde (with Karlshorst, p. 202) has 16,600 inhabitants. About 1 M. to the N E. of the station is the large public cemetery of Berlin (62 acres). — 5¹/₂ M. *Biesdorf* has a municipal hospital for epileptics. — At (10¹/₂ M) *Hoppegarten* is the chief race-course of Berlin (p. 30). — 14 M. *Fredersdorf* (branch-line to Rüdersdorf, see p. 202). — 17¹/₂ M. *Strausberg.*

Branch-line (3 M.) to the N. past a race-course to the town of **Strausberg** (7900 inhab ; Hôt. Stadtfeld, Restaurant Seebad, on the W. bank of the lake), which is pleasantly situated on the *Straus-See*, to the N. About 1¹/₂ M. to the N. of the town begins the *Blumen-Tal*, a somewhat lonely wood, intersected by two chains of lakelets. On its N.W. margin is *Tiefensee* (Spitzkrug), a station of the Wriezen railway (25 M from the Silesian Station).

28¹/₂ M. *Dahmsdorf-Muncheberg.*   A branch-line runs hence to (3 M.) —

Buckow *(Kronprinz; Bellevue,* R. 1¹/₂-2¹/₂ *M; Eck's Hôtel; Zentral-Hôtel),* with 2000 inhab , a favourite summer-resort. The pleasant lakes and well-wooded, picturesque hills of the neighbourhood have earned for it the title of the **Märkish Switzerland (Märkische Schweiz);* comp p. 204 Among the most picturesque points, to the N. of Buckow, are the *Bollersdorfer Höhe* (269 ft.; rfmts.), ¹/₂ hr to the N , above the *Schermutzel-See,* the *Silberkehle,* the two *Tornow Lakes,* and the *Pritzhagener Mühle* (restaurant).

Cycling Route. From Berlin to Buckow, 39 M. This is an attractive route, the road is good, though hilly; the first 5¹/₂ M. are paved. Start from the Alexander-Platz (prohibited streets, see p. 43) — 4¹/₃ M. *Friedrichsberg - Lichtenberg* — 5¹/₂ *Friedrichsfelde* — 7 M *Biesdorf* - 8 M. *Kaulsdorf* — 9¹/₂ M. *Malsdorf.* — 10³/₄ M. *Dahlwitz* (to the left, road to Hoppegarten). — 14¹/₂ M. *Vogelsdorf* — 17 M. *Tasdorf* (digression to the Rüdersdorfer Kalkberge). — 20 M *Herzfelde.* — 21³/₄ M *Lichtenow.* — 26¹/₄ M *Wilder Mann Inn* — 32 M. *Muncheberg* Then to the left via (36¹/₂ M) *Dahmsdorf* to (39 M) *Buckow.*

Return-route: 1¹/₄ M. *Bollersdorf.* — 3³/₄ M. *Ruhlsdorf.* — 8³/₄ M. *Strausberg.* Then keep to the right to (16¹/₂ M.) *Alt-Landsberg* — 19 M. *Seeberg.* — 21 M *Hönow.* — 24¹/₂ M. *Marzahn* — 31¹/₂ M. Berlin (Alexander-Platz).

f The **Spreewald,* 37 M. long and from ¹/₂ M. to 4¹/₂ M. broad, is watered by the Spree, which intersects it in a network of about 200 channels It is reached from Berlin by the Görlitz railway.

In natural beauty the *Lower Spreewald,* below Lübben, has the advantage in virtue of the wide expanses of deciduous trees that still cover part of it. In the *Upper Spreewald* no woods of any size are to be found except in the N.; the W. is a region of flat pasture-land, while the S.E. (Burg), which is tolerably well populated and has nearly all been brought under the plough, has more the general appearance of a well-wooded park Nursery gardening, cattle rearing, and fishing are the principal industries of the Wendish population, which has here retained its original language and customs. The women still wear a peculiar costume. The villages of Lehde and Leipe, in the pastoral region, are

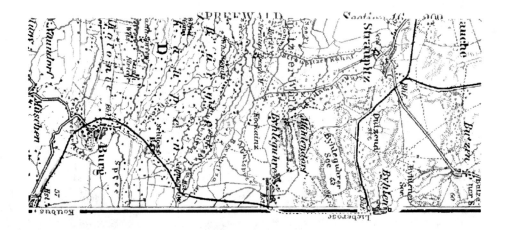

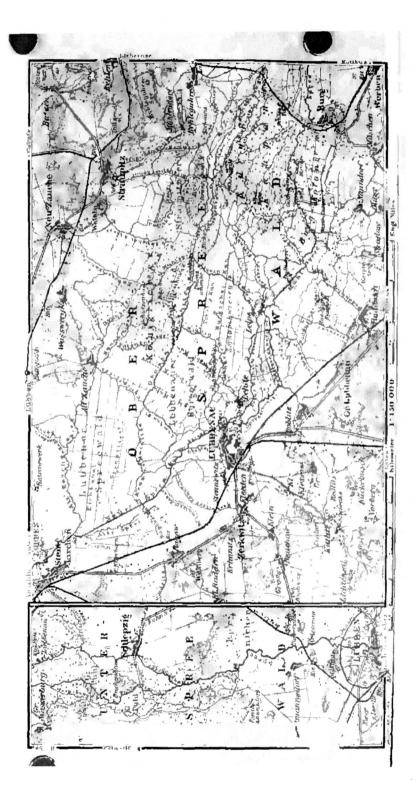

accessible only by water, or in winter over the ice. In the farming
district of Burg the widely scattered wooden houses may be reached on
foot, but many water-channels have to be crossed by curiously built
bridges. — A visit to the Spreewald is most conveniently made in May
or September. In summer the gnats are very troublesome.

RAILWAY TO LÜBBEN, 46½ M., in 1¾ hr. — To (17½ M.) *Königs-
Wusterhausen*, see p. 202.

46½ M. **Lübben** (*Stadt Berlin*, R. 1½-2½, D. 1½-2 *M*;
Goldener Stern, both very fair), an old town with 7200 inhab., is
surrounded by four arms of the *Spree*. Paul Gerhardt (p. 148), who
was archdeacon from 1668, died here in 1676 and is buried in the
parish-church, in front of which a monument, by Pfannschmidt,
was erected to him in 1907. Between the station and the (1 M.)
town, we pass an attractive grove with a bronze statue of Minister
von Mantenffel (d. 1882), unveiled in 1908.

Lübben is the best starting-point for an excursion in the LOWER
SPREEWALD. The most convenient plan is to proceed from Lübben
by boat (ample notice to the boatman should be given at the hotel)
viâ *Schlepzig* (Gottlieb's Hôtel zum Unterspreewald, R. 1-2, pens.
3-4 *M*) to the *Puhl* and *Gross-Wasserburg*, although by this
route the woods are not reached until 2 hrs. after starting. An
alternative plan is to drive to Schlepzig (1½ hr.; 5-7 *M*) and thence
take a boat. — From Gross-Wasserburg (inn) we may either return
by boat through the woods to the landing-place of *Hartmanns-
dorf*, and walk thence viâ this village to the (1½ hr.) station of
Lübben; or we may proceed by rail from the station of Hartmanns-
dorf, 1½ M. from the landing-place.

Those bound for the UPPER SPREEWALD go on by railway beyond
Lübben to (53½ M.) **Lübbenau** (*Brauner Hirsch, Deutsches
Haus*, both in the market-place; in summer rooms should be secured
beforehand), a little town with 3800 inhab. and a château and park
of Count Lynar. The boatmen of the Spreewald Society may be found
stationed at the E. end of the town (1 M. from the station) or may
be enquired for at the hotels. Tariff 60 pf. per hr. besides a retain-
ing-fee of 1 *M*, and 60 pf. more for every hour; if the boatman is
dismissed at Burg, 2 *M* 40 are due for his return-journey. The
usual boating-trip from Lübbenau (6 hrs., not incl. halts; fatiguing)
is that viâ *Lehde* (see below), the *Wotschofska Restaurant* (also
R., good), the forester's houses of *Kannomühle* and *Eiche* (small
restaurant near) situated in the woods, and then viâ the *Polenz-
Schenke Restaurant* and *Leipe* (inn) back to Lübbenau. — An idea
of the curious residential and domestic arrangements of the Spreewald may, however, be obtained by a trip (1 *M*) from Lübbenau
viâ the *Lübbenauer Kaupen* to the (½ hr.) village of *Lehde* (Inn
zum Fröhlichen Hecht, with an annexe for tourists. 36 R. at 1¾-
2¼, B. ¾ *M* the *Venice of the Spreewald*). An interesting
spectacle is offered on Sun. by the gay costumes of the Spreewald

women on their way to church at the village of **Burg** (*Inn zum Spreewald*, R. 1¹/₂, D. 1¹/₂-2 *M*, very fair, *Zur Bleiche*, both on the Muhlspree, respectively 50 and 30 min. from the village; *Schwarzer Adler, Koch*, both in the village) Intending spectators should leave Berlin on Sat. and take the Spreewald Railway (Cottbus branch-line) from Lubben to Burg (spend night) On they may on Sun. at an early hour proceed by boat viâ Leipe to Burg After the midday meal, they may take a boat from Burg viâ the forester's houses of Eiche, Kannomühle, etc. (the route mentioned on p. 209 in the reverse direction) to Lübbenau, and return to Berlin by an evening train.

List

of the more important German Architects, Painters, and Sculptors
of the 18th and 19th centuries, mentioned in the Handbook

Achenbach, Andreas. P., b. 1815 at Cassel

Achenbach, Oswald, P., brother of the preceding, 1827-1905, Düsseldorf

Achtermann, Wilhelm, S., b. 1799 at Münster, d. 1884 at Rome

Adam, Franz, P., b. 1815 at Milan, d. 1886 at Munich.

Adler, Friedrich, A., b. 1827 at Berlin.

Angeli, Heinrich von, P., b. 1840 at Ödenburg (Hungary)

Baisch, Hermann, P., b. 1846 at Dresden, d. 1894 at Carlsruhe

Bantzer, Karl, P., b. 1857 at Ziegenhain (Hesse)

Bartels, Hans von, P., b. 1856 at Hamburg.

Baucke, Heinrich, S., b. 1875 at Düsseldorf.

Baumbach, Max, S., b. 1859 at Wurzen.

Becker, Karl, P., 1820-1900, Berlin.

Begas, Adalbert, son of Karl B. the Elder, b. 1836 at Berlin, d. 1888 at Nervi.

Begas, Karl, the Elder, P., b. 1791 at Heinsberg, d. 1854 at Berlin.

Begas, Karl, the Younger, youngest son of the preceding, S., b. 1845 at Berlin.

Begas, Oskar, eldest son of Karl B. the Elder, P., 1828-83, Berlin.

Begas, Reinhold, son of Karl B the Elder, S., b 1831 at Berlin

Behrens, Christian, S., b. 1852 at Gotha

Benda, Julius, A., b 1838 at Rauden.

Bendemann, Eduard, P., b 1811 at Berlin, d. 1889 at Düsseldorf.

Biermann, Eduard, P., 1803-92, Berlin

Blaser, Gustav, S. b. 1813 at Düsseldorf, d. 1874 at Cannstatt

Blechen, Karl, P., b. 1798 at Cottbus, d. 1840 at Berlin.

Bleibtreu, Georg, P., b. 1828 at Xanten, d. 1892 at Berlin.

Bochmann, Gregor von, P., b 1850 in Esthonia.

Böcklin, Arnold, P., b 1827 at Bâle, d. 1901 at Fiesole, near Florence.

Boeckmann, Wilhelm, A., b. 1832 at Elberfeld, d. 1902 at Charlottenburg.

Boetticher, Karl, A., b 1806 at Nordhausen d. 1889 at Berlin

Bokelmann, Christ Ludw., P., b 1844 near Bremen, d. 1894 at Berlin

Boumann, Johannes, A., b 1706 at Amsterdam, d. 1776 at Potsdam

Bracht, Eugen, P., b 1842 at Morges on the Lake of Geneva

Braith, Anton, P., b. 1836 at Biberach

Brendel, Albert, P., b. 1827 at Berlin, d 1895 at Weimar

Brunow, Ludwig, S., b 1843 at Lutheran near Lubz (Mecklenburg-Schwerin)

Brütt, Adolf, S., b. 1855 at Kiel

Burger, Ludwig, P., b. 1825 at Cracow, d 1884 at Berlin

Buring, Johann Gottfried, A., b 1723 at Berlin.

Burkel, Heinrich, P., b. 1802 at Pirmasens, d. 1869 at Munich.

Burnitz, Karl Peter, P., 1824-86, Frankfort on the Main

Busch, Georg, S., b. 1862 at Hanau

Calandrelli, Al., S., 1831-1903, Berlin.

Camphausen, Wilhelm, P., 1818-85, Düsseldorf.

Cantian, A., 1794-1866, Berlin

Carstens, Asmus Jakob, P., b 1754 near Schleswig, d 1798 at Rome.

Cauer, Karl, S., b. 1828 at Bonn, d. 1885 at Kreuznach

Cauer, Ludwig, S., son of the preceding, b. 1866 at Kreuznach

Cornelius, Peter von, P. geb. ... ... Düsseldorf, ... 1867 at Berlin

Corinth, Louis, P., b 1858 at Tapiau

Cornelius, Peter von, P., b. 1783 at Düsseldorf, d. 1867 at Berlin

Cremer, Friedrich Albert, A., b 1824 at Wiesbaden, d. 1882.

Crola, Hugo, P., b 1841 at Ilsenburg.

Dahl, Joh, P., b 1788 at Bergen (Norway), d. 1857 at Dresden

Darnaut, Hugo, P., b. 1850 at Dessau

Defregger, Franz, P., b 1835 at Stronach in the Pusterthal

Dettmann, L, P., b. 1865 at Flensburg.

Diez, Robert, S., b 1844 at Possneck (Saxe-Meiningen)

Diez, Wilhelm von, P., b. 1839 at Bayreuth

Dill, Ludwig, P., b 1848 at Gernsbach.

Donndorf, Adolf, S., b 1835 at Weimar.

Doepler, Karl Emil, P., b. 1824 at Schnepfenthal

Drake, Friedrich, S., b. 1805 at Pyrmont, d. 1882 at Berlin.

Dreber, Heinrich, known as *Franz D.*, P., b. 1822 at Dresden, d 1875 at Rome.

Ducker, Eugen, P., b 1841 at Arensburg (Ösel Island).

Ebe, Gustav, A., b. 1834 at Halberstadt

Eberlein, Gustav, S., b 1847 at Spiekershausen near Münden.

Echtermeier, Karl, S., b. 1845 at Cassel

Eckmann, Otto, P., b 1865 at Hamburg, d 1902 at Badenweiler

Encke, Erdmann, S., b 1843 at Berlin, d. 1896 at Neu-Babelsberg.

Ende, Hermann, A., 1830-1907, Berlin

Engelhard, Friedrich Wilhelm, S., b 1813 at Grünhagen near Lüneburg, d 1902 at Hanover.

Enhuber, Karl von, P., b. 1811 at Hof (Oberfranken), d. 1867 at Munich.

Erdmannsdorf, Friedr. Wilh von, A., b. 1736 at Dresden, d. 1795 at Dessau

Ewald, Ernst, P., 1836-84, Berlin.

Fechner, Hans, P., b 1860 at Berlin.

Feuerbach, Anselm, P., b. 1829 at Speyer, d. 1880 at Venice.

Firle, Walther, P., b 1859 at Breslau

Fischer, Ferdinand August, S., and medallist, b 1805 at Berlin d 1866

Flamm, Albert, P., 1823-1906, Düsseldorf.

Flickel, Paul, P., 1852-1903, Berlin.

Franz, Julius, S., 1824-87, Berlin

Frenzel, Oskar, P., b. 1855 at Berlin

Friedrich, Kaspar David, P., 1774-1840, Dresden

Friedrich, Woldemar, P., b 1846 at Gnadau, near Magdeburg.

Friese, Richard, P., b 1854 at Gumbinnen.

Führich, Joseph von, P., b. 1800 at Kratzau in Bohemia, d 1876 at Vienna.

Gärtner, Eduard, P., 1801-77, Berlin

Gaul, August, S., b. 1867 at Gross-Auheim near Hanau

Gebhardt, Eduard von, P., b. 1838 at St. Johann (Esthonia).

Geiger, Nikolaus, S., b. 1849 at Lauingen, d. 1897 at Wilmersdorf.

Genelli, Bonaventura, P., b. 1798 at Berlin, d 1868 at Weimar.

Gentz, Heinrich, A., d. 1811 at Berlin

Gentz, Wilhelm, P., b 1822 at Neuruppin, d. 1890 at Berlin

Gerlach, Philipp, A., b. 1679 at Spandau, d. 1718 at Berlin.

Geselschap, Friedrich, P., b. 1835 at Wesel, d. 1898 at Rome.

Geyer, Otto, S., b. 1843 at Charlottenburg

Geyger, Ernst Moritz, S., b. 1861 at Rixdorf.

Gilly, Friedrich, A., b. 1717 at Altdamm, d 1800 at Carlsbad

Gleichen-Russwurm, Ludwig von, P., b. 1836 at Greifenstein in Bavaria, d. 1901 at Weimar

Gontard, Karl von, A., b 1731 at Mannheim, d. 1791 at Berlin.

Gosen, Phil. Theodor von, S., b. 1873 at Augsburg.

Götz, Johannes, S., b 1865 at Fürth

Graeb, Karl, P., 1816-84, Berlin.

Graeb, Paul, P., son of the preceding, 1842-92, Berlin.

Graef, Gustav, P., b. 1821 at Königsberg, d 1895 at Berlin.

Grael, Johann Friedr., A., b. 1708 at Quichtz (Silesia), d. 1740 at Bayreuth.

Graff, Anton, P., b. 1736 at Winterthur, d. 1813 at Dresden.

Gropius, Martin Karl Philipp, A., 1824-80, Berlin.

Groszheim, Karl von, A., b. 1841 at Lübeck.

Gude, Hans, P., b 1825 at Christiania. d 1903 at Berlin.

Gussow, Karl, P., b. 1843 at Havelberg.

Habermann, Hugo von, P., b. 1849 at Dillingen.

Hähnel, Ernst, S., 1811-91, Dresden.

Hagen, Hugo, S., d. 1871 at Berlin.

Haider, Karl, P., b. 1846 at Munich.

Harrach, Count Ferdinand, P., b. 1832 at Rosnochau (Silesia)

Hartzer, Karl Ferd., S., 1838-1906, Berlin.

Hasenclever, Johann Peter, P., b 1810 at Remscheid, d 1853 at Düsseldorf.

Hasenpflug, Karl, P., b 1802 at Berlin, d 1858 at Halberstadt

Haug, Robert, P., b 1857 at Stuttgart.

Hausmann, Karl, P., 1825-86, Hanau.

Henneberg, Rudolf, P., 1825-76, Brunswick.

Hennicke, Julius, A., b 1832, d. 1892 at Constance.

Hensel, Wilhelm, P., b. 1794 at Trebbin, d 1861 at Berlin.

Henseler, Ernst, P., b. 1852 at Meseritz.

Hermann, Karl Heinrich, P., b 1802 at Dresden, d 1880 at Berlin

Herrmann, Hans, P., b 1858 at Berlin.

Hertel, Albert, P., b 1843 at Berlin.

Hertel, Karl, P., b. 1837 at Breslau, d. 1895 at Düsseldorf.

Herter, Ernst, S., b 1846 at Berlin.

Hess, Peter von, P., b 1792 at Düsseldorf, d. 1871 at Munich.

Heuss, Eduard von, P., b 1808 at Oggersheim, d. 1880 near Mayence

Heyden, August von, P., b 1827 at Breslau, d 1897 at Berlin

Heyden, Otto, P., b. 1820 at Ducherow (Pom.), d. 1897 at Göttingen.

Hildebrand, Adolf, S., b 1847 at Marburg

Hildebrand, Ernst, P., b. 1833 at Falkenberg (Lower Lusatia)

Hildebrand, Theodor, P., b 1804 at Stettin, d 1874 at Düsseldorf

Hildebrandt, Eduard, P., b. 1818 at Dantsic, d. 1868 at Berlin.

Hildebrandt, Fritz, P., brother of the preceding, b 1819 at Dantsic, d. 1885 at Rome

Hilgers, Karl, S., b 1844 at Düsseldorf.

Hilgers, h . . . . dorf.

Hitz, Dora, P., b 1856 at Altdorf near Nuremberg

Hitzig, Friedrich, A., 1811-81, Berlin.

Hoffmann, Ludwig, A., b 1853 at Darmstadt

Hoffmeister, Heinz, S., b. 1851 at Saarlouis, d 1894 at Berlin.

Hofmann, Ludwig von, P., b 1861 at Darmstadt

Hoguet, Charles, P., 1821-70, Berlin

Hösel, Erich, S., b 1869 at Augsburg

Hosemann, Theodor, P., b 1807 at Brandenburg, d. 1875 at Berlin.

Hübner, Julius, P., b 1806 at Oels, d. 1882 at Loschwitz near Dresden.

Hübner, Karl, P., b. 1814 at Königsberg, d. 1879 at Düsseldorf

Hude, Hermann Philipp Wilhelm von der, A., b 1830 at Lübeck

Hundrieser, Emil, S., b 1846 at Königsberg

Hunten, Emil, P., b. 1827 at Paris, d. 1902 at Düsseldorf.

Ihne, Ernst Eberhard von, A., b 1848 at Elberfeld.

Jacob, Julius, P., b 1842 at Berlin.

Janensch, Gerhard, S., b 1860 at Zamborst in Pomerania.

Janssen, Karl, S., b 1853 at Düsseldorf

——, Peter, P., 1814-1908, Düsseldorf.

Jernberg, Olaf, P., b. 1855 at Düsseldorf.

Jordan, Rudolf, P., b. 1810 at Berlin, d. 1887 at Düsseldorf

Kaffsack, Jos., S., b 1849 at Ratisbon, d. 1891 at Berlin.

Kalckreuth, Count Stanislaus, P., b. 1821 at Koschmin, d 1894 at Munich.

——, Count Leopold, son of the preceding, P., b. 1855 at Düsseldorf

Kalide, Theodor, S., b 1801 at Königshütte, d 1863 at Gleiwitz

Kallmorgen, Friedrich, P., b 1856 at Altona.

Kameke, Otto von, P., b. 1826 at Stolp, d. 1899 at Berlin.

Kampf, Arthur, P., b. 1864 at Aix-la-Chapelle.

——, Eugen, P., b 1860 at Aix-la-Chapelle.

Kaulbach, Wilhelm von, P., b 1805 at Arolsen, d. 1874 at Munich.

Kayser, Heinrich, A., b. 1842 at Duisburg.

K . . K . . . . W . . baden,
b 1842
. . . .

Kiss, August, S., b. 1802 in Upper Silesia, d 1865 at Berlin.

Klimsch, Fritz, S , b 1870 at Frankfort

Klinger, Max, S. and P , b. 1857 at Leipsic

Kloeber, August von, P , b. 1793 at Breslau, d. 1864 at Berlin.

Knackfuss, Hermann Wilhelm Johann, P., b 1848 at Wissen near Siegburg

Knaus, Ludwig, P , b. 1829 at Wiesbaden.

Knille, Otto, P., b. 1832 at Osnabruck, d 1898 at Meran.

Knobelsdorff, Georg Wenzeslaus von, A & P, b 1699 at Kuckadel (Lusatia), d. 1753 at Berlin

Knoblauch, Eduard, A., b 1801, d 1865 at Berlin

Kobell, Wilhelm von, P , 1766-1855, Munich.

Koch, Georg Karl, P., b. 1857 at Berlin

Koch, Joseph Anton, P., b. 1768 in the Tyrol, d. 1839 at Rome.

Kokolski, Hermann, S, b. 1853 at Berlin.

Kolitz, Louis, P , b 1845 at Tilsit

Koner, Max, P., 1854-1900, Berlin

Kopf, Joseph von, S., b. 1827 at Unlingen, d. 1903 at Rome,

Kraus, August, S , b 1868 at Ruhrort

Kroner, Christian, P., b 1838 at Rinteln.

Kruger, Franz, P., b.1797 at Radegast near Cothen, d. 1857 at Berlin.

Kruse, Max, S , b 1854 at Berlin.

Kuehl, Gotthardt, P , b 1851 at Lubeck

Kuntz, Gustav, P , b. 1843 at Wildenfels (Saxony), d.1879 at Rome

Kyllmann, Walther, A., b. 1837 at Weyer near Wald

Langhans, Karl Ferdinand, A., b. 1781 at Breslau, d. 1869 at Berlin

—, *Karl Gotthard*, A , father of the preceding, b 1733 at Landeshut (Silesia), d 1808 at Gruneiche.

Lederer, Hugo, S , b 1871 at Znaim

Leibl, Wilhelm, P., b. 1844 at Cologne, d. 1900 at Wurzburg.

Leistikow, Walter, P , b. 1865 at Bromberg.

Lenbach, Franz von, P., b. 1836 at Schrobenhausen d. 1904 at Munich

Lepsius, Reinhold, P, b. 1857 at Berlin

Lessing, Karl Friedrich, P., b. 1808 at Breslau, d. 1880 at Carlsruhe.

—, *Konrad*, P., son of the preceding, b 1852 at Dusseldorf.

—, *Otto*, P. & S, son of Karl Friedrich L , b 1846 at Dusseldorf

Liebermann, Max, P., b. 1849 at Berlin.

Lier, Adolf, P , b 1826 at Herrnhut, d 1882 at Vahrn near Brixen

Lucae, Richard, A . 1829-77, Berlin

Ludwig, Karl, P., b 1839 at Rombild, d. 1901 at Berlin

Lugo, Emil, P., b. 1840 at Stockach, d. 1902 at Munich.

Lurssen, Eduard August, S., b.1840 at Kiel, d 1891 at Berlin.

Magnus, Ed., P., 1799-1872, Berlin.

Magnussen, Harro, S , b. 1861 at Hamm near Hamburg.

Maison, Rudolph, S , b 1851 at Ratisbon, d 1901 at Munich.

Makart, Hans, P., b 1840 at Salzburg, d 1884 at Vienna.

Manthe, Albert August Karl, S., b. 1847 at Angermunde.

Manzel, Ludwig, S , b 1858 at Kagendorf.

March, Otto, A , b 1845 at Charlottenburg-Berlin.

Marees, Hans von, P., b. 1837 at Elberfeld, d. 1887 at Rome.

Martersteig, Friedrich P., 1811-99, Weimar.

Max, Gabriel, P., b. 1840 at Prague

Mayer, Eduard, S., b. 1812 near Treves, d. 1881.

Mengs, Rafael, P , b 1728 at Aussig, d 1779 at Rome

Menzel, Adolf von, P., b. 1815 at Breslau, d. 1905 at Berlin.

Messel, Alfred, A., b. 1853 at Darmstadt.

Meurer, Moritz, P , b 1839 at Waldenburg (Saxony).

Meyer, Johann Georg (known as *Meyer von Bremen*), P., b. 1813 at Bremen, d 1886 at Berlin.

Meyer, Klaus, P , b. 1856 near Hanover.

Meyerheim, Eduard, P , b. 1808 at Dantsic, d. 1879 at Berlin.

Meyerheim, Paul, P., son of the preceding, b 1842 at Berlin.

Möckel, Gotthilf Ludwig, A., b. 1838 at Zwickau

Möller, Karl, S , b 1803 at Berlin, d. 1882

Moser, Julius, S., b. 1832 at Berlin.

Mucke, Heinrich P b. 1806 at Breslau, d. 1891 at Dusseldorf.

Muhlenbruch, J., P., b. 1856 at Trutzlatz (Pomerania).

Muller, Eduard, S., b. 1828 at Hildburghausen, d. 1895 at Rome.

—, *Viktor, P.,* 1829-79, Munich

Munthe, Ludwig, P., b. 1841 at Aaroen (Norway), d. 1896 at Düsseldorf

Neumann, Richard Gustav, S. & P., b. 1848 at Berlin.

Noster, Ludwig, P., b. 1859 at Friedeberg (Neumark).

Oeder, Georg, P., b. 1846 at Aix-la-Chapelle.

Olde, Hans, P., b. 1855 at Süderau (Holstein).

Orth, August A., b. 1828 at Windhausen near Seesen (Brunswick)

Ottmer, Karl Theodor, A. & P., b. 1800 at Brunswick, d. 1843 at Berlin.

Otto, Paul, S., 1816-93, Berlin

Otzen, Johannes, A., b. 1839 at Siesebye (Schleswig).

Overbeck, Friedrich, P., b. 1789 at Lübeck, d. 1869 at Rome.

Pankok, Bernhard, P., b. 1872 at Munster

Panzner, Georg Otto, S., b. 1853 at Konigstein (Saxony)

Persius, Ludwig, A., b. 1804 at Berlin, d. 1845 at Rome

Pettenkofen, August von, P., 1821-1889 Vienna.

Pfannschmidt, Friedrich Johann, S., b. 1864 at Berlin

—, *Gottfried, P.,* b. 1819 at Mühlhausen, d. 1887 at Berlin

Pfuhl, Johannes, S., b. 1846 at Lowenburg (Silesia).

Philippi, Peter, P., b. 1866 at Treves

Piglhein, Bruno, P., b. 1848 at Hamburg, d. 1894 at Munich

Piloty, Karl Theodor von, P., b. 1826 at Munich, d. 1886 at Ambach.

Piper, Carl, S., b. 1856 at Stettin.

Plockhorst, Bernhard, P., b. 1825 at Brunswick, d. 1907 at Berlin.

Pohle, Leon, P., b. 1819 at Leipsic, d. 1908 at Dresden

Pohlmann, Heinrich, S., b. 1839 at Scheventorf (Hanover)

Poppelmann, Peter, S., b. 1866 at Harsewinkel (Westphalia).

Prell, Hermann, P. and S., b. 1854 at Leipsic

Preller, Friedrich, the Elder, P., b. 1804 at Eisenach, d. 1878 at Weimar.

Preyer, Joh. . . . . at Rheyd . . . .

Rahl, Karl, P., 1812-65, Vienna.

Raschdorff, Julius, A., b. 1823 at Pless

Rau, Leopold, S., b. 1847 at Nuremberg, d. 1880 at Rome.

Rauch, Christian Daniel, S., b. 1777 at Arolsen, d. 1857 at Dresden.

Rayski, Ferdinand von, P., b. 1806 at Pegau, d. 1890 at Dresden

Rethel, Alfred, P., b. 1816 near Aix-la-Chapelle, d. 1859 at Düsseldorf.

Rheinhold, Hugo, S., b. 1853 at Oberlahnstein, d. 1900 at Berlin.

Richter, Gustav, P., 1823-84, Berlin

Richter, Ludwig, P., 1803-84, Dresden

Riedel, August, P., b. 1799 at Bayreuth, d. 1883 at Rome.

Riefstahl, Wilh., P., b. 1827 at Neustrelitz, d. 1888 at Munich

Rietschel, Ernst, S., b. 1804 at Pulsnitz, d. 1861 at Dresden

Rietschel, Ernst Wilhelm, P., 1821-1860, Munich

Ritter, Henry, P., b. 1816 at Montreal (Canada), d. 1853 at Düsseldorf

Rober, Ernst, P., b. 1849 at Elberfeld

—, *Fritz, P.,* brother of the preceding, b. 1851 at Elberfeld.

Rochling, Karl, P., b. 1855 at Saarbrucken

Rode, Christian Bernhard, P. & etcher, 1725-97, Berlin.

Romer, Bernhard, S., b. 1852 at Gross-Strehlitz (Silesia), d. 1891

Rottmann, Karl, P., b. 1798 near Heidelberg, d. 1850 at Munich

Rumann, W. von, S., b. 1850 at Hanover, d. 1906 at Ajaccio.

Ruths, Valentin, P., 1825-1905, Hamburg

Saltzmann, Carl, P., b. 1847 at Berlin.

Salzenberg, Wilhelm, A., b. 1803, d. 1887 at Montreux.

Sattler, Joseph, P., b. 1867 at Schrobenhausen (Bavaria).

Schadow, Gottfried, S., 1764-1850, Berlin.

—, *Wilhelm von, P.,* son of the preceding, b. 1789 at Berlin, d. 1862 at Düsseldorf.

Schafer, Karl, A., b. 1844 at Cassel

Schuller, E. Johann, P., b. 1844 at Wasungen, d. 1887 at Coburg.

Schaper, Friedrich, S., b. 1841 at Alsleben on the Saale

Schennis, Friedrich von, P., b. 1852 at Elberfeld

Scheuren, Kaspar, P., b 1810 at Aix-la-Chapelle, d. 1887 at Düsseldorf

Scheurenberg, Josef, P , b 1846 at Düsseldorf.

Schick, Rudolf, P., 1840-87, Berlin

Schievelbein, Hermann, S , 1817-67, Berlin.

Schindler, Emil, P . b 1842 at Vienna, d. 1892 at Sylt.

Schinkel, Karl Friedrich, A. & P., b. 1781 at Neuruppin, d. 1841 at Berlin

Schirmer, August Wilhelm, P , b. 1802 at Berlin, d. 1866 at Nyon.

, Johann Wilhelm, P., b 1807 at Jülich, d. 1863 at Carlsruhe.

Schleich, Eduard, the Elder, P., b 1812 at Harbach (Bavaria), d.1874 at Munich.

Schlüter, Andreas, A. & S., b. 1664 at Hamburg, d. 1714 at St. Petersburg.

, Karl, S., b. 1816 at Pinneberg, d 1884 at Dresden

Schmitson, Teutwart, P, b. 1830 at Frankfort-on-the-Main, d. 1863 at Vienna

Schnorr von Carolsfeld, Julius, P, b 1794 at Leipsic, d 1872 at Dresden

Scholl, Anton, S., b. 1837 at Mayence.

Scholtz, Julius, P., b 1825 at Breslau, d. 1893 at Dresden.

Schonleber, Gustav, P., b. 1851 at Bietigheim (Wurtemberg)

Schott, Walter, S., b 1861 at Ilsenburg.

Schrader, Julius, P , 1815-1900, Berlin

Schreyer, Adolf, P , b 1828 at Frankfort-on-the-Main, d 1899 at Cronberg

Schrödter, Adolf, P., b. 1805 at Schwedt, d 1875 at Carlsruhe.

Schuch, Karl, P , 1846-1903, Vienna

—, Werner, P.. b. 1843 at Hildesheim

Schuler, Karl, S , b. 1847 at Nuremberg, d. 1886 at Berlin.

Schulz, Moritz, S , b 1825 at Leobschütz, d. 1904 at Berlin

Schwechten, Franz Heinrich, A , b. 1841 at Cologne.

Schwenitz, Rudolf, S., 1839-96, Charlottenburg (Berlin)

Schwind, Moritz von P., b 1804 at Vienna, d. 1871 at Munich

Sehring, Bernhard, A , b 1855 at Adderitz.

Seidl, Gabriel, A , b. 1848 at Munich

Seitz, Rudolf, P., b 1842 at Munich

Siemering, Rudolf, S., b 1835 at Königsberg, d 1905 at Berlin.

Simm, Franz, P., b. 1853 at Vienna.

Simmler, Wilhelm Carl Melchior, P , b. 1840 at Geisenheim.

Skarbina, Franz, P , b.1849 at Berlin.

Sohn, Karl, the Elder, P , b. 1805 at Berlin, d. 1867 at Cologne

Soller, August, A., b. 1805 at Erfurt, d. 1853

Sommer, August, S., b. 1839 at Coburg.

Spangenberg, Gustav, P., b 1828 at Hamburg, d. 1891 at Berlin.

Sperl, Johann, P , b 1840 at Buch (Bavaria)

Spieker, Paul, A., b 1826 at Trarbach, d before 1890 (?) at Wiesbaden.

Spitzweg, Karl, P , 1808-85, Munich

Stahn, Otto, A , b 1859 at Berlin.

Starck, Constantin, S., b. 1866 at Riga

Statz, Vincenz, A , 1819-99, Cologne.

Stauffer (Bern), Karl, P. & S , b 1857 at Trubschachen, d. 1891 at Florence.

Steffeck, Karl, P , b. 1818 at Berlin, d 1890 at Königsberg.

Steinbruck, Eduard, P., b. 1803 at Magdeburg, d. 1882 at Landeck (Silesia)

Steinle, Eduard von, P , b 1810 at Vienna, d 1886 at Frankfort-on-the-Main

Stier, Hubert, A., b. 1838 at Berlin, d. 1907 at Hanover.

Stilke, Herm., P., 1804-60, Berlin.

Struck, Johann Heinrich, A , b 1805 at Buckeburg, d. 1880 at Berlin

Strassen, Melchior Anton zur, S., b 1832 at Münster (Westphalia), d 1896 at Leipsic

Stuck, Franz, P & S , b 1863 at Tettenweis (Bavaria).

Stuler, Friedrich August, A., b 1800 at Muhlhausen (Thuringia), d. 1865 at Berlin.

Sussmann - Hellborn, Louis, S., b 1828 at Berlin.

Taschner, Ignatius, S., b. 1871 at Kissingen

Thoma, Hans, P., b. 1839 at Bernau (Baden).

Tieck, Friedrich, S , 1776-1851, Berlin.

Tischbein, Friedrich, P., b. 1750 at Maestricht, d. 1812 at Heidelberg.

Tischbein, Joh. Heinrich, the Elder,
P., b. 1722 at Haina (Hesse), d.
1789 at Cassel.

Toberentz, Robert, S., b. 1849 at
Berlin, d. 1895 at Rostock.

Tondeur, Alexander, S., 1829-1905,
Berlin.

Troschel, Julius, S., b. 1813 at Berlin, d. 1863 at Rome.

Trübner, Wilhelm, P., b. 1851 at
Heidelberg

Tuaillon, Louis, S., b. 1862 at Berlin.

Uhlhaus, Joseph, S., b. 1857 at
Münster, d. 1901 at Düsseldorf.

Uechtritz-Steinkirch, Cuno von,
S., b. 1856 at Breslau.

Uhde, Fritz von, P., b. 1848 at
Wolkenburg (Saxony).

Unger, Max, S., b. 1854 at Berlin.

Uphues, Joseph, S., b. 1850 at Sassenberg (Westphalia).

Veit, Philipp, P., b. 1793 at Berlin,
d. 1877 at Mayence.

Vogel, Hugo, P., b. 1855 at Magdeburg.

Voigtländer, Rudolf von, P., b. 1851
at Brunswick.

Volkmann, Arthur, S., b. 1851 at
Leipsic

—, *Hans von,* P., b. 1860 at Halle

Volz, Hermann, S., b. 1847 at Carlsruhe.

Vordermeyer, Ludwig, S., b. 1868
at Munich.

Wach, Karl, P., 1787-1845, Berlin.

Wagenbauer, Max Jos., P., b. 1774
at Markt-Grafing, d. 1829 at
Munich.

Waldmüller, Ferd., P., 1793-1865,
Vienna

Wallot, Johann Paul, A., b. 1842
at Oppenheim on the Rhine.

Warthmüller, Robert, P., b. 1859
at Landsberg on the Warthe, d.
1895 at Berlin.

Wasemann, H. Fr, A., 1814-1879,
Berlin

Weidemann, Friedrich Wilhelm,
P., b. 1668 at Osterburg (Altmark), d. 1750 at Berlin.

Weishaupt, Victor, P., b. 1848 at
Munich, d. 1905 at Carlsruhe

Weitsch, Friedrich Georg, P., b 1758
at Brunswick, d. 1828 at Berlin.

Wenck, Ernst, S., b 1865 at Reppen

Werner, Anton von, P., b. 1843 at
Frankfort-on-the-Oder.

Werner, Fritz, P., 1827-1908, Berlin.

Wichmann, Karl Friedrich, S.,
b. 1775 at Potsdam, d 1836 at
Berlin

—, *Ludwig,* S., brother of the preceding, b 1781 at Potsdam, d. 1859
at Berlin.

Wiese, Max, P., b. 1846 at Dantsic

Wille, Fritz von, P., b 1860 at
Weimar.

Wittig, August, S., b. 1826 at
Meissen, d 1893 at Düsseldorf.

Wolff, Albert, S., b 1814 at NeuStrelitz, d. 1892 at Berlin

—, *Emil,* S., b 1802 at Berlin, d. 1879
at Rome

—, *Friedrich Wilhelm,* S., b. 1816
at Fehrbellin, d. 1887 at Berlin.

Wredow, August, S., b 1804 at
Brandenburg, d. 1891 at Berlin

Zügel, Heinrich, P., b 1850 at Murrhardt (Wurtemberg).

—, *Wilhelm,* son of the preceding,
S., b. 1876 at Munich

Zumbusch, Kaspar Clemens von,
S., b. 1830 at Herzebrock (Westphalia).

Index.

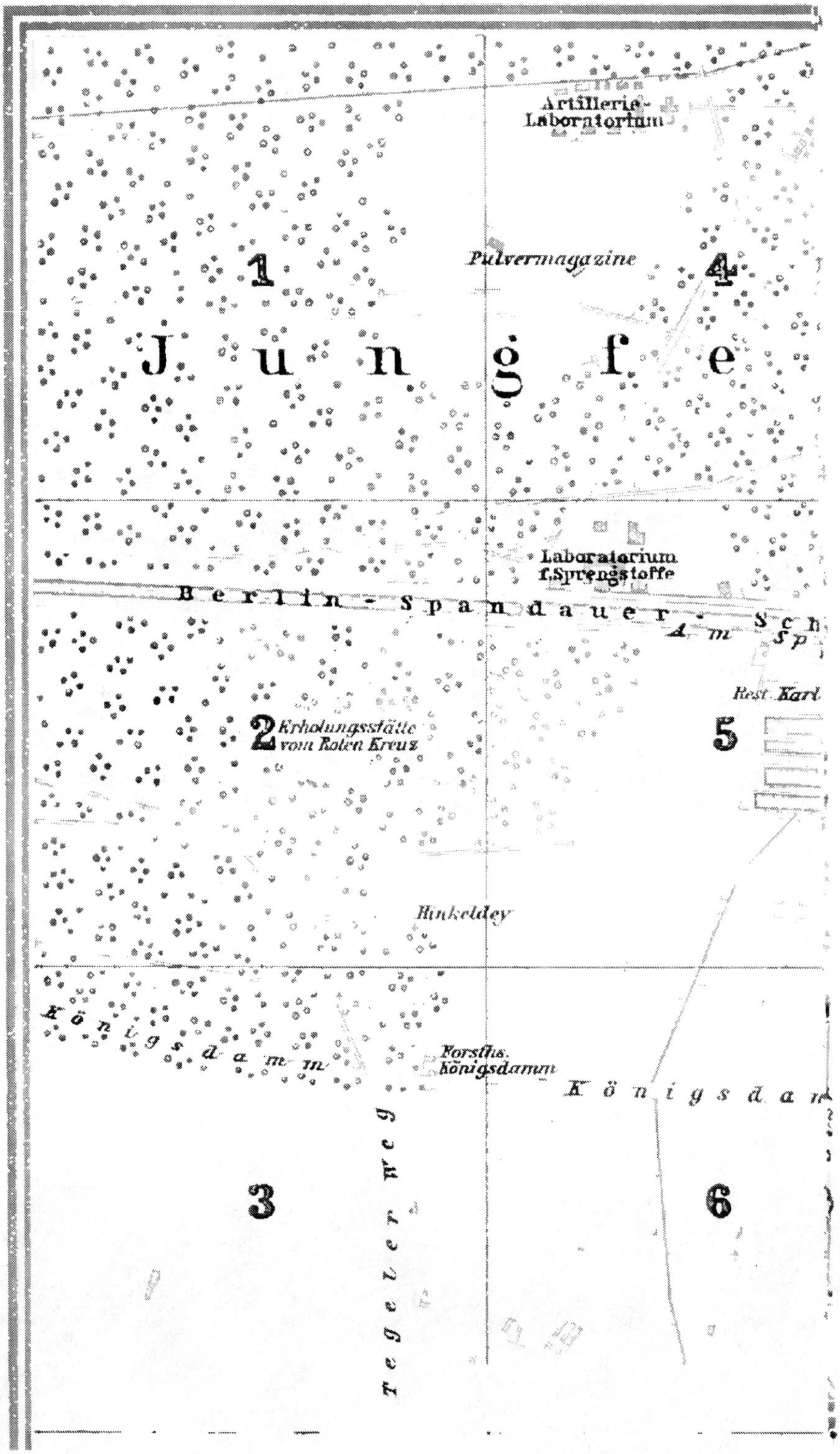

Artillerie-
Laboratorium

Pulvermagazine

1   **4**

J u n g f e

Laboratorium
f. Sprengstoffe

Berlin-Spandauer Sch

Am Sp

Rest. Karl

2 Erholungsstätte
vom Roten Kreuz

5

Hinkeldey

Königsdamm

Forsth.
Königsdamm

Königsdam

Tegeler weg

3

6

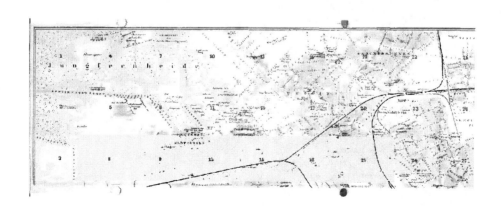

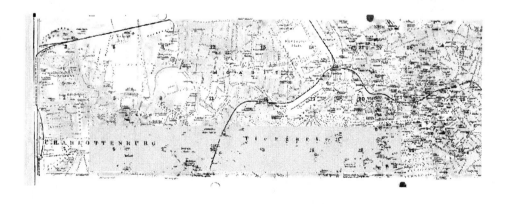

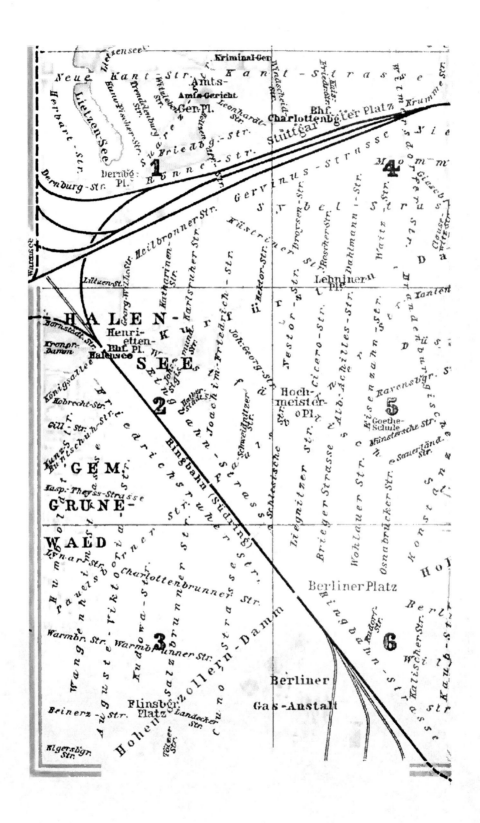

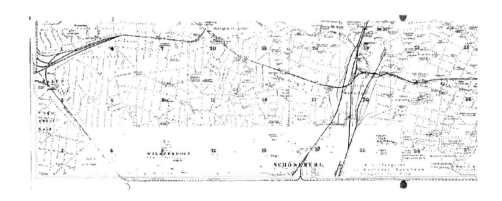

List of the Principal Streets, Squares, Public Buildings, Bridges, etc., of Berlin.

The large Map of Berlin, on the scale of 1:20,000, is divided into three sections, of which the uppermost is coloured *brown*, the central *red*, and the lowest *gray*. Each section contains 42 numbered squares. In the following index the capital letters B, R, G, following the name of a street or building, refer to the different sections, while the numbers correspond with those of the squares in each section. Thus, Admiral-Strasse will be found on the grey section, square 29. If the name sought for is also indicated on the Plan of the Inner Town printed in red (in the scale of 1:12,500; p. 54), this is shown by an 1 before the first perpendicular line. The numbering of the squares is so arranged, that squares in different sections bearing the same number adjoin each other. Thus, square 15 on the brown section finds its continuation towards the S. in square 15 on the red section.

The squares will also be useful for calculating distances, each side of a square being exactly a kilomètre (1093 yds., or about ²/₃ M.), while the diagonals if drawn would be 1531 yds.

The large Italics (*N, O, S, W, C.* etc.) following the names of the streets indicate the postal district to which the street belongs.

Abbreviations of names of districts and villages in the environs of Berlin: Box. = Boxhagen; Char. = Charlottenburg; Grun. = Grunewald; Hal. = Halensee; Plö. = Plötzensee; Rix. = Rixdorf; Rum. = Rummelsburg; Schmar. = Schmargendorf; Schön. = Schöneberg; Trep. = Treptow; Weis. = Weissensee; Wilm. = Wilmersdorf.

	B	R	G		B	R	G
Aalesunder-Str. *N* ..	25			Albertinen-Str.(Weis.)	37		
Abgeordnetenhaus ..		19	19	Albrecht-Str. *NW* . 1		20,23	
Academy, Agricultural		21		Albrecht-Achilles-Str.			
of Art 1	..	19		(Wilm.)	.	.	5
— of Science......	.	.	16	Alexander-Platz *C* . 1	.	29	
—, Military 1	.	20		— Str. *C (12-28a O)* 1	.	29	
— of Music	.	19		—, Kleine *C*	.	30	
—, Technical	.	7, 10		— Ufer *NW* ...	.	20,21	
Achenbach-Brücke ..	.	11		Alexandrinen-Str. *SW*			
— Str. *W*	.	.	10	*(30-101 S)*	.	.	26,25
Acker-Str. *N*	21,21	24		Allenstein-Str. *NO* ..	.	33	
Adalbert-Str. *SO* ...	.	.	28	Alsen-Brücke 1	.	20	
Adler-Str. *C* 1	.	25		— Platz 1	.	20	
Admiral-Str. *SO*	.	.	29	— Str. *NW* 1	.	20	
Admiralsgarten-Bad 1	.	23		Alt-Boxhagen	.	37	
Admiralty....... 1	.	19		Alt-Moabit *NW*	.	⎰11,12 ⎱11,17	
Adolf-Str. *N*	17						
Ahorn-Str. *D*			1	Alt-Schön...			11
Akazien-Str. *S*..			1	... *NO*		11	
Albert-Str. *(S* ...			1	... *D*			17

	B	R	G		B	R	G
Amalien-Haus			14	Bach-Str. *NW*		10	
— Strasse *C*		27		Bad-Str. *N*	19		
— — (Weis.)	34,37			Badensche-Strasse (Wilm.)			12
Amrumer-Str. *N*	11			Bahn-Str. (Schön.)...			18
Amsterdamer-Str. *N* .	14,16			Balten-Platz *O*		35	
Amtsgerichte, Berlin .	19	26,29	19,22	Bamberger-Str. *W* ..			11,12
—, Charlottenburg ..			1	Bandel-Str. *NW* ...		15	
—, Schöneberg....			15	Bar-Str. (Wilm.)....			6,9
Anatomie		21		Barbarossa-Platz *W* .			14
Andersen-Str. *N*	25			— Str. *W*			11,14
Andreas-Hof *O*		31		Bardeleben-Str. *NO*..		33,36	
— Platz *O*		31		Barfus-Str. *N*.....	13		
— Strasse *O*		31		Barnim-Str. *NO* ...		30	
— —, Kleine *O*		31		*Barracks:*			
Anhalt-Str. *SW*....			19,22	Cuirassier Guards .			24
Anklamer-Str. *N* ...	24,27			1st Dragoon Guards			23
Annen-Str. *S* I		28		2nd — —			26
Ansbacher-Str. *W*...			11,10	Emperor Alexander Guards I		23,29	
— —, Neue *W*			11	— Franz Guards ..			26
Anton-Platz (Weis.)	35			2nd Foot Guards . I		20,23	
Anton-Str. *N*	17			3rd Foot Guards ..			31
Antwerpener-Str. *N* .	14			4th — —		15,18	
Apostel-Paulus-Str. (Schön.)			15	Fusilier Guards...	21		
Aquarium I		20,23		1st Field Artillery Guards	15,18	15,18	
Architektenhaus....		19,22	19,22	3rd — —	18		
Arkona-Platz *N*	27			Pioneer Guards ...			31
Arminius-Platz *NW*.		12		Queen Augusta Grenadier Guards			24
Arndt-Str. *SW*....			24	1st Railway Reg. .			18
Arnim-Platz	25			2nd Uhlan Guards .		18	
Arnswalder-Pl. *NO*..		33		Balloon Division..	4,7		
Arsenal, Royal		23		Telegraph Battalion			35,38
Art, School of		29		Baruther-Str. *SW*...			23
Artillerie Laborato- rium	1			Bärwald-Brücke			26
— Prüfungskom- mission			11	— Strasse *S*			27,26
— Strasse *N*		23,24		Bastian-Str. *N*.....	19		
Artillery and Engin- eering School		10		Bau-Akademie....I		25	
Aschaffenburger-Str.*W*			11,12	Bauhof-Str. *NW*..I		23	
Askanischer-Platz*SW*		19		Bautzener-Str. *W*...			21
Augsburger-Str. *W*.			10,14	Bayerischer-Platz *W*.			12
August-Str. *N* (28- 59 *C*)		24,27		Bayerische-Str. (Wilm.)			5,8
Augusta-Brücke			19	Bayreuther-Str. *W*..			14,13
— Hospital		21		— —, Neue *W*			14
— Strasse (Wilm.) ..			9	Bechstein-Saal			19
Auguste-Victoria- Hospital (N.-Weis.)	34			Behm-Str. *N*	23,22		
— — Platz (Char.) ..			10	Behnsen-Str.(Pankow)	28		
— — Strasse (Schmar.)			3	Behren-Str. *W*....I		22	
Augustenburger- Platz *N*	14			Belfort-Str. (Weis.)..	38		
Ausstellungs-Park ..		17		Belforter-Str. *NO*...		30	
Automobile Club, Imperial I		19		Belle-Alliance-Brücke			23
				— Platz *SW*			23
				— Strasse *SW*....			24,23
				Bellermann-Str. *N* ..	22		
				Bellevue, Château ..		14	
Babelsberger-Platz		27,30		Bellevue Allee.....		16	
— Str. (Wilm.) ..			12	— Brücke		14	

	B	R	G
Cemeteries:			
French	21	24	
Friedrich-Werder	.	.	27
Garrison	17	27	
St. George's	34	30,35	
Invaliden	.	21	
Jerusalem	.	.	23,27
Johannes	8, 11		
St. Matthew's	.	.	18
Nazareth	11,17		
New	.	.	27
Sophien	22,24		
Central Market	.1	26	
Chamisso-Platz *SW*	.	.	24
Chancellery, Imperial	.	19	
Charité	.1	.	21
Charité-Str. *NW*	.1	20	
Charlotten-Str. *(1-22a*			
& 72-99 SW, 23-38			
& 46-71 W, 39-45			
NW)	.1	23,22	22
Charlottenbrunner-			
Strasse (Schmar.)	.	.	3
Charlottenburg	.	1,4,7	
— Mausoleum	.	2	
— Palace	.	2	
Charlottenburger-			
Brücke	.	10	
— Chaussée	.	10,13 / 16,19	
— Strasse (Weis.)	31,34		
Charlottenburger-Ufer		5,8, / 10	
(Char.)			
Chaussée-Str. *N*	21	21	
Chemical Institute	.	21	
Cherusker-Str.(Schön.)	.	.	18
Children's Hospital	16		
Chodowiecki-Str. *NO*	30,33		
Choriner-Str. *N*	27	27	
Christburger-Str. *NO*	30,33		
Christiania-Str. *N*	16,19		
Christinen-Str. *N*	.	27	
Christ-Str. (Char.)	.	2	
Churches:			
American	.	.	13,14
Andreas	.	31	
Apostel Paulus	.	.	15
Ascension	23		
Baptist Chapel	.1	28	
St. Bartholomew's	.	30	
Bethanien (Weis.)	34		
Bethlehem	.1	22	
Bonifatius	.	.	23
Capernaum	14		
Cathedral	.1	26	
Cath. Apostolic	.	.	25
Christ	.	.	22
Corpus Christi	.	16	
Dankes-Kirche	.	24	
Dom	1	26	

	B	R	G
Churches:			
Dorotheenstadt	.1	23	
Dreifaltigkeits	.1	22	
Elisabeth	24,27	24	
Emmaus	.	.	31
Emperor Frederick			
Memorial Church	.	13	
Emperor William			
Memorial Church	.	.	10
English	.1	23	
Erlöser (Rum.)	.	.	10
French	.1	22,25 / 26	
Friedens-Kirche	24		
Friedrich-Werder	.1	22	
Garrison	.1	26	
—, second	.	.	27
— (Rom. Cath.)	.	.	27
St. George's	.	29	
— (Engl.)	.1	23	
Gethsemane	.	29	
Gnaden-Kirche	.	21	
Golgotha	.	24	
St. Hedwig's	.1	22	
Heilands-Kirche	.	12	
Heilige-Geist	.	15	
Heilige-Kreuz	.	.	23
Herz Jesu	.	27	
Himmelfahrt	23		
Holy Ghost	.	26	
— Rood	.	.	23
Immanuel	30	30	
— Chapel	22		
Irvingite	.	.	25
Jacobi	.	.	25
Jerusalems	.	.	22,25
St. John's	.	15	
St. John the Evan-			
gelist's	.	21	
St. Joseph's	34		
Kloster-Kirche	.	29	
Lazarus	.	34	
Liebfrauen	.	.	35
St. Louis's	.	.	8
Luisen (Char.)	.	5	
Luisenstadt	.1	25	
St. Luke's	.	.	19
Luther	.	.	17
St. Mark's	.	32	
St. Martha's	.	.	32
St. Mary's	.1	26	
Matthäi	.	16	16
St. Matthias'	.	.	14
St. Mauritius'	.	10	
Melanchthon	.	.	26
St. Michael's	.	28	28
Nazareth	17		
New Church	.1	22	
—	.1	26	
Nordkirche	.	24	

	B	R	G
Churches:			
Old Evangelical (Schön.)			15
Old Lutheran			28
Parochial	I	29	
Passion			34
St. Paul's	19		
— (Rom. Cath.)		12	
St. Peter's	I	25	
Petrus	22		
Pfingst		35	
Philippus Apostel		21	
Pius		32	
Redeemer (Rum.)			40
Reformation		12	
Resurrection		32	
Sacred Heart		27	
Samaritan		38	
St. Sebastian's	21,24		
Segens	27		
Simeon's			25
Sophien		27	
St. Thomas's			31
Trinitatis (Char.)		4	
Trinity		22	
Twelve Apostles			16
Versöhnungs	24		
Zions	27		
Zwingli			37
Cicero-Str. (Wilm.)			5
Circus Busch	I	26	
— Schumann	I	23	
City Passage S		25,28	
Claudius-Str. NW		14	
Clausewitz-Str.(Char.)			4
Clinical Institutes .I		23	
Commandant's Residence	I	26	
Cornelius-Brücke			13
— Strasse W			13
Cösliner-Str. N	20		
Cothenius-Str. NO		36	
Courbière-Platz N	17		
— Strasse W			13
Crefelder-Str. NW		11	
Criminal Court		15,18	
Culm-Str. W			17
, Neue (Schön.)			17
Cuno-Str. (Schmar.)			3
Curtius-Str. N	28		
Cuvry Strasse SO			35
Cuxhavener-Str. NW		11	
Czarnikauer-Str. N	25		
Dahlmann-Str. (Char.)			4
Dalldorfer-Str. N	20		
Dammmühlen-Gebäude	I	25	
Danckelman Str (Char.)			1

	B	R	G
Dänen-Str. N	26		
Danziger-Str. N and NO	31,33		
Darmstädter Bank .I		26	
Darwin-Str. (Char.)		8	
Deaf and Dumb Asylum		27	
Demminer-Str. N	21,23		
Dennewitz-Platz W			17
— Strasse W			17
Deputies, Chamber of		19	19
Derfflinger-Str. W			16
Dernburg Platz(Char.)			1
— Str. (Char.)			1
Dessauer Str. SW			19
Deutsche Bank .I		22	
Deutschkroner - Str. NO		36	
Dieffenbach-Str. S			29
Diestelmeyer-Str. NO		35	
Diesterweg Str. NO	33		
Diet, Imperial		20	
Dircksen-Str. C .I		26,29	
Diskonto-Gesellschaft .I		22,23	
Dissecting Room		21	
Döberitzer-Str. NW		18	
Dolziger-Str. O		38	
Dom (Cathedral) .I		26	
Donau-Str. (Rix.)			33
Dönhoff-Platz SW .I		22,25	
Dorf-Str.(Lichtenberg)		40,41	
Dörnberg-Str. W			16
Dorotheen-Str. NW .I		20,23	
Dortmunder-Str. NW		11	
Dosse-Str. O		40	
Dove-Brücke		8	
— Strasse (Char.)		8	
Dragoner-Str. C		27	
Drake-Str. W		13	
Dreibund-Str. SW			21
Dresdener-Str. SO (21-118 S) .I		25	28
Dreyse-Str. NW		15	
Driesener-Str. N	25		
Drontheimer-Str. N	19		
Droysen-Str. (Char.)			4
Duncker-Str. N	29		
Düsseldorfer-Str.			5, 8
Ebeling-Str. O		35	
Ebers-Str. (Schön.)			48
Eberswalder-Str. N	27		
Eberts-Brücke .I		23	
Eberty-Str. O		35,36	
Eckernförder-Platz N	13		
Eckert-Str. O		35	
Ehrenberg-Str. O			34
Eichendorff Str. N	24		
Ei... Str. NO			38
E... Str. W			19

	B	R	G		B	R	G
Eisenacher-Str. W ..			15,14	Fehrbelliner-Str. N .	27	27	
Eisenbahn-Str. SO ..			31	Feilner-Str. NW ...			25
Eisenzahn-Str.(Wilm.)			5	Feld-Str. N	24		
Eiserne-Brücke ...I		23		Fenn-Str. N	18		
Eislebener-Str. W ..			10	Fenrig-Str. (Schön.) ..			15,18
Elberfelder-Str. NW.		11		Fichte-Str. S			29,30
Elbe-Str. (Rix.)			36	Fidicin-Str. SW ...			24
Elbinger-Str. NO ...	32	36		Finnländische-Str. N.	25		
Eldenaer-Str. O		38		Finow-Str. O		37,40	
Electricity Works ..	23			— (Rix.)			31
Elgersburger-Str. ...			3	Fire Brigade			25
Elisabeth-Brücke ..			28	Fischer-Brücke, An			
— Children's Hospital			30	der O I		25	
— Hospital	27		16	Fischer-Str. O I		25	
— Strasse NO		29		Flemming-Str. NW.		17	
— Ufer SO........			28,29	Flensburger-Str. NW		14	
Elsasser-Str. N		24		Flieder-Str. NO		29,30	
— — (Weis.)	35,38			Flinsberger-Platz			
Elsen-Str. SO			36,38	(Schmar.)			3
Elssholz-Str. W....			17	Flora-Platz		16	
Embassies:				Flotow-Str. NW ...		11	
America (office ..I		23		Flottwell-Str. W ...			19
Austria I		29		Föhrer-Str. N	15		
France I		20		Fontane-Promenade S			26
Great Britain ...I		19		Forckenbeck-Platz O		38	
Russia I		19,22		Forster-Str. SO			32
Spain ...I			16	Franken-Str. W....			14
Emdener-Str. NW ..		12		Frankfurter Allée O .		35,37	
Emperor and Empress				— Strasse, Grosse O			
Frederick Children's				(21-126 NO)		32	
Hospital	16			— —, Kleine NO ..		29	
— Memorial Foun-				— Tor		35	
dation (Char.)		2		Franklin-Str. (Char.).		8,11	
Emperor Frederick				Fransecki-Str. N and			
Museum.......I		23		NO.........	30		
Emser-Str. (Wilm.) ...			8	Französische-Str. WI		22	
Engel-Ufer SO			28	Fraunhofer-Str.			
Engineers' Head-				(Char.)........		7	
quarters			13	Frederick Orphanage .			41
Englische-Str. (Char.)		10		Freemasons' Lodges .		{ 5,23 / 25 }	14
Eosander-Str. (Char.)		5		Freiarche, Untere ...		10	
Erasmus-Str. NW ..		9		Freiarchen-Brücke,			
Erdmann-Str. (Schön.)			18	Obere			35
Erfurter-Str. (Schön.) .			12,15	Freienwalder-Str. N .	22		
Esmarch-Str. NO ...		33		Freiligrath-Str. S ...			26
Esplanade (Pankow) .	25			Freisinger-Str. W ...			14
Essener-Str. NW...		11		Friedberg-Str. (Char.)			1
Exchange I		26		Friedeberger-Str.			
Exerzier-Str. N	16			NO.........		33	
Exhibition Park ...		17		Friedel-Str. (Rix.) ...			32,33
Eylauer-Str. SW ...			21	Frieden-Str. NO....		30,32	
				Friedens-Allée I		20	
Falkenstein-Str. SO .			35,34	Friedrichs-Brücke..I		26	
Falk-Platz N	26			Friedrich-Str. (1-55 &			
Falkenberger-Str.	40			200-250 SW, 56-			
Fasanen-Str. W....		10	11,10	85a & 157-199 W,			
Fasanerie-Allée		13		86 to I & 157-156			
Fehmarn-Str. N	17			NW ..., N ...		22,23	22
Fehrbelliner Pl				New C ...I		26,29	
(Wilm.) .			5,8				

	B	R	G		B	R	G
Friedrich-Karl-Platz				Georg-Wilhelm-Str.			
(Char.)		2		(Hal.)			2, 1
Friedrich-Karl-Str. O		37		Gerhard-Str. NW		17	
— — Ufer NW		17,20		Gericht-Str. N		17,20	
Friedrichsberger-Str.				St. Gertraudt Hospital			20
NO		32		Gertraudten-Brücke I		25	
Friedrichsfelder-Str. O		31,34		— Strasse C		25	
Friedrichsgraeht C . I		25		Gervinus-Str. (Char.)			1,4
Friedrichshain NO		33		Gessler-Str. (Schön.)			18
—, Am NO		33		Gesundbrunnen	19,22		
Friedrichsruher-Str.				Giesebrecht-Str.			
(Schmar. & Hal.)			2, 3	(Char.)			4
Friedrichs-Str. (Weis.)	35,34			Gieseler-Str. (Wilm.)			9
Friedrich-Wilhelm-				Gill-Str. (Grun.)			2
Hospital	32,33	32		Gips-Str. C		27	
— — Strasse W		13	13	Gitschiner-Str. SW			
Friedrich-Wilhelm-				(13-14 S)			23,26
Viktoria-Stift			38	Gleditsch-Str. W			14,17
Friesen-Str. SW			24	Gleim-Str. N	26		
Fritsche-Str. (Char.)		2,1,4		Glogauer-Str. SO			32
Froben-Str. W			17	Gneisenau-Str. SW			
Froebel-Str. NO	33			(36-79 S)			23
Frucht-Str. O		31,34		Gneist-Str. N	29		
Fulda-Str. (Rix.)			33	Gnesener-Str. NO		36	
Fürbringer-Str. SW			23	Goeben-Str. W			17
Fürsten-Str. S			25	Goethe-Park (Char.)		4	
Fürstenberger-Str. N	27			— Str. (Char.)		4, 7	
Fürstenwalder-Str. NO	32			— — (Weis.)	31		
Fürther-Str. W			11,10	— — (Rum.)			40
				Gollnow-Str. NO		30,29	
Gabelsberger-Str. O		37,38		Golssener-Str. SW			27
Gäbler-Str. (Weis.)	31			Goltz-Str. W			14
Gabriel-Max-Str.(Rox.)		37		Gontard-Str. C . I		26	
Galvani-Str. (Char.)		8		Görlitzer-Strasse SO			32
Garde-du-Corps-Str.				— Ufer SO			35
(Char.)		2		Gormann-Str. C		27	
Garrison Hospital N	21			Gossler-Str. O			37
Garten-Platz N	21,24			Gossow-Str. W			11
— Strasse N	21,24	24		Goten-Str. (Schön.)			18
— — (Weis.)	40			Gothaer-Str. (Schön.)			15
— Weg (Plö.)	9			Gothenburger-Str. N	19,22		
Gärtner-Str. (Rox.)		37		Gotland-Str. N	25		
Gas Works	{ 18,21	6, 8	3,6,14	Gottsched-Str. N	16,19		
	32,33	31	26,27	Gotzkowsky-Brücke		11	
Gasteiner-Str. (Wilm.)			9	— Strasse NW		12	
Gaudy-Str. N	26,29			Graefe-Str. S			30,29
Gauss-Str. (Char.)		6		Gransecer-Str. N	27		
Geibel-Str. S			26	Graudenzer-Str. O		34	
Geisberg-Str. W			11,14	Graun-Str. N	26		
Gendarmen-Markt W I		22		Greifenhagener-Str. N	29,28		
General Pape-Str.				Greifswalder-Strasse			
(Schön.)			21	NO	33	30,33	
General Staff		20		Grenadier-Str. C		27	
General-Str. (Weis.)	31			Grenz-Str. N	20		
Genter-Str. N	14,17			Griebenow-Str. N	27		
Genthiner-Str. W			16	Grimm-Str. S			29
St. George's Hospital	16			Gröben-Ufer SO			34
Georgen-Str. N W I		2.		Gröbenau SO		7	7
Georgen-Kirch-Str				Gross- Str. N			
NO		23,40		Gross- Str.			23

	B	R	G		B	R	G
Grossbeeren-Str. *SW*	.	.	20,23	Habsburger Ufer *NW*	.	9, 8	
Grossfürsten-Platz ..	.	17		Hackescher Markt *C* 1	.	26	
Gross-Görschen-Str. *W*	.	.	17	Hafen-Platz *SW* ...	.	.	19
Grün-Str. *C* 1	.	25		— Strasse (Plö.)....	12		
— —, Neue *C* 1	.	25		Hagelsberger-Str. *SW*	.	.	20,23
— (Char.)	.	4		Hagenauer-Str. *N*..	30		
Grünauer-Str. *SO* ...	.	.	32	Halberstädter - Str.			
Grünberger-Str.(Box.)	.	37		(Hal.).........	.	.	2
Grüner Weg *O*	.	31		Haller-Str. (Char.) ..	.	8	
Grüner-Str. *C* 1	.	29		Hallesche-Strasse *SW*	.	.	19,22
Grunewald	.	.	2, 3	— Tor	.	.	23
Grunewald - Str.				— Ufer *SW*.....	.	.	19
(Schön.)........	.	.	12,15	Hamburger - Platz			
Grünstrassen-Brücke I	.	25		(Weis.)........	31,34		
Grünthaler-Str. *N* ...	22			— Strasse, Gr. *N*...	.	27	
Gryphius - Str. (Rum.)	.	37	37	— —, Kl. *N*.....	.	24	
Guard House, Royal I	.	23		— Tor	.	24	
Gubener-Str. *O*	.	34		Händel-Str. *NW*...	.	10,13	
Gnericke-Str. (Char.)	.	8		Handels-Hochschule I	.	26	
Guinea-Str. *N* 10,11				Handelskammer ...I	.	23	
Güntzel-Str. (Wilm.)	.	.	8, 11	Hannoversche-Str.			
Gürtel-Str. (Weis.) ..35,38				*NW*........	.	21	
— *O*	.	40		Hansa-Brücke	.	11	
Gustav-Adolf-Platz				— Platz *NW*	.	14	
(Char.)........	.	6		— Ufer *NW*.....	.	11	
— — Strasse (Weis.) 31				Hardenberg-Str. (Ch.)	.	7	10
Gustav-Meyer-Allée *N* 23				Harzer-Str. (Rix.) ...	.	.	36
Gustav - Müller - Str.				Hasenheide *S*	.	.	27,30
(Schön.)........	.	.	18	Haupt-Str. (Schön.) ..	.	.	15,18
Gymnasium:				Hausburg-Str. *O*...	.	36,38	
Askanisches	.	.	19,22	Hausvogtei-Platz *C* 1	.	22	
Augusta	.	7		Havel-Str. (Char.)...	.	5	
Bismarck......	.	.	8	Havelberger-Str. *NW*	15	15	
Französisches ...I	.	20		Health Office.....	.	14	
Friedrichs I	.	20,23		Heckmann-Ufer *SO* .	.	.	35
Friedrich-Werder..	.	11		Hedemann-Str. *SW*.	.	.	22
Friedrich-Wilhelm.	.	.	22	St. Hedwig's Hospital	.	24	
Graues Kloster ..I	.	29		Heide-Str. *NW*	18	18	
Hohenzollern	.	.	15	Heidelberger-Str. *SO*	.	.	36,39
Humboldt	.	24		Heidenfeld-Str. *O*...	.	36	
Joachimsthal	.	.	11	Heilbronner-Str. (Hal.)	.	.	1
Köllnisches I	.	28		— — *W* (Schön.) ..	.	.	11
Königsstadt	.	29		Heiligegeist Hospital	16		
Leibniz	.	.	31	Heiligegeist-Str. *C* I .	.	26	
Lessing	20			Heim-Str. *SW*	.	.	24
Luisen.........	.	15		Heinersdorfer-Strasse			
Luisenstadt	.	.	25	*NO*	.	30	
Mommsen	.	.	13	Heinrich-Platz *SO* ..	.	.	28
Prinz Heinrich ...	.	.	15	Hektor-Str. (Wilm.) .	.	.	2,1
Real-Gymnasium				Helenenhof (Rum.) ..	.	.	37
(Char.)	.	4		Helgoländer-Ufer *NW*	.	14	
Reform	.	.	7	Helm-Str. (Schön.) ..	.	.	18
Sophien	.	27		Helmholtz-Platz *N* ..	29		
Kaiser Wilhelm .I	.	19		— Strasse (Char.)...	.	8	
Werner Siemens ..	.	.	14	Helmstedter - Str.			
Gymnastic Institute,				(Wilm.)........	.	.	11
Central	21	21		Helsingforser-Platz *O*	.	34	
				Hennigsdorfer-Str. *N*	16		
Haberland-Str. *W* .	.	.	11	Henrietten-Platz(Hal.)	.	.	2
Habsburger-Str. *W*.	.	.	14	Herbart-Str. Char. .	.	.	1

	B	R	G
Herbert-Str. (Schön.) . .		.	18
Herder-Str. (Char.) . .		7	
Herkules-Brücke W . .		.	13
Hermann-Platz S . . .		.	30
— Strasse (Rix.)		.	30
Herrenhaus 1		19	
Herschel-Str. (Char.) . .		3	
Hertha-Str. (Pankow)	31		
Herwarth-Str. NW . .		17	
Hessische-Str. N . . .		21	
Hildebrandt-Str. W . .		16	
Hindersin-Str. NW. 1		20	
Hippodrome		10	
Hirschberger - Str. (Rum.)		.	40
Hirten-Str. C		27,30	
Historical Institute .		20	
Hitzig-Str. W		13	
Hobrecht-Brücke . . .		.	32
— Strasse (Rix.) . . .		.	29,32
— — (Grun. & Hal.) . .		.	2
Hoch-Str. N	20		
—, Neue N	20,21		
Hochmeister-Platz (Wilm.)		.	5
— Strasse N	30		
Hochstädter-Str. N .	16,17		
Höchste-Str. NO . . .		33	
Hoffmann-Str. SO . .		.	37
Hof-Str. (Neu-Hohen-schönhausen)	42		
Hofjäger-Allée W . .		13	
Hohenfriedberg-Str. (Schön.)		.	18
Hohenlohe-Str. O . .		.	37
Hohen-Schönhausener-Str. (Weis.)	40		
— — (Wilhelmsberg)	42		
Hohenstaufen-Platz S		.	29
— Strasse W		.	11,14
Hohenzollern Museum		23	
— Damm (Wilm.) . . .		.	6, 8
— Platz (Wilm.) . . .		.	8
— School		.	15
— Strasse W		16	
Hoher Steinweg C. 1		26	
Hollmann-Stift		24	
— Strasse SW		.	22
Holsteiner-Ufer NW .		14	
Holsteinische-Str. (Wilm.)		.	9, 8
Holtei-Str. (Rum.) . .		.	37
Holtzendorff-Str. (Char.)		.	1
Holy Ghost Hospital	16		
Holzgarten-Str. C. 1		25	
Holzmarkt-Str. O . . .		28	
Home Office, Imperial 1		19	
Hopfen-Brück.		10	

	B	R	G
Horn-Str. SW		.	20
Horstweg (Char.) . . .		1	
Hospital, Municipal, am Urban		.*	26
— (Alt-Moabit)		15	
— (Charlottenburg) . .		4, 5	
— (Friedrichshain) . .		33,36	
—, Jewish		24	
—, Rudolph Virchow .	14	.	
Hübner-Str. O		38	
Hufeland-Str. NO . . .		33	
Humboldt-Hain N . .	20,23		
— Strasse (Grun.) . . .		.	3, 2
Hussiten-Str. N . .	20,24		
Hutten-Str. NW		9	
Hydrographic Office .		16	16
Hygienic Institute . .		21	
Ibsen-Str. N	25		
Iffland-Str. O		28,29	
Immanuelkirch-Str. NO		30,33	
Infectious Diseases, Institute of	15		
Inn-Str. (Rix.)		.	36
Insel-Brücke		25	
— Strasse S 1		25	
Insterburg-Str. O . . .		35	
Insurance Office, Imperial		.	16
Invalidenhaus		21	
Invaliden-Str. N (45-97 NW)		17,18 / 21,21	
Island-Str. N	25		
Jablonski-Str. NO . .	30,33		
Jäger-Str. W 1		22	
— (Char.)		2	
—, Kleine C. . 1		25	
Jagow-Str. NW		11	
Jahn-Str. S		.	30
Jakob-Str., Alte SW (45-102 S)		25	22,25
— —, Neue S		25,28	
Jannowitz-Brücke . . .		28	
Jausa-Str. (Rix.) . . .		.	32
Jasmunder-Str. N . .	24		
Jenaer-Str. (Wilm.) .		.	11
Jerusalem Hospital . .		.	31
Jerusalemer - Str. SW (14-35 C) 1		22	
Joachim-Str. C. . . .		27	
Joachim-Friedrich-Str. (Hal.)		.	1, 2
Joachimsthaler-Str. W		.	10
Johann-Georg-Str. (Hal.)		.	2
Johannis-Str. N . . .		23	
Johannistisch SW . .		.	23

	B	R	G
Johanniter-Str. *SW*	.	.	26
Johann-Sigismund-Str. (Hal.)	.	.	2
Jordan-Str. *SO*	.	.	35
Joseph-Str. *SO*	.	28	28
Josty-Str. *NO*	.	30	
Jüden-Str. *C* . . I	.	26	
Jung-Str. *O*	.	37	
Jungfern-Brücke . . I		25	
— Heide	1,4,7		
— Steg (Plö.)	9		
Jauker-Str. *SW*	.	.	22
Jüterboger-Str. *SW*	.	.	24,27
Kaiser-Allée *W*	.	.	12,11
Kaiser-Damm (Char.)	.	1	
Kaiser-Str. *C*	.	29	
Kaiser-Franz-Grenadier-Platz *SO*	.	.	28
Kaiser-Friedrich-Museum . . . I	.	23	
— Platz *S*	.	.	27
Kaiser Friedrich-Str. (Schön.)	.	.	18
— (Rix.)	.	.	33
— (Char.)	.	5,4	4
— (Pankow)	28		
Kaiser Gallery *W* .I	.	22	
Kaiserhof-Str. *W* .I	.	22	
Kaiserin Augusta-Allée *NW*	.	6,9	
— Stift	.	5	
— Strasse *W*	.	13	13
Kaiser Wilhelm-Akademie	.	23	
— Brücke . . I	.	26	
— Platz (Weis.)	35		
— Strasse *C* .I	.	26	
— & Kaiserin Augusta Stift	16		
Kalandsgasse *C* .I	.	26	
Kalckreuth-Str. *W*	.	.	13
Kalischer-Str. (Wilm.)	.	.	6
Kameruner-Str. *N*	14		
Kammergericht	.	.	22
Kamminer-Str. (Char.)	.	2,6	
Kanal-Str. (Char.)	.	4	
— (Plö.)	9		
Kanonier-Str. *W* ..I	.	22	
Kant-Str. (Char.)	.	.	{ 1,4 / 7,10 }
— (Rnm.)	.	.	40
Karl-Str. *NW* . .I	.	20,23	
Karl-August-Platz (Char.)	.	4	
Karlsbad, Am *W*	.	.	16,19
Karlshof	5		
Karls-Platz I	.	20	
Karlsruher-Str. (Hal.)	.	.	1,2

	B	R	G
Karpfenteich-Str. (Rix.)	.	.	39
Kaspar-Theyss-Str. (Grun. & Schmar.)	.	.	2
Kastanien-Allée *N*	27		
Kastanien-Wäldchen I	.	23	
Katzbach-Str. *SW*	.	.	21
Katzler-Str. *W*	.	.	17
Kaub-Str. (Wilm.)			6
Kaufhaus des Westens	.	.	10,13
Keibel-Str. *NO* . . .I	.	29	
Keith-Str. *W*	.	.	13
Kemper-Platz *W* . .I	.	19	
Kepler-Str. (Char.)	.	.	6
Kessel-Str. *N*	.	.	21
Kiautschou-Str. *N*	15,18		
Kiefholz-Str. *SO*	.	.	35,39
Kieler-Str. *N*	18		
Kietzer Weg (Friedrichsberg)	.	.	40
Kirch-Platz (Char.)	.	5	
— Strasse *NW*	.	14	
— (Char.)	.	5,4	
Kirchbach-Str. *W*	.	.	17
Kirchhof-Str. *S*	.	.	27
— (Char.)	.	5	
Kleinbeeren-Str. *SW*	.	.	19,22
Kleine-Str. (Lichtenberg)	.	.	40
Kleist-Str. *W*	.	.	13
Kloeden-Str. *SW*	.	.	24
Klopstock-Str. *NW*	.	10,11	
Kloster-Str. *C* I	.	26	
Knesebeck-Str. *W*	.	7	7
Knie	.	7	
Kniprode-Str. *NO*	36	33,36	
Knobelsdorff-Str. (Char.)	.	1	
Koch-Str. *SW*	.	.	22
Kochhann-Str. *O*	.	35	
Kolberger-Str. *N*	20		
Köllnische Fischmarkt *C* . . . I	.	25	
Köllnischen Park, Am I	.	28	
Köllnische-Str. *C* . .I	.	25	
Köllnisches Ufer (Rix.)	.	.	36
Kolonie-Str. *N* . . .I	19		
Kolonnen-Str. (Schön.)	.	.	18
Kommandanten-Str. *SW (23-66 S)* . . I	.	25	25
Komturei-Platz *O*	.	35	
König-Str. *C* I	.	26	
— , Nene *NO* . . .I	.	29,30	
Königgrätzer-Str. *W (25-120 SW)* . . I	.	19	19,22
Königin Augusta-Str. *W*	.	.	16
Königin-Brücke	.	.	28
Königs-Allée (Grun.)	.	.	2

	B	R	G
Königsberger-Str. O .	.	34	
Königs-Chaussée (Weis.)	35,38		
Königsdamm (Plö.)	3,4,9		
Königsdamm-Brücke	12		
Königsgraben, Am, OI	.	26,29	
Königshofer-Str. (Wilm.)	.	.	11
Königs-Platz NW	.	20	
Königstor NO	.	30	
Königswache I	.	23	
Königsweg (Char.)	.	1	
— (Schön.)	.	.	18
Konstanzer-Str. (Wilm.)	.	.	6,5
Kopenhagener-Str. N	26		
Köpenicker-Brücke	.	31	31
— Landstrasse SO	.	.	38,39
— Strasse SO	.	28	31
Kopernikus-Str. O	.	34,37	
Kopisch-Str. SW	.	.	24
Koppen-Platz C	.	24,27	
— Strasse O (36-52 NO)	.	31,32	
Körner-Str. W	.	.	16
Kosche-Str.	42		
Köthener-Str. W	.	.	19
Kottbuser-Brücke	.	.	29
— Damm S	.	.	29,30
— Strasse SO	.	.	29
— Tor	.	.	28,29
Kottbuser-Ufer SO	.	.	29,32
Krausen-Str. W (20a-53 SW) . . I	.	22	
Krausnick-Str. N	.	23,24	
Kraut-Str. O	.	31	
Kremmener-Str. N	27		
Kreutziger-Str. O	.	37	
Kreuzberg SW	.	.	21
Kreuzberg-Str. SW	.	.	21
Kreuz-Str. C	.	25	
Kriegs-Akademie . . I	.	20	
Kriminal-Justizamt	.	15,18	
Krögel, Am C . . . I	.	25	
Kronen-Str. W . . . I	.	22	
Kronprinzen-Brücke I	.	20	
— Damm (Hal.)	.	.	2
— Palais I	.	23	
— Platz	.	40	
— Strasse O	.	40	
— — (Weis.)	35		
— Ufer NW . . . I	.	17,20	
Krossener-Str. (Box.)	.	37	
Krug-Allée, Neue	.	.	42
Kruume-Str. (Char.)	.	4	4
Krupp-Str. NW	.	15	
Kudowa-Str. (Schmar.)	.	.	3
Kugler-Str. N	28	.	
Kulmbacher-Str. W	.	.	11
Kunkel-Str. N	21,20		

	B	R	G
Kuno Fischer-Str. (Char.)	.	.	1
Kunstschule I	.	29	
Künstlerhaus I	.	19	
Kunz-Buntschuh-Str.	.	.	2
Kupfergraben, Am, N1	.	23	
Kur-Str. C I	.	25	
Kürassier-Str. SW	.	.	25
Kurfürsten-Allée (Char.)	.	7,10	
— Brücke I	.	26	
— Damm W (10-73 & 170-245 Char.; 74-169 Hal.)	.	.	{ 2,4 7,10
— Platz	.	17	
— Strasse W	.	.	13,16
Kurze-Str. C	.	29	
— — (Pankow)	28		
Küstriner-Platz O	.	31,34	
— Strasse (Wilm.)	.	.	1,4
Kyffhäuser-Str. W	.	.	14
Landecker-Str. (Schmar.)	.	.	3
Landgericht I	.	26,29	
— II	.	.	19,22
— III	.	3	
Landgrafen-Str. W	.	.	13
Landhaus-Str. (Wilm.)	.	.	12,11
Landsberger Allée NO	.	32,36	
— Strasse NO (35-88 C)	.	29,32	
— Tor	.	32	
Landshuter-Str. W	.	.	11
Landwehr Canal	.	8	
Landwehr-Str. NO	.	29	
Langenbeck-Str. NO	.	36	
Lange-Str. O	.	31	
Lange-Schuke-Stift	16		
Langhans-Str. (Weis.)	31,34		
Lankwitz-Str. SW	.	.	25
Laube-Str. (Rix.)	.	.	36
Lauenburger-Str. (Wilm.)	.	.	9
Lausitzer-Platz SO	.	.	31
— Strasse SO	.	.	32
Lazarus-Hospital	24		
Lebuser-Str. NO	.	32	
Lehder-Str. (Weis.)	31		
Lehniner-Platz (Wilm.)	.	.	4
Lehniner-Str. S	.	.	27
Lehrter-Str. NW	18	18	
Leibniz-Str. (Char.)	.	7	7
Leipziger-Platz W . I	.	19	
— Strasse W (43-89 SW) . . I	.	22	
— -, Alte C . . I	.	25	
Leun-Str. Rix.	.	.	33
Leubach-Str. Box.	.	.	37

	B	R	G		B	R	G
Lenné-Str. W I	.	19		Ludwigskirch-Platz			
Leonhard-Str. (Char.)	.	.	1	(Wilm.)	.	.	8
Leopold-Platz N ...	17			— Str. (Wilm.)	.	.	8
Lessing-Brücke	.	14		Luisen-Brücke	.	.	28
— Strasse NW	.	14		— Platz (Char.)	.	2	
— (Rum.)	.	.	40	— NW	.	21	
Lette-Str. N	29			— Strasse NW ...I	.	21,20	
Leutnants-Berg	10			— Ufer S	.	.	26,28
Levetzow-Str. NW	.	11		Luitpold-Str. W	.	.	14
Libauer-Str. O	.	34,37		Lüneburger-Str. NW	.	14,17	
Liberda-Str. (Rix.) ..	.	.	32	Lustgarten I	.	26	
Library, Royal ...I	.	22		Luther-Brücke	.	14	
—, University I	.	23		— Strasse W	.	.	13
Lichtenberg	.	41		Lütticher-Str. N ...	11		
Lichtenberger-Str. NO	.	32		Lützen-Str. (Wilm.)..	.	.	1
— — (Weis.)	37,38			Lützow-Brücke	.	.	16
Lichtenstein-Allée W	.	13		— Platz W	.	.	13
— Brücke........	.	13		— Strasse W....	.	.	16
Lichterfelder-Str. SW	.	.	21,24	— Ufer W	.	.	13,16
Liebenwalder-Str. N .	16			Lützower-Str. (Char.)	.	5	
Liebig-Str. O	.	38		Luxemburger-Str. N .	14,17		
Liegnitzer-Str. SO ..	.	.	32	Lychener-Str. N	30,29		
— — (Wilm.)	.	.	6, 5	Lynar-Str. N	18		
Liesen-Str. N	21			— (Grün.)	.	.	3
Lietzenburger-Str.							
(Wilm.)	.	.	7	Maassen-Str. W	.	.	13
Litzensee-Ufer (Char.)	.	.	1	Madai-Str. O	.	31	
Lietzmann-Str. NO ..	.	29		Magazin-Str. O	.	29	
Limburger-Str. N ..	14			— — (Char.)	.	2	
Linden, Unter den				Magdeburger-Platz W	.	16	
(1-37 W, 38-78 NW)				— Strasse W ...	.	16	
I	.	23		Maien-Str. W	.	.	13
Linden-Allée (Weis.)	37,38			Mainzer-Str. O	.	37	
— Strasse SW....	.	.	22	— — (Rix.)	.	.	33
Lindower-Str. N	17			Maison de Santé ...	.	.	18
Linien-Str. (1-100 &				Malmöer-Str. N ...	25,26		
241-250 NO, 11-105				Malplaquet-Str. N ..	16		
& 161-240 O, 106-	.	{ 24,27		Manitius-Str. (Rix.)	.	.	32
160 N)	.	{ 30		Mannheimer-Str.			
Link-Str. W	.	.	19	(Wilm.)	.	.	9
Lipaer-Str. (Wilm.) ..	.	.	11	Manstein-Str. W....	.	.	17
Lippehner Str. NO ..	.	33		Manteuffel-Str. SO ..	.	.	29,31
List-Str. SO	.	.	35	Marburger-Str. W..	.	.	10
Littauer-Str. O	.	34		March-Brücke (Char.)	.	8	
Loan Office	.	24		— Strasse (Char.) ...	.	7	
Lohmeyer-Str. (Char.)	.	5		Margareten-Str. W ..	.	16,19	
Lohmühlen-Str. SO..	.	.	35,33	Marheineke-Platz SW	.	.	24
Lortzing-Str. N	23			Mariannen-Platz SO .	.	.	28,31
Lothringen-Str.				— Strasse SO	.	.	29
(Weis.)	38			— Ufer SO	.	.	31
Lothringer-Str. N ...	.	27		Marien-Str. NW ...I	.	20	
Lottum-Str. N	.	27		Marienburger-Str. NO	30,33		
Löwen-Brücke	.	13		Mariendorfer-Str. SW	.	.	24
Löwe-Str. O	.	35		Markets:			
Lübbener-Str. SO...	.	.	32,31	I. (Central) ...	.	26	
Lübecker-Str. NW ..	.	15		II.	.	.	22
Luckauer-Str. S	.	.	28	III. I	.	22	
Luckenwalder-Str.				IV. I	.	20,23	
SW	.	.	19	V.	.	.	16
Lüderitz-Str. N	10,13			VI.	.	24	

	B	R	G		B	R	G
Railway-Stations:				Reichs-Post-Museum I	.	22	
Börse I	.	26		Reichs-Schatzamt .. I	.	22	
Charlottenburg ...	.	.	1	Reichtags-Gebäude . I	.	20	
Friedrich-Strasse .1	.	23		Reichstags-Platz NW	.	20	
Gesundbrunnen ...	23	.		— Ufer NW I	.	20	
Görlitz	.	.	32	Reichs-Versicherungs-			
Halensee	.	.	2	Amt	.	.	16
Jannowitz-Brücke .	.	28		Reinerz-Str. (Schmar.)	.	.	3
Jungfern-Heide ...	.	3		Reinickendorfer-Str. N	16	.	
Lehrte	.	18,21		Reis-Str. (Char.)	.	5	
Potsdam I	.	.	19	Rennbahn-Str. (Weis.)	37	.	
Putlitz-Strasse ...	15	.		Reuchlin-Str. NW ..	.	9	
Savigny-Platz	.	.	7	Reuter-Platz (Rix.) ...	.	.	33
Schöneberg	.	.	18	— Stift	19	.	
Silesian	.	21		— Strasse (Rix.) ...	.	.	33
Stettin	.	24		Revaler-Str. O	.	34,37	37
Stralau-Rummels-				Rheinsberger-Str. N	24,27	.	
burg	.	.	37,40	Rhinower-Str. N ...	26	.	
Tiergarten	.	10		Richard Wagner-Str.			
Treptow	.	.	38	NW	.	.	17
Wannsee	.	.	19	Richthofen-Str. O ...	.	.	35
Warschauer-Strasse	.	.	34	Riedemann-Str. (Char.)	8	.	
Wedding	19	.		Riehl-Str. (Char.) ...	.	1	
Westend	.	.	2	Rigaer-Str. O	.	.	38
Zoological Garden .	.	.	10	Ringbahn-Str. (Wilm.)	.	.	2, 6
Ramler-Str. N	23	.		Rittergasse C I	.	25	
Ranke-Str. W	.	.	10	Rittergut-Str. (Lich-			
Rathaus I	.	26		tenberg).......	.	41	
— at Charlottenburg.	.	5		Ritter-Str. S (38-83			
— Friedrichsberg .	.	40		SW)	.	.	25
— Wilmersdorf .	.	.	9	Rixdorf	.	.	33
Rathaus-Str. (Fried-				Roch-Str. C I	.	26	
richsberg)	.	40		Rochow-Str. O	.	.	37
Rathenower-Str. NW	15	15		Rodenberg-Str. N ...	28	.	
Ratibor-Str. SO	.	.	32	Röder-Platz (Lichten-			
Rauch-Museum.... I	.	26		berg)	.	12	
Rauch-Str. W	.	13		— Strasse	.	39,42	
Raumer-Str. N	29	.		Rognitz-Str. (Char.) .	.	1	
Raupach-Str. O	.	28		Rölke-Str. (Weis.)...	34	.	
Ravené's Picture Gal-				Romintener-Str. O ..	.	34	
lery I	.	25		Rönne-Str. (Char.)...	.	.	1
Ravené-Str. N	20	.		Röntgen-Str. (Char.) .	.	8	
Ravensberger-Str.				Roon-Str. NW I	.	20	
(Wilm.)	.	.	5	Rosberitz-Str.			
Record Office, Privy I	.	26		(Wilm.)	.	.	11
Regensburger-Str. W	.	.	11	Roscher-Str. (Char.) .	.	.	4
Regenten-Str. W ...	.	16	16	Rosen-Str. C I	.	26	
— (Wilm.)	.	.	12,11	Rosenheimer-Str. W .	.	.	15
Rehberge	13	.		Rosenthaler-Str. C .I	.	26,27	
Reichenberger-Str. SO	.	.	29,32	— —, Kleine, C ...	.	27	
Reichsamt des Innern I	.	19,20		— Tor	.	27	
Reichsbank I	.	22,25		Rosinen-Str. (Char.). .	.	8	
Reichs-Druckerei .	.	.	25	Rosmarin-Str. W . I	.	22	
Reichs-Eisenbahnamt	.	19		Ross-Str. C	.	25	
Reichs-Gesundheits-				— —, Neue, S ...I	.	25	
amt	.	14		Rostocker-Str. NW ..	.	9	
Reichs-Justizamt .. I	.	19		Rother-Str. O	.	.	34
Reichs-Kanzlei . .I	.	19		Rousseau Insel....	.	16	
Reichs-Marine amt . I	.	19		Rucker-Str. C	.	27	
Reichs-Postamt . I	.	22		Rückert-Str. Char. .	.	4	

	B	R	G
Rüdersdorfer-Str. O . .		31,34	
Rudolf-Platz O			37
— Strasse O			34
Rudolf Virchow Kran-kenhaus	14		
Rudorf-Str. (Wilm.) . .			6
Rügener-Str. N	23		
Ruheplatz-Str. N . . .	17		
Rummelsburg			40
Rummelsburger-Platz O			31
Strasse (Friedrichs-berg)		40	
Runge-Str. SO . . I		28	
Ruppiner-Str. N . . .	27		
Rütli-Str. (Rix.)			39
Ryke-Str. N	30		
Saarbrücker-Str. N . .		30	
Sächsische - Str. (Wilm.)			8
Sadowa-Str. (Wil.) . .			11
Saldern-Str. (Char.) . .		1	
Salomon-Str. (Weis.) .	31,34		
Salzbrunner-Str. (Schmar.)			3
Salzufer (Char.)		8, 10	
Salzwedeler-Str. NW	15		
Samariter-Platz O . .		38	
— Strasse O		37,38	
Samoa-Str. N . .	14,15		
Sander-Str. (Rix.) . . .			29,32
Sandkrug-Brücke . . .		21	
Sauerländer-Str. (Wilm.)			5
Savigny-Platz (Char.) .			7
Schadow-Str. NW . . I		20	
Schäfer-Str. SO . . I		28	
Schaudauer-Str. (Rix.)			36
Schaper-Str. W			10
Scharnhorst-Str. NW (12-31 N)	18,21		
Scharnweber-Str. O . .		37,40	
Scharren-Str. C . . I		25	
— (Char.)		2, 5	
Scheffel-Str. (Licht.) .		41	
Schelling-Str. W . . .			19
Schendelgasse C. . . .		27	
Scherenberg-Str. N . .	29,28		
Scherer-Str. N	17		
Schering-Str. N . . .	21		
Schickler-Str. O		28,29	
Schiffbauerdamm NW I		20,23	
Schill-Str. W . . .			13
Schiller-Platz W . . I		22	
— Strasse (Char.) . .	4, 7		
— — (Rum...			
Schilling-Br...			
Strasse . .			

	B	R	G
Schinke-Str. N			29
Schinkel-Platz W . . I		26,25	
Schivelbeiner-Str. N .	25		
Schlegel-Str. N		24	
Schleiden-Platz O . . .		40	
Schleiermacher-Str. S			27,26
Schlesischen Bahnhof, Am O . . .		31	
Schlesische Busch SO			35
— Strasse SO			31,35
— (Wilm.)			2, 5
— Tor			34
Schleswiger-Ufer NW		11	
Schleuse, An der . . I		25	
Schleusen-Brücke . . I		25	
Schliemann-Str. N .	30,29		
Schloss, Königl. C . .		26	
— (Char.)		2	
Schloss-Brücke . . . I		26	
— (Char.) I		5	
— Freiheit C . . . I		26	
— Platz C I		25,26	
— Strasse (Char.) . . .		2, 1	
Schlüter-Steg NW . I		23	
— Strasse (Char.) . . .		7	7
Schmid-Str. SO . . I		28	
Schmückert-Str. O . .			37
Schneidemühler-Str. NO		36	
Schöneberg			15,18
Schöneberger Brücke .			19
— Strasse SW			19
— Ufer W			16,19
Schonensehe-Str. N .	28		
Schönfliesser-Str. N .	25		
Schönhauser-Allée N .	29,30	27	
— Strasse, Alte C . .		27	
—, Neue C		26	
— Tor		27	
Schönholzer-Str. N . .	27		
Schöning-Str. N	13		
Schönlanker-Str. NO .		36	
Schönlein-Str. S			30,29
Schön-Str. (Weis.) . .	34		
Schönstedt-Str. N .	19,20		
School of Art		29	
— of Mines		21	
— of Music		10	16
Schramm-Str. (Wilm.)			9
Schreiner-Str. C		38	
Schröder-Str. N		24	
Schul-Str. N	16,17		
— (Char.)		5	
Schulzendorfer-Str. N	21		
Schumann-Str. NW I		20	
Schützen-Str. NW . I		22	
— Alte C . . I		29	
S...			
S...			
S. L...			14

	B	R	G		B	R	G
Schwartzkopff-Str. N .	21			Serauer-Str. SO			32,31
Schweden-Str. N ...	19			Spandauer-Brücke, An			
Schwedter-Str. N ...	26,27			der C I	.	26	
Schweidnitzer-Str.				— Schiffahrts-Kanal,			
(Hal.)	.	.	2	Am (Plö.)	5, 8		
Schwerin-Str. W ...	.	.	17	— Strasse C I	.	26	
Schwiebuser-Strasse				— (Char.)	.	2	
SW		.	21	— Weg I	4		
Sebastian-Str. S	.	25	25	Sparr-Platz N	17		
Secession, Exhibition				— Strasse N.....	17		
of the	.	7		Spener-Str. NW	.	14	
Sedan-Strasse (Schön.)	.	.	18	Speyer-Str. W (Schön.)	.	.	14
— (Weis.)......	35,38			Spichern-Str. W....	.	.	11
— Ufer SW			26	Spiekermann-Str.			
Seehandlung I	.	22		(Pankow).......	28,31		
Seelower-Str. N	25			Spielhagen-Str. (Char.)	.	4	
See-Str. N ..... {	11,14			Spindler-Brücke	.	25	
	16			Spindlershof I	.	25	
—, Grosse (Weis.) ..	37			Spittel-Markt C ...I	.	25	
Seestrassen-Brücke .	12			Spree-Str. C I	.	25	
Seeweg (Stralau) ...	.	.	41	— (Char.)	.	5, 4	
Seller-Str. N	18			Spreewald-Platz	.	.	32
Seminary, Gymnastic	.	.	22	Spreeweg	.	13,14	
Senefelder-Platz N .	.	30		Sprengel-Str. N	15,17		
— Strasse N	30,29			Staatsarchiv I	.	26	
Sesenheimer-Str.				Stables, Royal ...I	.	25	
(Char.)	.	4		Stadthaus I	.	26,29	
Seume-Str. (Rum.) ..	.	37		Stall-Str. (Char.)....	.	2	
Seydel-Str. C I	.	25		Stallschreiber-Str. S.	.	.	25
Seydlitz-Str. NW ...	.	18		Stargarder-Str. N . {	29,32		
Sibold-Str. S	.	.	27	(39-50 NO) ...I	33		
Sickingen-Str. NW .	.	9		Statistical Office, Im-			
Sieges-Allée I	.	19		perial		.	16
Sieges-Säule I	.	20		— —, Municipal ...	.	25	
Siegfried-Brücke ...	.	.	18	— —, Royal	.	.	22,25
— Str. (Schön.)	.	.	18	Stavanger-Str. N ...	25		
Siegmundshof NW ..	.	10		Steffen-Str. (Neu-			
Siemens-Str. NW ...	12	12		Hohenschönhausen)	42		
— Steg (Char.)	.	5		Steglitzer-Str. W ...	.	.	16
Sigmaringen-Str.				Stein-Platz (Char.) ..	.	7	
(Wilm.).........	.	.	9	— Strasse C	.	27	
Simeon-Str. SW	.	25		Steinmetz-Str. W....	.	.	17
Simon-Dach-Str. O ..	.	37		—, Neue (Schön.) ...	.	.	17,18
Simplon-Str. (Box.)..	.	37	37	Stendaler-Str. NW ..	.	15	
Simson-Str. NW ..I	.	20		Stephan-Platz NW ..	15	15	
Singing Academy ..I	.	23		— Strasse NW	15	15	
Skalitzer-Str. SO ...	.	.	29,31	Stern, Grosser	.	13	
Slaughter Houses....	.	38		—, Kleiner.......	.	16	
Soldiner-Str. N	22			Sternwarte	.	.	22
Solms-Str. SW.....	.	.	21,23	Stettiner Strasse N .	22		
Sommer-Str. NW ..I	.	20		— Tunnel N......	21		
— (Neu-Hohen-				Stockholmer-Str. N..	19		
schönhausen)	42			Stolpische-Str. N ...	25		
Sonnenburger-Str. N	26			Stralau	.	.	41
Sonntag-Str. (Box.)..	.	.	37	Stralauer-Allée O ..	.	.	34,37
Sophie-Charlotte-				— Brücke, An der C	.	28	
Platz (Char.)....	.	1		— Platz O	.	31	
— — Strasse (Char.) .	.	2, 1		— Strasse C I	.	25,28	
Sophien-Str. C	.	25		Stralsunder-Str. N ..	24		
— (Char.)	.	7		Strassburger-Str. N ..		30	

	B	R	G
Strassburger-Str.			
(Weis.) 35,38			
Strassmann-Str. *O* . . .	.	35	
Strausberger-Str. *NO*	.	32	
Strelitzer-Str. *N* . . .	24		
— — (Wilm.)	.	.	6, 9
Streu-Str. (Weis.) . { 31,34			
{ 35			
Strom-Str. *NW*	.	15	
Stubenrauch-Str.			
(Schön.)	.	.	18
Stüler-Str. *W*	.	13	
Stuttgarter-Platz			
(Char.).	.	.	4
Suarez-Str. (Char.) . .	.	1	1
Südufer *N* 12,15			
Swinemünder-Str. *N* .23,27			
Sylter-Str. *N* 11,12			
Synagogue, New . . .	.	24	
Synagogues	. { 5, 24		
{ 25,26			
{ 29			
Tal-Str. (Pankow) . .	31		
Tauben-Str. *W* . . .I	.	22	
Tauenzien-Str. *W* . . .	.	.	10
Tauroggener-Str.			
(Char.)	.	5, 6	
Technical High School	.	7, 10	
Tegeler-Str. *N*	17		
— Weg (Char.) . . .	3	3, 2	
Telegraph Office, Cen-			
tral I	.	22	
Teltow Court House .	.	.	16,19
Teltower-Strasse *SW*	.	.	20,23
Tempelherren-Str. *S* .	.	.	26
Tempelhofer Berg			
SW	.	.	24
— Feld	.	.	21,24
— Ufer *SW*	.	.	19,20
Teupitzer-Str. *SO* . . .	.	.	39
Tentoburger-Platz *N*	.	27	
Thaer-Str. *O*	.	35,38	
Thaler-Str.	5		
Theatres:			
Berliner	.	.	22
Deutsches I	.	20	
Hebbel	.	.	14
Kleines I	.	23	
Komische Oper . .I	.	23	
Lessing I	.	20	
Lortzing	.	.	23
Luisen	.	.	29
Metropol I	.	22	
Neues I	.	23	
Opera House I	.	23	
— —, N . .	.	1.	
Operetter . . I	.	2 .	
Reichsha . . . (	.	2 .	
Residenz	.		

	B	R	G
Theatres:			
Schiller-Theater Ost	.	28	
— — Charl. . . .	.	7	
Schauspielhaus . .I	.	22	
Thalia I	.	25	
Trianon I	.	23	
Westens, des	.	.	10
Zentral	.	.	25
Thielen-Brücke . . .	.	.	32
Thomasius-Str. *NW* .	.	14	
Thorner-Str. *NO* . . .	.	36,35	
Thurneysser-Str. *N* . .	19		
Tieck-Str. *N*	.	24	
Tiergarten	.	13,16	
— Strasse *W*	.	13,16	
— Ufer *W*	.	10	
Tietz's Stores I	.	22,20	
Tile Wardenberg-Str.			
NW	.	11	
Tilsiter-Str. *O*	.	35	
Togo-Str. *N* 10,13			
Tölzer-Str. (Schmar.) .	.	.	3
Torell-Str. *O*	.	34	
Torf-Str. *N*	15		
Town Hall	.	26	
Transvaal-Str. *N* . . .11,13			
Trebbiner-Str. *SW* . .	.	.	20
Trelleborger-Str.			
(Pankow)	28		
Trendelenburg-Str.			
(Char.).	.	.	1
Treptow	.	.	42
Treptower-Brücke . .	.	.	35
— Chaussée *SO*	.	.	38,42
— Str. *SO*	.	.	36,39
Treskow-Str. *N* and			
NO	30		
Trift-Str. *N* 14,17			
Tunnel-Str. (Stralau) .	.	.	41
Turiner-Str. *N* 16,17			
Türken-Str. *N*	13		
Turm-Str. *NW*	.	12,15	
Turnanstalt, Zentral .	21	21	
Turnhalle, Zentral . .	.	.	25,28
Turnplatz	.	.	30
Türrschmidt-Str.			
(Rum.).	.	.	40
Überfahrt-Str. *N* . .I	.	23	
Uckermark-Str.			
(Pankow)	31		
Uckermünder-Str. *N* .	25		
Ufer-Str. *N* 20,19			
Uhland-Str. *W*	.	.	7,8,9
Ulmen-Str. *W*	.	.	13,16
Union-Platz *NW* . . .	12	12	
. . . . . . *NW*	.	.	23
. . . . . .	.	.	23
. . . . .	.	.	23
. . . .	.	.	23

	B	R	G
Unterbaum-Str. NW 1	.	20	
Unterwasser-Str. C 1	.	25	
Urania	.	17	
—, New 1	.	22	
Urban, Am S	.	.	26
— Hafen	.	.	26
— Strasse S	.	.	{ 26,29 / 30 }
Usedom-Str. N	24		
Utrechter-Str. N	17		
Versöhnungs-Str. N	24		
Veteranen-Str. N	27	27	
Veterinary College	.	21	
Victualling Office	.	11	31
Viehhof, Zentral-	.	38	40
Viktoria-Brücke	.	.	16
— Luise-Platz	.	.	11,14
— Park	.	.	21
— Platz (Rum.)	.	.	40
— Strasse W 1	.	19	16
Vineta-Platz N	27		
Virchow-Str. NO	.	33,36	
Voigt-Str. O	.	10,41	.
Völker-Str. N	22		
Volta-Strasse N	24		
Von der Heydt-Brücke	.	.	16
— Strasse W	.	.	13
Vorberg-Str. (Schön.)	.	.	18
Voss-Str. W 1	.	19	
Wadzeck-Str. NO	.	30	
Waghäusler-Str. (Wilm.)	.	.	12
Waisen-Brücke 1	.	28	
Waisenhaus	.	.	25
Waisen-Str. C 1	.	29	
Waitz-Str. (Char.)	.	.	4
Waldeck Park	.	.	25
Waldemar-Str. SO	.	.	28
Waldenser-Str. NW	12		
Wald-Str. NW	12		
Wall-Str. C (28-31 S) 1	25		
— — (Char.)	14		
Wallner-Theater-Str. O	.	29,28	
Wangenheim-Str. (Grun.)	.	.	3, 2
Warmbrunner-Str. (Schmarg.)	.	.	3
Warschauer-Platz O	.	.	31
— Strasse	.	34	34
Wartburg-Platz (Schön.)	.	.	15
— Str. (Schön.)	.	.	12,15
Wartenberg-Str. (Friedrichsberg)	.	40	
Wartenburg-Str. SW	.	.	12
Wassergasse SO 3	.	28	
Wassertor-Str. S	.	.	25
Wassmann-Str. NO	.	29,32	
Water Works, Municipal	.	30	
Waterloo-Brücke SW	.	.	26
— Ufer SW	.	.	23
Watt-Str. N	21		
Weber-Str. NO	.	32	
Wedding-Platz N	18,21		
— Strasse N	20		
Wegely-Str. NW	.	10	
Wegener-Str. (Wilm.)	.	.	9
Weichsel-Platz (Rix.)	.	.	33,36
— Str. O	.	40	
— — (Rix.)	.	.	32
Weidendamm NW 1	.	23	
— Brücke 1	.	23	
Weidenweg O	.	35,38	
Weidinger-Str. C	.	30	
Weigand-Ufer (Rix.)	.	.	36
Weimarer-Str. (Char.)	.	1	
Weinbergsweg N	.	27	
Weinmeister-Str. C	.	27	
Wein-Str. NO	.	29,33	
Weisbach-Str. O	.	35	
Weissenburger-Str. N	30		
Weissensee	34		
—, Château	37		
Weissenseer Weg (Neu-Hohenschönhausen)	12	42	
Werderscher Markt W 1	.	22,25	
Werdersche Rosen-Str. W 1	.	22,25	
Werft-Str. NW	.	17	
Werner Siemens-Str. (Char.)	.	7, 8	
Werneuchener-Str. NO	.	33,36	
Wertheim's Emporium 1	.	19	
Weser-Str. O	.	37,40	
— (Rix.)	.	.	33,36
Westfälische Str. (Wilm. & Hal.)	.	.	2, 5
Weyding-Stift	.	32	
Wichert-Str. N	28,29		
Wichmann-Str. W	.	.	13
Wielef-Str. NW	.	12	
Wiebe-Str. NW	.	9	
Wieland-Str. (Char.)	.	.	7
Wiener-Brücke	.	.	35
— Strasse SO	.	.	32
Wiesen-Brücke	.	.	32
— Strasse N	20		
Wikinger Ufer NW	.	11	
Wildenbruch Platz Rix.	.	.	36
— Str. (Rix.)	.	.	36

CPSIA information can be obtained at www.ICGtesting.com
Printed in the USA
BVOW02s0956051114

373810BV00016B/213/P